THE BOOK OF JERRY FALWELL

THE BOOK OF JERRY FALWELL

FUNDAMENTALIST

LANGUAGE

AND POLITICS

Susan Friend Harding

PRINCETON UNIVERSITY PRESS

PRINCETON AND OXFORD

Second printing, and first paperback printing, 2001

Paperback ISBN 0-691-08958-2

The Library of Congress has cataloged the cloth edition of
this book as follows

Harding, Susan Friend.

The book of Jerry Falwell : fundamentalist language and politics /
Susan Harding.

p. cm.

Includes bibliographical references and index.

ISBN 0-691-05989-6 (cloth : alk. paper)

1. Fundamentalism.   2. Language and languages—Religious
aspects—Christianity.   3. Falwell, Jerry—Language.

4. Falwell, Jerry—Oratory. I. Title.

BT82.2.H36 2000

280'.4'097309048—dc21   99–045172

British Library Cataloging-in-Publication Data is available

This book has been composed in Bembo Typeface

Printed on acid-free paper. ∞

www.pup.princeton.edu

Printed in the United States of America

10 9 8 7 6 5 4 3 2

For Marco

Contents

Preface and Acknowledgments

A CULTURAL movement swept through many American fundamentalist communities during the 1980s. Under the leadership of the Reverend Jerry Falwell and allied preachers, millions of inerrant Bible believers broke old taboos constraining their interactions with outsiders, claimed new cultural territory, and refashioned themselves in church services, Bible studies, books and pamphlets, classrooms, families, daily life, and the public arena.[1] In the process, they altered what it meant to be a fundamentalist and reconfigured the larger fellowship of born-again Christians, the rules of national public discourse, and the meaning of modernity. This is a study of the language by which many fundamentalist Protestants and their allies transformed themselves during the 1980s from a marginal, antiworldly, separatist people into a visible and vocal public force.

When I visited Jerry Falwell's Thomas Road Baptist Church and Liberty Baptist College in Lynchburg, Virginia, for the first time in 1982, there was an excited sense of collective mission in the air, the evident euphoria of a people caught up in a larger historical drama. Everyone—women and men, young and old, students, church members, and pastors—was in high gear, eager, energized, and working overtime for the Lord. Gatherings were charged with a sense of fresh purpose, and at times even my conversations with church people seemed to take on added weight, as if they had become little arenas of cultural reform. The people I saw and talked to struck me not as tradition-bound, defensive, or fearful, but as a people aggressively asserting and reshaping themselves and their world against any and all who resisted them. Far from bunkering themselves, these fundamentalists seemed to have a vast appetite for worldly ideas and practices—sports, therapy, sex manuals, politics, glossy magazines, television, Disney special effects—which they appropriated selectively and Christianized with great skill and zeal.

The cultural aperture and agitation of this community lasted most of the decade. Much of the action took place inside the language of fundamentalism, for Bible-based language is the medium and the ritual practice through which born-again Christians are formed and reformed.

I had been in Lynchburg about six weeks when one of Jerry Falwell's co-pastors told him that I was in town doing research among his church people. Having been recently embarrassed by an undercover *Playgirl* interviewer, Falwell was scrutinizing outside investigators more carefully. He invited me to interview him, in effect, to vet me. I reluctantly agreed—reluctantly, because I had by then interviewed dozens of church people and pastors in Lynchburg and was coming to the conclusion that formal interviews, though useful in many ways, did not in themselves serve my emerging interest in Bible-based language as a social force. Interviews presume that language, in this case the speech of those interviewed, represents stable, preexisting realities. Interviews gather information, life stories, perceptions, opinions, motives, values—words, more and less apt and compelling, that tell of things outside themselves. But the Bible-based language of cultural ferment, or, for that matter, of everyday faith in Falwell's community, was more alive, less stable, more productive, at moments even prophetic. It "spoke forth" realities. I could not see how an interview with Falwell would help me understand the force, the creativity, the consequences of his Bible-based language.

But I had no choice; I had to interview Falwell if I wanted to continue my work. As I expected, he was a large and irrepressible man with a baritone voice and a commanding presence. He inquired about my project, my purpose, and my affiliations and apparently determined that I could cause him no harm. He settled into answering my questions, all of which he seemed to have heard before, in a way that portrayed him as a reasonable man, a responsible moral leader, a man who had made mistakes and learned from them and who was fulfilling his various missions with confidence and vigor.

Falwell said some things that might sound odd or ill-considered to outsiders, but in the end his infelicities were no more significant than they were surprising. To dwell on them would be to read his words literally, which completely misconstrues his, and their, power. Falwell inhabits a world generated by Bible-based stories, and his language has the creative quality of the Bible itself. Skeptics tend to read him as they would read the Bible, looking for discrepancies that reveal the ulterior motives and social conditions of its human authors. As a result, skeptics are blind, or deaf, to the Bible's generativity. Falwell's people read him, and the Bible, very differently—harmonizing contradictions and infelicities according to interpretive conventions that presume, and thus reveal, God's design. Their Bible, their preacher, is thus constantly creating new truth.

An outsider might call these unifying interpretive conventions a folk hermeneutics and poetics of the Bible; it is they that make the Bible true and Jesus real. A born-again believer would call them the Holy Spirit; it is he who enables the believer to discern the truth of the Bible and to have a conversational relationship with Jesus.

I was introduced to the Holy Spirit by the Reverend Melvin Campbell, who had been trained at Falwell's Bible Institute and was pastoring a small church in another part of town. Campbell witnessed to me at length about the saving grace of Jesus Christ. He told me what had happened to him just before he came to know the Lord: *I began to look at things and I realized there was something missing in my life. Because, though we've never seen God, we're still aware of the fact that he is present, we know he's there. And even though I wasn't saved I knew there was something bombarding my life that was beyond my power to see or really understand at the time.* The Holy Spirit was dealing with young Campbell, quickening his supernatural imagination, and the Holy Spirit dealt with me not long after I left Campbell's office.

That is, I began to acquire the language that Campbell and other pastors and church people spoke to me. I came to know what it meant to have a soul, a sin nature, a heart; to say "God spoke to me" and "Satan is real"; to see God's hand in everyday life and the daily news; to know there is no such thing as an accident, and that everything, no matter how painful or perplexing, has a purpose. I did not convert, but I was learning their language of faith. As I did, I realized that I had arrived in my field site, and that my site was not so much the community of Bible believers as it was their vernacular. For years, I stood at the crossroads that Campbell and others fashioned for me, in between being lost and being saved, listening. I made that psychic intersection between born-again and unborn-again languages and worlds my field site, my home away from home. That is where I needed to be in order to do my fieldwork, and it is where I invite you to go as you read this book. Standing in the gap between conscious belief and willful unbelief, in a place I call "narrative belief," opens up born-again language and makes available its complexity, its variety and creativity, and its agile force.

I visited Lynchburg a half dozen times during the 1980s, conducting a couple of hundred hours of formal interviews with pastors, church people, administrators, professors, and students, and spending many more hours in church services, Bible studies, classrooms, workshops, meetings, homes, and informal conversations. Through these encounters, I tried to learn how to hear Jerry Falwell as his people do, and I have translated that understanding into this account of how their language works. It is full of his words and theirs. In order to create a space in which to explore narrative belief, I have placed direct quotations of spoken and written texts in oblique print, for the most part reserving quotation marks for short phrases and the words of outsiders. I also frequently fold the community's idiomatic expressions into my language without marking them typographically. I invite you to take note of their expressions and to read their words carefully, for, again, the community's language is my field site. I try to use their words not as evidence for something else, but, with the aid of a medley of largely implicit literary approaches, to show how Bible-based language persuades and produces effects.[2]

I focus primarily on preacherly discourse because preachers command all the Bible-based poetic, rhetorical, and narrative skills which make their vernacular generative. Many church people, including church staff, develop the same skills to some degree, but my formal interviews with them generally elicited their secular, not their Bible-based, speech codes. As a result, I had relatively few recorded texts of the religious vernacular of church people to study. Nor was I comfortable subjecting their language to the kind of scrutiny I bring to bear on preacherly discourse. My conversations with church people felt private, while preachers are public figures who expect their words will be studied and discussed.

This account is, then, a course in the Bible-based language of fundamentalism for anyone willing to enter the world, the history, the motives, the logics, and the families it fashioned and refashioned in the 1980s. I focus on the language of preachers, above all Jerry Falwell, because preachers are master-speakers. As they teach their language through sermons, speeches, and writings and enact its stories in their lives, they mold their church into the Church, a living sequel to the Bible.

ACKNOWLEDGMENTS

I am greatly indebted to many people who helped me over the years as I carried out the research for and wrote this book. I am most grateful to Charlotte Gaylor and her family, who gave me shelter and taught me by example the meaning of a Christian family and home. And I thank the many men and women in Washington, D.C., and in Charlottesville and Lynchburg, Virginia, who talked to me and helped me find my way, most especially Melvin Campbell, Ed Dobson, Russell File, Ed Hindson, Nelson Keener, Rodney Kidd, Elmer Towns, and M. C. Wise.

My students and teaching assistants in Born-again Religion and Culture at the University of Michigan and the University of California, Santa Cruz, helped me open up, think through, and enjoy this subject and its materials in countless ways. So did many graduate students, research assistants, and typists, among them Brian Auten, Kelly Countryman, Jeffrey Donner, David Edwards, Jennifer Harding, Kristin Harding, John Hartigan, Amanda Patterson, Jenessa Radocchio, Stephen Reynolds, and Matt Wray.

So many friends, colleagues, and acquaintances have supported me intellectually in this project that I could not possibly name them all. Many have read and commented on earlier versions of some of the chapters gathered here. I thank you all, and most especially Harry Berger, Jr., Charles Bright, Sam Bowles, Daniel Boyarin, Margaret Brose, Wendy Brown, Judith Butler, Steve Caton, Ross Chambers, James Clifford, Chris Connery, Karen Cope, Carol Delaney, Clifford Geertz, Faye Ginsburg, Donna Haraway, Val Hartouni, Max Heirich, Bruce Mannheim, Shirley Nelson, Vicente Rafael, Richard Randolph, Rayna Rapp, Skip Rappaport, David Schneider, Jane Schneider, Joan Scott, Cynthia Sowers, Elizabeth Taylor, Anna Tsing, Timothy Weber, Hayden White, Harriet Whitehead, Ralph Williams, and Marilyn Young.

I single out and give special thanks to those who read and commented on the entire manuscript at some point along its way to publication: Nancy Ammerman, Don Brenneis, Bill Christian, James Ferguson, Emily Martin, Beth Pittenger, Mary Steedly, Robert Wuthnow, and an anonymous reader for the University of California Press. Frances Fitz-Gerald and Katie Stewart also read and commented upon the entire manuscript and its many earlier piecemeal incarnations. But more, they accompanied me as friends and intellectuals in this project from beginning to end in ways that stimulated and sustained me immeasurably. I would not have wanted to do it without them.

A number of people encouraged me at crucial moments, among them John Brademas, Charlotte Curtis, Lynn Eden, Walter Lippincott, Ellen Malcom, Calvin Skaggs, Alan Skolnikoff, and Alfred Sussman. And I am indebted for financial support along the way to the Woodrow Wilson International Center for Scholars; the University of Michigan; the Institute for Advanced Study; the University of California, Santa Cruz; the National Endowment for the Humanities; the University of California President's Research Fellowship in the Humanities; and the American Academy of Arts and Sciences Fundamentalism Project.

I am grateful to Mary Murrell at Princeton University Press for her superb editorial work as well as her encouragement, humor, and friendship. I thank Alice Calaprice for her excellent copyediting. Kathryn Chetkovich pulled me out of writing ruts many times in the last few years and gave me invaluable editorial advice and moral support. Many thanks to Richard Randolph for nimbly proofreading the galleys with me, and to Jon Keesey for producing an index worth reading.

My family has enabled me in every way throughout this long project. I thank you all, especially my mother and father, Elizabeth and Harold, and my son, Marco.

A Guide to Terms

THE TERM "fundamentalism" has two inflections in both scholarly and popular discourse on American religion. Sometimes, it refers to all supernaturalist, or "Bible-believing," Protestants. Other times, it refers to a particular subset of white Bible–believing Protestants who represent themselves as "militantly antimodernist."

Preachers of the latter subset vigorously sustained and articulated a critique of modern society during the mid-twentieth century. Many, including J. Frank Norris, Carl McIntire, John R. Rice, Bob Jones Sr., Bob Jones Jr., and early Jerry Falwell, avowed "separation" from worldly society. However, some of them also occasionally broke into and otherwise agitated at the boundaries of the political arena. When referring to the subset of self-declared fundamentalists, I will use a small "f."

The large-gauge inflection of "fundamentalism," which I will mark with a capital "F," refers not just to self-declared fundamentalists but more generally to Bible-believing Protestants, most of whom do not use the term globally to refer to themselves. They prefer instead to call themselves evangelicals, Bible-believing Christians, or simply Christians. It is outsiders, especially liberal Protestants, academics, and journalists, who call all those who believe that the supernatural claims of the Bible are true, "Fundamentalists." A Fundamentalist view of the Bible stands in contrast to a "Modern" view, which considers the Bible a product of human history and reads its supernatural claims as allegory, spiritual truth, or mythology.

Thus, small "f" fundamentalism is a term inside Bible-believing discourses, while capital "F" Fundamentalism, which includes all Bible-believing Protestants, is not; it is a Modernist concoction. I make a related distinction between "Modern," which means specifically not-Fundamentalist, and "modern," which refers more loosely to cultural practices associated with the development of capitalist society.

"Evangelical" also has two inflections in popular and academic discourse. One usage refers to evangelizing Protestants in general, including fundamentalists, and the other refers to a subset of those Protestants who fashioned a conscious fellowship in opposition to militant fundamentalism in the 1940s and 1950s. Which inflection applies in the account that follows is made clear by the context.

I use "born-again" and "Bible-believing" Christianity more or less interchangeably to refer to pentecostal and charismatic as well as fundamentalist and evangelical Protestants who mobilized politically and culturally in the 1980s.

THE BOOK OF JERRY FALWELL

Standing in the Gaps

Somebody had to take a stand. I think Dr. Falwell was the one to do it because he gets his wisdom and knowledge from God. That's why we're for him a hundred percent. It's not just his point of view. He goes back to God's word. None of us is perfect, and we don't worship Dr. Falwell, but we love him because he preaches the Bible. And right off the top of my head, I can't think of anything he's ever tried to do that was wrong, because he's inspired of God, and we just trust him.

—NANCY GODSEY, QUOTED IN WILLIAM MARTIN, 1996

EVERY YEAR around Halloween, the Youth Ministry of Thomas Road Baptist Church (TRBC) in Lynchburg, Virginia, sets up Scaremare, a Christian haunted house. The ministry converts an abandoned warehouse in a seedy part of town into an ensemble of creepy encounters with dying, death, and the saving grace of Jesus Christ. Each night for a week, wary visitors pick their way through a weedy, tombstone-strewn yard to the door where a zombie-butler intones, "Come, it is appointed." You enter the house through a dark, damp tunnel and move haltingly through a dozen rooms, each one a little disaster scene: the grisly aftermath of a plane crash; a mausoleum of open caskets; dead bodies hanging on hooks in a meat locker; a homeless overdosed heroin addict; a woman holding a huge snake that has bitten a man who is writhing in pain; a cage full of crazed, ragtag people grappling to get out; a collapsed Hyatt Regency hotel littered with dying and dead bodies; a truck-motorcycle wreck bursting with yet more mangled bodies.

Scaremare is quite effective. Thousands of local residents, most of them unsaved, pay a few dollars to tour the house in late October, and some come back night after night, year after year, to undergo anew the gruesome scenes. The dead and dying people are real, enacted by the church's high school students. There is "blood" all over and horrifying noises and screams all around. The floors and walls warp and wobble, and the dim lights flicker and disappear at the worst moments. You exit the building down a spiral slide and are ushered into a funeral tent where a counselor stands aside a casket covered with flowers. He delivers you a three-minute gospel message and invites you to ask Jesus Christ into your heart and receive the gift of eternal life. Then you shuffle out.

Although most tours end without anyone being saved, Dave Adams, TRBC's senior youth minister, who led me through Scaremare when I first visited his church in 1982, supposed that later on some would respond to the message about death and life that God had tucked into their hearts. Salvation was Scaremare's greatest goal, but, Adams told me, there were others. Scaremare made money. It kept kids off the streets. It was fun. It provided an alternative to hot dogs and hayrides and trick-or-treating. It took harvest time back from the devil and replaced the demon-filled message of Halloween with the biblical message "man dies, Christ saves." The idea, Adams said, was to mix the fun and special-effects of Walt Disney's Haunted Mansion, which was the inspiration for Scaremare, with the facts, namely, we die. *Scaremare is a piece of our church's philosophy in action. We don't practice a stay-at-home Christianity. We're militant and aggressive in getting out Christ's message.*

Scaremare as an evangelistic outreach was fundamental Baptist Christianity as usual. What seemed unusual, even striking, to me about it at the time was its willfully hybrid quality, its fusion of dissonant cultural practices. As Adams put it, Scaremare "mixed elements" from Christianity and the world. As it turned out, many of the church activities I witnessed during my stays in Lynchburg were exercises in this kind of cultural alchemy. I found them striking at first because TRBC was still then an avowedly fundamentalist church and claimed allegiance to the historic fundamentalist movement in America which preached separation from the world. I knew fundamentalists had recently become more politically engaged under the leadership of TRBC pastor Jerry Falwell, but I had no idea how aggressively they were transgressing other boundaries that separated themselves from the world.

A week after Scaremare, the Miss Liberty Homecoming Queen Pageant delivered the same message. TRBC had had its own school system, including Liberty Baptist College (LBC), for over a decade by then. Sports were heavily emphasized at the college, especially football. Along with football came Homecoming Day and its beauty pageant, but reinflected, as was Scaremare, to represent born-again Christian rather than secular values. Each year, Liberty seniors selected twenty-four single *senior ladies who best exemplified the "Spirit of Liberty" in every aspect of their lives.* One of them would be elected homecoming queen at the pageant—as they preferred to call the contest—which was held in Thomas Road's main sanctuary, its four thousand seats filled, on a Friday night. The program listed the half-worldly, half-Christian criteria used to winnow the initial list of contestants: *personality, college involvement, achievements, academic ability, Christian testimony, Christian service, ambition, and appearance.* And it defined "the philosophy of a Christian pageant" in the following way: *A pageant is an opportunity to present a display of exceptional quality. In Proverbs 31, the Scriptures say "Many daughters have done virtuously, but thou excellest them all." It goes on to say that, "Favor is deceitful and beauty is vain, but a woman who feareth the Lord, she shall be praised." This is not a beauty pageant as the world would have it in the physical sense, but it is a beautiful pageant in that it portrays godly women who possess the virtue talked about in Proverbs 31.*

For three hours, we watched a beauty contest that had been converted to Bible-believing Christianity. Like Scaremare, the amalgamation was quite effective. Of course, there were no swimsuits, but all the contestants paraded to "oohs" and "ahs" in their Sunday-best dresses. Later, the ten semi-finalists swirled before us in elegant evening gowns, and finally the queen was crowned with all the standard pomp. Apart from their singular faith in the saving grace of Christ, the contestants were— oddly in keeping with the liberal cultural politics of the times—somewhat diverse. Only nine of the twenty-four contestants were from southern states; twelve were from northern and western states, and three from foreign countries. Nor were all white; there were three women of color, including one African American woman from Long Island who was second runner-up. Two women had disabilities, including a woman with a stutter from Philadelphia—she was third runner-up. Miss Liberty 1982 was a very blond psychology major, musician, honor's student, and prayer leader from Sugar Land, Texas. Just before she was crowned, Jerry, as everyone called their pastor, bounded up on stage and announced *I'd like to tell you how to get your copy of the four-volume Living Bible.* He was loudly laughed off stage with great delight.

That same fall, the Sixth Annual Superconference at TRBC further broadcast the message, along with some of the means, of fundamentalist cultural reform. Several thousand pastors and church leaders attended five days of workshops, sermons, and special events organized by TRBC staff. In addition to the usual fundamentalist fare of workshops on soul winning, Sunday School, evangelistic preaching, and missions, the Superconference was marbled with world-consuming events and rhetorics. There was a four-day workshop on "Christian Counseling" which blended secular psychology and Christian doctrine. A "Social Outreach" workshop series introduced the Save-A-Baby Ministry, which provided shepherding homes and a group maternity home as *abortion alternatives your church could offer to the woman with a crisis pregnancy.* The Superconference also showcased the new national magazine, *The Fundamentalist Journal,* published by the Old-Time Gospel Hour. The magazine's glossy format, colorful, photo-filled pages, and snappy topical articles and opinion pieces gave the impression that it was the fundamentalist version of *Time* or *Newsweek,* which was precisely what the editors intended.

At the preaching services each evening of the Superconference, we were brought up-to-date on the unfolding events of the "Nebraska tragedy." State troopers had raided a small church in Louisville, Nebraska, after school board officials ordered a Christian day school closed for noncompliance with regulations. Pastors from the Nebraska area gathered in the church the night before the raid to pray and to chain themselves to the railings. We were told the pastors were *forcibly picked up* by the troopers, *carried out, and dumped on the sidewalk as they preached in full voice.* Ron Godwin from the Moral Majority had gone to Nebraska to keep Jerry Falwell in constant communication with the pastors and to videotape "the siege." Falwell explained that the state of Nebraska, in

Figure I.1 An early *Fundamentalist Journal* cover visually parodied secular values.

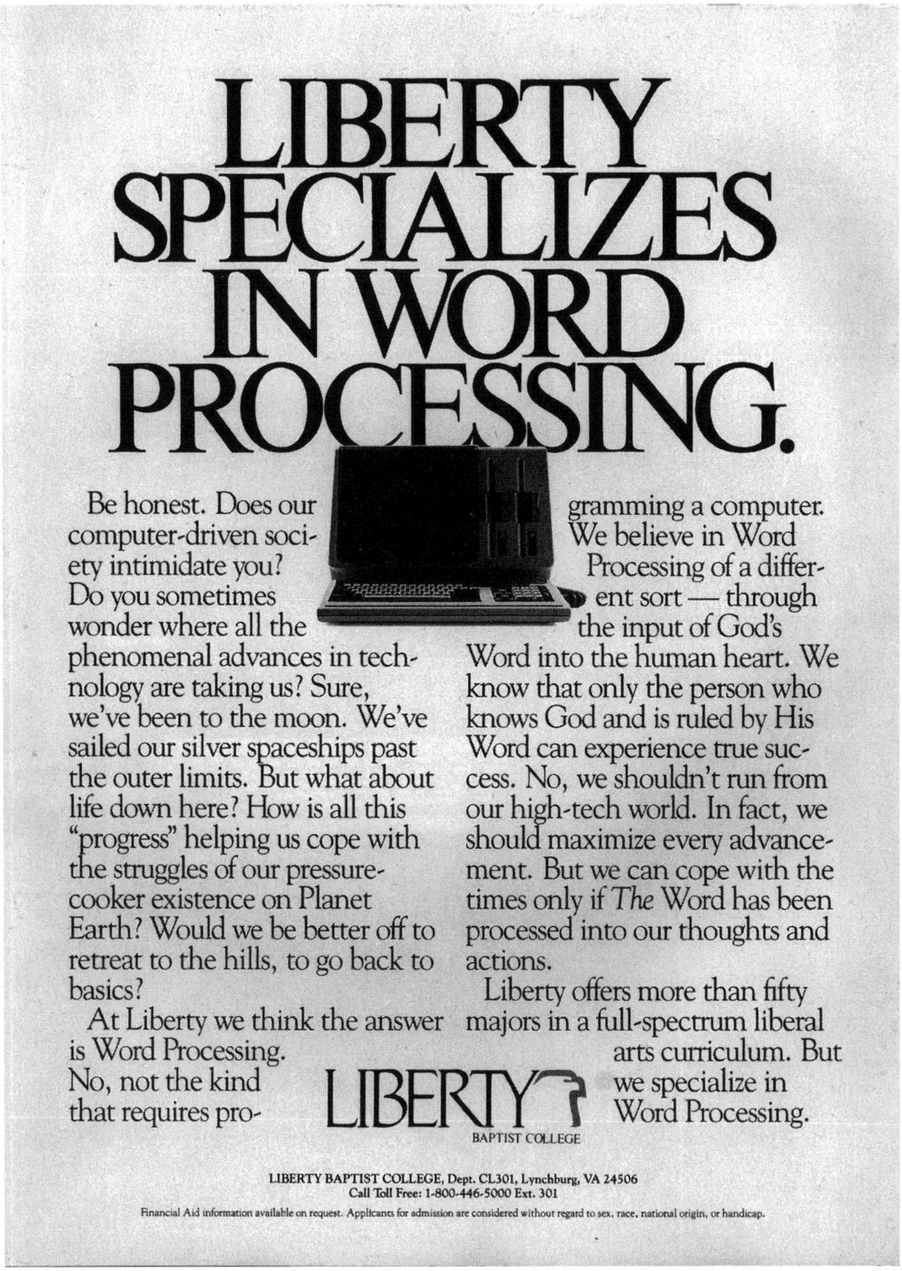

Figure I.2 A 1984 *Fundamentalist Journal* ad for Liberty Baptist College reappropriated the "word" in word processing.

league with the National Education Association, was violating religious freedom. *It's amazing what we've learned from feminists and the other side. Civil Rights people had the kind of backbone to stand up for their freedom, and Christians better have that kind of backbone too.*

When I first went to Lynchburg in 1982, I knew that fundamentalists under Jerry Falwell's leadership were in the process of breaking their separatist taboos against engaging in politics. Since I had gone to Lynchburg to study fundamentalist political activism, I looked for what I expected to find, namely, evidence of conventional kinds of politicking among his church people.

Cal Thomas and Ron Godwin, who ran the Moral Majority's Lynchburg office, told me about that organization's lobbying campaigns, but the only contact that church people seemed to have with it was through Falwell's sermonic asides and *The Moral Majority Report*, which was passed out each month in church lobbies. After some effort, I located and interviewed Sharon Overstreet, who had helped organize a bus trip of local churchwomen to Richmond to protest the Equal Rights Amendment in the late 1970s. She and another Thomas Road churchwoman also attended, as dissidents, the White House Conference on the Family in 1978. Neither of them, however, had continued on as pro-family activists. I attended a meeting in town of Women Exploited by Abortion, but the only Thomas Road churchwoman active in it was the one who had told me about it. Another churchwoman was active in the local Right to Life in 1982, and Falwell's church had just begun to send a busload or two of church people and college students to the Right to Life march in Washington, D.C., every year on the anniversary of *Roe v. Wade*. I met Lora and Steve Albacten, who were documenting the teaching of "humanist," "anti-Christian" values in the public schools. Patriotic songs were sung in church on several occasions by a chorus of college youth dressed in red, white, and blue. The Young Republicans had a table in the Liberty Baptist College student center, and various kinds of voting materials were distributed in the church lobby the Sunday before Election Day in November.

But that was about it. There were no big political meetings, no direct actions, no public political debates, no heated political conversations, and no partisan politics worth shaking a stick at. Apart from a dozen or so sometime activists, church people had remarkably little to say beyond agreeing with their pastor about pro-family political issues. Those issues were affecting their patterns of voting and sacrificial giving by 1982, but they had not generated the usual trappings of a political movement.

Eventually I realized that while I saw little in the way of routine or protest politics in Falwell's Lynchburg community, it was rife with another kind of politics, with what might be called cultural politics.

During the 1980s, Falwell delivered many politically charged sermons. He was an omnipresent spokesman and activist for the New Christian Right, and he headed the flagship conservative Christian political organization, the Moral Majority. But his project was never limited to electoral and legislative reform. He was also intent on cultural reform. Falwell's old and new ministries, his media projects, direct mail, audiotape and video series, books, magazines, newsletters, pamphlets, college programs and courses, concert tours, rallies, Bible studies, conferences, prayer groups, and many, many more kinds of activities produced by him and his one-thousand-strong staff—all were bent to the project of reforming old-fashioned, separatist fundamentalism. In effect, during the 1980s, Jerry Falwell turned his empire of ministries, including the Moral Majority, his church and university, the Old-Time Gospel Hour, and a half dozen other outreaches, into one large, long consciousness-raising meeting. This "meeting" was political in a broad sense of rearranging cultural power relations, but not in the narrow sense of conventional politicking. The agenda was to convert his people from "fundamentalists," whose only mission in American society was evangelism, into "conservative Christians," who would fight worldly battles and who sought worldly power and influence in the name of "Christian values."

God called many Protestant fundamentalists to save America during the 1980s. They had been aware since the 1960s that much of the country had sunk into a state of moral anarchy. The new revelation was that they were responsible for it, and thus for stanching the decline. As Bible-believing Christians, they, and only they, held the keys to America's moral order.

God further revealed that to save America, fundamentalists would have to do more than preach the gospel of the death, burial, and resurrection of Jesus Christ. God wanted fundamentalists to reenter, to reoccupy, the world. He urged them to educate themselves about the political process, to contribute money and time to moral causes, to participate in local, state, and national party politics, to vote for morally conservative candidates, and to run for public office. And he asked them to carry their moral agenda into every walk of life: to become high school biology teachers who would teach evolution from a creationist point of view; doctors, nurses, and hospital administrators who would oppose abortions; lawyers who would litigate on behalf of prayer in public schools; journalists and broadcasters who would make sure the Christian point of view was fairly represented in the news media.

There was nothing unusual about God's calling American Protestants to public action and social reform. Two hundred years earlier, he had encouraged some colonial Protestants to resist and rebel against British rule; at the same time, he summoned others to defend it. In the middle of the nineteenth century, God called on some Protestants to abolish slavery, others to preserve it. In this century, he counseled and nourished Protestants on both sides of the struggle over civil rights and racial inequality. He has very likely spoken in some manner to Protestants on the brink of every American war, urging some to fight, others to resist fighting. For that matter, God called some Protestants to work on behalf of the very reforms—abortion rights, gay rights, gender equality—that fundamentalists considered signs and agents of contemporary moral declension.

But nobody, least of all fundamentalists, expected fundamentalists to be called by God to engage in political action and social reform in the last quarter of the twentieth century. Their forefathers had done "battle royal" against modernism, Darwinism, worldly amusements (liquor, the theater, moving pictures, dance halls, flappers) and social vices (divorce, sex education, birth control, suffrage, women's clubs) early in the century. Having lost the war for public opinion as well as most of the battles, these early fundamentalists retreated from public life and declared themselves separated from the world. They disavowed denominations, politics, social reform, higher education, and most of the markers of worldly social status. They devoted themselves to building Bible-believing enclaves in which to live out what surely must be the last days of a lost and dying world before Christ returns. Many other theologically conservative Protestants—Adventists, Mormons, Jehovah's Witnesses, pentecostals, evangelicals, charismatics—also kept a relatively low public profile during much of the mid-twentieth century, but none so willfully, so self-righteously, so resolutely, as fundamentalists.[1]

It was preachers, evangelists, teachers, and writers—men and women whom God had anointed to speak for him—who helped Protestant fundamentalists discern their new calling in the 1980s. Above all, preachers, the master-speakers of Bible-based dialects, enabled fundamentalists to know God's updated will for them.[2]

Preachers "stand in the gap" between the language of the Christian Bible and the language of everyday life.[3] The Bible, which God wrote using human authors to pen his words, is for fundamentalists the sole source of his authority on earth. Preachers convert the ancient recorded speech of the Bible once again into spoken language, translating it into local theological and cultural idioms and placing present events inside the sequence of Biblical stories.[4] Church people, in their turn, borrow, customize, and reproduce the Bible-based speech of their preachers and other leaders in their daily lives. Preachers appropriate each other's sermons piecemeal and wholesale, while church people assimilate their preachers' language at the level of grammar, semantics, and style.

Religious traditions embodied in language may be preserved indefinitely under reiterative conditions such as these. Equally, alterations in what is spoken and how it is understood may occur very quickly. Indeed, individuals in communities bound by intense practices of speech mimesis may undergo in the space of a few years profound changes of collective speech that transform who they are, their social boundaries, and their worldly relations. Preachers, who are the nodes, the transformers, in the religious knowledge networks that articulate fundamentalist communities, are thus pivotal figures in moments of dramatic transformation.

Of all the leaders whom God used to call fundamentalists out of their self-imposed exile in the 1980s, the Reverend Jerry Falwell was by far the most renowned and effective.

Falwell was born in Lynchburg, a small city in central Virginia, in 1933. According to his testimony, his mother was a devout Christian and his father, an agnostic, an alcoholic, a bootlegger, and a successful small businessman. Falwell came to know Christ when he was eighteen and was shortly called by God to preach. He trained at Baptist Bible

Figure I.3 Thomas Road Baptist Church, main sanctuary. (From *The News and Advance*, Lynchburg.)

College in Springfield, Missouri, and founded Thomas Road Baptist Church in his hometown in 1956.

By the 1980s, Falwell had built a large, complex, and far-reaching ministry. TRBC claimed a membership of twenty thousand and a weekly attendance of eight thousand at its five regular services. Falwell was chancellor of Liberty Baptist College and Seminary, which became Liberty University in 1984, with some three thousand students. His educational system included as well the Lynchburg Christian Academy (a K–12 Christian day school), the Liberty Bible Institute, the Liberty Home Bible Institute (a national correspondence course), and the Liberty University School of LifeLong Learning (a national external degree program).

Falwell headed the Old-Time Gospel Hour (OTGH), which televised his sermons and television specials and aired his radio programs to millions of households through hundreds of local outlets all over the country.[5] The OTGH produced various periodic and special-issue publica-

Figure I.4 Jerry Falwell preaching at Thomas Road Baptist Church. (Photo courtesy of Lynn Hey.)

tions—magazines, books, newsletters, pamphlets. And it managed all of Falwell's multifaceted direct-mail fundraising appeals, which reached millions of conservative Christians and raised hundreds of millions of dollars during the 1980s.

Falwell oversaw a number of smaller, specialized ministries, among them a home for alcoholics, a home for unwed mothers, and a Christian counseling center. The counseling center had a staff of seven, four of whom had secular psychological training. According to its director, Ed Hindson, they treated about two thousand people a year.

Outside fundamentalist circles, Falwell was most widely known during the 1980s as the main media spokesman for the New Christian Right and founder of the the Moral Majority, the most visible public lobby for conservative Christian causes and a fund-raising organization with a mailing list of several million donors.

On behalf of his many ministries, Falwell traveled extensively during the 1980s, claiming to travel three thousand miles a week in his private jet. He delivered hundreds of sermons and talks in churches, public gatherings, and private meetings throughout the country every year. He made countless remarks at press conferences, luncheons, and dinners. He worked with brethren preachers to organize numerous local campaigns for moral reform. And he spoke each year at dozens of conferences of preachers, church leaders, and Christian broadcasters.

Falwell's combined ministries employed about one thousand men and women during the 1980s, and they included among them a number of ghostwriters, most of whom also worked for him as co-pastors, professors, or aides. They wrote or co-wrote many of Falwell's sermons and a dozen books and countless of articles and pamphlets that were published under his name.[6]

Falwell's fundamentalist empire was thus a formidable one as measured by standards of personnel, money, and organizational wherewithal. It was also an immense empire of words. Or rather, it was a factory of words, a veritable Bible-based language industry. Falwell's empire was, in effect, a hive of workshops, of sites of cultural production, that smelted, shaped, packaged, and distributed myriad fundamentalist rhetorics and narratives. For hundreds of hours every year, local church people and Liberty students heard, read, and studied Falwell's words and the words of those he had hired. Outside Lynchburg, several million people heard his public speeches, watched his television shows, listened to his radio broadcasts, and read his direct-mail and other publications. And, in the form of soundbites, interviews, and special reports, Falwell's words reached everyone in the country, whatever their persuasion, who read or heard the news at all during the 1980s. Falwell was thus exceptionally well poised not only to mobilize fundamentalists politically, but to transform, rearrange, and reposition fundamentalism itself.

Jerry Falwell had long applied worldly means to soul-winning ends. He came from a family of small businessmen and was steeped in a fundamentalist culture that privileged only two types of Christian masculinity: the

preacher and the businessman. He started his radio and television ministries the same year he founded his church, in 1956, and expanded them
both steadily into regional, then national, outreaches. American evangelism and business had been exchanging techniques for over a hundred
years.[7] So Falwell was specifically predisposed to adapt modern business
techniques and concepts to his evangelistic projects.[8]

In a 1971 defense of his aggressive church-building activities, Falwell
revealed his earthly inspiration: *Business is usually on the cutting edge of
innovation and change because of its quest for finances. Therefore the
church would be wise to look at business for a prediction of future innovation. The greatest innovation in the last twenty years is the development of the giant shopping centers. Here is the synergetic principle of
placing at least two or more services at one location to attract the custom-
ers. A combination of services of two large companies with small supporting stores has been the secret of the success of shopping centers. The
Thomas Road Baptist Church believes that the combined ministries of
several agencies in one church can not only attract the masses to the
gospel, but can better minister to each individual who comes.*[9]

During the 1970s, Falwell expanded his project, his mission, and by
the early 1980s his multifaceted ministries were directed as much toward
moving fundamentalism from the margins to the mainstream of American society as toward evangelism. The shift paralleled two major shifts in
his core constituency. In the 1970s, his growing college added more
highly educated students, faculty, and their families to his congregation.
By the 1980s, most of those attending Falwell's Sunday services had some
relationship to LBC, and his congregation was notably more middle class.
At the same time, through the work of the OTGH and, later, the Moral
Majority, Falwell became a national, rather than a Southern, preacher.

Early on, his cultural reform efforts seemed to be aimed at updating
and upscaling old-fashioned fundamentalism while retaining its distinctive features, to incorporate and enter worldly culture as fundamentalists
without assimilating to the norms of worldly middle-class culture. Gradually, however, the commitment to the peculiar identity and some of
the unambiguous markers of fundamentalism—its special jargon, its mili-
tance, its missionary zeal, its doctrinal scrupulosity, its hypermasculi-
nity—weakened. By the mid-1980s, Falwell was defining a "fundamentalist" as "an evangelical who was mad about something."[10] By the end

of the 1980s, though he still at times declared himself a "fundamentalist," Falwell was also calling himself an "evangelical" without any qualifications. Finally, in 1996, Falwell formally affiliated his church with the Southern Baptist Convention (SBC) historically an evangelical denomination though dominated by fundamentalists since 1979. The switch was not complete because his church continued to be listed as a member of the historic fundamentalist Baptist Bible Fellowship (BBF).[11] But, in the context of fundamentalism's constitutive disavowal of denominations, combined with Falwell's high profile as the emblematic fundamentalist preacher of the late twentieth century, Falwell's SBC affiliation marked a major turning point in the history of American fundamentalism.

It was the second such turning point inasmuch as the conversion of fundamentalists into evangelicals had happened once before. The very category "evangelical" as opposed to "fundamentalist" had been invented during the 1940s and 1950s.[12] At that time, a variety of conservative Protestant leaders, including many more world-friendly fundamentalists, fashioned an alternative set of parachurch organizations. They crafted a new "postfundamentalist" mindset that was avowedly not militant and not separatist and that was committed to a more nuanced understanding of biblical truth.[13] Most notably, they established the National Evangelical Association (NAE), *Christianity Today*, Fuller Seminary, Youth for Christ, and the Billy Graham Evangelistic Association.

The cultural movement Falwell led forty years later went in many of the same directions as the earlier movement had gone, but it strayed and differed in many important respects. Many of Falwell's faithful abandoned the label "fundamentalist," and their commitment to certain fundamentalist distinctives weakened, but they took a good measure of old-fashioned fundamentalism with them. Relative to the earlier generation of emerging evangelicals, Falwell's movement stopped halfway, refusing to budge and becoming more doctrinaire than ever on certain matters. Most vociferously, the 1980s fundamentalist reform movement drew a line in the sand on the matter of Bible truth or biblical inerrancy. Unlike the 1940s movement of fundamentalists out of their worldly retreat, this one insisted that preachers and lay people proclaim the Bible absolutely true. At the same time, its leaders defined new litmus tests of Bible truth—strict creationism, God's chain of command, God's absolute opposition to abortion and homosexuality—which buttressed the moral rhetorics they were crafting to defend Christian values in public life and to save America.

This second fundamentalist reform movement would have been a minor one had it been confined to Falwell's fundamentalist Baptist constituency. Instead, it converged with a parallel movement in the Southern Baptist Convention and the larger evangelical fellowship that realigned many evangelicals with some of the principles of fundamentalism. Together, the 1980s movements rearranged the boundary between fundamentalism and postwar evangelicalism, fashioning a new constituency composed of newly engaged fundamentalists under leaders such as Falwell and conservative evangelicals who were discontented with their more irenic leaders. United under the rubric "conservative," or "born-again Christians," they not only formed the core constituency of the New Christian Right and changed the shape and content of both fundamentalism and evangelicalism, but they changed the meaning of "modern America."

Jerry Falwell's following formed the core of the New Christian Right until the late 1980s, but the movement's overall claim to represent born-again Protestants generally depended on several dozen other national leaders and organizations. Among the movement's co-producers were the empires of the other national televangelists, most notably Pat Robertson, Jimmy Swaggart, and James Robison; a roster of nationally active but less visible preachers, including Charles Swindoll, Charles Stanley, Adrian Rogers, James D. Kennedy, W. A. Criswell, Greg Dixon, and John Gimenez; and several dozen parachurch organizations and their leaders, including Bill Bright, Demos Shakarian, Francis Schaeffer IV, Tim and Beverly LaHaye, Louis Sheldon, Donald Wildmon, Connie Marshner, and Gary Bauer.

Some of these men and women worked directly with Jerry Falwell, others had little or no contact with him but worked in parallel universes. They borrowed from different sources, merged voices from different traditions, reiterated speech from and to different constituencies, and created with him a panoply of partially overlapping registers of conservative Protestant moral indignation.[14] While Falwell refashioned and allied fundamentalists and conservative evangelicals, his co-belligerents refashioned and repositioned other born-again Protestants who could not abide

Falwell's rhetorics and whose rhetorics Falwell's following could not abide. Robertson, Swaggart, and Robison, for example, reached pentecostal and charismatic Protestants who parted with fundamentalists over gifts of the spirit and other doctrines. And Swindoll, Stanley, and other preachers reached more moderate evangelicals who disdained fundamentalism, even as voiced by Falwell, as excessively separatist, apocalyptic, biblically literalist, and anti-intellectual.

The same rubrics that allowed fundamentalists and conservative evangelicals to see themselves as allies—as "born-again" or "conservative" Christians—thus came to include many pentecostals, charismatics, and more moderate evangelicals as well.[15] The rubrics, or rather, the connecting tissues that animated them and enabled them to work as illusions of unity, had sources prior to the 1980s New Christian Right preachers. Most notably, forty years of ecumenical crusade evangelism by Billy Graham's organization, supplemented by the work of Bill Bright and many others, had renewed and reentrenched a shared elementary language of what counted as a Christian, namely, someone who had realized he was a sinner, asked Jesus to forgive him, and accepted Jesus into his heart as his personal savior.[16] Graham and Bright and other evangelists also taught Christians simply, without polemics, that the Bible is true and that Christ wanted them to spread his good news, too. They thus willfully worked against the grain of the many forces that divided theologically conservative Christians. However, although their spare messages were not sufficient to produce a felt sense of unity or collective national presence.

Then, in the mid-1970s, George Gallup, Jr., took a big step toward reaping the political potential of the shared elementary gospel speech. He polled Americans about their faith and found that over one-third of them described themselves as "born-again," defined as having experienced "a turning point in your life when you committed yourself to Jesus Christ." A third—which translated into 50 million adult Americans—agreed that "the Bible is the actual Word of God and is to be taken literally, word for word." Nearly half said that they had encouraged someone "to believe in Jesus Christ or to accept Him as his or her Savior."[17] The Gallup findings fused with other born-again headliners, namely, convicted Nixon adviser Chuck Colson's famous conversion and its narrative, Born-Again, and the nation's first born-again president, Jimmy Carter. The combined effect was to reveal a hitherto "hidden

Protestant majority" that was already in some sense manifesting itself in high political places. As fundamentalists, pentecostals, charismatics, and even evangelicals, these theologically conservative Protestants had until the late 1970s seen themselves as marginals, if not enclaves or scattered remnants, relative to a perceived liberal Protestant mainstream. Once they saw themselves, and were seen, as related to one another and, taken together, as the Protestant majority, their marginal days were numbered.

Jerry Falwell performed the final coup in this series when he dubbed them all the Moral Majority in 1979.[18] The extent of the organization's effects on elections and legislatures during the 1980s has been debated, but its effect on public perceptions, while even harder to measure, was indisputable. The "moral majority" moniker was a public relations stunt that kept on stunning its public for years. In two short words, Falwell marked the majority status of theological conservatives among Protestants, elided it with majority status among all Americans, established himself as that majority's apparent leader, aggressively "mixed" religion and politics, and claimed the right to reintegrate culturally disenfranchised fundamentalists into national public life.

Several other highly charged national public rituals followed in 1980 in which, it was said, religion and politics were inappropriately "mixed."[19] Presidential candidate Ronald Reagan spoke at the National Religious Broadcasters Convention, which was hosted that year by Jerry Falwell's Thomas Road Baptist Church. And John Giminez, Pat Robertson, Demos Shakarian, and Bill Bright gathered several hundred thousand born-again Christians—mostly evangelicals, pentecostals, and charismatics—on the Washington Mall for a "Washington for Jesus" rally. Pat Robertson considered the day of the march one of "America's Dates with Destiny."

Many times during that incredible day, I sat on the platform watching men and women of faith from all across the nation as they prayed. They were every color, every class, every denomination imaginable. They were chief executive officers of large corporations, and they were unemployed, blue-collar workers. They were old and young, rich and poor, well-dressed and shabby. But they were one, and their prayer for the nation was one prayer. And God was hearing and would answer their prayer. April 29, 1980, was the beginning of a spiritual revolution. And

I joined with the 500 thousand people in the Mall and the millions watching on television in praying that one day this same spiritual revolution would sweep the nation.[20]

As conservative Protestants commingled their religious and political imaginations in the Moral Majority, on the nation's Mall, and on the airwaves of television and radio, they tore up a tacit contract with modern America. The tacit contract, fashioned in the wake of the 1925 Scopes trial, specifically proscribed the "mixing" of ostensibly premodern, that is, Bible-believing, Protestant rhetorics and routine politics. It thus rendered the public arena and the nation as a whole "modern" in the sense of secular. The regime of public religiosity in America that spanned the mid-twentieth century culturally confined and politically quarantined fundamentalists above all, for it was they who most insistently spoke in tabooed biblical voices. It also constrained other theologically conservative Protestants who were less militant and did not call themselves "fundamentalists," but whom many other Americans lumped together with self-declared fundamentalists, labeling them all "Fundamentalists," with a capital "F."[21] Although largely self-imposed and self-policed, Bible-believing Protestants, and fundamentalists in particular, thus were in a kind of exile from American public life. As long as they remained in exile, accepting their pariah status as outsiders, as inferior, backward "others," they enabled other Americans to see themselves as modern, superior, and progressive.

Of course, the taboo on "mixing" religion and politics had never proscribed all public religious speech. Clichéd references to God were okay and were even required of public officials on certain occasions. Public speech and activism by religious leaders and organizations, such as the National Council of Churches and the National Association of Evangelicals, was okay as long as they kept their religious rhetorics and motives in the background.[22] Public pronouncements by certain venerable religious bodies, such as the Council of Catholic Bishops, even if they teemed with religious language, were acceptable. Nor had the manifest "mixing" of political and religious—audibly Bible-believing—rhetorics and activities been deemed inappropriate in the Civil Rights movement.

Or rather, only the segregationists objected to it. Such an objection was in fact the occasion of Jerry Falwell's first national appearance as a preacher in search of a larger public. In 1965, he widely distributed "Ministers and Marchers," a sermon in which he preached: *As far as the relationship of the church to the world, it can be expressed as simply as the three words which Paul gave Timothy—"preach the Word." We have a message of redeeming grace through a crucified and risen Lord. This message is designed to go right to the heart of man and there meet his deep spiritual need. Nowhere are we commissioned to reform the externals. We are not told to wage wars against bootleggers, liquor stores, gamblers, murderers, prostitutes, racketeers, prejudiced persons or institutions, or any other existing evil as such. I feel that we need to get off the streets and back into the pulpits and into our prayer rooms. I believe we need to rededicate ourselves to the great task of turning this world back to God. The preaching of the gospel is the only means by which this can be done.*[23]

It is not clear when Falwell began to change his mind about the propriety of preachers reforming externals and waging war against existing evils. Nor was his disavowal of ministerial activism an entirely genuine position at the time, for the sermon was itself an instance of a preacher extending his reach beyond the gospel, as were Falwell's more direct pronouncements on behalf of racial segregation.[24] Nevertheless, sometime in the early 1970s, Falwell's explicit position began to shift as he reached ever more aggressively beyond his region to fashion a national constituency by way of his national crusades, his college, and the Old-Time Gospel Hour. By 1976, he was preaching that *This idea of "religion and politics don't mix" was invented by the devil to keep Christians from running their own country.*[25] And Falwell was also aggressively practicing what he now preached, most overtly in his national crusades ("I Love America!," "America Back to God," and "Clean-up America") in which he attacked, among other "existing evils," the Equal Rights Amendment, homosexuality, pornography, and women's liberation. He joined Anita Bryant in her 1977 campaign against a gay rights ordinance in Dade County, Florida, and kept a close eye on the 1978 White House Conference on Families. Finally, in 1980, he specifically repudiated his position in "Ministers and Marchers," calling it "false prophecy."[26]

Thus Falwell, like many other white conservative Protestant preachers, had made forays into public life long before he formed the Moral Majority. But until then, such forays were seen as just that, outbreaks of

"religious extremism," of inappropriately political zeal by Fundamentalists—by Bible believers—of one sort or another, which would soon sub-
side. The formation of the Moral Majority was a willfull attack on just
this kind of thinking. It declared a rupture in the modern American
regime of public religiosity that had rendered illegitimate the participation of white conservative Protestants, and fundamentalists in particular,
in mainstream American cultural and political life since the Scopes trial
in 1925. Two things that had been kept apart for much of America's
mid-twentieth century—routine public activism and aggressive Bible-
believing Protestantism—were once again being re-fused.

    The regime of law, custom, and violence that separated black and
white Americans during much of this century is not comparable to the
regime of public opinion and anti-worldliness that separated fundamentalists, in particular, from modern Americans. But the effect of Falwell's
founding of the Moral Majority and equivalent barrier-breaking events
of the early 1980s was, at least momentarily, comparable to the effect of
the first black sit-ins at white drugstore counters in the South in 1960.
The escalating Civil Rights movement shocked many white Southern-
ers. As one writer described the response of white Charlestonians to a
strike by black hospital workers, "it was as if the tables walked out of
their dining rooms."[27] Likewise, the formation of New Christian Right
organizations shocked many non-born-again Christian Americans. It was
a modern nightmare come true.

Jerry Falwell often compared the New Christian Right to the Civil
Rights movement, as he did in his remarks about the "Nebraska tragedy"
at the 1982 Superconference when he hoped Christians would have the
kind of backbone to stand up for their freedom that *Civil Rights people
had.* On several occasions, I heard him qualify the comparison by denying that fundamentalists (who, by implication as well as in fact, were
virtually all white) were ever subject to anything like the discrimination
and prejudice that blacks endured before the Civil Rights movement.[28]
Still, the comparison was provocative. For one thing, as we have just
seen, white fundamentalist preachers, including Falwell, were among the
outspoken advocates of racial segregation in the 1950s and 1960s. Moreover, in terms of scale and the kinds of activism, several magnitudes of
difference separated the Civil Rights movement and the New Christian

Right as political movements. The Civil Rights movement relied on high-risk and high-cost direct actions and city and statewide campaigns, while most New Christian Right activism was routine, low-cost, no-risk electioneering and lobbying. And, no one, not even New Christian Right leaders, claimed that the New Christian Right had produced a great national orator such as was Martin Luther King, Jr.

If the comparison of the two movements had any merit, it was in the central role played in both cases by Protestant churches, parachurch organizations, pastoral networks, and preachers in mobilizing local, regional, and national constituencies in pursuit of political goals. Both movements were also specifically cultural reform movements mediated by preacherly language. Jerry Falwell was no Martin Luther King, Jr., but he was the major cobbler and distributor of the hybrid religious and political rhetorics that enabled hitherto unallied and inactive white conservative Protestants to see themselves as a singular political and moral force.

During the late 1950s and 1960s, Martin Luther King, Jr., molded the voices of disparate Protestant communities into one voice, speaking tirelessly for them for over a decade throughout the country, in places high and low, joining liberal whites as well as blacks into the cause of racial justice.[29] Preachers are not bound by intellectual property rights, and among them piracy is not a vice, it is a virtue. They may borrow aggressively from one another, appropriating exegeses, illustrations, stories, quotations, logics, style, tone, gestures, and even entire sermons without citation. Their skills of imitation and impersonation, and whom they choose to imitate and impersonate, in part determines their audience and their reach. King mastered, merged, and broadcast speech drawn not only from African American folk traditions, but also from the corpus of printed sermons by the most nationally renowned white liberal Protestant preachers from the 1920s to the 1950s. By shaping these varied sources into a moral vision and wellsprings for action, King simultaneously spoke to and moved both blacks and white liberals to action. King's speech was in turn reiterated by legions of other preachers, both black and white liberal, who customized it in thousands of local contexts and further enabled millions of otherwise unrelated Americans to hear, and in some measure acquire, a collective, transcendent voice regarding racial justice.

Comparable preacherly and popular practices of speech mimesis fashioned otherwise unrelated white conservative Protestants into the cause of preserving Christian values during the 1980s. There were differences. For one thing, no other preacher spanned traditions as historically and socially separated as did King. Jerry Falwell stitched together rhetorics and styles across the divide between (moderate) fundamentalist and (conservative) evangelical traditions, but the divide was recent in origin, partial at best, and always sustained a good deal of low-profile traffic back and forth. Also, Falwell was one among many; he was the most visible by far outside the world of white conservative Protestants, but inside that world his preeminence did not extend much beyond his fundamentalist and conservative evangelical followers. These are important differences, but they should not obscure the fundamental similarity between the two preachers in their role as pivotal figures in the dramatic transformation of their peoples.

In my adolescence and young adult years I don't remember hearing one person speak of the injustice of segregation. To the contrary, all my role models, including powerful church leaders, supported segregation.

I have never once considered myself a racist. Yet, looking back, I have to admit that I was one. Unfortunately, I was not quick enough or Christian enough or insightful enough to realize my condition until those days of tumult in the 1960s.

But believe me, it wasn't the Congress or the courts that changed my heart. [The] demonstrators, in spite of their courage, didn't move me to new compassion on behalf of my black brothers and sisters. The new laws and the loud protest marchers may have helped to enforce the change and to speed it up, but it was God's still small voice in my heart that was the real instrument of change and growth for me.

One Saturday morning in 1963 I sat in the end chair of Lee Baca's shoe-shine business on Main Street in Lynchburg. It was my Saturday morning ritual to have Lewis, an elderly black man, shine my shoes at 10 A.M.

"I heard your sermon on television last week, Reverend," Lewis said as he began dusting a week of dirt off my shoes. "I sure do like the way you preach."

"Why thank you, Lewis," I replied, looking closely at the thin, muscu-
lar man in his middle sixties whose curly gray hair framed his shiny,
smiling face.

Every week Lewis shared his faith with me. And every week I left his
chair feeling his ministry in my life. Then on that particular Saturday
morning Lewis asked me a question that he had never asked before.

"Say, Reverend," he began softly, so that no one else could hear,
"when am I going to be able to join that church of yours over on Thomas
Road?"

I felt like a boxer who had been punched directly in the stomach. For
the first time in years, I was speechless.

I puzzled over the question that next week and in the months that
followed. I had no good reason that Lewis could not join my church.
He was kind enough not to ask me for an explanation, because he knew
there was none. I had excuses, but I had no reason.[30]

Once, in 1980, Falwell was caught lying about an exchange between
himself and President Carter at a White House breakfast. Falwell claimed
that he had asked the president, "Sir, why do you have homosexuals on
your senior staff in the White House?" and that the president had replied
that he wanted to represent everyone. When audiotapes revealed that no
such exhange occurred, "Falwell tried to excuse his action by character-
izing what he had said as a 'parable' or an 'allegory'."[31] He asked, in
effect, that his words be read figuratively, not literally.

When I was in Lynchburg during the 1980s, that is exactly what I
learned to do with respect to Falwell's deeds as well as his words, and it
is what I ask my readers to do in the study that follows.

Falwell's story about God's beginning to change his heart about segregation through the voice of Lewis in 1963 is akin to with his other, more
contestable narrative efforts to backdate the end of his active opposition
to racial integration. Thomas Road Baptist Church welcomed its first
black family and baptized its first black member in its baptistry sometime
around 1970. But Falwell on numerous occasions, including in his 1982
interview with me, claimed blacks were admitted to TRBC in the early or
mid-1960s.[32] His retrospective accounts of the late 1950s and 1960s erase
the fact that he preached pro-segregation sermons.[33]

In his 1987 (ghostwritten) autobiography from which the story about
Lewis is drawn, Falwell portrayed himself as a victim of a racial regime

he did not make. He seemed baffled by a kneel-in on his church steps by members of the Congress on Racial Equality one Sunday in 1964. In 1967, the same year all public schools were required to implement integration plans, Falwell started his Christian day school. Although local clergy and the newspaper charged that the school had a whites-only policy, Falwell denied it. He claimed that the ban on school prayer, not the integration order, had inspired him to start the school, and that it was not a "segregation academy," even though only white students were admitted for the first few years.[34]

Falwell's denials and assertions, which, taken together, enabled him to claim his heart began to change about segregation in the early 1960s, trigger among skeptics a literalist reading that hunts for "the facts," for "objective evidence" that shows that Falwell was still a practicing segregationist until the late 1960s. The response is understandable, but it misses entirely the dimension of Falwell's speech that his faithful followers tune into. Not that they do not notice Falwell's factual sleights of hand—they probably do notice them—but they read them differently. For they understand, and they taught me to understand, that Falwell was, like King had been for his people, a postbiblical character who at once staged and enacted an unfolding, biblically framed drama. Falwell's speech is not like secular speech. He inhabits a world generated by Bible-based stories and, as a "man of God," his speech partakes of the generative quality of the Bible itself. He incessantly frames his life, if only lightly, in biblical terms, and his faithful followers read him as they read the Bible—not as already true, but as always coming true.

Falwell's tale of talking to Lewis that Saturday morning in 1963 incites skepticism at the same time it foils a literalist reading. He and Lewis were the only witnesses—Lewis spoke *softly, so that no one else could hear.* And Lewis is dead—*He was a faithful member of his own church until the day he died.* The tale also invites a figurative reading, one that attends to its form as much as its content. It resonates with other stories in Falwell's corpus of postsalvational conversions in which persons of lesser status (a woman reporter, his children, or an unsaved man)[35] deliver him a Word from God that changes his life. They are stories in which Falwell is momentarily humbled, rendered speechless, hears God's *still small voice,* and begins a new journey toward higher moral ground.

The Bible is full of such "type-scenes," stories "told two or three or more times about different characters, or sometimes even about the same character in different sets of circumstances." Moreover, they occur "at the crucial junctures in the lives of the heroes," and are "a means of attaching that moment to a larger pattern of historical and theological meaning."[36] Falwell's exchange with Lewis also echoes particular biblical characters— David, the king who sinned, was rebuked, and blessed again by God; and Jesus, washing his disciples' feet and saying to Simon Peter, "What I do thou knowest not; but thou shalt know hereafter" (John 13:7). And even his unreliability as a narrator—many of his church people remember Falwell's stands against integration in the 1960s—has a biblical ring to it, triggering the harmonizing interpretive practices in listeners and readers that convert "inconsistencies" into meaningful insights.[37]

These echoes and reverberations all lodge Falwell's life stories within a tradition of Bible-based narrative rites that fashion a fundamental Baptist version of apostolic authority. The interpretive tradition is literalist in the sense that it presumes the Bible to be true and literally God's Word, but the interpretive practices themselves are not simply literalist. The biblical text is considered fixed and inerrant, and it means what God intended it to mean, but discerning that meaning is not simple or sure or constant. The Bible is read within a complex, multidimensional, shifting field of fundamental Baptist (becoming evangelical) folk-narrative practices, and so are the lives of preachers and their peoples. The Bible is at once a closed canon and an open book, still alive, a living Word. Preachers and their peoples are third testaments, the authors of always unfolding chapters and verses.[38]

Jerry Falwell led his people during the 1980s toward a more open engagement with American society, culture, and politics, and he helped make that worldly engagement part of the definition of a true Bible-believing Christian. The following chapters trace the emergence of the composite cultural formation known as "born-again Christianity" in the 1980s from the point of view of one pivotal network of discourses. They show how an old-fashioned culturally and politically disenfranchised fundamentalism morphed into a nationally franchised "fundamentalist evangelicalism."

Part I examines, first, the language of witnessing, which produces fundamentalists and other true Bible believers, and, then, the language and imagery of the Scopes trial, which produced Fundamentalism, that is, Bible belief from the modern point of view. Part II examines the language and context of a series of local and national campaigns, events, and genres from Falwell's community in the 1970s and 1980s—preacher autobiographies, fund-raising, student revivial, the Moral Majority sermon, pro-life stories, creationism, Bible prophecy, and the televangelical scandals. In effect, I interpret sermons, speeches, pamphlets, journals, books, direct mail, videos, television broadcasts, meetings, conferences, and other verbal, visual, and performed texts and occasions as culturally productive rituals. They were the sites, or workshops, in which Falwell, his allies, and their communities recast and resituated themselves as a people in history.

Part One RITES OF ORIGINS

CHAPTER ONE

Speaking Is Believing

To be converted, to be regenerated, to receive grace, to experience religion, to gain assurance are so many phrases which denote the process, gradual or sudden, by which a self hitherto divided, and consciously wrong, inferior and unhappy, becomes unified and consciously right, superior and happy, in consequence of its firmer hold upon religious realities. This at least is what conversion signifies in general terms, whether or not we believe that direct divine operation is needed to bring such a moral change about.
—WILLIAM JAMES, 1906

DUSK had fallen by the time I left Jordan Baptist Church, but the light bothered my eyes as I looked around the parking lot for my car. It seemed as if everything had moved slightly. The church was on the outskirts of one of the poorer parts of Lynchburg, and I would have to zigzag across a half dozen big streets that bisect the city to get back to my motel. I knew I was in some kind of daze after my long talk with the Reverend Melvin Campbell. I usually am after an interview, and this one had been especially intense. Halfway across town, I stopped at a stop sign, then started into the intersection, and was very nearly smashed by a car that seemed to come upon me from nowhere very fast. I slammed on the brakes, sat stunned for a split second, and asked myself "What is God trying to tell me?"

It was my voice but not my language. I had been inhabited by the fundamental Baptist tongue I was investigating. As the Reverend Camp-bell might have put it, the Holy Spirit was dealing with me, speaking to my heart, bringing me under conviction. He was showing me that life is a passing thing, that death could take me in an instant, no matter how much control I fancied I had over my life, and that I should put my life in the Lord's hands before it was too late.

If we conceive of conversion as a process of acquiring a specific religious language or dialect, I was initiated into the first stage of fundamental Baptist conversion as I sat in my car that evening in Lynchburg, awash in apprehension and relief. The process starts when an unsaved listener begins to appropriate in his or her inner speech the saved speaker's language and its attendant view of the world. The speaker's language, now in the listener's voice, converts the listener's mind into a contested terrain, a divided self. At the moment of salvation, which may come quickly and easily, or much later after great inward turmoil, the listener becomes a speaker. The Christian tongue locks into some kind of central, controlling, dominant place; it has gone beyond the point of inhabiting the listener's mind to occupy the listener's identity. The Holy Spirit, the very Word of God, has come, as fundamental Baptists say, to indwell the heart of the believer, who may now publicly display in speech and action a personal, which is to say, conversational, relationship with God.

Conversion is an inner transformation which quickens the supernatural imagination as it places new believers within the central storied sequence of the Christian Bible and enables them to approach the Bible as a living reality. Conversion transfers narrative authority—the Holy Spirit—to the newly faithful as well as the wherewithal to narrate one's life in Christian terms. As we will see, the keys that unlock the Kingdom of God include Bible-based interpretive practices which Christians experience as the indwelling of the Holy Spirit.

Among fundamental Baptists, the gospel of Jesus Christ is the plan of salvation, the good news, God's gift to all mankind. Narrowly defined, the gospel is the story, the message, of Christ's death, burial, and resurrection. More broadly, it is the storied sequence that renders the Bible whole, unified. How does the language and performance of fundamental Baptist gospel preaching (and witnessing, testifying, evangelizing, spreading the Word) convict and convert the unsaved listener? How does it work as a rhetoric of conversion? Witnessing is rhetorical in two senses, namely, as an argument about the transformation of self that lost souls must undergo, and as a method of bringing about that change in those who listen to it. Fundamental Baptist witnessing is not just a monologue that constitutes its speaker as a culturally specific person; it is also a dialogue that reconstitutes its listeners. My focus is on this latter aspect, on witnessing as the practice, the rite and the rhetoric, of conversion.

William James speculated that those who experienced dramatic conversions might have been born with a "melancholy disposition," a chronically "divided" mind, or else they had drunk "too deep of the cup of bitterness."[1] Contemporary social scientists have also investigated converts to born-again Christianity for some indication of why they convert. The notion is, apparently, that those who convert are somehow susceptible, vulnerable, in need of something, so the question becomes: "Why? What's wrong? What's unsettling them?" Or, "What's setting them up? How have they been predisposed to convert?" Social scientists scrutinize the external psychological and social conditions of converts looking for clues, patterns, and causes. They have found evidence in converts' lives of psychological and social stress (due to marriage problems, loss of a job, imprisonment, adolescence, dating, serious illness or accidents, encounters with death, "role" transitions, moving to a new city, going to college, and so on). They have argued that converts were predisposed by previous conditioning (religious upbringing, education, class, gender), and by patterns of interpersonal influence (by converted kin, friends, mentors). These correlations are not satisfying explanations, however, because, among other things, none of the circumstances have been found with enough regularity among converts, and the same circumstances have been found among nonconverts with too much regularity.[2]

There is also considerable literature, both popular and academic, on how various ritual practices and psychological techniques trigger experiences that result in a conversion from one worldview, or mind-set, to another.[3] Distinct conversion methods (social seclusion, dramatic enactments, bodily markings, physical stress or pain, fasting, interrogation, chanting, silence, immobility, and so on) certainly pave the way for radical shifts in belief and commitment. However, this approach, at least when plied by those who see conversion as a kind of brainwashing, overlooks how persuasive in a quite unsensational way the recruiting rhetoric is. It overlooks the extent to which the language of conversion as such "divides" the mind and contributes to bringing about conversion. The presumption which I think accounts for this oversight, and which in more muted form also guides many social scientific studies, is that "nobody in their right mind would believe this stuff." Since "belief" is irrational, some sort of suspension of normal thinking must have taken place and caused the convert to lose his or her grip on reality.

Social scientists and professed unbelievers in general do not let themselves get close enough to "belief" to understand it, or, for that matter, even to see what it is. Men and women convert to fundamental Christianity because they become convinced that supernatural reality is a fact, that Christ is the literal Son of God, that he did rise from the dead and is alive today, that the Holy Spirit is speaking to them, that Jesus will enter their hearts if they acknowledge their sins, that they will have eternal life, that God is really real. To continue to think otherwise would be irrational; it is disbelief that is false and unthinking. The appropriate question then is: How does this supernatural order become real, known, experienced, and absolutely irrefutable?

Among conservative Protestants, and especially among fundamentalists, it is the Word, the gospel of Jesus Christ, written, spoken, heard, and read, that converts the unbeliever. The stresses, transitions, influences, conditioning, and techniques scrutinized by many social scientists do not in themselves "explain," do not "cause," conversion to Christ. All they do is increase the likelihood that a person might listen to the gospel; they may open or "prepare a person's heart." It is the Word of God, the gospel, and, believers would add, the Holy Spirit, God himself, that converts, that changes the heart.[4] We cannot understand fundamental Baptist conversion by looking only at what causes a person to listen to the gospel; the causes are innumerable. Rather, we must listen to the gospel with an open ear, and we must explore the interpretive practices that enable us to understand and accept what we hear.

Witnessing and preaching are the two main situations in which believers speak the gospel most intensely. Preaching—the sermon—is a formal oration addressed to a body of believers and nonbelievers by an ordained or anointed speaker in church services and revivals. Sermons occur in the context of clear ritual format, of a collective, sanctifying scenario in which the mode of interpretation is enacted. Witnessing is more informal and often occurs in the course of what appears to be no more than a conversation between the witness, who is *saved*, and an *unsaved* listener.

But it is no mere conversation. The witness and the unsaved "do not share a common understanding—either of the immediate situation or of reality more generally." Witnesses are "aware of this difference in understanding and self-consciously set out to change the views of those they address" and to create a "compelling religious reality completely at variance with their [listener's] experience."[5]

Witnessing aims to separate novice listeners from their prior, given reality, to constitute a new, previously unperceived or indistinct reality, and to impress that reality upon them, make it felt, heard, seen, known, undeniably real. The reality, or *truth*, constituted in witnessing is, in part, a linguistic one: the supernatural manifests itself as God's voice and his spirit is communicated and experienced through words. Much collective ritual among orthodox Protestants is likewise centered on words, on the Word. Especially among fundamentalists, church services and revivals are stripped of overt, imagistic, and sacramental material; relatively little happens visually, and spiritual realities are not communicated through sensuous, nonlinguistic means. In a way, witnessing is pure fundamentalist ritual, shorn of almost all distractions. It is the plainest, most concentrated method for revealing and transmitting the Word of God, one in which language is intensified, focused, and virtually shot at the unwashed listener.

Fundamentalists are by no means unique in their use of oratory to convert others. Their general techniques and some of the content of their conversion rhetoric are broadly shared among conservative Protestants. Indeed, the principle of conversion, of one person insinuating his or her mode of interpretation in the mind of another, informs all dialogue.[6] What distinguishes fundamental Baptists from others is the degree to which they have formalized rhetorical techniques for converting others, the precise and distinctly unconscious manner in which those techniques appropriate the listener's dialogic imagination, and the particular transformations of self evoked in the listener.

As I sat in that intersection contemplating my near collision, it was quite specifically the Reverend Campbell's language, his supernaturalizing mode of interpretation, that unfurled itself in my mind. I had intended to interview him that afternoon, but within the first few minutes of our talk, Campbell assumed control of the dialogue and reframed my appointment to interview him into his opportunity to witness to me for an hour and a half.

A witnessing session minimally includes the gospel story (an exegesis of the death, burial, and resurrection of Jesus Christ) and a confrontation between the witness and his or her listener in which the witness invites or exhorts the listener to receive Christ as his or her personal savior. Witnesses may also tell how they and others came to know the Lord as savior; they may testify (give accounts of encounters between themselves and God, and other narrative evidence of God's intervention in the natural world) and deliver other doctrinal exegeses (regarding, for example, heaven and hell, the origin and nature of sin, or the ways of Satan).

Witnessing, like evangelistic preaching, "is intended to create a spiritual crisis by calling to the fore one's desperate and lost conditions, which one may have been totally unaware of."[7] This crisis is the onset of the conversion process, what fundamentalists call "coming under conviction," and is based on a direct experience of the divine. You *know* when the Holy Spirit convicts you of, or makes you see, your sins. Conviction effects a deep sensation of one's own impurity and separation from God, or one's sinfulness, one's sin nature. And it engenders a sense that something has to be done about it. We shall see that the inner speech of convicted sinners is transformed as they are alienated from their previous voices (the old self, natural man); cast into a limbo (lost, in need, searching), that is to say, somehow in a liminal state, a state of confusion and speechlessness; and begin to hear a new voice (an inaudible voice, the Holy Spirit).

It is a kind of inner rite of passage that is completed when sinners are saved, or born-again, regenerated, washed in the blood of Christ. Salvation is experienced as a release from the bondage of sin and a personal reconciliation with God. A new self, or the spiritual man, emerges and the supernatural imagination is cut loose as the newborn Christian accepts the meaning of the gospel and begins to speak the language of Christ. In the words of Benetta Jules-Rosette, who studied among, and joined, the Apostles of John Maranke in Africa, conversion is "a powerful clash resulting from the shift from one realm of thought and action to another, a moment of specific *shock*. Under this shock, the very terms of physical existence seem to alter."[8]

The power of the Reverend Campbell's rhetoric to induce liminality was seconded in my case by several circumstances—I was on a number of margins. It was late in the afternoon, and his church was on the edge of town. We were in a corner of the church, his study, alone, on the edge of propriety. I was beginning my fieldwork. And Campbell seemed to me a peripheral character in my study. Having grown up with Jerry Falwell and trained to be a preacher at his Liberty Bible Institute, Campbell was in, but not quite of, Falwell's empire. His congregation appeared to consist largely of white working-class or unemployed men and women and their children. Jordan Baptist Church was, in his words, "a solid work," with about 350 members, and it sustained a number of outreaches, but Campbell and his congregation were not engaged in any of the political or cultural activism that earned Jerry Falwell a national reputation.

Campbell was a tall, trim, muscular man, his silvery gray hair piled up from his forehead in waves an inch or two high. He sat at his desk, I in a side chair, and he looked me in the eye the entire time we talked. Later I realized that most people who sat in the chair I was sitting in came to Campbell for spiritual help. I also realized he was eager to have me tape-record our conversation so that I might listen to it again and again should I prove too hard-hearted that afternoon to receive the help he offered me.

Born-again believers say that unbelievers cannot understand their faith. Jeanne Favret-Saada came to a similar conclusion while studying witchcraft in the Bocage region of France. "For anyone who wants to understand the meaning of [witchcraft] discourse, there is no solution but to practice it oneself, to become one's informant."[9] This is so, she tells us, because there are only two "positions" from which a person speaks or hears speech about witchcraft: bewitched and unwitcher; if you are neither, you will never hear others speaking the discourse.[10] The situation is, of course, quite different among fundamentalists. Gospel talk is public and targets outsiders, nonbelievers; but, as in witchcraft, there is no such thing as a neutral position, no place for an ethnographer who seeks "information." Either you are lost, or you are saved.

When I went to Lynchburg, I was naive enough to think I could be detached, that I could participate in the culture I was observing without partaking of it. I could come and stay for months, talk mainly to church people, attempt to "learn the culture," ask questions based on respect and knowledge; and still remain outside, separate, obscure about what I believed and disbelieved. But there was no such ground. I might think there was, but the church people did not, no matter what I said. It was inconceivable to them that anyone with an appetite for the gospel as great as mine was simply "gathering information," was just there "to write a book." No, I was searching. *God works in mysterious ways.* In my case, he seemed to be letting me find my way to him through this book I said I was writing about them. Several people told me as much; others just seemed amused when I told them what I was doing and gave me a look that suggested they knew better. My story about what I was doing there, instead of protecting me from "going native," located me in their world: I was a lost soul on the brink of salvation. And the Reverend Campbell spoke to me accordingly.

I asked him first how he became a pastor, and he took fifteen minutes to answer me. I had expected to get something akin to "information" or "facts," and he gave me a long story of personal transformation, one that began with how he had been saved and had served the Lord before he was called to preach. He never acknowledged my academic project and seemed to speak to me as if I were what they call a "nominal Christian," someone who might think she was a Christian but who had never been saved. He could assume I was not born-again simply because I did not indicate I was, as believers do when they meet, if only by a turn of phrase. Certainly, he was aware of himself as witnessing to me, and he had been trained, formally and informally, in soul-winning techniques, but his manner and his method seemed to draw more on unconscious intuition than deliberate design.

There were at least five distinct rhetorical movements in Campbell's witnessing talk that afternoon. He equated his present listener—me— with the listeners in his stories. He fashioned her as lost. He fashioned the gospel speaker—himself and others—as saved. He transformed lost listeners in his stories into gospel speakers. And he invited me to undergo the same transformation, the same narrative rite of passage, and become a gospel speaker. I will trace these movements by exhibiting and ex- panding on sequential pieces of Campbell's speech, hoping to show you, as much as tell you, what conversion and belief are among fundamental

Baptists. Unfortunately, in words flattened out on a page, we may hear
only suggestions of his Southern, fundamental Baptist accent, his peculiar
cadence, intonation, pausing, pitch, and stress.

I was saved when I was fifteen years old. I was a member of a Method-
ist church all of my life as a child. At the age of fifteen I still had not
heard the gospel story of Jesus Christ and how that he died for our sins.
I was instructed as a child coming up in the Methodist movement just
to live a good life, to be morally good and to maintain all of those particu-
lar statuses, and I would be okay. Now I was invited by a friend to visit
a Baptist church. . . . And this was an independent fundamental Baptist
church. And of course they had one of those hell-fire-and-damnation
preachers in there, and he got down on my case that night. And I began
to look at things and I realized there was something missing in my life.
Because, though we've never seen God, we're still aware of the fact that
he is present, we know he's there. And even though I wasn't saved I
knew there was something bombarding my life that was beyond my
power to see or really understand at the time. And I couldn't understand
why I wasn't receiving what I needed in a Methodist church. So after
attending about three of their services—and incidentally they were in
revival that week—then the spirit of God began to convict me about my
place in life and how that I was lost and had not yet turned my whole
life over to Christ, so I was saved that week, I went forward and gave
my heart to Christ. Now this is a process that some folks misconstrue
along the highways of life. "I put all the nine yards in that really belongs
there . . . ," they think often that this is all that's necessary. But I realized
that night there was a need in my life and that need was met, and so
much the spirit of God came to live in my heart. Now this is God's gift
to every person that receives Christ. So I joined that particular church
after about a month of visiting there. But I was first saved and then I
followed Christ to baptism, which I hadn't been baptized before. Of
course the Methodist church, they sprinkle, and I don't have any argu-
ment with them there, other than the fact that I believe the Bible teaches
immersion. And then after this, my life began to grow and materialize
into something that was real, something that I could really identify with.
That emptiness that was there before was now being replaced by some-
thing that had meaning and purpose in it. And I began to sense the need
of telling others about what had happened to me. And basically I think

perhaps the change could be detected in my life, as the Bible declares, that when a person is saved, the old man, the old person, or the character that they were passes away, and then they become a new creation in Christ Jesus. That is to say, they might be a character that may be drinking and cutting up and carrying on, and a variety of things that are ill toward God. All of these things began to dissolve away. I found that I had no desires for all these things, but then I began to abhor them. I actually began to hate them. And this was in accordance with the Scriptures, as I found out later. And then as my life began to mature in Christ I found that I too could win others to Christ the same way I was won: by simply telling them that there's a heaven to gain and a hell to shun.

In his conversion narrative, the Reverend Campbell defined being "lost" and being "saved" and how he moved from one position to the other. Lostness, he indicated, is a position from which you listen, and salvation is one from which you speak. Campbell began to pull me in and placed me into his narrative in the position of listener.

Numerous poetic and performance features teem on the surface of Campbell's speech. There are verse markers ("and" and "now"), special codes, figurative language, symbolic and metaphoric parallelism, and appeals to tradition. These features mark the text as an oral performance and indicate a special relationship between performer and listener. It is a relationship in which the performer assumes responsibility for a display of competence, indirectly instructs the listener about how to interpret messages, and invites, elicits, participation. These tactics bind the listener to the performer in a relationship of dependence and keep the listener caught up in the display.[11]

Campbell also communicated my relationship to his speech more directly through his use of pronouns (emphasis added): *I still had not heard the gospel story of Jesus Christ and how that he died for* our *sins. . . . Because, though* we've *never seen God,* we're *still aware of the fact that he is present,* we *know he's there.* Campbell continued to place me in his narrative during the rest of the time we talked by using the cooptive "we," and he frequently shifted his pronouns and at times used "you" ambiguously, as a personal and impersonal pronoun. His listener by these means became the subject of a whole range of presuppositions posited in such a way that they were difficult to resist.

At one point in this initial speech and at several points subsequently Campbell quite overtly identified me with his narrative listeners. The central, repeated narrative structure in his witnessing was a dialogic encounter between person and God, or between a lost listener and a saved speaker. The context of his witnessing, of course, was also conversational: Campbell and I were engaged in a dialogue, one in which he, who was saved, was speaking, and I, who was not saved, was listening. Early in his conversion narrative, Campbell began to collapse these parallel levels of conversational structure and thereby place me in his stories, in his speech:

Now I was invited by a friend to visit a Baptist church . . . and of course this was an independent fundamental Baptist church. And of course they had one of those hell-fire-and-damnation preachers in there, and he got down on my case that night. In describing his context the night he was converted, Campbell called attention to our—his and my— context. He too was a hell-fire-and-damnation preacher, and I, in effect, was informed that he would be getting down on my case and that I might be converted that afternoon. This was no mere innuendo: Campbell was thus aligning me and my encounter with him with the listening persons and their encounters with God in his stories. Whenever a saved speaker addressed a wayward listener, the speaker would also be addressing me. I too would be transfigured, if only by degrees, by the very act of listening to the Reverend Campbell.

Campbell reminded me of my position in his narrative several times. I heard it faintly when he said, *I found that I too could win others to Christ the same way I was won: by simply telling them that there's a heaven to gain and a hell to shun.* He was more explicit later, when he told me how he was called to preach.

Now when I had my calling at age twenty-nine, I was operating a service station. And I was in the station one afternoon, working on a car. And God did not speak to me with an audible voice, but he spoke to my heart. And there was a conversation going on much like the one that's here. I'm doing the talking and you're listening. And God was doing the talking and I was listening. I was down under the car, changing the oil, and . . . God was just dealing with me about doing this. And I said, "I can't do that." And much like Moses when the Word called him

to do something, he said, "I can't even talk." And God said, "Well, I'll
send your brother Aaron to help you." So every excuse I would come
up with, he would head me off by instructing me that he would do
something to meet my shortcomings. So I finally surrendered in the sense
of the word that afternoon.

If I had any doubt about where I belonged in Campbell's talk, this
story dispelled it. God spoke to him under his car that afternoon just as
Campbell was speaking to me in his office. I am the listener; he is the
speaker; that which transpires in his narrated dialogues shall somehow
transpire between us. Campbell also introduced and located me within
another parallel level of dialogic structure, between God and biblical
figures. I must listen to Campbell as long ago Moses, and much later
Campbell, listened to God. Clues such as these inform or, rather, persuade the listener that the witness's words, though they appear to be
about the witness and about other characters on the narrative surface, are
on a deep level about the listener: you, too, are a character in these
stories; these stories are about you.

Keeping in mind that much of what the Reverend Campbell said about
himself as he came "under conviction" also applied to his listener, let us
examine how he fashioned the lost soul, the sinner, the person in need
of salvation.

Young Campbell realized there was something missing in his life.
There was a need in his life. He was lost and had not yet turned his
whole life over to Christ. He was cutting up and carrying on, and doing
a variety of things that were ill toward God. He realized his life was
empty and lacked meaning; it was not maturing and growing into something that was real. Yet he knew there was something bombarding his life
beyond his power to see or really understand. Campbell was ostensibly
describing himself here, but because he had put me in his narrative in his
place, he was also describing me. Indeed, he was refashioning me.

Campbell's language emptied my life, my personality, and erased my
past. I was primarily distinguished by what I lacked and, given my lacking, by what I needed. I stood for absence, for void, yet I was aware of
something more, something missing, unseen, hidden. And I would come
to need that, to desire it, having been launched on a quest for affirmation
and revelation which may be achieved only through conversion. All this

was accomplished in me by implication and presupposition, not by direct argument. My consent was not sought; I was implicated, already enlisted as a collaborator, in my own metamorphosis.

As well as constituting the listener as a lost soul, Campbell in his conversion story began to fashion the speaker, the saved soul, as he narratively moved himself, you could say converted himself, from lost listener to a saved speaker of the Word of God.

The hell-fire-and-damnation preacher who got down on Campbell's case shortly became the spirit of God convicting him about his place in life—that he was lost and had not yet given his whole life over to Christ. He was saved, and he went forward and gave his heart to Christ, and the spirit of God came to live in his heart. His need was met. His life began to grow and materialize into something that was real, something that had meaning and purpose in it. His old character and its desires passed away. Then he began to sense the need of telling others about what had happened to him and found that he too could win others to Christ in the same way that he was won. The spirit of God first worked on Campbell and brought him under conviction, then entered and transformed him, and finally spoke through him to bring others under conviction.

God's spirit, the Holy Spirit, converts sinners, but he (the fundamental Baptist Holy Spirit is a male person) speaks through those who preach the gospel. Preachers speak the Word of God; God speaks through them. Campbell had started a church in a storefront after God called him, and on the first day of services, he wondered why anyone would come there to hear him preach. Later he realized *it was the Word of God they must come to hear, and not me. It's the Word of God that must cause the change.* The change is caused not by God as an external agent, but by the Word, the spirit, of God, which is internalized when a person accepts Christ. *By nature, Adam and Eve, you know, they caused the problem, but they invested into everyone of us that would be borned a similar nature. Now this nature can be wiped clean, it can be changed by once again instilling the spirit of God within us.* Here, according to Campbell, is how the Holy Spirit works his will. It's not that easy though.

Now I realize many times when I preach, the Bible says preaching is as of foolishness. But there is another agent working while I'm preaching. And he's the Holy Spirit. And he's the one that grips the heart. I could throw a rock at you and you could throw another one at me. But if I make a statement from the Word of God, and the Holy Spirit bears me up, and he begins to deal with your heart about it, then when we have parted company, he's still working, and I'm gone. Now until we're saved, he lives without us. But when we're saved, he comes to live within us, and this is what we mean by receiving the Lord into us. When he comes to live in us he comes in the form of the Holy Spirit. I've never seen him. But like a mother with a child, she's not seen her unborn baby, but she knows he's there. You say, "How does she know?" She feels life and movement within her. Now the spirit of God is like another voice, like another party. And he is not a figment of the imagination. But the Bible says, he's a real personality, a real person. And actually he can catch your next word and stop it, if you're sensitive to him. And if you're not, you put a piece of tape across his mouth, you can fold him back into the innermost rooms of your heart and give him no liberty. But if you let him, he becomes the tutor of your life, the instructor, the guide, the teacher. And he tells—now when I use the term "tells," he speaks to my heart and he gives me—you've seen the time when you would sense something and you couldn't really say another person was talking to you, but you sense you ought to do something. You were impressed to get up and go see somebody or something. All right, this is the way the Holy Spirit works with me. He impresses me. He moves upon my heart to do certain things. And sometimes he gives me spiritual discernment that's almost like reading another person's mind. Many times I've had people sit down to talk with me, and the Holy Spirit would almost link my mind up with theirs and tell me certain things. And I cannot explain it, but this is because he is a third part of the Godhead. In reality, it's God living within us. Now once he's in here, the things that I used to love to do—and I mean I had a real passion for some things before I got saved—and when he came to live within me, all of a sudden I found that I hated and despised those things. Well, it wasn't my flesh; it was Christ living within me that was despising those things because they were anti- and alien to his nature.

Fundamental Baptists, especially preachers, are acutely aware of the power of witnessing and of the gospel, of the rhetoric of conversion in general. They attribute its transforming power to the workings of the Holy Spirit, that is, to supernatural agencies, but when they describe how those agencies work, they invariably refer to words, to speaking and hearing and reading. In effect, in a coded way, they recognize language as a medium, even a subject, of religious experience, and they coach the unconverted in the linguistic dimension of conversion.

The Holy Spirit uses Campbell's speech, as it were, to remodel his listeners' inner speech. The Holy Spirit impresses on Campbell what to say and deals with the hearts of his listeners, bearing him up, after he's gone. The heart is contrasted with the head and seems to mark the difference between unconscious and conscious knowledge and belief. The Holy Spirit, the Word, works on the unconscious mind to bring the conscious mind under conviction. As listeners appropriate the gospel, the Holy Spirit penetrates the conscious mind and becomes another voice, a real person, who begins to recast their inner speech. After salvation, the voice of the Holy Spirit guides converts, gives them discernment, and seems to alter the very chemistry of desire.

The Reverend Campbell spelled out the moment of salvation elliptically in his own conversion narrative, and he elaborated it in his disquisition on the Holy Spirit. He also posited the moment of salvation in highly charged symbolic terms, in biblical exegeses on birth and death, flesh, spirit, blood, and sacrifice.

Campbell drew on well-established parallels in evangelical culture between narratives of Christ's death, or the gospel story, and conversion narratives, and between the cosmic order outlined in the Bible from the Garden of Eden to Calvary and the epic of each individual in the face of inevitable death. The gospel story defines the movement, the passage that all believers must endure, from suffering and dying (coming under conviction), to burial (silence, absence, void), and resurrection (converting, being reborn, eternal life). As God restored man to himself by sacrificing his son on the cross, so the unsaved may restore themselves to God by dying to their old selves and being born anew in Christ. All they need do is acknowledge their sin nature, accept that Christ died for their sins, and ask him into their hearts. It is these words, once genuinely spoken, that resurrect a dead soul, that instill in the newborn believer the Holy Spirit, the very voice of God.

Campbell began to elaborate the connection between the gospel story and salvation, as witnesses often do, by talking about Nicodemus, who came to visit Jesus one night and said to him, as Campbell put it, *Now you've got something that we've missed.*

Jesus said, "Nicodemus, I'm going to limit my words in talking to you. Listen carefully." He said, "Ye must be borned again. Ye must be borned again." And Nicodemus said, "How in the world can a man be born when he's old? Is it possible that I could enter again a second time into my mother's womb and be born?" Jesus said, "No, you didn't listen. I'm going to repeat one more time. . . . You must be borned again. . . . That which is born of flesh is flesh. That which is born of spirit is spirit. Marvel not that I say, you've already had one birth, but you need more. You need the birth that's going to change you from the one you received from Adam, which is a sinful nature. You've already experienced that first birth and you're full of yourself. But now you need the second birth, the one that will give you this indwelling of the spirit of God."

Now when I was born, I was born physically of my mother. Jesus said, "You must be borned of the water first, of the spirit second." . . . When a child is about to be born, it's first enclosed in the mother's womb. Is that true? [Yes.] *That water must be broke before the child can be born. Now this is a representation of the first birth. He said, "You must be born of the water first, Nicodemus. You've already been born, you're here." But then he said, "Now you must be born by the spirit." Your mother birthed you the first time. And your mother cannot give you this spiritual birth. So this must come from above. Now God gives this second birth.* [I ask, "How does the second birth change a person?"]

Okay, Susan, you have the characteristics and the traits of your mother and your father. True? ["Yes."] *All right. Now the second birth will give you the characteristics or the traits of the Father that birthed you. Now the first time when you were born, you couldn't help your mother. If your life had depended on it, you had to depend upon her strength to bring you into this world. True?* ["Yes."] *Now when we're saved, or borned again, this is absolutely and totally dependent upon God.*

Now where did the birth take place at? It had to be a birth of such a caliber that it had to take care of the whole world. And this was a place called Calvary. Jesus, when he was dying, was shedding his blood, and the Old Testament says that without the shedding of blood there is no remission, there can be no forgiveness for sin. So blood—the innocent—

and God typified this in the animal sacrifices of the Old Testament.
When Adam and Eve sinned, Genesis 3:21 said he slew innocent animals.
And he took the skin off these animals, and he covered their nakedness,
which is the type of giving them a covering which is representative of
righteousness, and the blood was used to atone for their sins. . . . Atone-
ment means to cover, and the blood of the animals of the Old Testament
typified one day that Christ would come, shed his blood, but then this
blood, this blood being shed now, brings about redemption and not
atonement, which is a temporal covering. For thousands of years, the
Jews under the Mosaic economy offered up sacrifice of animals—you've
probably read that—and they did this because this was representative of
one day a coming Savior.

You remember the incident in Exodus [sic], about how Abraham
went to offer his son Isaac on Mount Moriah. And the Bible says that
Isaac the son said, "Father"—he didn't know what was going on—he
said, "Here's the altar, here's the wood, here's the knife, here's the fire,
but where's the sacrifice? Where's the lamb?" And Abraham said, "My
son, God himself shall provide a sacrifice. A lamb." Now we go down
several thousand years into the future, and John the Baptist, when he
saw Jesus Christ for the first time, he told the disciples that were with
him, he said, "Behold, take a look. Here is the lamb of God that will
take away the sins of the world." And the lamb of God was Jesus Christ.
Of course, Isaac was not slain. There was a ram caught in the thicket
which was a type of substitution. So Jesus Christ died in my place as a
substitution for me.

According to Billy Graham, "the conquest of death is the ultimate
goal of Christianity," and victory is achieved when sinners are born again
and the spirit of God is instilled in them.[12] Rebirth is totally dependent
upon the grace of God, as a baby is totally dependent on its mother for
its birth. Symbolically, Campbell first moved his listener from the first
birth, the mother, flesh, and water breaking, to the second birth, the
Father, spirit, and blood shed. The second (spirit/male) birth takes over,
subverts, and cancels out the consequences of the first (flesh/female)
birth, releasing the sinner from the wages of sin, death. The womb of
the second birth was the cross at Calvary. Christ mediated between the
first (flesh/female) and second (spirit/male) birth and created the possibility of reconciliation with God.

After spelling out the contrast between the first and the second birth, Campbell moved deeper into a discussion of blood, of the innocent. The blood of animals sacrificed under the law of Moses was a temporal, or a temporary and earthly, covering (atonement). The blood of Christ provided eternal, heavenly remission from sin (redemption). Through animal sacrifice, humans asked God's forgiveness and might stay his judgment, but they were still condemned to die. Only the self-sacrifice of God himself could lift the curse of Adam and Eve and overturn the Mosaic economy. God gave to man that which he had not asked Abraham to give, his only son, his own flesh and blood, and so made available eternal life to those who would believe. God no longer asks the blood of animals from men and women. He asks for repentance and faith in the saving grace of Christ. A sacrifice is still due, namely, the flesh-bound self of the first birth, which is offered up in the act of believing.

Animal blood is linked to spiritual death; it can only cover sin (separation from God, death) and nakedness (meaninglessness, void); and it only represents, or typifies, righteousness (order, reunion with God) and a coming Savior. Christ's blood actually saves men and women from spiritual death; Christ's death substitutes for them and creates eternal life. Here Campbell was using the New Testament to overtake, subvert, and transform the Old Testament; he seemed to suggest that "Mosaic" sacrifice only approximated, or signaled to, God, while born-again sacrifice relates directly to and reunites one with God.

On a symbolic level, Campbell argued that it was Christ's blood that made this transition possible. But narratively, that is, looking at the form his argument took on the surface of his whole juxtaposition of stories, Campbell emphasized the importance of spoken language, of dialogue, in making the passage from one world to the next. He repeatedly relied on dialogue—between Jesus and Nicodemus, himself and me, Isaac and Abraham, John the Baptist and the disciples—to set up the dilemma of human choice. In this respect, he was speaking as much within Old as New Testament tradition. Old Testament writers used "narration-through-dialogue" to highlight "human will confronted with alternatives which it may choose on its own or submit to divine intervention. Articulated language provides the indispensable model for defining [the] rhythm of political or historical alternatives, question and response, creaturely uncertainty over against the Creator's intermittently revealed design, because in the biblical view of reality words underlie reality."[13] And it is through spoken dialogue, through witnessing, that each sinner is confronted with and makes the choice to accept or reject Christ.

The Reverend Campbell concluded an hour of virtually uninterrupted talk with a veritable gospel poem that fully realized the complex, holistic meaning of blood as birth and death and emphasized the mutuality of the sacrifice and reconciliation between humans and God. Campbell's speech is strikingly biblical here—in fact, much of it is a rephrasing of several verses from the Old Testament Book of Ezekiel—though as elsewhere he converts the Hebrew text to New Testament ends.[14]

My birth, it belongs to God. God made me. And then Paul said, "When I've been saved, I've been bought with a price." What was that price? His life at Calvary. That's what he gave for me. He ransomed me out of the, you might say, the slave markets of sin and brought me into a right relationship. And when I was unworthy, the Bible said he loved me. When I was wretched and naked, when I was borned, the prophets said it was like I was thrown out onto the ground. I had not been washed in salt. I had not been suppled [washed in water]. *I had not been bathed in olive oil. I was laying there in my own blood, dying. And when he saw me, there was nothing about me that really made me desirable. Yet he looked beyond all of my faults and saw my needs, and he come, and he loved me, and he died for me. And he even made it available so that I could know this, and when I come to that knowledge, I had no alternative but to want to run to the one that loved me. Because nobody had ever cared for me like Jesus. And that's about the size of the story. Nobody.*

Campbell then turned to me and asked, *Now Susan, let me ask you a question. Do you know Christ as your personal savior?* He asked me several more questions. *Do you believe in God? What if you died today?* Then he told me a story of a man he buried a few weeks before who had choked to death on some food. *Had no idea he would be sent out into eternity. . . . Life is just an uncertain thing.* He inquired again into my faith. *Have you ever sensed the presence of God?* Then he told me about a man who, at forty, lamented that he'd been looking for a wife for so long. Campbell told him, *I think God has sent you the right woman, probably twenty times, and you turned her down.* He said the man had overlooked the orchid and all the other beautiful flowers while looking for a rose. *Can you identify with that?*

Then Campbell brought his exhortation to a rather stunning conclusion.

Now if in this life, the Bible says, only we have hope, then we of all men are most miserable. But you see my life, my hope, is in the life to come, and I realize this life is a passing thing. Jeremiah says it's like a vapor. It appears but for a little while, and then vanishes. We know how uncertain life is. We're just not sure how long things are going to go. I went to work one morning. I had some work to do on a Saturday morning. And one of my sons was fourteen years old. And the other one was fifteen years old. And we got up that morning. And I went in, and I rassled with my son and rassled him out of bed, the one that was fourteen. And we got up that morning and ate breakfast. We opened the Word of God. We read and we prayed together as a family, my wife, my two sons, and I. And I went on to do that work that morning. It was a Saturday. And I had something I wanted to move. And I was operating a crane. And I accidentally killed him that morning. And I looked at God, and I said, "Lord, you told me in your Word that all things work together for good to those that love you, especially those that are called according to your purpose." And I said, "I've served you faithfully. And I've loved you. And I've given you my heart, my life, my soul, given you everything about me. And now I can't understand this, why you've taken my son." And God didn't speak with a voice that I heard with my ear but he spoke to my heart. He said, "Melvin, you know maybe you don't understand what I've done at this particular time, but, can you accept it?" And I said, "yes sir, I can accept it." And Susan, when I made that statement, and I settled that in my own heart, and I said "Lord, I accept it though I don't understand it," I don't know where to say it came from other than that God gave it to me, but he gave me a peace in my soul. And I have not questioned it since.

Now I went and shared it with my wife. I said, "Shelby," I said, "God said all things would work together for the good to us because we loved him." And she said basically the same thing I did, "Well, I don't understand. This isn't good." But I said, "Yeah, but God said it is good." And I shared with her, and when I shared this with her, she came of the same opinion. And we watched them close the casket on that little fellow and my, he was just super. I mean, he was almost my heart throb, you know, that was my baby. And yet he died in my arms. And yet I looked at God and I said, "Lord, I'm going to love you if you take my other son. I'm going to love you if you take my wife. I'm going to love you if you take my health, if you strip me of everything I've got, I'm going to love you."

Now I'm saying that because, Susan, he is real. This is not mythology. I'm forty-six years old, and I'm no fool. God is alive. And his son lives in my heart. And I'd love for him to live in your heart. Of all that I could give or think of ever giving over to you, I hope that what we've talked about here today will help you make that decision, to let him come into your heart, and then he will be your tutor. And he'll instruct you in things that perhaps I've stumbled over today. Sometimes the vocabulary may not be appropriate to really describe the depth and the detail of the things that need to be said. But this is where the Holy Spirit can make intercession for us. The Bible says with groanings and utterings that we just cannot utter. I may miss something, but he'll bring it out. I may present something, and you don't understand it. But he will reveal it to you. This is what the whole thing is about.

Campbell began his ultimate narrative on a note of wistful resignation. Life is a passing thing, a vapor; it's here for a little while and then vanishes. Without pause, he shifted into a homey story about getting his sons up one Saturday morning, opening and reading the Word of God, and going out to work in the yard. Then in a split second he delivered a narrative shock: *And I accidentally killed him that morning.* The sentence disrupts his story. It startles his listener. But before it is absorbed, Campbell shifts to the real point—his conversation with God. God asked Melvin Campbell to accept what he, God, had asked Abraham to accept and what he, God himself, was willing to give: his son's death. And Melvin obeyed: *Yes, sir. I can accept it.* This sentence, in a moment as extreme and extraordinary as the tragic death of his son by his own hand, is what God asked of him to restore order in himself and in the world. By speaking his obedience, his submission to God's will, they were reconciled, and Campbell received in return peace in his soul, an eager willingness to give still more. The same gifts, he concluded, awaited me, if only I too would accept Christ. *This is what the whole thing is about.*

The unborn-again listener wants to know more about Campbell and Campbell's son, not about God's son. How did the boy die? How did

Campbell really feel about it? What about his pain? His sorrow? His guilt? How could he speak to a stranger about what could be the most tragic moment in his life with such spareness, such calm, such calculation? The dialogues with God and with his wife sound like cloaks concealing what he really must have felt. At best, they ring of reinterpretation, of a retrospective story Campbell tells—one that, as he himself suggests, renders him at peace with his loss. The unregenerate listener interrogates Campbell's story as if it were a system of verbal clues about something outside itself—about the tragic event, his raw experience, the unmediated emotions of the moment, or his subsequent effort to recover and reintegrate—and finds the story distinctly odd, choppy, suspiciously elusive.

In contrast, the born-again believer, or the unbeliever who is being born-again, listens to the cadence and phrasing of Campbell's words, to the esthetic shape of his story and the multidimensional biblical universe it presupposes, and hears nothing but the truth, that is, the world evoked, the world constituted, by the story. Campbell's tale sounds homespun, but its threads are thousands of years old. In the story's rich weave are echoes of the trials of Job, and paraphrasings of David's songs in Psalms and of Paul's letters to the Romans and the Phillippians. Many of the literary devices that distinguish Hebrew scripture are also audible—the strategic use of "now" and "and"; the laconic pace; the use of minimal detail to establish time, place, character, and relationships; the characteristic rush of biblical narrative toward an essential moment; auspicious shifts and gaps that engage interpretive attention; the privileging of dialogue over narration to reveal character; and the repetiton of key dialogue and the movement of action-response.[15] Campbell's supple mastery of biblical conventions authorize him as a "man of God," a man who breathed life into God's Word and whom God's Word breathed to life. But what made his story truly captivating and potentially transformative was its placement at the end of a sequence of biblical stories which, looking back, fashioned a series of interlocking sacrificial altars, and, looking forward, fashioned one upon which a sacrifice was due. This sequence, the sacrificial passage, was formed in his disquisition on the Old Testament stories of Adam and Eve, and Abraham and Isaac, and on the New Testament story of Christ's death at Calvary.

Campbell summed up the narrative economy laid down by those stories: *Now here's the entire Bible and its economy coming together. For
four thousand years of the Old Testament, they offered up blood sacrifices. Now all of this together, combined, typified one day a coming
hope. They looked through the offering of the blood one day to Calvary. . . . They looked forward and believed that he would* [die for us],
*and I look back and believed that he did, and we all focus at a place called
Calvary and realize why he died.*

Campbell called attention here to the way in which Bible-believing
Christians make connections among the storied events, both biblical and
historical. The interpretive links between his juxtaposed stories—between the animal blood shed at Eden and Mount Moriah and the divine
blood shed at Calvary, and between Christ's self-sacrifice and ours—
were "typological," or "figural," links. Old Testament storied events
"typify" the central story of the New Testament. The skins that covered
Adam and Eve and the blood of animals slain in the Old Testament were
a "type" of righteousness, of redemption. Earlier events are types of later
events. That is, earlier events prefigure later events, and later events complete, or fulfill, earlier, incomplete events. In figural interpretation, "an
event on earth signifies not only itself but at the same time another,
which it predicts or confirms. . . . The connection between occurrences
is not regarded as primarily a chronological or causal development but as
a oneness within the divine plan, of which all occurrences are parts and
reflections."[16] There is no distinction between biblical and historical stories here. Both are "events on earth" related by figuration, enabling
Christians to envision "the real world as formed by the sequence told by
the biblical stories."[17]

Adam's sin called forth a sacrifice of animals to cover him with their
skins. Abraham's obedience called forth the ram to substitute for Isaac.
Both stories, or events, are interpreted as incomplete. Animal sacrifice
only atones, only provides a temporal covering, a substitute for the ultimate sacrifice—death—that is due. When Christ made the ultimate
sacrifice upon the cross for all mankind, he completed, he filled the gaps
in, all the prior stories. In the same instant, he opened a gap that must
be closed. Christ's death raised a question that must be answered by all
those who come after: Whom did Christ die for? In answering, "He died

for me," and in sacrificing their old selves to Christ, Campbell and all believers close the gap; they fulfill or complete the story. Simultaneously, their self-sacrifice poses the question anew to all who have not sacrificed themselves.

Not long after his exposé of our right relationship to Calvary, Campbell inquired into my beliefs and found, mostly from what was not said, that I was unlikely to be convinced that afternoon that Christ died for me. From then on his talk led in a zigzagging but steady fashion toward his sacrificing his own son for me in order to strike home his message one last time. In doing so, he set up a figural sequence of sacrifice stories, from Abraham and Isaac, to Christ's passion, to his own terrible tale, a sequence that looked forward with hope to the next story, my own self-sacrifice of faith.

Campbell wanted his listener to understand that she, her life, bore the same relationship to the story of Christ's sacrifice that that story bore to the story of Abraham and Isaac. Her story would fulfill Christ's in the same way that Christ's fulfilled the Old Testament tale. The moment of salvation is precisely the moment when a lost soul realizes that Christ died for *you.* Suddenly, the story of Calvary, the Bible as a whole, becomes "relevant." The context in which biblical stories are meaningful and the context of one's personal life collapse into each other, and the fusion evokes a sense of great insight, of miracle. All of these stories are speaking to you. These stories are God speaking to you.

More specifically, you stand in the same relation to the ram as Isaac did. The ram died in his stead. The lamb, Christ, died in your stead. This connection between stories/events is established through a sense of incompleteness, of "something missing." Isaac fashioned the gap in the form of a question: "Where's the sacrifice?" According to Campbell, Christ answered that question, completed that story, as he became the sacrifice that was due. Campbell acknowledged the gap in Christ's story by answering the implicit question, *Why did Christ die? Christ died for us,* so that we might live forever. We "complete" the story of Christ, we determine the meaning of Christ's death.

Campbell's final story about his son's death replicated the biblical stories in the obvious thematic sense—a father sacrifices his son. But the connection was not merely allusive. It is also figural. Campbell's story fulfilled Christ's, which fulfilled Abraham's. Campbell, like Abraham, like God himself, was willing to sacrifice his son in accordance with God's plan. But like their stories, his too was incomplete. It evoked a haunting sense of something missing. Why did Campbell's son die? Or, more precisely given the typological sequence, for whom did Campbell's son die? The answer, of course, had already been provided as well by the previous stories. He died for me. The Reverend Campbell sacrificed his son, narratively speaking, for me.

Through the cumulative pattern of his Bible-based storytelling that afternoon, Campbell created a space for me to take responsibility, and feel responsible, for determining the meaning of his son's death. That I owed him something, and what it was, and what I would receive in turn, was one of the last things the Reverend Campbell made clear to me: *Of all that I could give you or think of ever giving over to you, I hope that what we've talked about here today will help you make that decision, to let him come into your heart, and then he will be your tutor.* Campbell had fashioned access to a divine pattern of history for me, and the only question remaining was, would I accept it?

If conversion is a process of acquiring a specific religious language and witnessing is a conservative Protestant rite of conversion, then, if you are willing to be witnessed to, if you are seriously willing to listen to the gospel, you have begun to convert. Listening to the gospel initiates lost souls into the Word, the language of God.

The single most important unconscious clue I gave Campbell that I was "susceptible" to conversion was that I was willing to listen to the gospel. Crises, transitions, and upbringing as such do not lead you to convert. They may make you more likely to listen, and anything that makes you more likely to listen, including the work of ethnography, is actually what makes you susceptible.

"Susceptible" implies passivity, but I was not passively listening to Campbell. I was struggling mightily against the grain of my ignorance and incredulity to make sense of what he was saying. His language was so intense and strange, yet deceptively plain and familiar, full of complex nuances and pushes and pulls, that I had no time, no spare inner speech, to interpret him consciously, to rework what he said into my own words as he talked. I just gripped my chair, as it were, and took his words in straight. I was willfully uncritical as well in the sense that I wanted to understand, as best I could, his words from his point of view, to assume his position, to make his speech mine.[18] It was not exactly what Campbell said that brought me under conviction; it is that I took it up, merely by listening to him actively and uncritically.[19]

The membrane between disbelief and belief is much thinner than we think. All I had to do was to listen to my witness and to struggle to understand him. Just doing so did not make me a fundamental Baptist born-again believer, but it drew me across that membrane in tiny ways so that I began to acquire the knowledge and vision and sensibilities, to share the experience, of a believer. Believers and disbelievers assert there is no middle ground: you are either one or the other. You cannot both believe and disbelieve. But that is precisely what it means to be "under conviction." You do not believe in the sense of public declarations, but you gradually come to respond to, interpret, and act in the world as if you were a believer. It is a state of unconscious belief, experienced with more or less turmoil and anxiety, depending on how strong your disbelieving voices are. It also depends for the ethnographer on how adamant your colleagues are about the "dangers" of doing "this kind of fieldwork." I was given to think my credibility depended on my resisting any experience of born-again belief. The irony is that this space between belief and disbelief, or rather the paradoxical space of overlap, is also the space of ethnography. We must enter it to do our work.[20]

Campbell's testimony was a hodgepodge of stories sewn together with the scarlet thread of redemption, not a series of "logical" or "empirical" arguments. He persuaded me narratively. Disbelief is a conscious refusal to accept a particular version of reality, and believing involves the conscious acceptance of "doctrines," of particular claims about reality and one's relationship to it. But disbelief is also, in the case of evangelical Christianity at least, an unconscious refusal to participate in a particular narrative mode of knowing reality. Likewise, belief also involves an unconscious willingness to join a narrative tradition, a way of knowing and being through Bible-based storytelling and listening. You cannot tell born-again stories, you cannot fashion them, without acknowledging belief, but you can hear them, you can absorb them, and that's how you "believe" when you are under conviction. You get caught up in the stories, no matter what your conscious beliefs and disbeliefs are.

I was caught up in the Reverend Campbell's stories—I had "caught" his language—enough to hear God speak to me when I almost collided with another car that afternoon. Indeed, the near-accident did not seem like an accident at all, for there is no such thing as a coincidence in born-again culture; God's hand is everywhere. Gospel talk casts in your subliminal mind, your heart, a Bible-based sense of options poised to trigger God's speech, given a context in which you seem to have a choice to submit to God's will or ply your own. Preachers construct such contexts verbally, and life presents them virtually every day—those gaps in the ordinary, when the seams split and you encounter the unknown, the unexpected, the uncontrollable, the irrational, the uncanny, the miraculous. These are moments ripe for supernatural harvesting, moments when fear or awe mutes your natural voices and God may speak, offering you the opportunity to speak back.

Coming under conviction (listening to gospel stories or voices) is easy compared to being saved (speaking, telling stories). When you come under conviction, you cross through a membrane into belief; when you get saved, you cross another membrane out of disbelief. This passage is more problematic for some lost souls, for what outsiders would say were reasons of education, class, or intellect, and insiders would say was hardness of the heart, pride, or the work of the devil. However you explain it, getting saved among fundamental Baptists involves publicly giving up disbelief, not just suspending it, but disavowing it. It involves accepting born-again belief in the sense of acquiring new knowledge of reality that quickens the supernatural imagination and yields a conversational relationship to God. Born-again knowledge becomes the centering principle of your identity, your personal and public life, your view of human nature and history. And it involves joining a particular narrative tradition to which you willingly submit your past, present, and future as a speaker.

One more reason Campbell was a compelling witness was the extent to which, and eloquence with which, he gave his life, narratively speaking, to the language of Christ. This willingness to submit one's life to God, to narrate one's experience and fashion stories out of it in dialogue with God's will and biblical truths, makes God, and his Word, most real and known and irrefutable to oneself and to one's listener. Campbell understood this, at least intuitively, well enough to tell me about killing

his son just before his final appeal on behalf of my soul. The story dis-
armed me because he said he had killed his own son, because he so crisply
gave up his grief and his guilt to God, and because he was telling me, a
stranger and an outsider, about it. He sacrificed his own son to his narrative tradition with a calm assurance, a peace of heart, that I still find
difficult to accept. Often that afternoon I found myself at a loss for words
as Campbell narratively generated what for me were novel grounds for
knowing and for speaking, but the story of his son's death struck me
dumb. He might as well have gone up in a puff of smoke.

A cynic, second-guessing Campbell's motives, would say he was manipulative, that he used this painful story to "get to" his listener. But
from within born-again culture, this telling was the ultimate evidence of
belief, Campbell's moment of maximum authenticity. If he told me the
story for effect, it was to effect the reality of God in me. What God said
to him and he said to God in that tragic moment meant that God is
absolutely real. This was his own conclusion: *Now I'm saying that,
Susan, because he is real. This is not mythology. I'm forty-six years old,
and I'm no fool. God is alive. And his son lives in my heart.*

Among fundamentalist Baptists, the Holy Spirit brings you under conviction by speaking to your heart. Once you are saved, the Holy Spirit
assumes your voice, speaks through you, and begins to rephrase your
life. Listening to the gospel enables you to experience belief, as it were,
vicariously. But generative belief, belief that indisputably transfigures you
and your reality, belief that becomes you, comes only through speech:
speaking is believing.

CHAPTER TWO

Fundamentalist Exile

Heave an egg out of a Pullman window, and you will hit a
Fundamentalist almost anywhere in the United States today.
—H. L. MENCKEN

HEAVE an egg into the annals of modern America and you will hit an account of the Scopes trial of 1925. Contemporary accounts of the trial, including most of the national news coverage, in effect, legitimized the exile of Fundamentalists—Bible-believing Protestants generally—from public life and thus helped make America modern in the sense of "secular."[1] The public rhetorics that refashioned a heterogeneous array of conservative Protestants into an unitary cultural "other," into Fundamentalism with a capital "F," were not invented in the Scopes trial. But they were unfurled in that court battle more vividly, more widely, more sensationally, and more disparagingly than ever before. And, for over fifty years after the trial, its highly charged images and story lines have cycled through journalistic and academic accounts, high school textbooks, novels, plays, and movies as if they were matters of fact.[2]

The public rhetorics that exiled Fundamentalists and defined modern America as a secular nation emerged out of late nineteenth and early twentieth century debates over the validity of biblical literalism and the public worthiness of the theologically conservative Protestants who proclaimed the Bible literally and absolutely true. The debates turned into contests for power and influence all over the country, in universities, public schools, seminaries, denominations, legislatures, courts, elections, the press, and local and national literatures. The outcomes of the contests were mixed and unstable until the late 1920s when, in the aftermath of the Scopes trial, conservative Protestants, or Fundamentalists, separated out. They left their denominations and formed new organizations uncontaminated by modern theology; they declared social reform hopeless; and they disavowed all manner of modern sociability. Thus they began their collaboration with a definition of modern America as secular and hence off-limits to biblical literal rhetorics and practices. They accepted their designation as premodern, as unfit for modern cultural and political life.

Articulated in the form of academic knowledge, media images, literature, and popular stereotypes, the presumption that modern America was secular prevailed as national common sense for over fifty years. The presumption was grounded in an escalating string of oppositions between Fundamentalist and Modern—between supernaturalist and reasoning, backward and progressive, ignorant and educated, rural and cosmopolitan, anti-intellectual and intellectual, superstitious and scientific, duped and skeptical, bigoted and tolerant, dogmatic and thinking, absolutist and questioning, authoritarian and democratic.[3] The totalizing opposition between Fundamentalist and Modern in turn emplotted a progressive history. Fundamentalism was a rigid, homogeneous thing stuck in the past, and modernity was the multifaceted, ever-changing face of the future. The central story line of this history, both folk and official, anticipated the increasing marginalization, if not the disappearance, of Fundamentalism, and supernatural religiosity generally, in America.

The modern point of view in America emerged in part from its caricature of conservative Protestants as Fundamentalists. They were the "them" who enabled the modern "us." You cannot reason with them. They actually believe the Bible is literally true. They are clinging to traditions. They are reacting against rapid social change. They cannot survive in a modern world. Such attitudes, clichés, images, and plots not only licensed the de facto disenfranchisement of conservative Protestants, they also chartered the public dominance of secular and theologically liberal and moderate voices in mid-twentieth century America.

In the late 1970s and 1980s, conservative Protestants, including self-described fundamentalists, challenged and rewrote this charter, the social contract of American secular modernity. Through myriad legal, political, and cultural contests, whether won or lost, conservative Protestants released themselves symbolically from the terms of the implicit social contract which disenfranchised them. In effect, they overturned the cultural verdict of the Scopes trial as they broke free of and dramatically revised the heavily freighted modernist imagery and logic this verdict had condensed.

Contemporary conservative Protestants put various labels on their opponents in these contests—they were liberals, secular humanists, feminists, homosexuals, pornographers, abortionists, and, all together, emissaries of Satan. But they also struggled against an unnamed opponent, present in every public combat, namely, national common sense and, more specifically, the cultural verdict rendered most memorably in the Scopes trial, which had exiled them from public life. As a way of making the disenfranchising imagery and logic of the Scopes trial more apparent, more tangible, let us return to the scene of the trial, trace how its cultural judgment was fashioned and performed, and thus how, in effect, "Fundamentalists" became the quintessential modern American outsiders.

The core drama of the Scopes trial is, much like an origin myth, remarkably stable. It invariably zeroes in on the image of two big old white men arguing about the Bible in a southern courthouse on a sultry summer afternoon. The story may be bent on behalf of various agendas, but the paradoxical verdict is always the same. The Bible, the old man defending it, and the Fundamentalists lost the cultural battle, even though they won their legal case by convicting John Scopes of the crime of teaching evolution. Especially in early accounts of the Scopes trial, the word and all persons and things called "Fundamentalist" were riddled with pejorative connotations. Those who interrogated the literal Bible, those who won the cultural battle even though they lost their legal case, carried off the valued connotations.[4]

Before the Scopes trial, it was unclear which of the opposed terms, Fundamentalist or Modern, would be the winner and which the loser, which was superior and which was inferior, which term represented the universal and the future and which the residual, that which was passing away. In the early decades of the twentieth century, two loose and fluid Protestant coalitions—most commonly dubbed liberal and conservative—fought for control over doctrinal statements, seminaries, missions, and, effectively, as it turned out, the prevailing definition of Protestant Christianity. They were, in other words, still struggling to determine which view of Christianity would be dominant within American Protestantism. The activists in both camps were minorities who represented themselves as the center, as speaking for the majority, and both tried to stigmatize their opponents as marginal, the infiltrator, the upstart, the violator of order and all that was truly Christian.[5]

While some of the religious polemics of the period were blunt and deprecatory, most were restrained and even erudite, and overall the tone was one of serious debate about matters of monumental importance. When the Reverend Curtis Lee Laws invented the term "fundamentalist" in 1920, it was taken up as an honorific by his Baptist and Presbyterian colleagues who swore to do "battle royal for the fundamentals of the faith."[6] It and other labels ascribed to each side acquired more unsavory connotations in the course of some very heated denominational struggles, but until the Scopes trial, neither liberal nor conservative Protestants succeeded in taking over and tainting their opponents' definition of themselves. Each side was able to sustain its own version, or versions, of events, and the accounts on both sides could only anticipate—they could not assume—victory.

Alongside the intensifying denominational fights that agitated Northern cities in the early 1920s, some conservative Protestant ministers allied with politicians in the South to provoke a string of legislative fights over the teaching of evolution and the status of Genesis in public schools. The political debates were more charged, more acrimonious than their religious counterparts, having been taken up, on one side, as the main battle royal of self-declared fundamentalist preachers and laymen under the leadership of William Jennings Bryan and, on the other side, by liberal lawyers, scientists, politicians, and journalists in alliance with politically outspoken liberal ministers. The legislative debates produced partial victories for fundamentalists in several states, and in 1925 Tennessee passed a law that represented full victory: evolution was cast as denying the Genesis account, thus as anti-biblical and anti-Christian, and its teaching was prohibited, actually criminalized, in schools funded by the state. In July, just a few months after the law was implemented, it was challenged in the trial of biology teacher John T. Scopes.

Even before the Scopes trial began, participants and observers proclaimed that it would be the decisive battle that would settle once and
for all which side would win the contest between religious liberals and
conservatives in both arenas of their struggle—church and state. The
remarkable thing is that it did just that. All accounts agree, regardless of
the point of view of the author, that the Scopes trial "climaxed" the
controversy, which was thereafter known as the Fundamentalist (not the
conservative Protestant, not the Modernist) controversy, and that it was
a decisive "defeat" for what then came to be called the Fundamentalist
movement.[7] Indeed, the Scopes trial was inscribed as "the end" of the
movement, even though the denominational debates and legislative battles persisted into the 1930s.

After the trial, a relatively unnuanced modernist version of what was
thereafter known as Fundamentalism became both popular and official
history. It did not abolish fundamentalist—or conservative—versions of
events so much as encapsulate them. Conservative Protestant versions of
the Scopes trial and the events of the 1920s acquired a kind of double
vision in which they, conservative Protestants, were at once victims and
critics of modernist insinuations. Their own histories of the period were
thereafter marked by an essentially modernist trajectory, with a sense of
the inevitability of their defeat, at least on earth.[8] The Scopes trial was
thus a moment of narrative encapsulation, a moment in which the cultural story of one people was subordinated to and reframed by the terms
of another. Narrative encapsulation marks cultural dominance, and it is
in this sense that the Scopes trial constituted the beginning of a half century of liberal Protestant and secular dominion in America.

How, more precisely, did the Scopes trial produce this narrative effect?

The Scopes trial was a representational event. It was a complex, multilayered, polyvocal, open-ended cultural process in which participants, including self-appointed observers, created and contested representations
of themselves, each other, and the event.

In the beginning, the legal range of the trial was the constitutional
challenge imagined by the national officers of the American Civil Liberties Union (ACLU) in New York City who were looking for a test case
of the Tennessee law and the men of Dayton, Tennessee, who concocted

the Scopes test. However, within weeks of the initial challenge the con-
tours of the case mushroomed. Roger Baldwin, director of the ACLU,
described in retrospect what happened when William Jennings Bryan
offered to appear as counsel for the attorney general of Tennessee: "It
was immediately apparent what kind of trial it would be: the Good Book
against Darwin, bigotry against science, or, as popularly put, God against
the monkeys. With Bryan for the prosecution, it was almost inevitable
that Clarence Darrow should volunteer for the defense. Darrow was
well known as an agnostic; he frequently wrote and lectured on the
subject, ridiculing many of the Old Testament myths. . . . The legal issues
faded into obscurity against the vivid advocacies of an unquestioning
faith and of a rational and probing common sense. Bryan threw his
challenge to the defense lawyers, stating, 'These gentlemen . . . did not
come here to try this case. They came here to try revealed religion. I am
here to defend it. . . . I am simply trying to protect the Word of God
against the greatest atheist or agnostic in the United States.' And Darrow
replied to him, 'We have the purpose of preventing bigots and ignora-
muses from controlling the education of the United States and you know
it, and that is all.'"[9]

The entry of Bryan, then Darrow, to the Scopes case catapulted it into
the arena of national debate over evolution and the Bible, over science
and religion.

Although Roger Baldwin's language tilted in favor of the pro-science
camp, he, like virtually all who wrote about the trial, portrayed it as a
fair fight. Each side was represented by a nationally renowned oratorical
giant. Both points of view would be articulated at their extremes, and
so, it seemed, were nicely balanced and positioned to frame the event,
the contest, in the most dramatic mutually exclusive terms. Bryan was
prepared to convict evolution as heresy and to defend the Bible as truth;
Darrow to convict the Bible as wrong and defend evolution as fact. Finally, neither man hesitated to deploy powerful ad hominem arguments
against his adversary. Darrow used Bryan's rural, populist, Southern alliances against him, and Bryan accused Darrow and his team of Yankee
interventionism and big-city, fancy-credential elitism.

Everybody had a stake in the trial's looking like a fair fight between
Darrow and Bryan, evolution and the Bible, science and religion, other-

wise it could not have produced an authentic winner and loser. But it was not a fair fight. The sides were not equally represented; their representations were not equal in that some traveled farther than others. The representations that circulated in the courtroom seemed to be equally matched. The representations that traveled around the town were tilted toward orthodoxy, and those that traveled to midsized cities around the country varied somewhat depending on who was in editorial control, but the narrative of the trial was delivered in the main by the voices of the national news service writers.[10] Their voices and those of big-city newspaper correspondents produced most of the representations that left Dayton and spread around the nation and abroad, and they were dominated by the pro-science camp. Just as the case against Scopes was largely settled before the fact in the court of law, the case against biblical orthodoxy in the court of national public opinion was largely settled before the fact by this representational imbalance.

The Scopes trial was a spectacular media event from the moment Bryan and Darrow signed on and converted it, in Bryan's words, into "a duel to the death" between evolution and Christianity. Radio Station WGN, an outlet of the *Chicago Tribune*, made it the occasion of the first national radio hookup, so that news from Dayton, in the courtroom and on the streets, was broadcast live all over the country for two weeks. In addition, over one hundred, some said two hundred, newspaper reporters and photographers from all the big cities (two from London) descended on Dayton, a town of 1,800 in the hills of Tennessee, northeast of Chattanooga. No doubt many of the journalists considered themselves Christians. Some of them may even have harbored doubts about evolution, and a few wrote with sympathy for the orthodox cause. But none of them identified with the fundamentalist standard, and overall their reportage composed an unrelenting, at times unbridled, rendition of the modern point of view. In the 1920s, dozens of conservative Protestant journals and bulletins had national circulations, but they did not send observers to Dayton. Some did not comment on the trial at all, and others described it briefly and belatedly, mainly as another instance of liberals' attacking the Bible or the unfortunate prelude to William Jennings Bryan's death. The trial was thus constituted for most Americans by the national press from the modern point of view. The conservative Protestant point of view, spoken in its own voices, was erased and then rein-scribed within and encapsulated by pro-modern story lines in the daily news read and heard around the country and abroad.

On the eve of the trial, the *New York Times* set the major narrative frame by describing Scopes as "a mere figure over which will joust the forces of evolution and religion, Fundamentalism and Modernism, liberalism and conservatism."[11] Most of the *Times* story, however, was not con-cerned with such lofty issues, but rather with minutely detailed depic-tions of Bryan preaching "in the hills" to "plain folk" and the "cranks and freaks who flocked to Dayton" for the trial. Subsequent trial cover-age bulged with such side stories—some days they seemed like the main stories—which progressively homogenized, stigmatized, and appro-priated the voice of fundamentalists, "the plain folk," "the throngs from the hills."

That the *New York Times* considered itself fair-minded compared to the *Baltimore Evening Sun*'s H. L. Mencken was suggested by a side story entitled "Mencken Epithets Rouse Dayton's Ire."[12] Specifically, the *Times* reported, Daytonians were irked by Mencken's calling them "gap-ing primates," "yokels," "peasants," "hillbillies," "Babbits," "morons," and "mountaineers." Mencken's pieces were indeed excessive, ribald, Rabelaisian parodies of both rural America and Protestant orthodoxy. The two were almost indelibly fused in his writing. One of his stories, a rambling account of a healing revival in the hills, peaked with this de-scription of a preacher praying for a penitent: "Words spouted out from his lips like bullets from a machine gun. . . . Suddenly he rose to his feet, threw back his head and began to speak in tongues—blub-blub-blub, gurgle-gurgle-gurgle. His voice rose to a higher register. The climax was a shrill inarticulate squawk, like that of a man throttled. He fell headlong across the pyramid of supplicants. A comic scene? Somehow, no. The poor half wits were too horribly in earnest. It was like peeping through a knothole at the writhings of a people in pain."[13]

Mencken was not much more restrained when he was back in Dayton focusing on the trial. He spent much of his verbal excesses on Bryan— the precise details of his dress, his appetite, his corpulence, his somber face, his anxious glaring gaze. Darrow was, in contrast, the unembellished hero of Mencken's stories, a master in court, a source of terror in the town. "All the local sorcerers predict that a bolt from heaven will fetch him in the end."[14] On the day Scopes was found guilty, Mencken summed up the trial like this: "The Scopes trial, from the start, has been carried on in a manner exactly fitted to the anti-evolution law and the simian imbecility under it. There hasn't been the slightest pretense of decorum. The rustic judge, a candidate for re-election, has postured before the yokels like a clown in a ten-cent side show, and almost every word he has uttered has been an undisguised appeal to their prejudices and superstitions. . . . Darrow has lost the case. It was lost long before he came to Dayton. But it seems he has nonetheless performed a great public service by fighting to the finish and in a perfectly serious way. Let no one mistake it for comedy, farcical though it may be in all its details. It serves notice on the country that Neanderthal man is organizing in these forlorn backwaters of the land, led by a fanatic, rid of sense and devoid of conscience."[15]

The circus metaphor audible in Mencken's summation was widespread, especially in the local color stories that embellished accounts of the legal proceedings. The *New York Times* described Dayton on the eve of the trial as "half circus and half a revival meeting," and the next day as a "carnival in which religion and business had become strangely mixed."[16] Indeed, it was not entirely a metaphor. John Scopes recalled in his memoirs that "everybody was doing business" in Dayton during his trial—stores peddled monkey commodities (little cotton apes, a soda drink called Monkey Fizz, a "simian watch fob"), and the streets were filled with vendors of hot dogs, lemonade, books and pamphlets, religion and biology. "There was never anything like this. It was a carnival from start to finish. Every Bible-shouting, psalm-singing pulpit hero in the state poured out of the hills . . . and they came from outside the state too. . . . Some professional circus performers, who must have felt at home, brought two chimpanzees. The air was filled with shouting from early morning until late into the night."[17]

In this rendering of the carnivalesque scene in Dayton, Scopes's point of view was, like that of most national reporters, a modern one in the sense that he cast himself as an observer of, not a participant in, the spectacle. Circus performers actually did come to town, and a side-show ambiance did pervade all the proceedings, but not everyone was inside the spectacle. The journalists, lawyers, scientists, and otherwise liberal-minded men and women who flocked to Dayton, even Scopes himself, were not reckoned—did not reckon themselves—inside the carnival. They *witnessed* it. The town, and the trial, "happened to them." They were somehow outside their stories, the speakers, not the spoken of, of this history. The titles of Mencken's dispatches from Dayton went so far as to inscribe explicitly the events on him: "Impossibility of Obtaining Fair Jury Insures Scopes' Conviction, Mencken Says." "Yearning Mountaineers' Souls Need Reconversion Nightly, Mencken Finds."

While the Tennessee town and countryside seemed to present themselves to the press as a modern nightmare—as the spectacle of premodernity—the trial was more wily, harder to nail down as transparent evidence of Modern superiority, at least until the last day. Mencken's final dispatch, the relatively somber meditation on the meaning of Scopes's conviction cited above, was hardly triumphal, but then he actually wrote it before the last day of testimony in the trial. Mencken left early expecting that the only remaining event was the jury's inevitable guilty verdict. Indeed, part of what made the last day of testimony so dramatic was that nobody expected it. Although Darrow and his team had obviously planned for it, they too were galvanized when Bryan accepted Darrow's request that he, Bryan, take the stand as an expert witness on the Bible. Unexpected, it was also the moment everybody had been waiting for, a duel to the death, it turned out, quite literally. Or so it seemed. All primary and secondary accounts I have examined, including those written by conservative Protestants, represent the encounter as a decisive moment in which Darrow (science) beat Bryan (the Bible). Here, briefly, is how the encounter is generally represented.

The courtroom was so crowded on the last day that the judge, fearing the building might collapse, convened court outdoors. On a platform set up for visiting revivalists, Clarence Darrow interrogated William Jennings Bryan for two hours about the precise accuracy of well-known Bible stories and about his knowledge of science and history. Bryan did not know that the "big fish" that swallowed Jonah in the Old Testament was called a "whale" in the New Testament. He did not know what would happen to the earth if "the sun stood still," or where Cain got his wife. He did not know that Bishop Ussher's widely accepted date of the Creation, 4004 B.C., was a calculation, not a quotation, from the

Bible. He did not know how the serpent moved before God made it crawl on its belly. Darrow established that (the authors of the Book of) Joshua believed the sun revolved around the earth, yet Bryan acknowledged that he believed the earth revolved around the sun. In what became the most notorious exchange, Darrow led Bryan six times to say that he did not think the six "days" of creation were "necessarily" twenty-four-hour days.

Darrow spliced his biblical thrusts with inquiries that impugned Bryan's knowledge, indeed, his intelligence, repeatedly inducing Bryan to confess his ignorance of scholarly knowledge. The interrogation concluded with the following exchange:

> MR. BRYAN: Your Honor, I think I can shorten this testimony. The only
> purpose Mr. Darrow has is to slur at the Bible, but I will answer his
> questions. . . . I want the world to know that this man, who does not
> believe in God, is trying to use a court in Tennessee—
> MR. DARROW: I object to that.
> MR. BRYAN: To slur at it, and, while it will require time, I am willing to
> take it.
> MR. DARROW: I object to your statement. I am examining you on your
> fool ideas that no intelligent Christian on earth believes.[18]

Mr. Darrow and Mr. Bryan were at this point both standing and shaking their fists at each other; the judge abruptly adjourned court until the next morning. Many spectators, including townspeople who had previously cheered Bryan on, thronged around Darrow to congratulate him on his performance. Bryan, left alone, watched and waited until a few people broke away from the crowd and spoke to him. If Bryan thought Darrow had beaten him, he never admitted it, not even to his wife. Five days later he died during an afternoon nap.

My telling of the story figures the climactic encounter in the courthouse as Bryan's defeat, but it could be represented as his victory: as the occasion of a man's standing up publicly for the Bible, for God, taking upon himself the ridicule and scorn of all unbelievers; as an unambiguous demonstration that evolutionary thought was an attack on true Christianity, on Bible believers. Darrow could be cast as a shameless man who "hated" the Bible, a bigot who mocked the common man and persecuted the Great Commoner. Bryan could be etched in our memories as a hero who exposed a villain. At the end of the Scopes trial, and at several points during it, Bryan seemed to be constructing himself and the event in these terms, but no one else took up his story line.[19]

Of course, pro-science and pro-Bible accounts inflected the events of the last days of the trial differently. Modern voices construed them most literally, as bearing intrinsic, obvious meanings—namely, that Darrow beat Bryan because science is superior to biblical religion; that the truth simply won out; that Darrow revealed Bryan's ignorance and quite properly found the Bible guilty of not representing reality. Even Bryan admitted, so the modern story goes, that the Bible could not be, word for word, literally true, and his death proved that he knew he was wrong, profoundly outwitted and outmoded, whether he admitted it or not. The people of Dayton even recognized the truth. The *New York Times* reported: "These Tennesseans were enjoying a fight. That an ideal of a great man, a Biblical scholar, an authority on religion, was being dispelled seemed to make no difference. They grinned with amusement and expectation, until the next blow by one side or the other came, and then they guffawed again. And finally, when Mr. Bryan, pressed harder and harder by Mr. Darrow, confessed he did not believe everything in the Bible should be taken literally, the crowd howled".[20]

Pro-Bible narratives of the interrogation usually passed over the details and moved on to discuss the way the encounter was represented in the newspapers and the extent to which journalists, in their stories, converted a bad situation into a rout. According to the Reverend R. M. Ramsay, writing for the *Presbyterian & Herald and Presbyter* in August 1925: "When the trial was over, and everyone saw that the [Scopes' conviction] was just as every sensible, unbiased judge who knew the facts knew it would turn out, then the newspaper reporters raised a great noise of ridicule about the awful scene when Lawyer Darrow questioned Mr. Bryan about his beliefs." Ramsay described Darrow's line of questioning as "repulsive, abusive, ignorant, tiresome twaddle about Bible questions that no true student of God's Holy Word would ever think fit to answer."[21]

The Reverend Ramsay's point of view was savvy and hostile but nonetheless presupposed Bryan's defeat and hence collaborated in constructing the trial as a modernist victory. Modern accounts of the Scopes trial, no matter how gloating or unself-critical, could not have by themselves constituted the trial as literally meaning the triumph of modernity.

Fundamentalists read the trial, specifically Darrow's interrogation, in essentially the same way, and it was the overlap, the convergence of the two story lines, that produced the sensation that the modern version of events had literally come true. Bryan lost in terms of fundamentalist expectations because he failed to defend the Bible according to code, which required active, aggressive Bible quoting, an ability to parry all "infidel objections" and "standard village atheist questions," and, finally, a willingness to assert that every claim, every word, every jot and tittle in the Bible was literally true. In each respect, Bryan broke the pose of absolute biblical literalism, and that amounted to his publicly betraying fundamentalism as well as the Bible, Christianity, and God.

Although Bryan's Bible-believing brethren were devastated by his testimony about the six days of Creation, they did not think it proved he was not really a biblical literalist. The prevailing consensus among Protestants—laity, pastors, and theologians—at the time was that the "days" of Creation were "ages," not twenty-four-hour days, and this interpretation, along with numerous other metaphorical readings, was regarded as properly literal. The problem for Bible believers was that Darrow's interrogation converged with a rhetorical ploy that Bible-believing preachers used to police each other, a ploy which awarded the higher ground to a preacher who could establish his biblical interpretation as "more literal" than another's. Darrow succeeded in proving that Bryan's views were not consistent with his modernist caricature of biblical literalism which assumed that each word in the Bible was always, and only, to be understood in its narrowest, most literal sense. Thus Bryan's testimony was devastating because Darrow, in his interrogation regarding the six days and other Bible passages, used the rules of fundamentalist rhetorical combat to impugn Bryan's status as a strict Bible believer. The fundamentalist audience was trapped; they could not contest the outcome of the duel because it conformed to their own rules.

That might well have been enough to have rendered the trial a defeat in fundamentalist eyes, but then Bryan died, definitively extinguishing any residual hope that he might recoup his loss to Darrow and providing, as deaths do, an ultimate sense of ending. A story takes shape in relation to its ending, the endpoint from which to look back upon events as if they had led up to it. (Imagine, for example, how the story of the Scopes trial would have changed for both sides had Bryan survived and Darrow been struck by lightning on his way home from the trial.) Bryan's death figured as the last event in fundamentalist as well as modern accounts of the Scopes trial, and most narrators elaborated it as unambiguous evidence of Bryan's loss, his utter humiliation. Darrow's words, it seemed, were deadly; Bryan had, it appeared, internalized the stigma, and it killed him. Insofar as Bryan stood for Fundamentalism, his death also marked the definitive end of the movement.

Darrow's interrogation of Bryan was spellbinding and, joined with Bryan's timely death, positively mythic because of the narrative fusion that occurred in its wake, indeed, seemed even to occur in the event itself. It was the moment in which "Fundamentalists" got caught up in the modernist narrative. They were captured by its terms; the modernist story encapsulated their story. It was the moment when Fundamentalists saw themselves, as well as were seen, as acting out, in the body of William Jennings Bryan, modernist preconceptions and scenarios. In effect, under the sign "Fundamentalist," Protestants who believed the Bible was true were "othered," they were rendered cultural outsiders, not simply in the numerous accounts of the trial that poured out for years afterwards but in the event itself. Fundamentalists were othered "live" in the Scopes trial. They were present and participated in the event which stigmatized them, cast them out of public life, marked them as a category of inferior persons whose very existence required explanation. The event also constituted, in and after the fact, an apotheosis of the modern gaze, its authorial point of view, its knowing voice, its teleological privilege, its right to exist without explanation.

The Scopes trial was the first "cultural workshop" that produced the social contract which exiled conservative—in the sense of Bible-believing and Christ-professing—Protestants from the nation's public life, but it was by no means the last. Modern secular hegemony was produced over and over again during subsequent decades. In their theories, story lines, plots, and images, the nation's scholars, journalists, novelists, playwrights, and filmmakers most explicitly articulated modern America as a world in which Fundamentalists figured as stigmatized outsiders.[22] The terms of secular modernity were also written into a wide array of laws, court decisions, government policies, decrees, and regulations, codes of etiquette, customs, practices, and commonsense presuppositions that structured national public discourses.

Some conservative Protestants, looking back on their recent history, have seen a vast, all-pervading, evil (literally, guided by Satan) conspiracy by secular humanists to take over America from its rightful Christian heirs.[23] It is easy enough to counter this theory. For one thing, there is no evidence for a secular humanist conspiracy, sinister or otherwise. For another, the theory erases the ways in which conservative Protestants, especially and most aggressively fundamentalists, collaborated in their own cultural and political exile. It also suggests that their absence makes America secular, as if there were no other faiths present. The regime of public religiosity that prevailed during America's midcentury was secular in the limited sense that, for the most part, at least at the national level, signs of religious partisanship were voluntarily suppressed. The regime was indeed all-pervasive, but it was also incomplete, partial, fragile, and, at times and places, seriously contested.

The regime of secular modernity did however put a special onus on conservative Protestants, above all on those who called themselves fundamentalists, insofar as they had come to stand for religious partisanship and their exclusion was seen as essential for the survival of a secular, or "tolerant," America. One form this exclusion took, one which testifies to the power of the regime, was the illusion, especially widespread among the nation's intelligentsia, that conservative, Bible-believing Protestantism—that is, Fundamentalism—was unchanging, homogeneous, and gradually disappearing.

We know now that strict Bible belief in America did not diminish but rather flourished during the middle half of the twentieth century; also that it was always more heterogeneous, more urban, more middle class, more educated, and more nationally engaged than it was represented to be in popular and academic discourses; and that it became more heterogeneous, urban, upwardly mobile, educated, and nationally engaged—right along with the rest of the country—after World War II.[24] The whole period after the Scopes trial has been revisited and opened up in new ways, revealing a history of steady institutional growth and diversification—of pastoral networks, parachurch organizations and superchurches, schools and colleges, book and magazine publishing industries,

radio, television and direct-mail operations—yielding a dense, sophisticated, multicentered national cultural infrastructure.

The midcentury history of even the emblematic Fundamentalists, the
independent fundamental Baptists, was one of extraordinary growth, increasing heterogeneity, and transformation. Between the 1930s and
1980, Baptist churches repeatedly withdrew from national denominations for their "alleged liberalism" and formed or joined "independent"
networks of churches with their own, "separated" seminaries and mission
bodies.[25] The largest and longest-lived networks were the General Association of Regular Baptist Churches, the Conservative Baptist Association of America, the New Testament Association of Independent Baptists, the Fundamental Baptist Fellowship, the Orthodox Baptists, the
Southwide Baptist Fellowship, the World Baptist Fellowship, and the
Baptist Bible Fellowship. By the early 1970s these networks comprised
nearly nine thousand churches with over 1.5 million members.[26] One of
the fastest growing among them was the Baptist Bible Fellowship (BBF)
which had nearly 1,800 churches and 750,000 members. According to a
1971 list of the one hundred largest Sunday Schools (that is, attendance
at the midmorning Sunday service which instructs adults and children in
the Bible), twenty-three were BBF churches, including Jerry Falwell's
Thomas Road Baptist Church.[27] By the early 1980s, the BBF had nearly
3000 churches and well over one million members.[28]

Both fundamentalism and pentecostalism gave rise to new, upwardly
mobile movements after World War II that began the process of re-
mainstreaming conservative, Bible-believing Protestants socially and of
challenging their exile from public life.

Pentecostalism emerged out of a series of revivals around the turn of
the century marked by outbreaks of gifts of the spirit, that is, speaking in
tongues, prophecy, healing, and other signs of "second blessing." Pentecostals, like fundamentalists, left their denominations and formed new
organizations. While eschewing fundamentalist polemics about Biblical
truth and separation, they took Biblical truth and the virtue of holy living
for granted and were lumped together with fundamentalists by outsiders
as profoundly "antimodern." However, inexplicably from the point of
view of outsiders, pentecostal gifts of the spirit began to break out in
nonpentecostal churches, both conservative and mainline in the 1960s.

As the gifts of the spirit spread, the movement became known as the charismatic movement.[29]

In a very different form, fundamentalism gave rise to its own expansive movement during the 1940s and 1950s. During World War II, several hundred moderate fundamentalist leaders began to fashion a new "conscious fellowship," calling it evangelicalism, to distinguish themselves from separatist fundamentalists.[30] The founding act of their movement was the formation of the National Association of Evangelicals (NAE) in 1942, and in subsequent years evangelicals fashioned and took over leadership of dozens of major parachurch organizations.[31]

Especially with regard to its posture toward American politics and culture, evangelicalism was a radical departure from its fundamentalist roots. Evangelical leaders and organizations—many of them, enough to characterize the movement as a whole—routinely discussed and debated social problems and public policies among themselves and made substantial forays into the national public arena. Aside from the NAE, which was a public lobby on a par with the National Council of Churches, they started, in the 1950s, the national "prayer breakfast movement" that regularly gathered members of Congress and preachers, and evangelist Billy Graham became the spiritual counselor of choice for the postwar generation of U.S. presidents.[32] Charismatics were almost as publicly active as evangelicals through the Full Gospel Businessmen's Fellowship International, the National Prayer Breakfasts, the NAE, and other organizations. Washington, D.C., in the early 1970s under the Nixon administration, was a beehive of charismatic activity in the form of small prayer groups that networked politicians, staff, and other professionals. Or so we gather from Charles Colson's Born-Again, a book-length testimony of the Watergate scandals and the saving grace of Christ, which gave many Americans the first glimpse of how active conservative, supernaturalist Protestants were in high places hitherto considered hopelessly secular.

Both the charismatic and evangelical movements laid the ground for the dramatic reenfranchisement of Bible-believing Protestantism in the 1980s, but neither constituted a break with the regime of secular modernity. Both movements limited their effectiveness in certain ways. Their leaders refrained from overtly "mixing" religion and politics in public venues or events, avoided partisan activities, and restricted themselves to private "fellowshipping" activities and to lobbying along the lines already established by mainline church organizations. In these ways, they collaborated with secular modernity's presumption that the public arena was off-limits to openly Bible-believing voices. Some progress was made toward reenfranchisement, but conservative Protestants were still marginalized. Their position was not so much one of accommodation to the larger national culture as it was strategic coexistence.[33]

Not that there was no politicking outside these constraints by conservative Protestants between 1925 and 1975. Indeed, there was a good deal of it, especially at the local level, and its frequency and scale increased in the postwar period. During the 1950s, Christian anticommunist crusades and the John Birch Society mobilized many fundamentalists, and they also provided much support on behalf of segregation in the South during the 1960s. There were major battles over textbooks and curricula in the 1960s and early 1970s—most notably over the sex education curriculum in Anaheim, California, in 1968; the Kanawha County, West Virginia, textbook controversy in 1974; and over the National Science Foundation's "Man: A Course of Study" (MACOS) curriculum in the mid-1970s.[34] Conservative Protestants were among the most active and organized opponents of the Equal Rights Amendment (ERA) and were responsible for its defeat in many states in the early 1970s. There were countless smaller contests around the country, and conservative Protestants formed dozens of lobbies and organizations to represent their interests and publicly promote their points of view.

In retrospect, it is clear that there were many challenges during its midcentury heyday, but none of them constituted a break with the regime of secular modernity. Either the activists themselves limited their moves in ways that preserved the rule of public secularity, or, when they did not, their moves were willfully episodic or otherwise policed back into the margins. Separatist fundamentalists in particular seemed to operate in ways that actively sustained the story of secular modernity. Aside from their vociferous, hyperbolic polemics about biblical inerrancy, periodic public outbreaks by fundamentalist preachers on moralistic, anticommunist, anti-Catholic, or anti-Semitic crusades unambiguously confirmed, from the modern point of view, the unfitness of all Protestant Bible-believers for modern life. It was as if there were a weird kind of contract between fundamentalists and the mainstream. Much of the power of fundamentalists in the public arena came from the extent to which they were a modern nightmare come true, but public appearances also triggered fierce remarginalizing practices that discredited them and limited their efficacy. This, of course, is the dilemma of marginality, of having the power only to disrupt the mainstream in ways that trigger a reinstallation of constraints, revised and updated. So the marginalization of fundamentalists was incomplete, but its incompleteness worked in a way to reproduce modern secular hegemony, enlisting fundamentalists as active collaborators in their own marginalization.

During the 1980s, Bible-believing, white Protestant Christians in America broke through the array of cultural barriers that had quarantined them from other Americans for half a century. Suddenly, their old-fashioned kind of Christianity—Fundamentalism—seemed to be everywhere. A half dozen national televangelists—Jerry Falwell, Pat Robertson, Jimmy Swaggart, Jim and Tammy Faye Bakker, James Robison—were the most visible leaders of this movement, this permeation, transporting images and voices of God-fearing Christians into living rooms all over the country. Their television and radio programs filled the airwaves, and for nearly a decade they were staple subjects and topics in news broadcasts, talk shows, television specials, newspapers, and national magazines. And they also were key figures in the formation of organizations—the Moral Majority, the Religious Roundtable, and Christian Voice—that marked their movement as unabashedly political.

Many observers argued at the time that the public and political actions of conservative Protestants in the 1980s were but another episode of religious zeal that would play itself out eventually, and then the country would be back on track. That is, we would once again settle back into being a nation in which modern, secular values dominate the public life without notable challenge. This view became harder to sustain as the decade wore on, and by now, it seems clear that during the 1980s we were witnessing instead a major realignment of public religiosity in America.[35] The realignment was not a changing of the guard—conservative Protestants did not come to dominate public life—but they reentered public life. They returned from exile. Marginalized groups were main-streamed, but mainstream groups were not marginalized. In the new regime of public religiosity, power and authority are less centered. More dramatically, one of the stories that gave shape to modern America, the story of the progressive secularization of national life, lost its essential protagonist, the excluded Fundamentalist other.

The episode of New Christian Right activism of the 1980s was not an "eruption," after which its perpetrators would withdraw from public life, but a "rupture" that produced something new and enduring. True, most of the national televangelical empires that dominated the public face of Protestant orthodoxy in the 1980s declined and largely disappeared from national view. But their decline did not requarantine conservative Protestant Christianity because the televangelists and their many and varied compatriot leaders and organizations had forged a new hybrid, a new Christian chimera, an unstable but enduring intersection of religious discourses. The new formation was part fundamentalist, part pentecostal, part charismatic, part evangelical, and then something else in a way that none of its parts had been: morally outraged, socially engaged, and routinely politically active. The hybrid was christened in 1976, before its parts had quite come together, in the media hype around Charles Colson's spectacular conversion and Jimmy Carter's professions of faith: born-again Christianity.

Born-again Christianity was a composite formation, more like a mixture than a compound. The styles, voices, and distinctive features of its component parts were still operative: it was a partial unity. In other words, the cultural formation was composed of hyphenated, old-fashioned white conservative Protestants—of fundamentalist born-agains, evangelical born-agains, pentecostal born-agains, and charismatic born-agains. The parts retained their separate cultural and theological identities, but they also forged new jointly held rhetorics focused on specific moral, social, and political issues (the ERA, pornography, abortion, homosexuality, creation science, public school curricula, television sex and violence, rock 'n' roll). A new Christian folk sociology emerged in the form of a widely shared multifaceted critique of secular humanism. Longstanding Christian folk theories of history—various premillennialisms which envision the return of Jesus Christ to rule a one thousand-year kingdom—were variously deployed to refashion the end-time, that is, current history, as a time for worldly Christian activism.

This hybrid creature, born-again Christianity, was unstable in the sense that it was composed of theologically discrete parts and that its parts were internally riven. But it was stable in the sense that it generated an enduring organizational and oratorical public presence, one sufficiently permanent and persuasive to constitute a break with the story, indeed, the history, of modernity in America, a storied history that posited increasing secularization as a major theme of the twentieth century. "Secularization" had meant, among other things, the separation—or segregation—of supernaturalist Protestants, or, more precisely, of supernaturalist Protestant rhetorics, from public life. This rhetorical segregation, as we have seen, depended most heavily on conservative Protestants themselves—they policed themselves, or, again, more precisely, their Bible-based voices—out of the political arena and civil society. The emergence of born-again Christianity marked the end of this secularizing collaboration. Born-again Christian rhetorics, by definition, sutured up the two things kept apart, by definition, under the regime of secular modernity—routine political activism and aggressive, Bible-based supernaturalism.

Part II of this study tracks the emergence of this new composite form of publicly permeating supernatural white Protestant born-again Christianity, from the point of view of one of its component parts, namely, fundamentalism. More specifically, it traces the emergence of born-again Christianity in Jerry Falwell's fundamental Baptist community.

My focus is not on the political activism of Falwell's community—not on the Moral Majority or on other New Christian Right organizations. Nor is it on televangelism, on the Old-Time Gospel Hour or the other religious media empires that dominated the news in the 1980s. Rather, my focus is on the oratory, on the rhetorics and narratives, on the internal cultural work that ended conservative white Protestant collaboration with the terms of secular modernity. The separation particularly of fundamentalists from worldly society before 1980 depended on cultural constraints and taboos and a nexus of self-representations that subjectively situated, Bible-believing, Christians outside current history and the national culture. And their political activation during the 1980s derived from and generated complex rhetorical and narrative processes that loos-

ened those constraints, broke taboos, and culturally reinscribed and politically repositioned Bible-believing Christians. As they rerepresented
themselves to themselves and to others, intense worldly engagement
gradually became (once again) part of the very definition of being a true
Christian.[36] Strict Bible belief and aggressive social activism had once
again been fused in white Protestant America.

Part Two RITES OF REVISION

CHAPTER THREE

The Art of Jerry Falwell

*What is it like, the biblical writers seek to know through their art,
to be a human being with a divided consciousness—intermittently
loving your brother but hating him even more; resentful or perhaps
contemptuous of your father but also capable of the deepest filial
regard; stumbling between disastrous ignorance and imperfect
knowledge; fiercely asserting your own independence but caught in
a tissue of events divinely contrived; outwardly a definite character
and inwardly an unstable vortex of greed, ambition, jealousy, lust,
piety, courage, compassion, and much more?*

—ROBERT ALTER, 1981

T HE TELEVANGELICAL preachers of the 1980s
emerged out of the populist apostolic tradition in America. The tradition
enables preachers to enact, believers to recognize, and skeptics to scorn
charismatic religious authority. The televangelists were all authorized by
more formal means as well, but their extraordinary reputations depended
on continuous evidence of miraculous action in their lives and works.
They produced this evidence by constantly narrating themselves in terms
of Bible-based story cycles which made manifest their divine election.[1]
What counts as a miracle or a sign of election in these apostolic story
cycles varies, but one thing all miracles have in common is semantic
risk or ambiguity, some sort of excess or gap that demands interpretive
attention and engagement, choices which place one inside or outside the
faith at hand.

An interpretive gap or excess is a silence or an anomaly in a story that incites the imagination by failing to meet expectations, a little like a clue in a murder mystery; or an odd sound at night, downstairs, near the back door; or two friends gazing at each other a bit too long and longingly to be "just friends." A miraculous gap or excess fails to meet worldly expectations in a way that opens up a space for supernatural action. A lifelong drunkard sobers up after he receives Jesus Christ into his heart. A believer's fatal cancer goes into spontaneous remission. A ministry is spared certain destruction when a hurricane abruptly veers north. The ultimate miracle, of course, is that Jesus Christ died on the cross so that all mankind might have eternal life.

Necessarily, there is something incredible—in the simple sense of unbelievable—about a miracle, if only because the disbelief of outsiders is a precondition of miraculous action. But believers too, even though they know miracles happen, must weigh the evidence in each instance and judge a miraculous claim true or false. And therein lies a certain source of instability in all miracle-based ministries. They depend on faith constantly constructed out of intrinsically dubious claims. They are built on ambiguous figures and events composed of narrative gaps, excesses, and indeterminacies which the faithful must ceaselessly close, suppress, and fix in the name of God.

The 1980s televangelists were masters of this kind of narrative instability. Each elaborated a lifelong corpus of personal testimonies, sermons, official biographies, and (mostly ghostwritten) autobiographies that were framed by the general conventions of the apostolic tradition and by the terms of their particular folk-theological traditions. The televangelists plied the staple stories of the apostolic tradition which testified to their special election by God—great soul-winning feats, the extraordinary entrepreneurial and organizational zeal needed to build a great ministry, superhuman stamina, a phenomenal memory for faces and names, verbatim recollection of countless Bible passages, and, of course, the ability to triumph in the face of worldly defeats and criticism.

The testimonies of the pentecostal and charismatic televangelists such as Jimmy Swaggart, Jim and Tammy Faye Bakker, and Pat Robertson abound with evidence of their own miraculous gifts and of the miraculous actions of God in their lives.

In sync with the Arminian pulse of reversible, hence repeatable, salvation, pentecostals Swaggart and the Bakkers punctuated their autobiographies with episodes of moral backsliding, devil wrestling, and deep spiritual crisis.[2] Swaggart tells us in *To Cross a River* that, after giving his life to the Lord in his teens, he shot pool, rolled dice, boxed, stole from his uncle, and, under the influence of the devil, played the piano with his cousin Jerry Lee Lewis.[3] In *Move That Mountain!*, Jim Bakker describes a terrible tragedy that led him finally to surrender his life completely to God. At age eighteen, he slipped out of church during the altar call *with a cute blonde named Sandy*, and they cruised around town in his father's Cadillac listening to rock 'n' roll music. As they returned to the church, *it seemed as if the car bumped against something like the curb.* Jim leapt out and saw the Sunday School director holding *the battered form of a little boy. . . . Both wheels of the heavy Cadillac had completely run over his body crushing his lungs immediately. I began to cry.* I had killed a child. *The life went out of me.*[4]

The charismatic Bapist Pat Robertson set his life story within a more Calvinist, once-saved–always-saved, frame of irreversible salvation. Pat never backslid out of salvation according to his tales in *Shout It from the Housetops*, but God used his wife Dede many times to test his faith. And God sent many powerful and influential men his way who enabled his progressive baptism by the Holy Spirit and who thus mediated his receiving charisms, or miracle-making gifts of the spirit.[5]

Jerry Falwell's independent Baptist fundamentalism, like Robertson's Southern Baptist roots, framed his salvation as irreversible. But Falwell's tradition brooked none of Robertson's pentecostal notions regarding the miraculous works of the Spirit. So Falwell could not, in his auto-biographical corpus, avail himself of the moral latitude and histrionics allowed pentecostal and charismatic preachers in producing their authority. Nor could he claim any embodied miracle-making gifts of the Holy Spirit such as healing, divine prophecy, words of knowledge, and exorcism. Falwell's fundamentalism, however, gave him the ample stage of personal character, of judgment, integrity, and ethics, upon which to script doubts and qualms and queries about himself that would tax and trouble the hearts of those who followed him.

Falwell's autobiographical corpus, both as he enacted and as he narrated it, bristled with misdeeds, bad characters, and an edge of zealotry. His agnostic father was a bootlegger who shot and killed his younger brother and drank himself to death. Before he converted, Jerry was a "prankster" and neighborhood "gang leader." As a preacher, from the very inception of his ministry in 1956, he was surrounded by a chorus of criticism, controversy, protest, and litigation. Outsiders as well as insiders recognize that such features frame Falwell as a classic fundamentalist preacher—militant, bold, at times intemperate, a slightly dangerous man, a man, who, as contemporary fundamentalists would say, was sold-out on Christ. And insiders, especially those who sit in the pews of the Thomas Road Baptist Church year after year, steeped in fundamentalist versions of the apostolic interpretive code, hearing over and over again his tales of grace in the midst of misconduct, chronicle a still more complex and troubling figure.[6]

Fundamental Baptist interpretation rests on a poetics of faith—absolute faith—not a hermeneutics of suspicion.[7] The Bible is entirely true in the ordinary sense of accurately depicting historical events. The rule of inerrancy extends, not explicitly and by no means irrevocably (as it does to the Bible), to preachers and other "men of God." Specifically, everything Jerry Falwell authors is true. But truth is not automatic, transparent, unmediated. It is the outcome of continuous exegetical exchanges between the Bible and its readers, a preacher and his people. A preacher's God-given authority, like the absolute truth of the Bible, is produced by a community of believers through its interpretive practices. It is as if Falwell, in his varied storied manifestations, were telling his followers, "Read me as you read the Bible. I appear in many versions. There are differences between the versions, and there are awkward silences and anomalies within them. My tales are troubled and they are troubling. Harmonize my discrepancies. Close my gaps. Overcome my troubles. Make me whole. Make me true."

The stories within Jerry Falwell's corpus place him deep within the cycles of divine election of Christian and Hebrew biblical traditions.[8] Together, these traditions fashion a field of narrative gaps and excesses, a perilous contrapuntal movement of wavering, at times wobbly, story lines from which Jerry Falwell continuously emerges as a complex, mercurial, irreducibly ambiguous man of God.[9] For his people, the co-pro-

Figure 3.1 This Old-Time Gospel Hour direct-mail solicitation set Jerry Falwell's 1987 autobiography in a sequence with the Bible.

ducers of this transformation, Falwell becomes "a course on miracles." The narrative interactions that bind Falwell and his faithful, though not marked as miracles, partake of the same structure. He produces the gaps, the anomalies, the excesses, the apertures for the uncanny, and his people produce faith by harmonizing his discrepancies. Moreover, as we shall see, these miraculous exchanges not only convert trouble into truth, doubt into certainty, deception into special election; they may, under the right circumstances, convert a poor, powerless preacher into a multi-million dollar powerhouse for God.

During the peak years of his national fame, from 1980 to 1987, Jerry Falwell often posed as the innocent victim of bad press, as if his notoriety were a figment of the journalistic imagination. Certainly, he was the subject of enormous attention on the part of academics and political opponents as well as journalists, and much of that attention was critical, some of it scathing. However, a review of Falwell's (auto)biographical corpus, that is, the vast assembly of speech and text he himself authored and authorized, reveals that Jerry Falwell had always cast himself as a man with a troubled, and troubling, reputation. Even story cycles regarding his early years—as a child growing up in the 1930s and 1940s, as a teenager and college student, as a young man courting his wife and a young pastor founding his church—even these stories are riven with anomalies, unanswered questions, lapses, and character flaws. The little alarms, gaps, and excesses of these apparently artless tales located Falwell squarely in the biblical canon, revealing him to be a distinctly artful man; a man who knows what he wants because someone else has it and who will get what he wants by any means necessary; and also a man distinctly protected and blessed, because he invariably gets away with things he ought not and gets what he wants at the expense of others. The early tales thus fashion Falwell as a latter-day Jacob.

The biblical story of Jacob begins in his mother's womb where "the children struggle within her," and the Lord told Rebekah, "Two nations are in thy womb, and two manner of people shall be separated from thy bowels; and the one people shall be stronger than the other people; and the elder shall serve the younger" (Genesis 25:22–24). The younger twin emerged from the womb "grasping his brother's heel, so he was named

Jacob," a name that means "he supplants" (Genesis 25:26 and 27:36). It was said Esau, the older twin, was a "cunning hunter" and preferred by his father, Isaac, while Rebekah and God preferred Jacob, "a plain man." Yet it was Jacob who proved to be cunning and Esau plain. Jacob convinced Esau to sell his birthright for a bowl of stew, and then Rebekah and Jacob tricked Isaac into blessing Jacob, in effect stealing Esau's inheritance as well as birthright. These and subsequent tales clinch the fundamental ambiguity of Jacob, the usurper, the deceiver, the humiliator, to whom God delivered great wealth and eternal dominion over Israel.

Echoing Jacob's tales, Jerry Falwell is framed, and frames himself, in Jacob's crafty shadow throughout his own corpus of stories, sometimes obliquely, sometimes clearly, and sometimes, as in the cycle of stories regarding his very early years, explicitly.

THE TWIN CYCLE

As Jacob and Esau, Jerry and Gene Falwell were born twins. Like Jacob, Jerry demonstrated a certain impatience early in life, announced the glossy, large-format photo-essay, *Jerry Falwell: Man of Vision*, which was distributed nationally by Falwell's Old-Time Gospel Hour ministry in 1980.[10] Stories separating and ranking the twins pepper Falwell's growing-up stories, most elaborately in his 1987 ghostwritten autobiography, *Strength for the Journey*.

Jerry and Gene were not identical twins; Gene grew bigger and stronger earlier, while Jerry was a skinny boy. *Dad was afraid that I would grow soft, so the fights between us were strictly regulated for me to win. I've often wondered why Gene seemed so willing to go along with those lopsided, unfair rules.*[11] Jerry's second-grade teacher also inexplicably separated him out and privileged him: *I skipped grade two and advanced one class ahead of Gene that second year.*[12] His only memory of elementary school was *that awful moment when my brother Gene and I were separated by our second-grade teacher, Mrs. Hunter. She didn't think I belonged in the second grade; so, with the principal's approval, she skipped me on to the third. From that day on, my brother and I were in different classes. We never knew exactly why she advanced me one whole year.*[13] And then one day, to everyone's surprise, their father, an agnostic, stood Jerry and Gene on a table in his office in front of a roomful of his employees and *put one hand on Gene's head and one hand on mine. Then he said, "Gene will be my farmer and Jerry will be my preacher."*[14]

These twin stories directly locate Jerry in Jacob's narrative lineage. Two subsequent story cycles, one recounting his "youthful pranks" and the other narrating his conversion, engagement, and church founding, develop Jerry's dubious nature as a man who could humiliate, deceive, and steal, a law unto himself, a man who would supplant his rivals by any means. And yet, waters parted all around Falwell as he grew up. We come to understand that Jerry is someone special, not a perfect man, not a bad man, but a man not bound by ordinary constraints, a man somehow protected.

THE PRANKSTER CYCLE

I could not resist an occasional practical joke. I knew I would pay the consequences when I teased or tormented a student or a teacher— especially a teacher. And though it cost me plenty, I entered into each new prank with abandon. And though this might sound like a halfhearted attempt at self-defense some of my victims deserved it.

I shall never forget one particular teacher who will remain unnamed. He was a mean little man who pranced about our physical ed classes squeaking out orders, humiliating students, and generally trying to lord it over us. I led the growing resistance movement to this teacher and his prissy falsetto ways. . . .

One sixth-period class, he humiliated a rather unathletic student on the basketball court. After the boy ran to the showers crying, our teacher turned on the rest of us. Suddenly I tackled him and began to wrestle him toward the sports equipment storage room. Two other students finally helped me subdue him, while the rest of the class looked on in shocked surprise. Inside the storage room, I pinned him to the floor. With the aid of my classmates, I pulled off his britches and left him pantless in a bin of basketballs.

After locking the gym teacher in his own storage area, I took his pants to the school's main bulletin board in the front lobby and pinned them up with a note reading "Mr. ———'s britches." When Jerry was called into the principal's office the next day, the principal *didn't say a thing. Apparently he was trying so hard not to laugh that he was afraid to speak. He didn't appreciate this teacher either.* [He tried to lecture Jerry but] *lost his poise and began to laugh uncontrollably. He laughed so hard he almost fell out of his chair.*[15]

Falwell portrayed himself here as a precocious foe of unjust homosexual authority. The teacher *pranced;* he was *squeaking out orders;* he had *prissy falsetto ways.* And Jerry's prank was sexually humiliating in triplicate—he pulled off the teacher's britches, left him pantless in a bin of basketballs, and pinned his britches to the school's main bulletin board. Falwell published this tale in 1987 so it became retrospectively a prefiguring of a role he had by then fulfilled. In retrospect, however, from the point of view of a man who fashioned himself a national moral leader, even a great statesman, the prefigure was not an entirely flattering one. In the end, Jerry's macho action went too far. It partook of that which he protested: It was he who seemed mean-spirited, he who humiliated another person. And he got away with it, indeed, was rewarded by the principal's uncontrollable laughter. The story was another instance of the figure of Jerry-as-Jacob: an impatient, imperfect, impertinent man who won favor in spite of his flaws.[16]

Jerry's most oft-told prank, the last "harmless" prank of his high school years, *resulted in rather dire consequences for me and for thirty-two members of my high school football team.* At the beginning of his senior year, Jerry broke into the school safe, found the color code for cafeteria meal tickets, and handed out tickets for free meals to his teammates for the entire year. *It was meant to be a joke. The school made money charging a one-dollar entrance fee to our football games. We were just getting our share, or so we thought. . . . We thought it all a lark, but the principal and the local law-enforcement agencies considered it a serious felony. . . . The financial loss amounted to several thousand dollars, and the parents were asked to pay back in equal shares the total losses. . . .* The principal told Jerry he could not give the valedictory address that year. *"We can't have a petty thief deliver Brookville's honors speech, now can we?"*[17]

As usual, Jerry disclaims willful wrongdoing. The scam was just a joke, a lark, another one of his harmless pranks. But the disclaimers rattle against other details and phrases. The principal and police considered it a serious felony. Jerry was a petty thief. Yet he did not go to jail, and the parents paid for the cost of the prank. His only penalty was not being allowed to deliver the Valediction. The combination bespeaks Jerry's nascent righteousness, as if it were clear early on that it was up to him to decide right from wrong, that his moral compass was sovereign. Narrative gaps were opened that will be opened again and again: Is Jerry Falwell above the law? When does a harmless prank become theft? In the early 1970s, when Falwell was accused by the Securities and Exchange Commission of illegally selling $6.5 million in church bonds, he said it was an "honest mistake." When does an honest mistake become fraud and deceit? Is Jerry Falwell above the law?

The tales of Jerry's childhood and adolesence established him as a mysteriously separated-out, lifted-up, let-off young man with a wild and wily streak. Subsequent stories of his young adulthood that narrate his courtship, his conversion, and his church founding set his supplanting nature still more firmly.

THE MACEL CYCLE

According to Elmer Towns, Falwell's first authorized biographer, Macel Pate was playing the piano and Dolores Clark the organ at Park Avenue Baptist Church the night Jerry Falwell and his best friend, Jim Moon, got saved. Jerry told Jim he was going to ask Dolores out, and Jim picked Macel, *the most beautiful girl he had ever seen.* But *both boys married the opposite choice they made that night.*[18] Jerry made up his mind about Macel right away, but Macel was already engaged to be married. When Jerry went off to Baptist Bible College a few months later, he found himself rooming with the fellow who was engaged to Macel Pate. Undaunted, without telling his roommate, Jerry wrote love letters to Macel. *Jerry confessed that it took him until Christmas to get the other ring off her finger. When asked how he did it, Falwell shyly remarked, "My roommate gave me his letters to Macel to mail; I just didn't do it."*[19] After college, Jerry let Macel stall their marriage for a year and a half. Then, *He gave her an ultimatum, "now or never." Macel still didn't respond,* so Jerry *began dating another girl. The next time Jerry*

called the Pate residence, Macel said "Do you still want to get married?"
"Yes . . . when?" Macel indicated, "As soon as possible."[20]

Had Jerry's courtship story, as told by Elmer Towns, omitted certain details and foregrounded others, he would have given us a marriage-by-conquest tale. Instead, he gave us a marriage-by-deceit tale. He dated and married the girl his best friend wanted to date and his college roommate planned to marry. He doubly deceived his roommate and manipulated Macel into deciding to marry him as soon as possible. Two turns of phrase in Towns's account—Jerry *confessed* that it took him a year to break the engagement, and he "shyly remarked" that he'd thrown away his roommate's letters to Macel—called attention to Jerry's self-awareness of foul play. He stole Macel, he knows it, and he lets everyone know he knows it.

THE CHURCH-FOUNDING CYCLE

Jerry Falwell founded Thomas Road Baptist Church in 1956 with thirty-five charter members, a moment in his life, along with his moment of salvation in 1952, which he recalled almost every time he preached. Oft-recalled, but, unlike his salvation experience, rarely elaborated, though some of those charter members, including Jim Moon, Macel Pate Falwell, and the Pate family, are leading figures in the church. It took Falwell a long time to work out, and work in, the kinks in the story, judging from the slow, belabored pace with which he eked out the details of the church's founding in his written (auto)biographies between 1971 and 1987.

In his 1971 authorized biography of Falwell, Elmer Towns noted simply that thirty-five members from Park Avenue Baptist Church, where Jerry had been saved, asked him to start a new church after he graduated from Baptist Bible College. Falwell spoke to the Park Avenue pastor, "felt the pastor was agreeable," and decided to plant a church in Lynchburg.[21] In 1979, Falwell's second official biography, by Gerald Strober and Ruth Tomszac, opened a gap in the story: *Some men who Jerry greatly respected advised him not to start the church in his hometown.* He was troubled, prayed for two weeks, and was given closure: *God made him willing to lose even his best friends on earth in order to do what he felt the Lord wanted.*[22] In 1984, Falwell's semiunauthorized biographer, Dinesh D'Souza (Falwell apparently did not commission D'Souza, but he read and approved D'Souza's manuscript before it was published), reported that "Falwell was horrified" by the invitation from Park Avenue dissidents to found a church and tried to resolve differences between them and Pastor Wood, but Wood was "unconcerned about the dissidents."[23]

Finally, in Falwell's 1987 autobiography, a fuller and much more richly disturbing account emerged. First of all, it turned out that Macel's original suitor was not only Jerry's Bible college roommate but also Pastor Donnelson's wife's brother. Donnelson, the Park Avenue pastor under whom Jerry was saved, had resigned due to unspecified "growing problems," about which Jerry and Macel corresponded regularly. Jerry said he knew the perfect man to fill the bill: Frank Wood, his good friend, at Baptist Bible College.[24] When Jerry finished college and returned home, he found that "the transition between Donnelson and the new pastor had not been smooth."[25] Again, Falwell never specified the nature of the problem.[26] The dissidents asked Wood to resign, he refused, and when they asked Jerry to found a church with them, Jerry "was shocked"—even though he had participated in the group's deliberations from the beginning.[27]

Jerry prayed and determined that God wanted him to stay a few months and help the dissidents get started, but *before making my final decision, I called the pastor and asked to see him.* [Pastor Wood] *listened silently while I reasoned on behalf of the new church.* After an hour, Wood excused himself, consulted by phone with Baptist Bible Fellowship headquarters in Springfield, and when he returned, he was no longer willing to cooperate. BBF officials advised Falwell that his *plan to begin another church in Lynchburg was "unacceptable" and that the only acceptable option I had was "to leave town immediately and to let them* [the dissenters] *go."* We never learn in any of Falwell's numerous accounts of this moment exactly why the BBF considered his plan unacceptable, although there may have been an unwritten rule against intracivic rivalry.[28] But Jerry by now felt, *if I let them scare me away, I would be moving against the voice of God, who I felt was calling me to stay in Lynchburg. . . . How lonely I felt that day, deciding against all the advice of the authority figures in my life. But I had prayed and thought long enough.*[29]

Pastor Wood publicly criticized Jerry and *the word quickly spread to Springfield and throughout our little fellowship to key pastors and powerful Baptist leaders in the country.* Because Jerry stuck with his plan to start a second BBF church in Lynchburg, he was "excommunicated," cut off from his pastoral fellowship, its members, and its meetings. He was disfellowshipped. . . . *Those were terrible times for me. . . . It was at that time that God began dealing with me about belonging to Him alone and not to anything else on this earth.* Falwell sought refuge in the Psalms. *This man* [David] *whom God loved best had been confronted by the prophet, repudiated by the people, and rejected by his family and friends. . . . Though I hadn't disobeyed the Lord in the same way King David had, I needed the same kind of comfort and strength that David sang about in the Psalms. . . .* [The] *men who rejected me were good men. But they allowed their zeal for a movement to get ahead of the Spirit of God in their hearts and lives. We have long since corrected all that. After fifteen years of isolation, the gap has been bridged again. We support the fellowship, are members of good standing of that body. . . .* [But] *I spent fifteen years alone and cut off. . . . I learned during those fifteen long years that I didn't need a fellowship to guide me. I didn't need a program to follow or a book of outlines to depend upon. I didn't need a headquarters or a hierarchy to trust in. Jesus Christ was all of that for me.*[30]

Of course, church foundings are often fractious events, and disfellowshipping happens. In this particular cycle of stories, Falwell invariably closes up the gaps he opens by repeatedly stating that God willed him to start Thomas Road Baptist Church. The question is, why does Falwell narrate the gaps, why does he stitch holes in his stories to begin with?

In this, as in other story cycles, the indubitability of Falwell's election combines with accumulating doubts about his character, his motives, the means to his ends, and with the particular pattern of rivalrous desire. David, with whom Jerry aligns himself, was of course another figure who fulfilled Jacob, another manifestly flawed founding biblical father. Jerry Falwell let us know that he supplanted, displaced, and overrode Pastor Wood, the church in which he was saved, and his Baptist Bible Fellowship, just as he had done with Macel's fiancé, Jim Moon, his high school authorities, the police, and his twin brother. This is the basic pattern of his early life stories: God wanted Jerry to have what, by some reckoning, belonged to others. "The elder shall serve the younger," and "the last shall be first." It is an ancient biblical pattern, often allegorized as the overthrow of primogeniture, a pattern that is at once authorizing and agitating, a magic formula that, properly wielded, yields charismatic religious authority.

I have focused thus far on Jerry Falwell's stories of his early years. Rather than reading them literally, I have read them as his people do, productively, as producing character traits, narrative tensions, and plot lines that fashioned Falwell as a postbiblical figure. The mere resemblance to Jacob did not lend him authority so much as did Falwell's Bible-based orchestration of a system of narrative gaps. The storied gaps—the excesses and silences, the unnecessary details and spareness—captured attention, induced interpretive action, and wove semiotic webs between a preacher and his people. In effect, through the stories of his early years, Falwell taught his people a mode of interpretation, a poetics of faith, that would sustain and constitute him, and them, in his middle and later years.

A different cluster of controversies gave a distinct shape to each decade of Falwell's ministry. In the late 1950s and 1960s, Falwell fashioned friends and enemies in Lynchburg in response to his defense of racial segregation and his techniques of superaggressive church-building and saturation evangelism. In the 1970s, as we will see, Falwell "walked through the shadow of death" when the Securities and Exchange Commission charged him with fraud and deceit in the sale of church bonds. The national fund-raising campaigns that Falwell designed to pull him out of that crisis were also troubling as they gradually became a crucial means by which he evolved out of the mold of an old-fashioned separatist (and pro-segregation) fundamentalist preacher into a new, relatively more moderate and openly political mold. In the 1980s, Falwell further taxed his people's faith in him via the Moral Majority, to which there were principled and practical objections. Some wondered if his role as a high-profile spokesman for the New Christian Right was too "political" for a pastor, and his hectic schedule seriously competed with his pastoral obligations. Many of his church people felt that Falwell's suit against Larry Flynt and *Hustler* magazine was as unseemly as the offending cartoon (portraying Falwell's mother in an outhouse) which inspired the suit. Many church people were also alarmed when Falwell assumed a center-stage role in the televangelical scandals of 1987–1988 by taking over Jim Bakker's organization, Praise the Lord (PTL) for they wished to keep their distance from both the scandals and the pentecostal practices of PTL. In the early 1990s, Falwell's most highly publicized excess took the form of *The Clinton Chronicles*, a videotape of lurid gossip and innuendo about the Whitewater case, Bill and Hillary Clinton, and their friends and associates.

Below the surface of these public controversies, Falwell produced many more layers of trouble. On each of my half-dozen trips to Lynchburg from 1982 to 1989, I found that Falwell was scandalizing— was provoking the doubts of—his church people and co-workers in one way or another. Some of them were bothered by his financial and business ethics. Most of the many millions of dollars Falwell raised for his college, a home for unwed mothers, and other specific causes were used instead to support his television ministry; but such financial diversions, to the extent that they were known, were not troubling. His people were more troubled by the fact that his ministries were chronically overspent. They did not pay their vendors on time. They downsized without mercy. Moreover, some of the men Falwell hired to run the business and finance side of his ministries had criminal records. And then there were the periodic lawsuits. In 1986, for example, the Old-Time Gospel Hour was sued by an eighty-one-year-old widow for misappropriating money from her "nest egg," which she had entrusted to the ministry.

Falwell's management of Liberty Baptist College, which became Liberty University in 1984, was another constant source of controversy. It was said that he maintained absolute control but was hardly ever around. That he allowed charismatic students, Hollywood movies, and Christian rock 'n' roll on campus. That he built multimillion dollar sports facilities while academic facilities languished. That star athletes got special treatment when they broke the rules.

Thomas Road Baptist Church had passed its prime as a source of controversy by the mid-1980s, but even there Falwell could still agitate. His most scandalous decision was to institute a "tithe-or-quit" policy to deal with his ministry's sharp financial downturn in 1989. Falwell proposed that all of the thousand or so men and women who worked for his combined ministries be required to give 10 percent of their income to Thomas Road, or they would have to quit their jobs. Many who worked in Falwell's various ministries attended, and tithed to, smaller Baptist churches in the area, so they were most dismayed. But there was a general outcry in response to the idea of requiring staff—school teachers, janitors, secretaries, professors, data processors, cafeteria workers, financial officers—to tithe to a particular church as a condition of work. It seemed a very un-Baptist, a most un-Christian, thing to do.

Sometimes Falwell's church people and co-workers succeeded in pulling him back from a brink. Criticism from within his church, at least in part, stopped Falwell from speaking out in favor of segregation and led him, eventually, to allow blacks into his church, schools, and college. He disbanded the Moral Majority in 1986, at least in part, so that he could return full time to his duties as church pastor and college president, as many of his co-pastors and church people urged him to do.[31] He withdrew his tithe-or-quit policy shortly after he announced it. But even in the wake of such retreats, his people wondered about his motives. Had Falwell realized he was wrong? Or had he looked at his balance sheet and discovered that his position was hurting him financially? Or that too many people were prepared to leave, or had left, his church and quit their jobs rather than accept his views, his absenteeism, his policies?

People did leave, of course, at all levels, especially in the late 1980s, but what makes Falwell's scandalous actions productive is that they also bound people to him. Even those who were driven away had once been captivated. Falwell's church people and co-workers did not accept him uncritically. On the contrary, their acceptance was always provisional, always in need of renewal. It was the outcome of continuous interpretive labor, of wrestling with the doubts and qualms Falwell generated, of overcoming them, of having—of making—faith in spite of them. In this way, Jerry Falwell, like other preachers who have emerged from the American apostolic tradition, was an ongoing, collaborative work of rhetorical art.

So far we have considered how Falwell's stories and his deeds call for interpretive actions that fill in narrative gaps and bind his people to him by enlisting them in the making of his reputation. A preacher's corpus of life stories is not the only preacherly discourse that works in this way.

Sermons and gospel rhetorics—rhetorics that fashion particular born-again Christian points of view—may also wobble and weave in ways that make faith by challenging it. Falwell's preaching, spoken and written, openly challenged and changed the faith of his people in many ways that are traced in subsequent chapters. Before going on, though, let us consider one more corpus through which Falwell tested his people's faith, namely, his campaigns against moral wrongdoing, which sometimes seemed to go so far themselves as to do wrong, or at least partake of others' wrongdoing. That was the nature of the uneasiness he produced by his suit againt Larry Flynt, by his involvement in the Bakker scandal, and by *The Clinton Chronicles*. And Falwell often tottered rhetorically on the brink of moral contamination in his campaigns against sexual excess.

Falwell came particularly close to consorting with an enemy in a made-for-TV sermon called "A Look inside the Cup" produced in 1982, during the peak years of his extended campaign to "clean up America."[32] For one long hour, Falwell described and displayed dozens of attacks on him and his efforts to reverse the tide of moral decay in America, asking his faithful followers over and over to *please write a check . . . for a thousand dollars, a hundred dollars, ten dollars, whatever you can do . . . right now. Please help me. Make your check payable to The Old-Time Gospel Hour. Help me financially. I need a financial miracle. Help me, do it today.* In its content, the program was an intense appeal to sustain Falwell's fight against abortion, homosexual rights, heterosexual promiscuity, pornography, and other sex-related sins. But the form of his appeal moved in the opposite direction, couched as it was in unusually personal and intimate language. To enjoin his audience to sacrifice themselves financially, Falwell sacrificed himself narratively. He told them he was, like Christ, drinking a cup of suffering and taking on the sins of the world so that others might be free. He revealed his own suffering, and then asked his listeners to join him in that place of suffering, that very special, private place, where they would be alone with him.

The television program opened with Jerry Falwell sitting in his radio studio in the basement of his home in Lynchburg, Virginia, reading from Matthew 26:38–39 about Jesus in the Garden of Gethsemane on the eve of his crucifixion: *Then saith he unto them "My soul is exceedingly sorrowful, even unto death: tarry ye here, and watch with me." And he went a little farther, and fell on his face, and prayed, saying, "O my*

Father, if it be possible, let this cup pass from me." Falwell paused and proposed to take his audience into that cup, to look inside his own bitter cup for the next hour, to listen to the protesters demonstrating against him—*the Nazis, the Communists, the atheists, the God haters, the homosexuals and the feminists*—to share his heartaches and heartbreaks.

Falwell read a few more verses from Matthew 26 and then he said: *This is the story of Jesus Christ in the Garden of Gethsemane. This is my radio station, in the basement of my home. I call this my inner sanctum sometimes. You've really got to want to come here to get here, because this is way down in the basement. You walk through my wife's laundry room to get here. I've sound-proofed the room here, put a few books in it, not many. . . . This is where I pray, come alone every day to meet with the Lord, in his Word. This is where I come to do radio broadcasts.*

Falwell elaborated the parallel meetings that take place in his inner sanctum between himself and the Lord in prayer, and between himself and his listeners via radio. And then he asked: *What was that cup? What cup was the Lord talking about here? I think the Lord Jesus looked into the cup of suffering ahead of him when . . . he who knew no sin would become sin. . . . I think inside that cup he also saw that . . . for the first time in all eternity he would be separated from his Holy Father. . . . It was a bitter cup. . . . And he drank of that bitter cup until the last dregs. . . . We all have a cup to drink from, a cup of suffering, anguish, loneliness, hurt. I've prayerfully decided to spend this hour . . . taking you into my inner sanctum, into this little radio studio, my study, in the basement of my home, to let you look inside my cup with me. . . . Just as our Lord who set the example two thousand years ago, I'm willing to drink the cup . . . I'm willing to pay the price . . . Let's look inside the cup today.*

I've told you that this room, this study, this studio is my garden where I come to look into my cup every day. I come to this garden alone once a day at least. Don Norman is going to sing for us now a very beautiful song that says it better than I, "I come to the garden alone."

> I come to the garden alone
> While the dew is still on the roses
> And the voice I hear falling on my ear
> The son of God discloses.

And he walks with me
And he talks with me
And he tells me I am his own
And the joy we share as we tarry there
None other has ever known.
And he speaks and the sound of his voice
Is so sweet the birds hush their singing
And the melody that he gave to me
Within my heart is ringing.
And he walks with me
And he talks with me
And he tells me I am his own
And the joy we share as we tarry there
None other has ever known.

Falwell not only described and displayed his bitter cup, he rhetorically performed it. Metaphorically speaking, as he invited his followers into his cup, his garden, his inner sanctum, his private place, in his basement, on the other side of his wife's laundry room, [he] *took on the sins of the world*, [he was] *separated for a brief time from His Father*, he became that which he was not, he became sin. The sin is not named, but it is referenced obliquely by the vague but insistently repetitive sexual suggestiveness of his figures of speech. Falwell drew his followers into *my cup, my inner sanctum, my private place*. Once inside, he offered them a way out, the chance to call forth another miracle, if only they would enable him to persevere by sending him a sacrificial gift—*a thousand dollars, a hundred, or even ten*.

Falwell is here, once again, a complex, internally troubled, chronically unstable production. His seductively escalating figures of speech—his cup/studio/basement/garden/ private place—are another instance of the more general narrative process by which evangelistic preachers create themselves. It is a process, both languaged and enacted, in which a preacher's seaminess, his moral oscillations, his predilection for at least the appearance of wrongdoing is productive, not a side effect; is necessary, not incidental.

Narratively speaking, power does not corrupt in the apostolic tradition. Rather, corruption, in the sense of a constant generation of doubts and qualms about actions, words, and motives, is a route to and a source of power and authority. The narrative generation of sin in order to extirpate it—of gaps in order to close them, discrepancies in order to harmonize them, excesses in order to regulate them, indeterminacies in order to fix them—is a piece of a specifically fundamental Protestant populist apostolic tradition. The character—and often the ministry, as well, of many great fundamentalist preachers—is dual in nature. The pattern of repeated undecidability-which-demands-decisions produces intense narrative relationships between the preacher and those who would follow him. Believers must decide to believe in him over and over, must ceaselessly read the gaps not as ploys or lies or sins, but as little miracles, as signs of election, as the travails of a monumental man, and in so doing, join him in a kind of divine complicity.

CHAPTER FOUR

Sacrificial Economics

Since the world truly rendered by combining biblical narratives into
one was indeed the one and only real world, it must in principle
. . . embrace the experience of any present age and reader. Not only
was it possible for him to fit himself into that world, he was to see
his disposition, his actions and passions, the shape of his own life
as well as that of his era's events as figures in that storied world.
—HANS FREI, 1974

ALL PREACHERS must persuade their peoples to
support their ministries financially, and the televangelists of the 1980s
persuaded them to do so on a scale unparalleled in American history.
The three biggest "electronic churches," those of Pat Robertson, Jimmy
Swaggart, and Jim and Tammy Faye Bakker, together raised almost $500
million annually before the PTL crisis in 1987.[1] Falwell's ministry was
second tier in terms of annual income, raising nearly $100 million at its
peak in the mid-1980s.[2]

In 1970, when church membership reached 20,000, Falwell's ministry
earned about $1 million a year, most of it coming from church member
tithes. Turnover in membership brought in more up-scale families in
subsequent years, which increased the ministry's income from tithing,
but only marginally. Almost all the additional income Falwell's ministry
earned during the 1970s and 1980s came from sacrificial giving, from
contributions made by his growing national audience above and beyond
whatever they contributed to their local churches. After the Moral Majority was founded, total ministry income doubled between 1980 and

1986.[3] Relatively speaking, however, income growth during the 1970s was even more impressive—from $1 million in 1970, to $22–23 million in 1977, to $51 million in 1980. It was in this period, in particular between 1973 and 1977, that Falwell transformed himself and his ministry into figures worthy of great sacrificial giving. How did he do it?

Mom cried, Jerry Falwell wrote in his 1987 autobiography, *when she heard that 2,500 students and the faculty of our growing college met in the freezing snow on Candler's Mountain in a "miracle rally" to pray that one day a great Christian university would stand upon that place.*[4] A few weeks before the rally, in January 1977, the furnace broke down at Timberlake Middle School, a condemned building where Falwell's "growing college" had been meeting for several years. The furnace could be fixed, but the school was slated to be torn down that summer. Falwell would have to move his campusless college again, yet *God seemed to slam every door shut in the effort to provide a temporary campus for Liberty Baptist College. It became obvious to Jerry that God was driving him back to a very special mountain.*[5]

Those who braved the winter elements and so moved Falwell's mother that day on Candler's (later renamed by Falwell, Liberty) Mountain were praying specifically for a financial miracle, one that would enable them to build a permanent campus on that special mountain. *They sang the victory song, "I Want This Mountain," prayed, and claimed Liberty Mountain by faith. They asked God to enable them to eliminate all unsecured indebtedness by February 28, 1977, so that contractors could begin buildings for LBC's 1977–78 academic year.*[6] The "unsecured indebtedness" amounted to $2.3 million. By the end of February, Thomas Road Baptist Church had received $2.5 million over operating expenses, just what they had prayed for and then some. *It was evidently the miraculous working of God.*[7]

By fall of 1977, two buildings were completed and others were in progress. Building continued through the academic year, but not fast enough to suit Falwell or to accommodate the one thousand entering freshmen who arrived in August 1978. At the college's first chapel service that year, held outdoors for want of space, Falwell delivered another miracle appeal, one that doubled his grasp (asking for $5 million in a little over a month) and drew an exceptionally big biblical mantle onto his shoulders. According to Falwell's biographers, here is how Jerry Falwell explained the seriousness of the situation to the thousands of students:

"Our world is in trouble today. That is why you are here to train and prepare to minister in a world of more than four billion people who desperately need Jesus Christ. This summer we have experienced the constant threat of postal strikes, which has affected our offerings. The cost of our Clean Up America Campaign has been tremendous, but we could not, nor can we ever, stop proclaiming righteousness in our nation. Thus you see unfinished buildings that you desperately need. We serve a prayer-answering God. We have gathered on this mountain today for a prayer meeting. We desperately need $5 million and have come to ask God to supply that need by September 24, which I have set aside as 'Miracle Day'."

Then Jerry stood in the August sun and preached a message from the Book of Joshua. He described the people of Israel and their situation as they faced the high strong walls of Jericho. The Thomas Road Baptist Church was facing similar obstacles.

"The Jews had come through four hundred years of bondage. God delivered them from the Red Sea by the hand of Moses, and after forty years of wandering in the wilderness, delivered them from the river Jordan by the hand of Joshua. They had come far by faith, but now, having arrived in the Promised Land, they found the walls of Jericho immovable. The inhabitants of Jericho had been reported to Joshua to be 'giants.' Everything seemed lost to the children of God. Defeat seemed imminent.

"Liberty Mountain is our Promised Land. For many years we have prayed for this thirty-five hundred acres of sanctified property. After twenty-two years of miracles, we have arrived on Liberty Mountain. But now we find ourselves looking up at the high walls of bills and unfinished buildings. A miracle is needed."

The students listened attentively as their chancellor told how Joshua met the unseen Captain. The Lord assured Joshua of victory and gave him the plan for it. The Jews were told to march around the walls once a day for six days. Then, on the seventh day, they were to march around seven times. The men of war were to march up front. The seven priests with trumpets of rams' horns were to march directly behind them each day, sounding the trumpets all the way. The ark of the covenant would be carried in their midst. The congregation was to follow the ark.

Drawing an analogy between men of war and prayer warriors, Jerry called for thousands of local prayer warriors to "walk point," symbolic of those who go first into battle. He asked millions who were watching by television to do the same. He assured the prayer warriors that, as they circled the walls of impossibility, the preachers at Thomas Road would keep preaching and sounding forth the message of the gospel. He asked Christians of North America to join with him on this trek of faith and pray with them for a miracle.

On each of the six days preceding the September 24 "Miracle Day," Jerry drove along the circumference road of Liberty Mountain, an 11.3 mile trip. He began at the main entrance of the college and prayed continually as he drove. On Sunday, September 24, Jerry rose early and encircled the mountain seven times—79.1 miles—before the early church service at Thomas Road. The offering that day and from the previous six weeks totaled more than $7 million. Two million dollars more than what had been prayed for. People stood and wept and praised God who loves to answer the prayers of his people.[8]

Whether or not Jerry's circling the mountain those mornings, and the prayer warriors praying, moved God to bless the ministry with $7 million, we may still ask how the sermon moved men and women to give sacrificially. Not that Falwell's sermon on the mountain, in and of itself, moved millions who were watching to send in all that money. The sermon was one piece of a much larger campaign that included other sermons, television and radio spots, and direct mail. Moreover, it is a time-honored practice among fund-raisers to juggle the figures, not necessarily lying about how much was raised, but, say, including money promised, or borrowed, or raised by some other means, or at an earlier date, in the total.

We do know two things, however. First, Falwell's ministry raised large amounts of money, surely many millions, on behalf of Liberty Baptist College (LBC) throughout the 1970s, especially during the period 1973–1977, when his total ministry income first began to leap forward quite remarkably. The annual revenue appears to have grown sixfold in four years, from approximately $3.5 to $23 million.[9] Second, a good deal of that money did indeed come from the audiences reached by the LBC fund-raising campaigns. Falwell's appeals, including the Jericho campaign, yielded a great deal of money. Divine intervention aside, what accounts for the force of Falwell's fund-raising campaigns?

Certainly, there were many factors at work. Falwell's fund-raising appeals tapped into preexisting interests among his constituents, interests he and his co-pastors had a hand in constituting. He told them things they wanted to hear about Liberty Baptist College—that hemlines and hairlines were carefully monitored there, and that, unlike other colleges, Liberty was a place where students learned to love America and respect authority. While Liberty was not *of the world*, it was at the same time *in the world*—it would give its students access to credentialed degrees, better jobs, still higher education. And then, too, Falwell's appeals followed tried-and-true fund-raising formulas, creating a sense of crisis and impending doom if contributions were not forthcoming. And of course Falwell was, for those who listened to him faithfully, a figure of authority, and authority depends on obedience. Falwell's asking for money, and his people's giving it to him, enacted his authority.

But what about the specifically religious language of Falwell's fund-raising campaigns? If we attend closely to the language of Falwell's campaigns and listen to it as his faithful followers might, what sounds like "fund-raising" to an unbelieving ear becomes "sacrificial giving." The money raised by a preacher has more in common with the biblical blood of lambs than with what gets spent in stores or raised in a secular telethon. In an important way, the whole point of giving to a God-led ministry is to vacate the commercial economy and to enter another realm, a Christ-centered gospel, or sacrificial, economy in which material expectations are transformed. If we attend to what Falwell said, we may, ultimately, glimpse that other realm.

On the mountainside, under the August sun, Jerry Falwell recounted to the entering class of 1978 and his Old-Time Gospel Hour audience the story of Joshua and Jericho as history, not legend, or myth, or parable. God parted the waters of the Red Sea for Moses and of the River Jordan for Joshua. The Lord (the "unseen Captain") visited Joshua and gave him a victory plan which he and his warriors and priests carried out to the letter, circling the city once each morning for six days and seven times on the seventh day. The walls of Jericho fell down flat when the people shouted and the priests blew the trumpets, and the Israelites took the city and utterly destroyed all that was in it. God kept his promise to Joshua, who had faithfully carried out his plan.

From the beginning, Falwell, and his biographers, interlaced Joshua's tale with a second, contemporary story that reiterated with exquisite precision and updated details the same tests of faith and imagination evoked by the first. *Liberty Mountain is our Promised Land*, Falwell told his gathered church. On the brink of conquest, they faced great obstacles, *high walls of bills and unfinished buildings.* A miracle was needed. Falwell's plan mimicked the plan that God gave Joshua when he confronted the walls of Jericho. He asked his local and television prayer warriors to go into battle and circle the walls of impossibility, praying for a miracle. Falwell drove around the mountain (11.3 miles), praying each day before "Miracle Day" for six days, and on the seventh day, he compassed it seven times (79.1 miles). And the offering that day and from the previous weeks totaled $7 million. God had once again answered the prayers of his people.

Both these stories, the story of Joshua and the story of Jerry, are "absolutely true." Indeed, they are not simply "true stories," they are "storied events." As we have seen, event and story in fundamentalist discourse have not been torn asunder. Biblical narrators, past and present, tell histories, the way things actually happened. Their stories are literally true in the sense that they do not represent history, they *are* history. Likewise, the connections that anointed narrators propose between one story, such as Joshua's, and another, such as Jerry's, are not mere filaments of interpretation tying tales together in some folk fantasy. They are historical tissues, sinews of divine purpose, design and will that join concrete events across millennia.

The people gathered on Liberty Mountain in August, those who heard Falwell's sermon broadcast a few weeks later on the Old-Time Gospel Hour, and those who read its rendering in Strober and Tomczak's biography, filtered his appeal through a dense mesh of presuppositions. Their interpretive filter consisted of other tellings of Joshua's tale, including the biblical text and a variety of commentaries on the story; a set of side texts and contexts—other stories and storied situations in Falwell's discursive church which framed and infilled his appeal that sunny afternoon; and a characteristically fundamental Baptist set of preconceptions about how juxtaposed stories, their characters, and their outcomes are related as divinely designed events. Here are a few intimations of what those who listened and read might have brought to bear upon Falwell's appeal.

Fundamental Baptists read the story of Joshua and Jericho as a tale of God's omniscience and of the victorious life and blessings which await those who are faithful and obedient to God. God told Joshua before the final battle, *I have given into thine hand Jericho.* In announcing this certainty before the fact, God, according to Falwell's *Liberty Bible Commentary*, showed himself to be *above time, and that which is yet future for us is present for Him. What was for Joshua yet to happen in the capturing of Jericho, was for God already an accomplished fact.*[10] Still, the accomplishment of that fact depended on Joshua and Israel's blind obedience: *God's mysterious methods are not always understandable to us. But God does not ask us to understand them; rather, He asks us to obey them. Israel at the fall of Jericho is a good example of this truth. Although God's methods were mysterious, nevertheless Israel trusted them explicitly . . . ; followed them exactly . . . ; employed them enthusiastically . . . ; continued them expectantly . . . ; and accomplished them entirely. . . . God's work, done in God's way, always has God's blessing.*[11]

The Old Testament tale of tumbling walls is also simultaneously read as a prefiguration, a typification, of Christ's victory and of Christians' victory through Christ.[12] Paul told the Corinthians (I Corinthians 6:11) that the wilderness experiences of the Israelites "happened unto them for examples: and they are written for our admonition."[13] Joshua specifically is a type, or shadow, of Christ. "The types are but a 'shadow of good things to come and not the very image of the things' [Hebrews 10:1]; and therefore, like all shadows, they give but an imperfect representation."[14] Also, like a shadow, the relation between it and that which casts it is metonymic: A type is a sort of a model of the thing it refers to. It has certain characteristics of the real thing.[15] The *Liberty Bible Commentary* compares a "type" to the mark or imprint left by an engraving tool. A type is a copy of the original and the perfect, master original, which came after, yet came before, all the Old Testament figures, who anticipated him imperfectly, was Christ. Moses typified Christ as the one who delivered his people from bondage, which typified sin, and Joshua typified Christ as the one who gave entrance to the Promised Land, which typified all earthly blessings of God and Heaven itself.[16]

As the Reverend Melvin Campbell taught us, both the Old and New Testaments foreshadow the persons, events, and things in the world in much the same way that the Old Testament foreshadows, provides "the very alphabet of the language" for, the New Testament.[17] The terms "foreshadow" and "typify," "fulfill" and "complete," have passed out of vogue in this century.[18] But preachers, especially conservative Baptist preachers, still teach their people to read the Bible and to interpret their lives and current history typologically. They may use other terms, such as *applying the Bible to daily life*, and *drawing parallels*, and *pointing out analogies between the Bible and current history*. In his 1978 appeal, Falwell drew "parallels" and pointed out "analogies" between his financial Jericho and the story of Joshua, but, as we shall see, his logic, as in many other fundamental Baptist applications of the Bible, was as figural, or typological, as if he were reading the Old Testament through the New.

Falwell had drawn on the story of Joshua in his preaching before 1978, and those contemporary prefigurings also informed his later application. Unfortunately, the public archive of his early sermons is thin, but one of the few which is accessible in fact draws a parallel with the story of Joshua very much at odds with the one Falwell drew on Liberty Mountain.

Falwell delivered "Ministers and Marchers" at Thomas Road Baptist Church in March 1965 and widely distributed it as a pamphlet through fundamentalist networks. Sometime around 1970, after he began to back away from his defense of segregation and to build a national audience, Falwell recalled all copies of his earlier sermons so that they could not be used against him. Because it had been distributed far and wide, "Ministers and Marchers" was the only sermon from the 1960s to survive the recall.[19] In that sermon, Falwell preached against preachers who engaged in politics, and specifically, against the preachers, black and white, who led the Civil Rights movement. Among other objections, Falwell objected to the pro-civil rights preachers' efforts to prove Christians should *lead people out of bondage in situations where they are being discriminated against* by lifting out of the Bible such instances as Moses leading the Jews out of Egypt. Such an application of the exodus story, he argued, was not acceptable, because Christians, according to type, have already crossed over the Jordan into the Promised Land. Christians, in other words, have already completed the exodus story.

The 400 years of Egyptian bondage is a type of the sinner's experience before he is converted. We all live in bondage to sin until we know the truth of the new birth. When the Jews came out of Egypt, they immediately came into forty years of wilderness wandering. This is a parallel of our infant and carnal Christian life as we struggle before learning the lessons of faith and rest in God. If church leaders are going to use Moses and the Jews in Egypt as a justification for what they are doing today with the negro in the South, they should also go on and tell the Jews that they are going to lead them in forty years of wandering in which everyone of them will die. That is exactly what happened to all of the Jews. Only Caleb and Joshua lived through that experience. Then, a new generation went into the Promised Land. The Promised Land is a parallel to the victorious Christian life on the earthly level, and our eventual Heaven on the eternal plain. To try to force any other meaning than this is simply making the Bible say what you want it to say.

Falwell's 1965 and 1978 narrations of Joshua show that typology is sufficiently flexible to enable diametrically opposed applications. In the first instance, Joshua's story, like Moses' story, was already complete for Christians. In the second, Falwell caught Christians up in a new completion of the story. More germane for our purposes, however, we may glimpse here one of the mechanisms by which Falwell transformed himself gradually during the 1970s into a preacher who engaged in politics, namely, by retypologizing himself. He not only drew on different biblical prefigures, but also reversed his earlier applications, so that instead of removing Christians from public life, they licensed world-building, world-changing activities.

The mountain was another type, or application, tucked between the lines of Falwell's sermon and of Strober and Tomczak's account. The phrases *a very special place* and *thirty-five hundred acres of sanctified property*, which Falwell used to describe Liberty Mountain, were charged up with biblical connotations during the mid-1970s.

In February 1976, a promotion appeared in the church publication *Faith Aflame* entitled THERE'S SOMETHING ABOUT A MOUNTAIN *that makes it hold such an important place in Scripture*. The title runs across two pages against an equally expansive backdrop of a mountain with the sun, presumably rising, behind its peak. A sidebar lists the scriptural mountains:

- Noah's ark came to rest on a mountain
- Abraham took Isaac to a mountain to be offered as a sacrifice
- God gave the ten commandments to Moses on a mountain
- Moses viewed the Promised Land from a mountain
- Elijah challenged the priests of Baal on a mountain
- Jesus gave us the great "sermon on the mount" on a mountain
- Jesus was transfigured on a mountain
- Jesus was crucified on a mountain
- Jesus ascended on a mountain
- Jesus is coming again to a mountain

The text of the promotion, five columns of it, began: WHAT GREAT SIGNIFICANCE DOES A MOUNTAIN HAVE TODAY? In 1972 God made available to Liberty Baptist College a beautiful tract of mountain land near Lynchburg which could become our world headquarters if Christians everywhere catch this vision. Since the humble beginning of our ministries in 1956, God has always moved in miraculous ways to bless and expand this work far beyond our expectations.

The promotion then identified Jerry Falwell as the man God called to lead his people to his mountain, described the sacrificial giving of wonderful people from all walks of life that had built his ministry thus far, and revealed the new vision—to "claim the mountain" in 1976. Just before it moved on to an intensely typologized appeal for money, the promotion paused for a moment, albeit guarded, of fundamentalist "health and wealth" theology: Yes, we want that mountain; we want to claim it for God in 1976 and we're going to ask you to "stake a claim" for the land. . . . Be much in prayer for us in this step of faith. Remember, LUKE 6:38 ["Give, and it shall be given unto you. . . ."] really does work. Stake your claim now. God just might give you a gold mine of blessings—materially and spiritually.

The promotion concluded by quoting Dr. Harold Willmington, dean of Thomas Road Bible Institute: We are in a parallel situation to the Jews in the days of Haggai the prophet. [God had brought poverty on the Jews then because they provided for themselves] while the house of God was lying on the mountain in waste: God commanded them to "GO UP TO THE MOUNTAIN, and bring wood, and build the house; AND I WILL TAKE PLEASURE IN IT, AND I WILL BE GLORIFIED, saith the Lord." This is

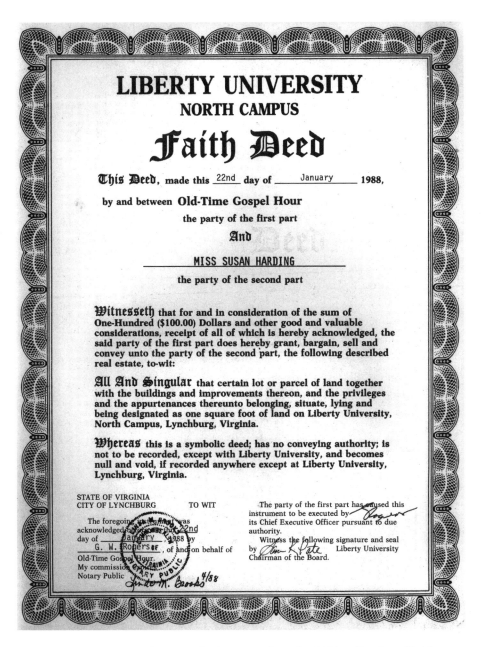

LIBERTY UNIVERSITY
NORTH CAMPUS

Faith Deed

This Deed, made this ___22nd___ day of _____January_____ 1988,

by and between **Old-Time Gospel Hour**

the party of the first part

And

MISS SUSAN HARDING

the party of the second part

Witnesseth that for and in consideration of the sum of One-Hundred ($100.00) Dollars and other good and valuable considerations, receipt of all of which is hereby acknowledged, the said party of the first part does hereby grant, bargain, sell and convey unto the party of the second part, the following described real estate, to-wit:

All And Singular that certain lot or parcel of land together with the buildings and improvements thereon, and the privileges and the appurtenances thereunto belonging, situate, lying and being designated as one square foot of land on Liberty University, North Campus, Lynchburg, Virginia.

Whereas this is a symbolic deed; has no conveying authority; is not to be recorded, except with Liberty University, and becomes null and void, if recorded anywhere except at Liberty University, Lynchburg, Virginia.

STATE OF VIRGINIA
CITY OF LYNCHBURG   TO WIT

The foregoing instrument was acknowledged before me this 22nd day of ___January___, 1988 by ___G. W. Rogers___, of and on behalf of Old-Time Gospel Hour.
My commission expires.
Notary Public

The party of the first part has caused this instrument to be executed by its Chief Executive Officer pursuant to due authority.
Witness the following signature and seal by _____ Liberty University Chairman of the Board.

Figure 4.1 An OTGH direct–mail solicitation from the 1980s offered sacrificial givers another opportunity to stake a claim in Liberty Mountain.

*what God wants on Liberty Mountain today and He promised to bless
those who obey his words. . . .*

*These are solemn words by the God of heaven. If Pastor Jerry Falwell
and the ministries need a "house of God" that will enable many thousands to worship the Lord together on the mountain, IT MUST BE
BUILT. . . .*

*We believe Christians everywhere WILL FOLLOW THIS EXAMPLE: for in
chapter 2, verse 9 [of Haggai] we read: "The glory of this latter house
shall be greater than the former. . . ." Isn't that fantastic? The present
progress we have made will seem small compared to what God will do
in "His new house" which must be built. For we can expect, as did the
people of Haggai's day, that God will bless us. Here's the promise—
Haggai 2:19: ". . . from this day will I bless you." Get in on this blessing!
Stake a claim on God's Mountain.*

This and other fund-raising appeals, circulated in the mid-1970s, saturated Liberty Mountain and Falwell's vision of it with biblical allusions.
Jerry was not only Joshua, but partook of Noah, Abraham, Moses, Elijah,
Haggai, and Christ himself. His gathered church resembled their gatherings, their peoples. His and his church's trials, persecutions, sacrifices,
and triumphs fulfilled theirs. As their prayers were answered, so would
be those of his church, *for we can expect, as did the people of Haggai's
day, that God will bless us.*

One more monumental, still unfolding, and deeply troubling storied situation informed Falwell's audience that afternoon on the grassy slope,
one that had pitched him into the big leagues as a persecuted figure. The
$2.3 million unsecured indebtedness of which Falwell finally absolved
himself in February 1977 was the remnant of the "most traumatic" crisis
his ministry had ever faced.[20] In the summer of 1973, the Securities and
Exchange Commission (SEC) sued Thomas Road Baptist Church for
fraud and deceit in the sale of church bonds and declared it insolvent
and unable to redeem the bonds. The church had sold $6.5 million worth
of bonds to 1,632 investors in twenty-five states in 1971–1973 with an
inaccurate prospectus, and the church's ledgers had not been kept up to
date.[21] *Nobody could tell exactly how much had been raised by the
church or where the money had come from and where it was going.*[22]
The worst accusations were officially cleared up fairly quickly in August

1973 when a federal judge dropped the fraud and deceit charge and cleared TRBC and Falwell of any willful wrongdoing, but the court placed the church's financial operations under the supervision of five local businessmen until all its unsecured indebtedness (totaling $16 million) was eliminated.

Liberty Baptist College was very much implicated in all this trouble. The Candler's Mountain property was a big financial leap for Falwell when he bought it around 1970, committing his ministry to a $1.25 million mortgage.[23] Building LBC into an accredited fundamental Baptist college as well as launching a national television and radio ministry, the Old-Time Gospel Hour, were even bigger commitments, and it was they that inspired the bond sale as a quick means of raising millions of dollars. Although LBC figured from the beginning in a panoply of appeals, almost all the money went into building the Old-Time Gospel Hour network. The idea was that the increased watershed of contributors created by the Old-Time Gospel Hour would eventually fund the college.[24] And it did, but not substantially until 1977 when the last of the $16 million debt was retired.

Later, Falwell could say that the SEC scandal was an educational period for Thomas Road because *it forced us to move from a one-horse church to a corporate position.*[25] His ministry cut overhead costs, hired professional accountants, public relations experts, and an ad agency to coordinate fund-raising, and they adopted cost-efficient procedures of buying radio and television time.[26] Falwell also considered it a kind of spiritual turning point: *Looking back, Jerry says this was the church's most crucial period. The SEC crisis was a time not only of testing but also preparation for greater service and accomplishment. The church learned never to fear any opponent. . . . Jerry comments now [1979], "These ministries have been down through the valley of the shadow of death. Christ had to bring me to the place where I relinquished control of my total ministry and offered it to Him. . . . Financially and legally, we were beaten upon every side. We learned how to call upon God, for He alone is able. . . . I can honestly say that . . . valley was the turning point in our ministry. It has been a miracle. Spiritually, it has been a transforming time, for God has taught us how to conquer through prayer. I am so glad there is no problem so big, so overwhelming, but what God is up to the task.*[27]

VOLUME 10   NO. 3   FEBRUARY 22

SOUL WINNING . . .

J. O. GROOMS

TREASURE PATH TO SOUL WINNING
book by Rev. J. O. Grooms is
being shipped by the hundreds
to pastors and churches a-
cross America.

This book is the key to
Scripture memorization and
prepares the Christian for
aggressive personal soul winning.

A special offer on the books
has been extended through the
month of March. Pastors and
churches wishing to initiate
a Scripture memorization ,
soul winning course should
write to:

SOUL WINNING COURSE
Jerry Falwell Evangelistic
Association, P. O. Box 1111,
Lynchburg, Virginia, 24505.

Complete course information
will be sent immediately.

**TREASURE ISLAND YOUTH
CAMP OPENS SATURDAY
JUNE 12th**

FALWELL ANNOUNCES NEWEST ADDITION TO TRBC MINISTRIES

In his midweek address to the congregation of Thomas Road
Baptist Church February 17th, Dr. Jerry Falwell announced the
founding of LYNCHBURG BAPTIST COLLEGE. The school, designed to teach practical courses for Christian workers, will also have
a full academic range of courses. "Training pastors, missionaries,
Sunday School workers, church musicians, administrators, evangelists, secretaries", Falwell said, "will be our main purpose".

In making the announcement Dr. Falwell stated that one of
America's best known Christian educators, Dr. Elmer Towns, would
be Vice President and Academic Dean of Lynchburg Baptist College.

DR. ELMER TOWNS HEADS FACULTY

Towns, author of the best seller, THE TEN
LARGEST SUNDAY SCHOOLS AND WHAT
MAKES THEM GROW, is currently Associate
Professor of Christian Education at Trinity Evangelical Divinity School, Deerfield, Illinois. He is
also Sunday School editor of Christian Life Magazine.

Those wishing catalogs may write:
LYNCHBURG BAPTIST COLLEGE, P. O. Box 657,
Lynchburg, Virginia 24505.

Dr. Falwell stated that the college's first classes would be held
in the fall of 1971.

The college will occupy part of the educational facilities of
Thomas Road Baptist Church.

BONDS

NOW

AVAILABLE

8%

Limited Amount
Available

Registered Mortgage Improvement
Bonds Issued By

**Thomas Road
Baptist Church**

Interest Payable Semi-Annually
Phone Collect 703 239-9281
Mrs. Hogan
Nights and Weekends 847-7316

Figure 4.2 A 1971 TRBC publication, *Word of Life*, announced both the church
bond campaign and the founding of Liberty Baptist College.

The spiritual transformation was also a rhetorical transformation. It appears that it was on this journey through the valley of the shadow of death that Falwell acquired ever-larger biblical prefigures.

Falwell's evangelist friend and mentor, B. R. Lakin, was attending a conference when the SEC announced its charges in April 1973. He was driving from Lynchburg to West Virginia when, as he related to Jerry, *"God told me to come back here to help you." Old Dr. Lakin spent the week. There was nothing he could do legally to end our troubles. But he ministered personally to my own tired spirit. He retold the Old Testament stories about ancient clashes between the government and the prophets. He reminded me of the New Testament stand the apostles and first-century Christians had to take against kings, governors, courts, and ruling bodies. He dragged out all his best dramatic accounts of the prophets and the priests, the martyrs and the saints. And he inspired me through the telling.*[28]

Take a fearless stand, Jerry, Lakin said, and Jerry did. Probably not for the first time, but perhaps with more conviction than ever, Falwell claimed *the devil is after us,* and he cast himself as under siege by the big guns on the SEC and by a hostile national press. A humble and thoroughly innocent servant of God, broken-hearted and contrite, Jerry interceded ceaselessly for his church. *After hours of prayer, Jerry would rise and smile peacefully, more convinced than ever that God had placed His hand on Thomas Road Baptist Church in a very special way.*[29]

Over the following years, as we have seen in his college fund-raising appeals, Falwell clearly took to heart Lakin's prefigurings. In 1975, he led a seven-month anti-debt road show with the LBC chorale for his Old-Time Gospel Hour audience scattered across the country. It further enlarged his image of self-sacrifice. *"Jerry was away from his family for days at a time* [a student on the tour reported] *and got very little sleep; yet he never complained. . . . Some criticized Jerry in those days for asking for money. But we who knew him knew that he never asked for a dime for himself. He asked for us, for LBC students, who needed a Christian education."*[30]

One evening after a rally in Seattle, Falwell and a few students reportedly went to an adjacent hall to see the tail end of a Led Zepplin concert that had earlier disturbed their own meeting. *There they witnessed a horrifying scene. Thousands of young men and women were lying on the floor, engaged in every filthy act imaginable. The discordant sounds were deafening. On the stage the rock star hero of thousands of American young people stood with outstretched arms in front of a cross, with psychedelic, fluorescent lights twirling around him.*[31]

Jerry felt in a small measure the tremendous weight of sin that was placed on Jesus Christ at the cross, and his heart ached. He resolved anew to help young Christians *turn this country upside down for Christ.*[32]

The following year, the nation's bicentennial, Falwell organized another massive tour, this one called "I Love America." The rallies were hugely successful, at once ballooning his audience, reputation, and income. It was in his stump sermon on that tour, "America Back to God," that Falwell began most audibly to assume the political mantle and voice of the Old Testament prophets. *What has gone wrong? What has happened to this great republic? We have forsaken the God of our fathers. The prophet Isaiah said that our sins separate us from God. The Bible is replete with stories of nations that forgot God and paid the eternal consequences. . . . Our country needs healing. Will you be one of a consecrated few who will bear the burden for revival and pray, "O, God, save our nation. O, God, give us a revival. O, God, speak to our leaders?" The destiny of our nation awaits your answer.*[33]

When the SEC barred Falwell from borrowing money from friends, he felt he had two alternatives: disband the college and the Old-Time Gospel Hour or ask God for a miracle.[34] He asked God for a miracle, and Falwell's end of the bargain, evidently, was to expand his place in biblical rhetoric and narrative immensely—as a man of action, and ultimately of politics, as well as a man of words. The SEC scandal, in other words, was one means by which God was leading and preparing Jerry Falwell for a political role. The Old-Time Gospel Hour tour became the "I Love America" rallies, which became the "Clean Up America" campaign, which became the "America, You're Too Young To Die!" extravaganza, which, finally, became the "Moral Majority" campaign. In 1987, Falwell wrote regarding the SEC suit that God had used *the entire ugly event to teach us important lessons that we desperately needed to learn if we were to be ready for the even greater future he was planning.*[35] By then Falwell was fashioning himself as the Paul and the early church (*facing their own investigation and persecution by the Roman emperor*) and Christ himself (*Jesus, too, had suffered from similar headlines. . . .*

With every triumph there is crucifixion).[36] In addition, Falwell had by then mastered the biblical language to convert defeat into victory, death into life, and debt into wealth.

So, a lot more was happening than met the eye on that mountainside in August 1978 when Jerry Falwell preached from the Book of Joshua. He and his prayer meeting were informed, or infilled, by other Joshuas, other prophets, other mountains, other Jerichos. All that came before, in some measure, prefigured him that afternoon, and his story completed and fulfilled them.

More specifically, Falwell's circling Liberty Mountain in prayer and in his car completed Joshua's victory. God spoke to him through the story of Jericho as plainly as he, the unseen Captain, had spoken to Joshua that night thousands of years before. He gave them each a plan of victory, and God's plans never fail, because their outcomes are, from God's vantage, already an accomplished fact. God always looks back, he always speaks from the point of view of the end of history, when everything has indeed already happened. Jerry's encompassing the mountain that morning was not magical; it did not induce God to act on his ministry's behalf. His circling was submissive, an act of obedience and sacrifice. It was Jerry enacting God's plan for him, Jerry, in that moment of crisis, and God's work, done in God's way, always had God's blessing. If God told Jerry to build a house of God on Liberty Mountain, it must be built.

All this translates into money rather elegantly and, under the influence of a master preacher such as Falwell, amply. The appeal, no matter how it is biblically adorned, sounds to the unborn-again ear like mere money-raising. But the biblical attire is everything to the faithful. An appeal for sacrificial giving catches them up in a sacred enactment of core gospel meanings. Just as Joshua obeyed God and was, necessarily, blessed, so was Jerry, and so will they be. They too will complete Joshua's story, not only through prayer but through sacrificial giving. We may be certain that Jerry explicitly asked for money from his television and radio audience after his Joshua exegesis, and even had he not, everyone would have understood that obedience to God in this instance included sending in money to Falwell's ministry.

Faithful Christians—and fundamental Baptists are among the more faithful in this respect—sacrifice themselves narratively, in their conduct, and financially to God. Their gifts of money, like their gifts of words and habits, do not go to any man or ministry, but go directly to God and represent obedience to him. As Ed Dobson, one of Falwell's principal co-pastors, explained in a sermon on stewardship, *Giving is worshipping God. We're not giving to a church or person or ministry when we give, but to God. God has a ledger with a debit column and a credit column, and God credits every gift. God does miracles because people give sacrificially.*

God, for his part, always blesses those who obey him, and blesses them abundantly. The whole of Christianity is giving. One year the Thomas Road Baptist Church adopted Luke 6:38 as their theme verse: *"Give, and it shall be given unto you; good measure, pressed down, and shaken together, and running over, shall men give into your bosom. For with the same measure that ye mete withal it shall be measured to you again."* As thousands of members gave sacrificially, they learned that God will be no man's debtor. Each found that God gave back to them far more than they had given.[37]

Money, like the blood of Old Testament animals or the blood of Christ, is a sacrifice given to God and representing obedience to him. God, in turn, blesses, financially and in other ways, those who obey. Again, the gifts do not induce God to give back; they are not efficacious.[38] Men are not getting God to act for them; God is getting men to act for him. And God blesses those who fulfill his plan. The $7 million in Jerry's coffers on February 28, 1978, had not effectively come from his people but from God, who blessed his ministry because he and his people had done God's work in God's way. Men and women sacrificially give money to God, and God gives money to men and women, above all to great men of God such as the Reverend Falwell: that is the gospel economy.

Falwell's empire—virtually all that radiates out from his local church— was built out of these sacrificial rites of offering. The church itself was built on and sustained by tithes, 10 percent of the annual income of members, money which already belongs to God and is not considered a gift. Everything else, the entire contributed income of the Old-Time Gospel Hour, represented sacrificial giving, and, as Falwell has said, *no one has given sacrificially until he has gone beyond ten percent.*[39] The $1 million Thomas Road budget in 1970 was mostly made up of tithes. A good deal of the $3.5–$7 million budget for 1973 probably came from the bond sale. Most of the total revenue for 1977, about $20 million, on the other hand, came from sacrificial offerings, which fired the ministry's phenomenal growth after 1973.

From the beginning, Jerry Falwell curried and lured big financial backers, but, until the late 1980s at least, most of his Old-Time Gospel Hour income came from small contributors, people living on earned incomes for whom a gift to Falwell meant a material as well as figural sacrifice. When Falwell asked for $5 million in August 1978, he had a good idea that he would get that much, given receipts from previous months, and because many of his contributors, as members of a variety of clubs, were committed to giving a fixed sum each month. In the 1970s, there were, among others, Faith Partners, Founders, Doorkeepers, the Pastor's Team, Station Sponsors, and members of the I Love America Club and the Ten Thousand Club. And then there were special appeals—for emergency relief, missionary work, on behalf of patriotism, and against pornography and homosexuality. There were banquets and rallies and tours and many opportunities for Christian stewardship—a Christian will, a life income agreement, a transfer of life insurance policies to the Lord, or a living memorial to a departed loved one.[40]

Money from all these sources was lumped together when Falwell announced the success of a fund-raising appeal and, indeed, in the ministry's spending practices as well. Most of the money from all appeals, of necessity, fed the machinery that raised the money to begin with. But most contributors were distant from and oblivious to these details. More to the point, sacrificial giving is a kind of submission to the Lord. It involves a relinquishing of control to God, for he alone is able. It is precisely good not to know exactly where the money goes, so that it goes into a void of sorts, seemingly out of human hands.[41] If a contributor is financially strapped, the gift is even more meaningful. It is more of a literal sacrifice, and the sense of escape from irksome budgetary constraints is heightened. Fundamental Baptists, the middling and wealthy as well as the poor, try to be careful financial managers, routinely treating themselves to seminars and tapes and manuals that pique their consciousness about the finite flow of money in and out of their hands. Giving sacrificially breaks them out of those cycles, and the sweet release may give them a taste of divine things to come, at the same time it allies them with God in his concrete miraculous work on earth.

A people gives its church many gifts, of course—sociability, services, creativity, loyalty, prayers, and more—and all of them, insofar as they are free gifts, function, like tithes and sacrificial offerings, outside the market economy, according to noncommercial logic. They generate an invisible world, a kingdom of the spirit, in which God is worshipped continuously through all sorts of sacrificial giving and God blesses people with *good measure, pressed down, and shaken together, and running over.* Born-again believers want very much to get in on this blessing, and for Falwell's electronic church the only tangible gift they can give, and thus receive the blessing for giving, is money.

That Falwell's empire and its financing were surrounded by skeptics— a hermeneutic of suspicion—from the beginning was part of what made it all work so well. The outside, worldly, cynical voice would say his fund-raising was gimmickry, fleecing, hucksterism, nothing but a con game. Even among believers, among Falwell's hometown followers, his image as a man of God was shadowed by misgivings, a secondary image of him as a small-time Southern merchant who struck it rich by indulging in dubious, often reckless, occasionally sublegal business practices.

As long as Falwell was able to juggle his double image, the tension worked for him by creating the grounds for a leap of faith, for it was precisely the transfiguration from the realm of the worldly image into the divine that believers effected when they gave to his ministry. *God does miracles because people give sacrificially,* because they obey God and act on faith, because they step out on a limb for God, and the shakier the limb, the firmer the faith, the greater the blessing.[42] In the early 1970s, Falwell turned the most skeptical moment his ministry had ever faced to his escalating advantage by harnessing the generative power of his opposition. As his opposition metamorphosed from hometown critics into the federal government and the national media, his ministry and its mission were likewise enlarged. Falwell's harness was the figural rhetoric which cast him as a prophet-apostle-martyr-saint, sacrificing himself and speaking for God, and whose people *must* respond with sacrificial gifts according to God's plan.

CHAPTER FIVE

Cultural Exodus

History will have to record that Jerry Falwell was a significant, if not the significant, individual in bringing fundamentalists back into being a recognized nation.

—NELSON KEENER, 1984 INTERVIEW

A S AN INDEPENDENT, unaffiliated fundamental Baptist preacher, Jerry Falwell during the 1970s was able to mix freely with preachers aligned with various networks, and he found many of them increasingly willing to mix with one another.[1] In his 1976 "America Back to God" crusade sermon, Falwell claimed that he was meeting monthly with some forty well-known fundamentalist preachers—among them John R. Rice, Jack Hyles, Lee Robertson, and J. Vernon McGee. Fundamentalists, or born-again believers, as he was beginning to call them, were America's *salt of the earth*, its *preservative*, and he reckoned at the time that there were some *45–50 million grains of salt in these United States.*[2]

Falwell was a frequent guest speaker at his colleagues' churches and conferences during this period, and John R. Rice provided him his most far-reaching venues. Rice was descended from the same fundamental Baptist preaching lineage as Falwell, a lineage founded by J. Frank Norris, perhaps the most renowned militantly separatist fundamentalist preacher of the 1930s and 1940s. But unlike Norris, and like Falwell, Rice was determined to extend his reach and influence beyond a narrow band of affiliated fundamental Baptists. To this end, Rice built the country's largest-circulating fundamentalist tabloid, *Sword of the Lord*, which had

300,000 subscribers at the time of his death in 1980.[3] He also held preaching conferences that drew pastors, evangelists, and students from a wide spectrum of fundamental Baptist networks, including the Baptist Bible Fellowship, Southside Baptist Fellowship, Bob Jones University, and the General Association of Regular Baptists Fellowship.

In 1979, Sword of the Lord Publications published and distributed a collection of revival sermons which Falwell had deliverd at Sword of the Lord conferences during the mid-1970s. *These messages were delivered primarily to preachers*, according to Falwell in his introduction, and they tell us a good deal about his thinking at the time. One of his constant refrains dwelt on the 1976 Gallup poll report to the effect that 34 percent of adult Americans professed to be saved, or born-again. They were Falwell's 45–50 million grains of salt. In his sermon "Seven Things Corrupting America," Falwell added on another 25 million boys and girls under age 18 and thus claimed that a grand total of 75 million Americans know Christ.

Many of these people are in liberal churches where nothing is being said or done of any scriptural worth on Sunday or any other time. Some of these people are in no church at all. Many millions of them are in fundamental churches. All I am saying to you, and what I continually say to our preacher boys at Liberty Baptist College is, they are out there. We have an obligation not only to hear them say they are born again, that they believe in the Bible, and that they share their faith, but we have an obligation to get them into good Bible-believing, soul-winning churches. . . . Those 75 million Americans, adult and below, are a mighty force of God in this generation if properly taught, trained and disciplined. I look on us preachers as that army of mobilizers and spiritual organizers who have to go out like the labor union and find them and bring them into our camp, teach them the Word of God, train them in the way of God, and set their souls on fire.[4]

Falwell's appeal here and in his other revival sermons of the period had two audiences, old-fashioned separatists and preachers chafing at their own separatist taboos. On the one hand, we hear an ardent soul winner and discipliner, and on the other hand, a respected leader asking his colleagues to rethink their mission and their methods in ways that conflicted with historic fundamentalism's exclusive commitment to evangelization and separation. In "Let Us Reach the World Together,"

he preached on behalf of fundamentalist ecumenicism, urging his colleagues to stop fighting with one another over *who to eat with and who
not to eat with, and who to have write for you and who to have preach
for you, and where you should and should not preach.*[5] While still defending holy living and biblical separation in principle, he deplored its
excesses, especially when it resulted in a falling-out among preachers. In
"A Day of Many Solomons," Falwell observed that *at Liberty Baptist
College, we require short hair for boys. By short hair we mean that it
has to be off the ears, cannot touch the collar and cannot get over the
eyes. For others, short means a little bit higher than that, and for others,
they want to skin and peel the head. God bless you! But let's not fight
over the length.*[6]

Why should fundamentalist preachers unite? Falwell, to be sure, said,
*It is high time we got down to the business of reaching a dying world
for a living Savior.* But he also told his colleagues in "A Day of Many
Solomons" that *we have to rebuild a nation. For too long, we have sat
back and said politics are for the people in Washington, business is for
those on Wall Street, and religion is our business. But the fact is, you
cannot separate the sacred and the secular. We need to train men of God
in our schools who can go on to Congress, can go on to be directors in
the largest corporations, who can become the lawyers and the businessmen and those important people in tomorrow's United States. If we are
going to turn this country around, we have to get God's people mobilized in the right direction and we must do it quickly.*

*Did you know that the largest single minority block in the United
States that has never been capitalized on by anybody is the fundamentalist
movement? If all the fundamentalists knew who to vote for and did it
together, we could elect anybody. If every one of these people could be
intelligently taught and mobilized, brother, we could turn this nation
upside down for God!*

*We preachers have to teach some Solomons how to build a new na-
tional house. This nation has to be rebuilt. It has gone to pot, it is literally
falling apart at the seams. And our young people and thousands like them
can do something about it, if there are some men of war [Davids] like us
behind them who maybe have shed a little blood along the way, who
will teach them how to do it, who will pay the price and make the
sacrifice to see that they know how to do it.*[7]

Indeed, Falwell had by this time shed a little blood. He first attracted the attention of the nation's media in 1976 after he read presidential candidate Jimmy Carter's *Playboy* interview. Carter, in an apparent effort to seem both humble and complex, admitted that "I've looked on a lot of women with lust. I've committed adultery in my heart many times. This is something that God recognizes I will do—and I have done it— and God forgives me for it. But that doesn't mean that I condemn some- one who not only looks on a woman with lust but who leaves his wife and shacks up with someone out of wedlock. . . . Christ says, Don't con- sider yourself better than someone else because one guy screws a whole bunch of women while the other guy is loyal to his wife."[8]

Carter's remarks produced a considerable hullabaloo, and Falwell de- scribed his part in it in his Sword of the Lord sermon, "Seven Things Corrupting America." The *Washington Post* and CBS Morning News aired Falwell's views on Carter's infelicitous remarks shortly after they appeared. In addition, Falwell taped two television programs of his own that were scheduled for airing the following week. *Mr. Carter's forces began immediately contacting all of our television outlets, threatening that if they aired the programs they would be in violation of FCC rules and regulations. I immediately got Dr. John Rice, Dr. Jack Hyles, Dr. John Rawlings, and Dr. Bill Dowell* [fundamentalist preachers with na- tional reputations] *together. We went to Washington and called a press conference at the National Press Club and I said, "I resent anybody in Washington, or anybody trying to go to Washington, silencing and muz- zling a preacher of the Gospel from preaching his moral convictions."*

The controversy about Carter's remarks in *Playboy* marked the begin- ning of the end of the evangelical romance with America's first self- described "born-again" president. Likewise, it was the beginning of Fal- well's march toward the Moral Majority. He was in fact first approached that year, in 1976, by a group of conservative leaders, among them How- ard Phillips, Paul Weyrich, and Richard Viguerie. They proposed Fal- well create an organization that would mobilize fundamentalists and evangelicals as voters. He declined, but the idea apparently took root.[9] He not only began to preach more openly toward such an end, he took some initial steps, joining singer Anita Bryant in her crusade against the homosexual rights ordinances in Dade County, Florida, in 1977 and 1978 and lending some support in Virginia to efforts to block the ERA amendment and protest the White House Conferences on the Family in 1978. Finally, in spring of 1979, after meeting again with conservative leaders, Falwell announced the formation of the Moral Majority.

The language of the Moral Majority was an important stage of fundamentalist transformation during the 1980s, as we shall see in the next chapter. However, the more important stage for enacting fundamentalist cultural reform, as opposed to political engagement, was the language of Falwell's total ministry. During the 1970s, Falwell had helped to close the ranks among a broad spectrum of fundamentalists. During the 1980s, he divided them down the middle, hiving off those who would forsake much of their biblical separation from the world, and allying them with conservative evangelicals who were already more at ease in the world but had lately become alarmed about its moral state and the prospect of accommodating to it. This alliance, which formed the core of the New Christian Right in the 1980s, was as much a cultural merger as it was a political pact among leaders.

To carry out his side of the merger, Falwell bent his sermons and his ministries, old and new, his media projects, direct mail, tape and video series, books, magazines, newsletters, pamphlets, concert tours, rallies, Bible studies, conferences, and prayer groups to the task of reforming fundamentalism. The main venue, however, was Liberty Baptist College. It was there, in his college (and, later, university), that the rhetorics were fashioned and aired that would relax the matrix of social and cultural rules, taboos, and practices that had demobilized fundamentalists for fifty years in the name of holy living and biblical separation.

Rituals are routinized public events that reproduce implicit cultural assumptions, points of view, and social relations. Rituals also always alter cultural assumptions, points of view, and social relations, for no reiteration is ever an exact replication. Under some circumstances, as a result of changes in ritual form, content, or context, rituals become sites of more cultural transformation than reproduction. When multiple rituals, new and old, become sites in which implicit cultural assumptions, points of view, and social relations are willfully challenged and reconfigured on a broad scale, a cultural movement is under way.

This is what happened in Jerry Falwell's community during the 1980s. Sermons, chapel services, classes, Bible studies, and other events opened up oratorically and became mixing grounds for idioms, ideas, attitudes, and self-representations that hitherto had been kept separate. It was in these ritual crucibles, and most especially in their fusions of moderate fundamentalist and conservative evangelical narrative and rhetorical practices, that the Moral Majority's postfundamentalist, born-again Christian constituency was forged.

At the center of these fusions were two key figures, the fundamentalist (proto-evangelical) Jerry Falwell, and the (ex-fundamentalist) evangelical Francis Schaeffer IV. Schaeffer, twenty years Falwell's senior, had been a dedicated separatist Presbyterian pastor and evangelist in his early years. He worked closely with the militant fundamentalist Carl McIntire for two decades, until the 1950s, when he broke from McIntire and his organizations. During the 1960s, Schaeffer and his wife, Edith, set up a Christian retreat and study center, L'Abri, in Switzerland. L'Abri was geared primarily toward college and graduate students, and it established for Schaeffer a reputation that was novel, even radical, at the time, namely, that of an intellectually respectable evangelical who was also a biblical inerrantist. During the 1970s, Schaeffer, his wife, and eldest son, Franky, developed a multifaceted Christian critique of American culture in dozens of lecture tours. They also emerged as leading critics of moderate evangelicalism's "compromises with the world." In his earlier militant days, the elder Schaeffer might have attacked his lax brethren in unforgiving terms. Working alongside his wife and son, however, Schaeffer developed a more irenic style. They devoted themselves to convincing the many evangelicals who were troubled by the social and moral problems of the times that uncompromising biblical inerrancy was not only intellectually respectable but also the only true Christian position.

Francis Schaeffer IV saw one of Jerry Falwell's special televised broadcasts on one of his trips to the United States in 1978, and he recognized his potential for building a broad fundamentalist-evangelical alliance.[10] The two men arranged to meet and quickly agreed to join forces. As their oratorical forefingers touched and twined over the following years, both Schaeffer's and Falwell's reputations as national moral leaders mushroomed. Falwell's people in particular acquired a new sense of confidence and intellectual self-respect. Schaeffer's wife, Edith, also a speaker and author of many books, contributed to the transfiguration. And so did their son Franky, through his books, films, and speeches.

Evangelists come and go in the yearly cycle of a church or Bible college, and every once in a while one sparks a revival. It may take the form
of an outbreak of newfound faith, a reawakening of routinized faith, a
dedication to new feats of faith, or, most often, a mixture of all kinds of
quickenings. The experience of those awakened may be deeply exhilarating and wildly transformative. Listen, for example, to the expansive thrill
of Shirley Nelson's fictional midwestern Bible college student, Jo Fuller,
who was revived one afternoon: *For some reason an idea came to life
for Jo as she listened. She thought she understood for the first time God's
love for humanity, and what it meant to be Christlike, a person of re-
source, on whom others could draw for strength and faith. . . . What
followed next was a startling hunger. . . . She thought if she could swal-
low the Bible whole it would not be enough. . . . Her idea of prayer
began to change as well. It was like breathing, she found, a running,
unbroken contact with Christ. . . . She talked of Him more freely now
and said the words "the Lord" without effort. All at once it was not hard
at all to pray out loud in prayer bands and fellowships. . . . She felt like
a house swept clean. . . . She never, never wanted to come down off this
mountaintop, back to the valley of her old defeated life.*[11]

Sometimes the effects of revival are more complex and confusing, or
even alarming. An evangelist, in order to save or rededicate his listeners,
must first convince them they are lost, or at least lapsed, and there are
ample and powerful rhetorical conventions for so persuading them.
When the evangelist follows those conventions, the awakening may produce some turbulence, but the terrain that is opened up before the eyes
of converts is in many ways already familiar. On the other hand, if an
evangelist, under the right circumstances, targets the rhetorical conventions as such, he may produce, or participate in, a more fundamental
reformulation of what it means to be faithful.

That is what happened in Lynchburg in October 1982, when Franky
Schaeffer delivered a Monday morning chapel sermon at Liberty Baptist
College. Having just arrived in town, I missed the service, but there was
no escaping its aftermath. Everyone I met who had heard, or heard about,
Schaeffer's sermon talked about it for weeks, poring over its implications
and debating its points. Since an audiotape of the sermon was immedi-

ately available, those of us who missed it live quickly had a chance to partake of the original event.

Franky Schaeffer's topic that Monday morning was, innocently enough, "Christianity Is Truth Rather than Religion." Introduced as the son of renowned evangelist Francis Schaeffer IV and a well-known filmmaker and author in his own right, young Schaeffer made several heavy-handed jokes at his host's and audience's expense before he plunged into his topic. The jokes set the tone and tension of his talk that would pull his audience in two opposing directions, seducing them with his informal style and offhand familiarity, and scathing them with his biting, sometimes irreverent and sarcastic wit. He also established a rhythm common in revivalistic preaching, an oscillation so rapid between humorous light banter and heart-stopping seriousness that the two virtually merge.

Franky Schaeffer told his audience that it was *an honor to be here in Salt Lake City—I've never seen so many Mormons before. [Laughter] You're not Mormons? Well, what are you? Baptists? Okay. . . . I was just kidding. . . . I know you're not Mormons because you don't look funny enough. [Laughter] Sort of strange, right? Kind of odd, you know. But not that strange.* Then he carried on about how nice it was *to have a captive audience to speak to. I could go on for three or four hours. . . . There's iron grills over the back door. . . . Look, steel shutters come down over the thing. [Laughter, applause] . . . Which is great because there's nowhere you can go, you see. And when I tell you the terms for getting out of here, in terms of fund-raising, the kind of collection I want to take, and everything, after about hour three, you'll basically pay anything. It's a form of extortion. [Laughter]* Finally, he mused briefly that *the nice thing about speaking to a Christian audience is that we have our own private language, don't we? . . . It's nice to have a private language. I remember when I was a kid trying to learn Pig Latin, remember that? [Laughter] Now we have our own language that no one else can understand. And, for instance, if a fellow believer tells you they have something to share with you, don't expect any money. [Laughter] That's not what they are talking about. On the other hand, if they ask you to pray for them, well, in a lot of cases, it's time to start thinking about how much you're going to give. [Laughter] Okay, so . . . rather than talking in terms that are understandable, we can just use these phrases and cut through a lot of red tape, which brings me to my topic this morning, which is, Christianity is truth rather than religion.*

Now, there are two ways of looking at your faith, and one is to look at it as a religion and the other way is truth. Now, the difference between truth and religion is that religion depends on some sort of religious experience—salvation, whatever—and this experience then so-called "changes your life," whatever, and you live this way instead of that way. Now if you approach Christianity as truth, however, it's a very different subject.

To give you one example, the most basic being the existence of God, let's say. Either God is objectively there whether you believe in him or not, or he isn't. Now, if God is really there and the Creator, it wouldn't matter if there were any people who believed in him or not, he would still be there. And if Christianity is a mere religion, then God, his existence, depends on us believing in him. Do you understand the difference? . . . After a brief aside composed of more barbs directed as his audience, Schaeffer resumed laying out his central thesis.

If we regard Christianity as truth, we have to see that we have missed the path in an enormous area in the way we do things as Christians. About a hundred years ago there was a movement came about called the pietistic movement. And this movement unfortunately left us a legacy which goes something like this. Life is divided into two big categories, spiritual and the unspiritual. There is the worldly, and there is the Christian. Now, seek through the Bible as you will, you will not find this division in the Bible. The Bible is the book of truth which writes to the whole man where he is in his human condition. The Bible presents the good, the bad, the ugly, the truth of the situation. In that sense it's not a spiritual book, it's not a religious book, it's a book of history.

Now, what happens when you divide life into compartments and use false divisions is you get into crazy situations. You have so-called full-time Christian work and ministry and evangelism and so forth over here. This is somehow regarded as higher, to be desired after. Then you have everything else over here, like filmmakers and all the other second-class citizens in the Christian world, up here. And what this leads to first of all is a lot of personal frustration. But secondly it leads to the situation we found ourselves in in the twentieth century, which is that we're somehow on the outside looking in and complaining bitterly be-

*cause we're not being taken seriously and we're not having our Christian
beliefs listened to, and there's no way we can influence our culture, and
so forth.*

*To give you an example, think of the following. Where do you think
someone would have more influence for the cause of Christ, and I don't
mean evangelism, I mean truth [Pause], in this world? If you had two
students, and one became an evangelist, say a TV preacher or something,
and the other went on and became the editor of the* New York Times,
*who do you think would be doing more, or could do more, or would
be in a position to do more, to change the perception of Christianity in
our culture? If you have two people, and you have one person going to
Bible school and another going to medical school, and the one going to
medical school becomes a surgeon and chief in a hospital, and the one
going to Bible school becomes a minister, who do you think has more
chance to actually affect the course of our country in the area of something like abortion? [Pause, mumbling] If you have two people, and they
both have filmmaking talent, and one goes off and makes, quote, Christian movies, and the other goes off and makes really good films in Hollywood that are successful commercially, but because he is a Christian the
underlying philosophy of what he believes runs through those films. The
person who makes Christian films is making low-budget amateur whatever, and they are somehow spiritual because they come out from Gospel
Films rather than United Artists or whoever. But who do you think is
reaching the world in which we live?*

For a long, exhilarating, agitating hour, Franky Schaeffer reiterated
and elaborated these points, lacing his lesson with vivid illustrations, acute
phrases, and an incisive wit directed squarely between the eyes of his
audience. He mocked the spiritual practices and language of the gathered
fundamentalists, explicitly attacking the conscious and unconscious habits that made them culturally distinctive and that grounded their sense of
superiority in the world.

Schaeffer's attack on what he called "pietism" had several fronts. Most
broadly, he attacked the mapping of the world into spiritual and unspiritual things, words, activities, and professions. He demeaned the code
words, the holy jargon, that peppered fundamentalist discourse, constantly identifying its speakers as true Christians. And he deplored the
absolute elevation among fundamentalists of the ministry, missionary

work, and evangelism above all other professions and tasks. Mincing no words, Schaeffer's assaults on folk fundamentalism were so bold and blunt that they rang in his listeners' ears even as they laughed and applauded him. It was a lot of fun, but very dangerous, and it was disturbingly hard to tell for sure as he went on and on whether his wild ride would prove in the end to be constructive or destructive, God-led or devil-driven.

Let's listen more closely to the case Schaeffer made against pietism.

Look at some of the language that's grown up surrounding this whole idea of separating life into compartments of full-time this and that. We talk about surrendering to the ministry. This conjures up an image of some guy being handcuffed and dragged kicking out of one of the doors. This isn't the way I would like to go into anything. I don't want to surrender to anything. You don't sort of give up and go into the ministry because God's sort of after you, and you know what you really wanted to do is be a journalist and be the editor of your newspaper, but instead you're going to do something higher. You're going to give it up and surrender. If you're pursuing that mentality all it does is lead to the mediocrity we find in the Christian world. Because we have a whole bunch of people who through guilt and spiritual but non-Biblical persuasion are being pushed into fields and avenues and so forth that are somehow portrayed as higher instead of following off from the true calling God gives them. . . .

There's nothing spiritual about things just because they happen to be surrounded by holy jargon and trappings. The only thing it is truly spiritual for a Christian to do is to follow God's will in his life where that leads. That is your calling. . . .

Now to me it's not a question of seeing ministry as less, or cut off, no, I have quite a different perspective. I see all of life as one part of the ministry of the gospel. Now, when someone says, well, you're a Christian doctor, what do you do about being a Christian physician. If all he answers is, "Well, I go to prayer meetings and I witness to my patients," that's not necessarily being a Christian physician. To be a Christian in your field means to take a stand in the field that you're in in the way that only you can. Passing out tracts or witnessing on street corners, which I sometimes suspect is more akin to kind of Christian mugging [Laughter], is not necessarily what God wants you to do. It doesn't matter that it seems more superficially spiritual. . . .

You know, people talk about blasphemy. Just as an example of the baggage I'm talking about, they talk about the fact that they don't like some word in a movie or . . . they think that, or that they don't watch this because somebody swore or something like that. OK, that may be true or whatever, but let me tell you something that isn't said very much in the area that concerns us. In terms of taking God's name in vain, we're, our camp, are the blasphemers. I'll tell you how. We trivialize it. "Praise the Lord this," "Praise the Lord that." "God told me to do this," "I'm this," "Jesus laid this on my heart," "Di di bam bam bam bam." We use those words like the secular world uses curse words. We just dress up our lives in window dressing. There is nothing spiritual about bandying God's name about.

I can't stand that kind of talk. I have people come up to me and say, "Well, I don't think you're very spiritual." What they mean is that they are not hearing all the lingo. "Praise God for this, that, and the other." Of course there is a place for that. But if Christianity is truth and God is really there, we don't need to do this stuff to make ourselves feel Christian. He's there whether you feel spiritual today or not. It's got nothing to do with that.

So I think that's a good example of the kind of baggage that we brought along. It's a cultural, it's like a, sort of our own form of jive if you like. [Laughter] Then we go around and say, well, why doesn't the world understand anything we're saying, or whatever. Because we're speaking a foreign language! We're like an island in this culture, and we keep building higher walls and trying to shut it all out, and films are banned but we allow television, and then suddenly somebody says "But ding ding," and you can't build the wall high enough. You can't shut the whole world out. So it becomes an absurdity.

. . . The window dressing means nothing. It's the reality of what your life is that's important. So it's no more or less an indication of someone's spirituality if they use all kinds of jargon, or if they are obvious about their devotions, or if they have a particular system of Bible reading, or if they get up every morning and do this that and the other, or da da da, whatever. The Chinese burn joss sticks in front of idols; they have ritual. That's the whole difference between Christianity as truth and religion. Ours is not a religion of ritual; it's a religion where our truth gets into the very being of where we are and affects our life in every area.

At the end of his sermon, Schaeffer questioned the meaning of salvation itself. *One last word to think about. This is a big one. Salvation. Salvation. You know, we talk about witnessing, saving souls, and the whole bit. I have a very hard saying for you. I'll probably be wrestled to the ground as soon as I say this. I wonder how many people are really going to be in heaven that we keep chalking up on our blackboards as being saved. I wonder how many of you sitting here are going to leave this college some day and wander off, having taken more of the baggage than the substance, and you look at it and it all looks stupid and you throw the baby out with the bath water. . . .*

And when we preach a shallow, easy, quick, get saved, kneel down, ask Jesus into your heart, bam, that's it, off to the next, stamp on the back of the head, and hand him his regulation uniform, three laws here, bam, six rules, get his name on the computer list, hey. This all may build huge organizations but there's no guarantee any of these people are going to show up in heaven. 'Cause you can't cheapen God's currency. We have deflated it. . . . And I'll tell you something, you know the truth of what I'm saying is right. You read the polls. There's supposed to be all these 60, 50 million Christians. Then look around at the country. Do you think if all these people understood the gospel, the fullness of it, we'd be in the mess we're in? They've been given a cheap gospel and we have a cheap Christianity. So think about what salvation means. . . .

We come stamping in with our little evangelistic messages and we're talking to a generation that doesn't even know whether truth exists. We're speaking a foreign language. We say "believe on Jesus Christ and be saved." Many twentieth-century people don't know if there's a way to believe on anything. They don't even know if they are there, ultimately, they don't have any touch with reality. Look at our crazy culture; it's a very complicated mess out there. You can't just go out there and drop tracts over the battlements and then go home again. So salvation is something we have to say, "What do we mean by that word?"

Franky Schaeffer also attacked local pieties about the Bible, comparing them to *what the Bible really says*. By the time he was finished, he had all but cast local Bible authorities in the garb of *Catholic foppery* and was calling for another Protestant Reformation.

We have to realize that the Bible does not reflect this dividing of life into compartments. There is no such thing as full-time Christian service in the Bible. There are only Christians and non-Christians. For instance, in the New Testament we find that two tax collectors became Christians, Zacchaeus and Matthew. And we find that Christ told one to go back and continue collecting taxes for the government but to pay back what he had stolen and do so honestly in the future. And the other was called into so-called full-time Christian service and became an apostle. But then what we don't find is a verse afterwards saying well this guy surrendered to the ministry and this fellow went back into the secular world. They are both portrayed as equally doing what God asked them to do. Not one higher and the other lower. . . .

This [false teaching] is a very crazy mentality. Because we don't see it in Scripture. Read the Bible. Not as a religious book, but a book of history. And what do you find in the Bible? You find all sorts of different people in all sorts of different walks of life, the good, the bad, the ugly, very few perfect, except Christ. You do not find sort of a whitewash of spiritual jargon. You don't find everything divided into neat little categories. It's a much more real and human book. And I think if the Bible itself in its form reflected where much of our Christian thinking's gone in this area, instead of being the rich thousand-page book of diverse human experience and wealth and beauty and truth that it is, it would probably be reduced to a three-page pamphlet printed in words of one syllable presenting a simple gospel quote unquote with maybe a scratch and sniff section on the back to kind of give us a good feeling when we read it. [Laughter] But see, the real Bible is not like this. It's not a little spiritual pamphlet. It's the fundamental basis of truth. . . .

And my father, I think, has a very wise statement that he pounded into my head. . . . It's this saying, and that is there are two ways to destroy the absolutes of Scripture. One is the way the liberals do it, and one is the way we do it. The liberals destroy it by taking away pieces, higher criticism, the whole bit; it's a very obvious thing. We destroy it by adding stuff. You see, there's two ways to devalue the word of God. One is take away from it directly; the other is to bring all your own baggage and rules and regulations and everything that aren't in the Bible and say these are equal with the Ten Commandments, this is the truth here. . . .

You see we all like to give what we're saying the respectability of Scripture. That's why most sermons and most Christian teaching, or much of it, unfortunately, consists of one thing. You figure out what you want to say, then you find out which verses in the Bible taken out of context will support it. [Applause] That's how we use it. That's why I quote very little Scripture when I speak, unless it's in an actual situation like a sermon on Sunday where the job is to open the Word. For the simple reason that I think that most of the time it's window dressing, and I like to lean the other way.

Schaeffer placed the gospel, evangelism, and the Bible's words narrowly construed in the background; the foreground, he argued, God's living text, was *the whole world*. These parallel moves were most intensely rendered in two perplexing tales in which atheists, one of them a Jew, turned out to be more Christian than church-going gospel-believers:

Now, if an atheist says to you, "Rain is wet," and a Christian comes up to you and says, "No, no, rain is dry," who's made the more Christian statement? The atheist has. For the simple reason that God made the real world and at that point the atheist isn't saved and the Christian lost, but in recognizing that water is wet and not dry, he's recognizing the reality of that little part of the world God made. In other words, something is not necessarily more true just 'cause its dressed up in spiritual terms. If you've got a Christian who says "No, no, water is dry, praise the Lord, this has been laid on my heart," and whatever else [Laughter, applause], so what? You know, it's window dressing. It's like people coming up to you and saying, "You know, well, the Lord has put this on my heart for you and so forth." Usually the response to that is, "Hey, mind your own business." It doesn't matter that they dress it up in spiritual terms. [Laughter] If it's not true, it's not true. So the atheistic Jew who hides another Jew from being executed by the Nazis at that point is more Christian than the S.S. guard who goes to chapel. It doesn't matter if he's dressing up what he does in Christian terms.

Liberty Baptist College was in a turmoil for the week following Franky Schaeffer's sermon. So was Jerry Falwell's church, because the faculty and student body comprised a substantial portion of the Thomas Road Baptist Church congregation. Schaeffer's sermon seemed to be on the tip of everyone's tongue as they debated what he said, what he meant, and whether he was right.

That "Christianity is truth not religion" was a familiar thought in a fundamental Baptist community, as was a critique of excessively experiential religion. However, in finer focus, Franky Schaeffer's message was out of tune with the community in at least three important ways, only one of which could be absorbed without turmoil. His first odd, but acceptable, rhetorical move was to ground the truth of Christianity in the existence of God, not in Christ's death, burial, and resurrection. In fact, Franky Schaeffer's father had preached just that message two years earlier at Thomas Road. The elder Schaeffer began "What Really Is Christianity?" by saying that *Christianity does not begin with a statement of Christ as Savior. Christianity begins with the objective existence of the infinite personal God of the Bible.* Stated and elaborated as such, the claim could be assimilated by all but theologians as an elaboration of a taken-for-granted assumption. It did not scan as a difference that made a difference, even though, from a doctrinal point of view, it was a latter-day Calvinism, with a more Presbyterian or Reformed than fundamental Baptist accent.

Franky Schaeffer's second message, on the other hand, aggressively disoriented his fundamental Baptist audience in 1982. He told them over and over that many of their most cherished daily habits and preferences of faith were just religion, cultural baggage, window dressing, jive, blasphemy, bondage, not biblically grounded truth. And who among them would have guessed that pietism was the source of this unbiblical excess baggage? Those in the audience who knew any nineteenth-century church history must have wondered what Schaeffer was talking about. German pietism was a seventeenth-century movement that influenced the Arminian branch more than the Calvinist branch of American Protestantism. Was he talking about the Keswickian Higher Life movement, which advocated "holy living"? Or the dispensational premillennialist movement with its emphasis on separation from the world? Both were nineteenth-century movements that shaped what became Baptist fundamentalism.

By calling pietism a nineteenth-century movement, Schaeffer implied that it was an identifiable folk or theological movement. However, his examples all seemed to be drawn from contemporary cultural dialects, from layers of shared unconscious knowledge, rather than from any formal or informal theologizing. Moreover, in the local fundamental Baptist dialect, pietism meant something else—it was used to describe practices which emphasized the "experience of faith" and a "heart knowledge" of God. While such practices were not bad in themselves, they were considered to run a risk of excess emotionalism unless tempered and submitted to "head knowledge," which was a fundamental Baptist strong suit. Pietism, in short, as it was understood locally, was a problem elsewhere, in other Christian—specifically, charismatic and pentecostal—communities.[12]

Underneath all these disorienting semantic currents on the surface of his speech, it was nevertheless quite clear that Franky Schaeffer was criticizing everyday fundamentalist separatism—its code words, its gung-ho evangelism, its peculiar status anxieties, its sense of unsullied superiority vis-à-vis the world. By labeling these practices pietism, Schaeffer subverted his audience's resistance to what was in fact a very specific critique of fundamentalist separatism. Everyone in Schaeffer's audience already agreed that heart-oriented experiential Christianity was a problem. What had never occurred to them was that they, their beliefs, their separatism, was a part of *that* problem. And worse, their pietistic practices were outside biblical truth. They were not, and never had been, doing what God really wanted them to do.

Schaeffer's third line of attack amounted to his running into the temple and smashing the idols of the gospel and gospel preaching. In this Schaeffer seemed ruthless, so unlikely was it that he was saying what he was saying. Early on he queried quite reasonably, *Where do you think someone would have more influence for the cause of Christ?* But what did he mean when he added, in reference to *the cause of Christ—And I don't mean evangelism, I mean truth?* What is the difference? What could Christianity or truth or the cause of Christ possibly mean if not the message of the gospel, the saving grace of Christ's death, burial, and resurrection? It was one thing to censure emotional conversions, holy mumbo jumbo, and the local spiritual status hierarchy, but how could he even separate, let alone contrast, salvation and the truth?

And then, how could he turn the little verbal submissions to Christ that pepper their daily speech into curse words? How could he raise the editor of the *New York Times* over a television preacher with Jerry Falwell sitting on the podium behind him? And what on earth did Jerry Falwell, whose declared mission was world evangelization, think of what Franky Schaeffer said?

During the week following Schaeffer's chapel sermon, extra counseling sessions with pastors and Christian psychologists were scheduled to deal with the questions, conflicts, and anxieties it provoked. Falwell's two right-hand men, Ed Hindson and Ed Dobson, who were both college professors and church co-pastors, carefully managed a special Wednesday night church service for students. Another college professor, William Matheny, preached the sermon and, without mentioning Schaeffer's name, directly addressed the controversy roiling the student body. Many students thought Schaeffer had said, in effect, that real Christians do not witness to the world for Christ. So Matheny preached on the story of Silas and Paul, who proclaimed Christ and would not deny him even under the threat of death. Of course, Matheny said, a Christian doctor must be the best doctor he could be, but he should also witness to other doctors. The altar call after the sermon was especially moving, as dozens of students poured forth in an atmosphere charged with tearful emotion.

I met M. C. Wise, a missionary student at Liberty Baptist Seminary, for coffee at Howard Johnson's after that Wednesday night service. An older student who had worked for several years as Falwell's press secretary, Wise was comfortable with what she thought Schaeffer had said, though she was worried, along with Hindson, Dobson, Matheny, and others, that Schaeffer had been misunderstood by many students. Schaeffer, she said, did not say "don't witness." He was preaching against separatism, against separation from the world. Wise said it was a hard message for many students and church people to hear because they assumed their faith depended on worldly separation, that exposure to the world would rob them of their faith. But she thought many others were ready to hear Schaeffer's message. Quoting a local ditty, *we don't smoke, we don't chew, and we don't go with girls that do*, Wise defined separatism in terms of the personal, or parietal, rules which still in the early 1980s circumscribed Christian dress, comportment, and social life. Such taboos, like the spiritual jargon which further distinguished Christians from non-Christians, should not be abandoned completely. But otherwise, Wise agreed with Schaeffer: Christians, if they were going to *change the perception of Christianity in our culture and affect the course of our country*, had to stop using jargon and parietal rules to separate themselves publicly and to mark their spiritual superiority. For her, the heart of Schaeffer's message was in the ways he linked up professional education and Christian activism as a mission field, and in this respect she thought he was simply articulating the vision that Jerry Falwell had for LBC. The task of good Christians was not to avoid the world, but to infiltrate it. This was the part of Schaeffer's sermon that spoke most directly to Wise and students like her:

The Lord has given each one of us specific talents and ideas and callings, none are higher or lower. None are more right or less right. The point is to be in line with what God wants you personally to do. I think it's a tragedy that people are sent off to Bible school, some of whom ought to be in journalism school. We sit and we complain about the Supreme Court. Well, I'll tell you something, if thirty years ago, Christian, parents had been saying, hey, if my son has a talent for law, then for him, his Christian ministry is the law, then maybe we'd have a majority on the Supreme Court, and back in '73 when the abortion decision came out we wouldn't have to be picketing because our men would have been there. [Applause]

The point is we have to fight a kind of guerrilla warfare here. And that is we have to infiltrate, we have to infiltrate the enemy camp. And you're not going to infiltrate anything by standing up saying, "Okay, here I am, shoot at me." That's what we do. We go in and we wear our spirituality on our sleeves. But we don't get it into the areas of life we're working in. The right thing to do, I think, is for each one to find the calling God wants them to do, and for us to stop using all this lingo to try to windowdress certain professions that have been designated as higher and then lay this whole sort of guilt trip on everybody else, saying, "Well what's the matter?" You know, "I'm not going to the mission field," or this, "I just want to be a good nurse." Well, good for you. And when you're a nurse, give patients the kind of care that God would have you give them. Blow the whistle on the abortionist who does the late-term abortion. Argue with the head nurse who says we're going to starve Baby Doe to death this week. This is being the salt of

*the earth in your area. And let the person who is called to the ministry
go do that, but never be forced into something because it's called
"more spiritual."*

In the end, it seemed many students, staff, and church people were able,
like M. C. Wise, to harmonize the messages Jerry Falwell was delivering
to his people and the one Franky Schaeffer delivered to them that fall.
The differences, conflicts, and even contradictions between them could
be reconciled. The messages were not ultimately antagonistic. Indeed,
they fed off each other. In this respect, the relationship between the two
men was, or became, the typical one between a powerful evangelist and
local preachers. The evangelist quickens and reinvigorates faith, which
local preachers tame, channel, and build into churches.

As we have seen, Jerry Falwell was himself a master at rearranging in
minute, sometimes quite unsettling ways, the fundamental Baptist vernacular so that his people might attach their faith to him and stretch its
definition to include new messages and missions. But he had his limits.
He could urge his students to go out into the world and fight for all kinds
of causes, but he always reined that message in by saying that the purpose
of those fights was to advance the ultimate cause of world evangelization.
Gospel preaching and witnessing would "re-separate" true Christians
even as they entered the world. The result of Falwell's double message
was that LBC was composed of two overlapping subcultures in 1982, a
still dominant subculture that privileged gospel-spreading practices, and
an emergent, barely articulate subculture that was converting worldly
professions into mission fields. What Franky Schaeffer's sermon and its
aftermath accomplished was to articulate and open up the breach between the two subcultures for all to see. It also further demoted evangelism in relation to professionalist pursuits on campus.

Franky Schaeffer made perfect sense within the context of his father's
eccentric blending of Princeton biblical inerrancy and Reconstruction
theology, but at LBC he came across like a bull in a china shop. Falwell's
colleagues and students in the aftermath had to whittle away the parts of
his message that had had a fruitful shock value initially, that had opened
up semantic gaps if not chasms, but that might do damage in the long
run. And they had to hold on to the parts of his message that jibed with
the leading edges of what was happening at the college and Falwell's

ministries in general, that is, with the ways in which they were already breaking the taboos and habits that Schaeffer deplored. As usual, Falwell himself, through his works, provided the acceptable semiotic model of excess and restraint.

Falwell had long violated the strict fundamentalist code that policed preachers' associations and specifically enjoined them from any contact with not only noninerrantists but also biblical inerrantists who had contact with noninerrantists. Falwell thus proudly claimed that many Catholics, Jews, and, those consummate apostates, Mormons, were among the members of the Moral Majority.[13] Again, Falwell had always taken the liberty of commenting on political and moral issues of the day, but the scale of his "mixing" politics and religion reached new levels in the 1980s. Most definitively, his founding and leadership of the Moral Majority was a major breach both of strict fundamentalism and of dispensational premillennialism, which denounced social action of any kind as a hopelessly lost cause and, because modern public life was Satan's den, it was spiritually dangerous as well.

In addition to the Moral Majority, Thomas Road Baptist Church and the Old-Time Gospel Hour launched in the 1980s new ministries that wobbled on the edge of both social action and secularism—a maternity home and adoption agency (Liberty Godparent Home), an agency which gave secondhand clothes to needy families (Family Center), and a psychological counseling center staffed by Christian psychologists. Granted, these services could be assimilated as extensions of TRBC's old-fashioned fundamentalist out-reach ministries such as the home for alcoholic men (Elim Home). All those who used these services were continuously urged to get saved, and they were given detailed instructions about what they had to do under their immediate circumstances to be saved. But these new venues were nonetheless a stretch for historic fundamentalism insofar as they took on some of the trappings of social reform and appropriated secular rhetorics hitherto held at a distance.

Finally, there was the college itself. It had undergone a rapid evolution since it was founded in the 1970s: from a little Bible college (Lynchburg Bible College) to a liberal arts college (Liberty Baptist College, LBC) in the early 1980s to a university (Liberty University) by 1984. In the process, the college curriculum added courses and programs never before seen at a self-declared fundamentalist institution and was willfully preparing students to enter graduate and professional programs, and ultimately professions, such as the law, communications, government, and public school teaching, once considered impious if not wicked.

There was one public demonstration by fundamental Baptist students on the college campus in 1982. Some Liberty Baptist seminary students (everybody called them "preacher boys") picketed the college movie theater after the administration decided to allow the theater to show *Star Wars*, the first non-Christian movie ever shown on campus. In effect, by showing the film, the administration broke a cultural taboo, as well as repealed an official policy against showing worldly films, that is, films not made by Christians, narrowly defined. Not that any old worldly film could be shown—all were strictly vetted—but another symbolically loaded wall had been breached. The college's relaxing, always modestly, of this and other social regulations on campus signified that, while the behaviors at stake were still matters that required personal discretion, they were no longer defining features of the community.

Presumably, the seminary students who picketed the theater had envisioned themselves becoming pastors whose identities were linked to customary fundamentalist constraints, such as the taboo on watching commercial films, and to the kind of communities such constraints defined. But the aspiring pastors no doubt also registered the deeper significance of the campus administration's relaxing of the ban on movies. It was another piece of the larger cultural reconfiguration within Baptist fundamentalism. It, and other myriad microshifts, represented and would effect a redistribution of prestige that would diminish the social value of full-time Christian service. The superior status of preachers depended in part on the corporate moral superiority of their communities which was enacted through customary speech and behavior that publicly marked, or separated, them. Downgrading the customs to matters of personal preference diminished them as pastors. Pastoring a church would become just like any other profession, the same as, no higher than, for example, the ones Franky Schaeffer dwelled on—journalism, law, medicine, and filmmaking.

Schaeffer, in his chapel sermon that fall, was gleefully explicit about this redistribution of prestige. Jerry Falwell was more ambivalent. He continued to preach inspirational messages to his young Timothys as if they were his pride and joy, but the avowed mission of the educational system he was building was the training of young men and women for Christian service in all areas. Although, for Falwell, Christian service included old-time witnessing, he and Schaeffer were allied in the same basic project: dismantling the complex of psychological, social, and intellectual constraints and taboos that discouraged fundamental Christians from entering upper-middle-class professions. Not only should fundamental Christians become doctors, nurses, lawyers, jurists, legislators, journalists, producers, directors, news anchors, public school teachers, professors, and so on, they should also excel in their professions and use them as platforms to *be the salt of the earth*, and *to take a stand in the field that you're in in the way that only you can.*

The *Star Wars* picket at LBC was a reactionary moment in the broader cultural movement that refashioned Falwell's fundamental Baptists and their allies during the 1980s. From a "religious" angle, Falwell, Schaeffer, and other conservative Christian leaders argued for a wider definition of the mission field and of witnessing for Christ. From a "political" angle, they argued for a wider definition of the arena of politics and of what counts as political action. Either way, throughout the 1980s they and their allies encouraged and enabled a kind of born-again Christian cultural diaspora, a movement out of exile and into the world, giving them access to and voice in the broad spectrum of middle-class institutions that shape and produce American culture, society, and politics.

Converting fundamentalists away from worldly separation and toward worldly engagement was one dimension of the cultural movement afoot in Falwell's community during the 1980s. Enlisting fundamentalists in an active alliance, indeed, a cultural merger, with conservative evangelicals was the other major dimension. Franky Schaeffer's sermon implicitly enacted this project, and Falwell's commitment to it was by that time already explicitly manifest in the form of the *Fundamentalist Journal*, a slick monthly magazine with a national circulation published from 1981 to 1987.[14] The same year the *Fundamentalist Journal* began publication, Falwell published a book, *The Fundamentalist Phenomenon*, in which he presented his own version of the past, present, and future of fundamentalism. Largely written by his lead co-pastors, Ed Dobson and Ed Hindson, the book's central analytic task was to redraw the boundary between evangelicals and fundamentalists. Each group, the authors argued, contained true believers, and *there were no real doctrinal distinctions between the two.*[15] And each group contained wayward elements: worldly evangelicals, on the one hand, who were drifting toward theological and social liberalism, and, on the other hand, hyperfundamentalists, who were drifting toward total isolation and cynicism. Falwell concluded his account with two lengthy appeals to the more moderate and true believers in each community.

The first appeal, to fundamentalists, asserted Jerry Falwell's commitment to biblical infallibility and separation, both personal and ecclesiastical, and then urged his brethren at large, many of whom still harbored reservations about the Moral Majority, to engage with *the political process and the social life of our country* [in order to reach] *the whole person for the cause of Christ.* He also urged them to collaborate with others, evangelicals in particular, working for the same cause. *We must extend our vision to evangelize the world in our lifetime. We must stop being so negative and critical of everyone who is trying to reach people with the Gospel but does not wear our label.*[16]

The second appeal, to evangelicals, asserted again that *there is little difference theologically between Fundamentalists and Evangelicals.* Falwell and his co-pastors noted that evangelicals were more tolerant of varying viewpoints, and that even evangelical pastors were worried that this tolerance was leading some of their brethren *dangerously close to moderate Liberalism.* To those who would resist that drift he issued his appeal: *We appeal to our evangelical brethren to stand with us for the truth of the Gospel in this hour when America needs us most. Stop looking down your theological and ecclesiastical noses at your fundamentalist brethren. Non-Evangelicals view Evangelicals and Fundamentalists as alike anyhow. We have so much in common. Only the radicals among us (to the left and to the right) divide us. I say it is time we denied the "lunatic fringe" of our movements and worked for a great conservative crusade to turn America back to God. We do not need organic unity. Such is not necessary to achieve a mutual appreciation and respect. . . .*

You talk much of love, but often you have only words of bitter contempt for those of us who call ourselves Fundamentalists. Do not be embarrassed because we believe the same things you do. Acknowledge us. Accept us as Bible-believing brethren who love the same Christ you love. Let us work to reach the world for Christ.[17]

In 1982, Carl F. H. Henry, among the most eminent evangelical spokesmen in the country, convened at his home a luncheon meeting of fundamentalist and evangelical leaders. He called the meeting, he said, *in response to the invitation given by Jerry Falwell in his volume, The Fundamentalist Phenomenon.*"[18] Jerry Falwell, Francis Schaeffer IV, and three top pastors and professors from Falwell's community—Ed Hindson, Ed Dobson, and Pierre Gillerman (president of LBC)—were among the sixteen present. In addition to Henry, founding editor of *Christianity Today*, the current editor, Kenneth Kantzer, attended, along with the heads or former heads of organizations as diverse as Dallas Theological Seminary, Wheaton College, the National Association of Evangelicals, and the Independent Fundamental Churches of America.[19]

From the unofficial notes taken by Kenneth Kantzer, it seemed Carl Henry's agenda was to ensure that any new cooperation among evangelicals and fundamentalists included a theologically broader range of evangelicals than those gathered represented. Henry also advocated their cooperation in the area of relief for the world's poor, hungry, and destitute. The discussion, however, quickly eclipsed Henry's agenda and circulated around the issues that preoccupied Jerry Falwell and Francis Schaeffer.

Jerry Falwell started the meeting off by sorting fundamentalists into two factions: those allied with Bob Jones Jr., who were opposed to cooperation; and the rest, whom Falwell claimed were 80–85 percent of fundamentalists and whose leadership at least privately favored cooperation. He declared that a truce was in place between the leaders of the two factions—specifically, he said that he did not publicly argue with Bob Jones Jr., and his allies, and that Bob Jones Jr. had agreed to stop attacking him. With respect to evangelicalism, according to Kantzer's notes, Falwell's stated goal was *to recognize evangelicals as brothers, to work together with them when he can, and to show respect for them before the world. He said that he believed, as healing occurs, the differences between them would disappear.* Francis Schaeffer, who also spoke at some length at the meeting, was more pointed in his remarks. He exhorted evangelicals to confront the *opponents of basic Biblical truth*, not fundamentalists. *We are one as brothers in Christ. If someone attacks my brother, he attacks me. We must both defend basic fundamentalist positions, including inerrancy.* By the time the meeting adjourned, *the group agreed on the necessity to cultivate personal friendship among*

*Evangelical and Fundamentalist leaders. They will promise to be respon-
sible to defend each other. Evangelicals need to present Falwell fairly and
favorably.* In short, Jerry Falwell had arrived, so to speak, within the
upper echelons of evangelicalism and had secured the terms of another
truce, the truce essential to the formation of the core constituency of the
New Christian Right, to the realignment of evangelicalism and fundamentalism, and to their ultimate overturning of the cultural verdict of
the Scopes trial.

Falwell, the Schaeffers, and their fundamentalist allies during the early
1980s pared separatism down to its ecclesiastical essence. They believed,
as Schaeffer put it in the 1982 meeting of evangelical and fundamentalist
leaders at Henry's home, in *ecclesiastical separation on the issue of inerrancy* and *the purity of the visible church,* but they repudiated or relativized other kinds of separation. Preachers who refrained from any association with noninerrantist preachers, or with inerrantist preachers who
associated with noninerrantist preachers, were hyperseparatists, the
lunatic fringe. Various forms of personal, or behavioral, separation from
the world were based on convictions, in some cases, doctrines, but they
were not doctrinal fundamentals, not scriptural. Ultimately, they were
cultural and personal preferences, not absolutes, and therefore were subject to change.

Falwell, the Schaeffers, and others, as they stripped away these inessen-
tial separations, never openly worried about the problem of assimilation.
Others did, among them critics like the conservative fundamentalist Bob
Jones Jr., and skeptics like the evangelical historian Ronald Wells, who
predicted that fundamentalism could not "sustain a significant countercultural style" as it exposed itself to "modernity's most powerful agents:
universities, professions, upper social classes, and urban lifestyles."[20] Fundamentalists deep in the cultural throes of deseparating, such as those
caught up in the aftermath of Franky Schaeffer's sermon, worried about
assimilation, too. Although the leaders like Falwell rarely addressed the
problem directly, they knew their constituencies had qualms. In the 1982
meeting, Falwell acknowledged that *everyone is held back by his constituency,* and the fears he expressed about evangelicalism's drift toward
liberalism was a fear of assimilation, a fear that Christians were being lost
to the world.

Instead of preaching directly on the problem of assimilation, Falwell and other fundamentalist leaders addressed the problem by interlacing virtually every step they made into the world with ways of staying out of the world. That was one function of Falwell's unrelenting emphasis on gospel preaching and witnessing. As long as fundamentalists kept talking about Christ's saving grace, no matter where they were or what they were doing, they would separate themselves out as true Christians. Conservative evangelical leaders like the Schaeffers also provided manifold ways in which Christians might distinguish themselves, albeit more minutely, now inside the enemy camp. For the Schaeffers, the proper Christian mission was a more general and more confrontational witnessing on behalf of God's truth, but the social and experiential effect would be the same—a doctor, a nurse, a lawyer, a filmmaker would make a distinctively Christian mark even if no Scripture were ever cited. By both means, in slightly different ways, true Christians would emerge over and over from the daily rites through which they gave witness to the inerrant truth of God and God's Word.

Even so, these little rites would have likely failed to preserve true Christians were it not for the fact that, by the time the born-again Christian cultural diaspora of the 1980s sent inerrant Bible-believers into the vast professional middle-class reaches of America, an equally vast cultural and institutional infrastructure had come into place that would reproduce them socially. An alternative educational system from kindergarten to college was already established, and graduate and professional schools had been launched. Numerous conservative Christian organizations provided an alternative subculture for Bible-believing students in major secular colleges and universities around the country. There were conservative Christian bookstores, novels, comics, concerts, movies, singers (rock 'n' roll, heavy metal, and rap, as well as gospel), actors, sport stars, coaches, psychologists, and public intellectuals. Many towns had a *Christian Yellow Pages* so that Bible-believers could find like-minded plumbers, car salesmen, veterinarians, and dentists. And sorting out the good from the bad and the ugly in the secular world had itself become a major born-again Christian industry. Bookshelves, audiotape and video selections, sermons, and workshops overflowed with critiques—of secular television, movies, public schools, day care, popular music, the news and the news media, contemporary lifestyles, government—of any and everything a

Bible-believer might encounter and find perplexing in the modern world. In the case of movies and television, there were even manuals on how to watch secular programs and films from a Christian point of view. In other words, an explicit born-again Christian "cultural criticism" was emerging.

Whether explicitly or implicitly, born-again Christians were being aggressively trained in techniques of interpreting and remaking the modern religious and secular worlds from a Christian point of view. The cultural walls of separation were torn down but not destroyed in the 1980s. They were miniaturized, multiplied, and internalized.

CHAPTER SIX

The Moral Majority Jeremiad

For much of American history, delivering sermons, listening to
them, and discussing them were the principal intellectual activities
for most people. . . . [The sermon's] significance lay both in the
inexpressible collective religious experience it provided and also in its
capacity to affect the stance people took on public issues, even on
issues not specifically mentioned in it.
—EDMUND S. MORGAN, 1999

ONE EVENING in June 1986, several thousand people from the Detroit area came to hear Jerry Falwell preach at Temple Baptist Church in the white working-class suburb of Redford. Falwell's topic was "The Spiritual Renaissance in America." His sermon was one of a series delivered by guest preachers as part of Temple's Summer Bible Conference. The church auditorium, built in the early 1960s when fundamental Baptists were just beginning to feel more at ease in America, was comfortable and colorful. Our pews were sky-blue movie theater seats. The choir robes matched the bright yellow carpets. A red, white, and blue banner hung above the pulpit proclaiming "LIBERTY." As the organ belted out "Stand Up for Jesus," we stood up and sang along. A procession of fundamental Baptist preachers entered from stage right, joining their voices to ours. Three big, bulbous, blue-suited men led the procession—Temple Baptist Church's pastor, Truman Dollar; the assistant pastor, Joe Wade; and the evening's guest preacher, Jerry Falwell.

The audience on the night Falwell spoke was, as far as I could see, all white, predominantly middle-aged or older, a mix of blue- and white-collar men and women, mostly couples.[1] About half were church members and the rest of us were visitors—Joe Wade asked visitors to raise their hands—most probably from other fundamental Baptist churches in the area. Everyone seemed comfortable with the milieu. Even I, tucked away in the middle of the church with my notebook and tape recorder, and the ABC Nightline crew up front, filming the occasion, seemed to fit right into the swing of things.

Many of us had heard a version of the sermon Falwell was about to deliver. Not only was he a frequent guest preacher at Temple Baptist Church, but this was his stump sermon. By then he had preached it in some form or another hundreds, perhaps thousands, of times all over the country for over a decade. In one version or another, he preached the sermon on his "America Back to God," "I Love America," "Clean Up America," and "Moral Majority" crusades, and he delivered it many more times each year when he visited churches as their guest preacher. Essentially the same message had been otherwise published many more times in myriad ways—in *America Can Be Saved, How to Clean Up America, Listen America!*, and several dozen Old-Time Gospel Hour publications. Nevertheless, there was a festive air of expectancy and excitement in the church, a sense that we were present for an event that was still making history.

Temple Baptist Church had its own considerable historical legacy which informed the occasion. Pastor Truman Dollar was among the leaders of the Baptist Bible Fellowship (BBF), the fundamentalist pastoral network that provided much of the national leadership infrastructure for the Moral Majority. Dollar, who had been a classmate of Falwell's at Baptist Bible College in the early 1950s, was also one of the founders of the Moral Majority in 1979, and he was still one of its leading spokesmen in 1986. (He fell from grace two years later after confessing that he had made lewd phone calls to a former churchwoman in Kansas City.)[2] Earlier in the century, from 1934 to 1952, Temple was pastored by J. Frank Norris, a Texan who virtually made the mold of a fiery fundamentalist preacher and in many ways prefigured Jerry Falwell. (Norris never fell from grace but came close, after he shot and killed a man in his church study.)[3] Norris fashioned the national network of fundamental Baptist preachers which, through a hostile breakaway, gave rise to the BBF, which in turn gave shape to the Moral Majority.

Jerry Falwell's Moral Majority stump sermon did in fact make history every time he delivered it. It was, for one thing, a rite of political passage—it publicly enacted the end of the militant separation and the reenfranchisement of fundamentalists in America. It also was a piece of the formation of 1980s born-again Christianity insofar as it fused certain fundamentalist and evangelical public rhetorics. The rhetorics reflected varied theological strains that both united and divided the two traditions, but one thing they all had in common was that they were spoken from a specifically male point of view. Both fundamentalism and the modern evangelical movement had been Christian men's movements from their beginnings, that is, movements led by conservative Protestant male leaders who self-consciously articulated a male point of view intent on protecting and cultivating male headship at home and in the church. Some evangelicals reconsidered these positions during the 1970s in light of feminist critiques and social changes that seemed to relativize male headship. However, many, perhaps most, evangelicals became caught up, along with many fundamentalists, by the wave of male-centered indignation generated by the Moral Majority and related rhetorics. The resulting movement was reactionary in several senses, but it did not simply entrench the status quo. In the name of preserving traditional Christian family values, Falwell's Moral Majority sermons renegotiated the meaning and implications of gender in both home and church. In all, the Moral Majority corpus was a virtuoso performance of the flexible absolutism that made fundamentalism such a formidable rhetorical force under both modern and late modern social conditions.

As Falwell approached the Temple Baptist Church pulpit on that warm summer evening, the men and women seated around me seemed to settle in for a delightful and edifying evening. Sometimes they amened and chuckled as if they were listening to an old friend recount a favorite tale. Other times, they seemed to hold their breath as if watching a dramatic uplifting epic unfold. I, on the other hand, felt increasingly disappointed, headachy, irritated, lost, and dismayed. I had hoped that by listening to Falwell deliver this sermon live, I would come to a better understanding of how his oratory produced his national moral authority and leadership in the 1980s. Falwell's sermon that night, instead of giving me fresh insights, stopped my thoughts. My mind went blank. Within

minutes and for the duration of his sermon, I felt as outside the community of fundamental Baptist belief as I ever had.

Eventually, I came to understand that the capacity of Falwell's rhetoric
to expel outsiders such as me, to viscerally define and exclude us, was
one aspect of its power. Unlike witnessing rhetoric, which both constitutes "lost" outsiders and invites them in—indeed, steadily paves the way
and prepares a house for them—Falwell's Moral Majority rhetoric
brooked no liminal listeners. It was advanced, industrial strength, conservative born-again Christianity. No lost souls, only the saved and surrendered, need apply. This essay examines both sides of this coin—how
Falwell's stump rhetoric included and transformed insiders, and how it
excluded and agitated outsiders. But first, let us recall some of Falwell's
1986 Temple Baptist Church sermon, "The Spiritual Renaissance in
America."

By the time Pastor Wade introduced Falwell, we had undergone a half-
hour of hymns, gospel solos, announcements, and the offering. Falwell
joked around, named local names, and boasted about his ministry and
his family for a while. He paused, cited a Bible chapter and verse (Mark
10:14), and gave us a glimpse of his sermon topic. *You and I happen to
be living in historic times. There has never been in our history, in modern history, a time when a nation, the great nation of America, that God
could make a spiritual turn-around such as is occurring in this country.
America is in the midst of spiritual renaissance.*

Then, without a pause, Falwell veered off into a lengthy, at times quite
scrambled, recitation of his latest forays into worldly politics. *Last night
in the United States Congress—I was in Lynchburg preaching to our
congregation. . . . We had just had prayer for a vote that was going down
to Congress on aid the president requested to somehow prevent the So-
viet-Cuban takeover of Central America, which should've been a 435
to nothing vote, but at least at 8:30, just as I was concluding the message
and we'd just prayed about it, a note was passed in that by 221 to 209
the House of Representative had passed the Edwards Amendment in
support of the president's efforts to put an end to Communist aggression
and occupation south of our borders. That's not the end. But it's an
indication of what is happening in our country.*

Falwell next described his difficulty in making a call to the Department of Education the day before because the phone lines were tied up *by Bible-believing Christians across the country lobbying their particular congressman to vote for freedom.* He talked about the new appointments to the Supreme Court that might make *the unborn in this country safe into the twenty-first century.* He noted that he had debated *Penthouse* publisher Bob Guccioni on TV talk shows four times in the last two months. He told us about the drugstore chains that had decided *to remove the garbage* [pornography] *from their shelves.* And he cited his recent comment to the press commending the Meese Commission for its *courageous and correct study of the awful blight of pornography. And I would say congratulations for courageous action that has been a part of correcting this issue in the country.*

These "exciting things" convinced Falwell—and evidently those seated around me that night—that the country was *in the throes of spiritual rebirth. We've got a long way to go, there is much to be done, but we have bottomed out of those dark ages, the two decades of the sixties and the seventies, the dark ages of the, the dark ages of the twentieth century, are past now. The country is making a rebound. There's a wave of religious and political and social conservatism that no one can deny and that portends very good things for the future of the United States of America. God bless you and all you are doing, keep on doing it.*

After a short quip about the governor of Michigan, Falwell turned to the Old Testament. *Nehemiah, chapter 2. The man of God, Nehemiah, who had been in exile as were all the Jews, and then miraculously liberated and dispatched to Jerusalem to rebuild the wall. The wall that was burned with fire, the gates that were down. To restore the spirit of the people who were in affliction and humiliation. And as he went around, to the Holy City, to restore that city, Nehemiah, chapter 2, verse 10, says he encountered serious opposition.*

That opposition, Nehemiah 2, verse 10, "When Sanballat, the Horonite, and Tobiah the servant, the Ammonite," if you read the rest of it you'd find Gesham, the Arabian, there, when "they heard of it," that is, of Nehemiah and a few good men and their effort to go rebuild the gates of the walls of Jerusalem and restore the people to dignity, when they heard of, "it grieved them exceedingly." Why? "That there was

come a man to seek the welfare of the children of Israel." "There was
come a man to seek the welfare of the children." It displeased these
enemies of God, because a man, Nehemiah, had determined that the
children need help and I shall be God's instrument to deliver that help.

And I return to Mark 10:14, Jesus says "Suffer," allow, "the little chil-
dren to come unto me." Why? Because "for such is the kingdom of
God." There is a global war in progress tonight against the little children.
A global war against the little children.

Falwell thus opened the body of his sermon. He set aside the hopeful
signs of spiritual renaissance, of revival and victory, and launched into
his catalog of contemporary worldly sins and Satanic designs. Though
Falwell presented each woe as an instance of a global war against the
children, his focus in all but one instance was on America. And, except
for divorce, all the sins Falwell discussed were properties of secular
America, of the lives of men and women who were the explicit outsiders
to his oratory.

Falwell told us that his commitment to bring an end to the violence,
to the biological holocaust, the abortion of the unborn, was second only
to his commitment to preach the gospel. Planned Parenthood, having
used our tax dollars to . . . perform more abortions each year than any
other one organization, was mainly responsible. Better named, I think,
Planned Unparenthood. If you listen to them, you'll never be a parent.
You'll kill all the babies. It'll take tax dollars to do it, they call it
family planning. [Laughter] It's the same kind of family planning Adolph
Hitler did five decades ago, and unfortunately they're held in high es-
teem. The most abominable organization in America today, I believe
sincerely, in the eyes of God, is Planned Parenthood. . . . I would liken
this biological holocaust to the Hitler era, something that speaks harsh
language. It is time to speak harsh language when you're dealing with a
bloody generation that has no respect for human life. And you should
not be afraid to make people mad. You don't change things if you don't
make people mad.

Falwell next evoked images of another battle in Satan's war against the
children, the drug industry, which he said was not only a major problem
in Detroit but also in Lynchburg. It was hooking kids in college, high
school, and even elementary school. Little children are being given drugs.
He recommended that any time anyone was convicted of any sort of

drug-related crime, *that we immediately confiscate all their earthly hold-ings, take everything away from them personally, so that no matter how much money they are making, they lose it all with every infraction and have to start all over again.*

Then he rather abruptly turned to *the sex maniacs in our society. Kidnapping. One of our pastors, a graduate from Liberty Seminary, just went to Long Island to start a church. Doing a great job. His beautiful family. One of his children a little four-year-old, blond, big blue eyes, just a doll. He arrived there and said they went down to stock up on groceries, went into one of the grocery stores, that one of the gentlemen very graciously came over, one of the gentlemen working there, came over to them and said, "Listen, don't let this little girl walk around this store. Blond, blue-eyed, four year, three year, four-year-old girls are going at a very high price at the kiddy porn and the prostitution market. And your child will disappear instantly. You hold that child. Don't walk through here with that child in one aisle and you in another at the gro-cery store." Isn't that a tragic thing, terrible thing? . . .*

Then we look at teenage suicide, teenage suicide in this country. And suicide even below teens today. The sadistic music, the heavy metal . . . you know, parents would be shocked if they knew the words, the lyrics, of the songs their children listen to. And, and I, as a pastor of 22,000 people, have preached many a funeral of a young person who committed suicide and almost always while listening over and over again to a re-cording. And these music merchants who have gotten into the basest of situations. And thank God for those congressional wives in Washington who started a campaign against it. The minds of little children are cap-tured, usually the drug and the music world all are merged, and that little life, a part of the satanic design to destroy our little children.

And then starvation. All over this world, not just in the inner-cities of this country. You say, "Well there's just not enough food." Well, that's a lot of baloney, there's plenty of food. God's always provided enough for his people. It is there, the problem is people. Sinful human beings. Whether it be in Ethiopia, where a Marxist government blows up trucks like organizations like ours have, or in Mozambique, or in Zimbabwe, or Angola, or Chad, or Latin America. Sinful human beings who enrich themselves at the expense of little children, satanic emissaries in the global war against the little children.

And the list went on. Falwell denounced child abuse. He decried at length the tragedy of single-parent homes, citing the scourge of divorce as its main cause. He attacked the sin of homosexuality and its acceptance by our society, mocking the notion that homosexuals are *a bona fide, God-created, God-ordained, minority . . . like blacks, like Hispanics, like women.*

Then there is parental neglect. And then the secularistic and amoral instruction. . . . There's been a total secularizing of our society and the impression being left with our boys and girls, that this is not a nation under God, and in fact this is a secular nation like the Soviet Union, like Red China, like Cuba, like Nicaragua, and so on. Not true. And this is a nation under God built on the Judeo-Christian ethic, the principles of the Old and the New Testament.

Why is this secularizing taking place? It is a part of the global conquest against our little children, to teach them there's nothing absolutely right or absolutely wrong, there are no absolutes in society, that there is no infallible Bible, there's no biblical standard of righteousness, that situational ethics is the better code for successful living. If it feels good, do it. And you know, and I know, that once you adopt that philosophy and join that secular society, you also become victimized by every other problem today that is destroying our young people.

And finally, *There is hardly a press conference in which someone doesn't ask me, "Do you believe AIDS is God's judgment against homosexuals?" I always say, "No, I don't believe that. I believe it is God's judgment against America, for endorsing immorality, even embracing it." I believe it is God's judgment against the whole society. AIDS is out of control, as is herpes, as are many of the social diseases and all of it is the judgment of God upon the society that has forgotten Him. It is all the negative side, part of this global war against the little children.*

His account of America's sins completed, Falwell talked for another twenty minutes, reiterating his hope that *this country is on the upswing,* cautioning that *we have a monumental task ahead of us,* and adding two more dimensions to his vision of current history. He told us the nation's moral crisis was a piece of divine history. *We could have the greatest harvest of souls in the history of the church. . . . These are the most glorious days of opportunity for Christian witness the world has ever known.* For, Falwell said, he was *convinced that we are in the last days,* that *this may be the last generation* before Christ comes to *rapture* his church, the body of true believers.

Falwell, finally, told us that what happened in America would change the world. *You know whatever happens in the U.S., pretty soon it jumps the Atlantic, the Pacific. . . . If we could have a spiritual awakening in America, that begins with a deep national conviction because of our sins, 2 Chronicles 7:14, we could have a divine healing in America and a spiritual awakening that would glorify Christ and promote holiness and change the national lifestyle. And it isn't revival if it doesn't change the national lifestyle. That is why I say you cannot separate the sacred from the secular. Everything is sacred to God, you and your work, that is sacred to God, your family is sacred to God, your work is sacred to God, your health is sacred to God. You can't separate the two. And I'm convinced that what is happening in America today is a part of a spiritual awakening. . . . That's going to impact the world. And no bamboo or iron curtain will keep God out.*

. . . We can see it. This global war against the little children brought to an end. And before the trumpet sounds and the church is called away before great tribulation, I would have lived to see hundreds of millions swept into the kingdom of God. And that is why we ought to be, that is our reason for existence. None other.

Jerry Falwell's Moral Majority sermons were jeremiads, or Protestant political sermons. Named for the Old Testament prophet Jeremiah, a jeremiad laments the moral condition of a people, foresees cataclysmic consequences, and calls for dramatic moral reform and revival. The Puritans brought the jeremiad tradition to America, and it became a staple of colonial and early American preaching. It waxed and waned during the course of subsequent American history, undergoing various adaptations as it gave shape and substance not only to political oratory, both religious and secular, but also to American literature, especially in the nineteenth century.[4] Falwell's Moral Majority stump sermon generally and his oration at Temple Baptist Church in 1986 in particular evince several of the basic features of the classic Puritan jeremiad.

At Temple Baptist Church, Falwell fashioned himself in the image of an Old Testament prophet, amplified it with a New Testament moral voice, and embodied it in a half dozen sketches of his political promi-

nence and activism. As he read chapter and verse from the Books of
Nehemiah and Mark, he mingled his voice with the prophetic voices
of Nehemiah and Jesus and figured himself as their heir, their current
fulfillment. Like Nehemiah, Falwell will *rebuild the wall . . . the little
children need help and I shall be God's instrument to deliver that help.*
Along with Jesus, he will *suffer, allow the little children to come unto
him.* Falwell's opening medley of forays into the public arena demonstrated his efficacy as a national moral leader who was standing up, speaking out, and being counted. Falwell was closing up the *breach in the
wall,* he was *standing in the gap,* for God.

Falwell likewise followed the jeremiad form in his listing of the nation's woes. Such a tally of moral complaints, or laments, was the core
of the Puritan jeremiad. National sins jeopardize a people's covenant
with God, so Falwell's casting of AIDS as *a judgment of God against
America for endorsing immorality* and for having *forgotten him* was a
crucial term in the jeremiad equation. When God's people—as he had
just fashioned America in talking about the destructive effects of *secularistic and amoral instruction*—fall away from him, he delivers his wrath
upon them. According to the jeremiad formula, there is hope, God's
judgment may be stayed, if God's people return to him. The returning,
or as Falwell put it, the *revival* or *spiritual renaissance,* included not only
soul winning and church building but also taking *a stand in this society
for the traditional family, for family values. . . . Somehow, some way,
we've got to recapture the visions, the dreams, of making family once
again the cornerstone of our society.*

The prophet's point of view, the sins of a people, the impending wrath
of God, the call to repentance and reform—these features distinguish the
jeremiad but do not describe its force. Jerry Falwell's jeremiad was history
making because it performed the political activism it advocated. And
both its speaker and listeners were engaged in the performance because a
preacher and his people are bound by the conventions of speech mimesis.
Christians who sat under Falwell's Moral Majority preaching underwent
the transformation he represented. His jeremiad, spoken and heard, was
a rite of passage. It returned fundamentalism from public exile. It recom-
mitted evangelicalism to certain fundamentals. It erased boundaries between moderate fundamentalism and conservative evangelicalism; it unified conservative Christians.

Overall, in his corpus of jeremiad sermons, Falwell stressed, and enacted, the end of three kinds of fundamentalist separation. Early on, in the middle and late 1970s, he argued against and helped dismantle hyperseparatist codes that prevented fundamentalist preachers from fellowshipping. He then launched a critique of fundamentalist codes of personal separation insofar as they discouraged church people from pursuing careers in public education, higher education, entertainment, journalism, law, and other venues of popular and public culture making. Around 1980, he took on the taboos that maintained their political exile and converted his jeremiad into a platform, a vehicle, for their reentry into politics. In 1986, Falwell opened his Temple Baptist Church jeremiad with a string of political vignettes—about the Edwards Amendment, about Christians tying up phone lines to the Department of Education, about debating Bob Guccioni on national television. Each one was for his fundamentalist listeners a flip of the switch, from "off" to "on," with respect to their preacher's political engagement. And, because he was their surrogate, each time their preacher voiced his political activism, his faithful listeners also partook of it. They too were transformed, moved, from outside to inside the public arena.

During the 1940s and 1950s, fundamentalists and conservative Protestants under the leadership of Billy Graham, Carl Henry, Harold Okenga, and others, fashioning themselves as evangelicals, performed a similar transformation. They too returned to public life, but with a significant difference. They disavowed their militancy as well as various forms of separation. Falwell and his co-belligerents, on the other hand, took their militancy with them. *It is time to speak harsh language. . . . And you should not be afraid to make people mad. You don't change things if you don't make people mad.* Falwell pushed—and fashioned new— rhetorical buttons marked militant, angry, harsh, uncompromising, admonishing. These were sufficient gestures to convince many if not most fundamentalists that Falwell was still a full-fledged fundamentalist, which enabled him to reenfranchise fundamentalism and fundamentalists, at the same time as he reached out to evangelicals disgruntled with their more moderate leaders.

Falwell also spoke specifically fundamentalist rhetorics—regarding the inerrant Bible, the last days, and Communist aggression—sufficiently to assure both outsiders as well as insiders that he was an undiluted fundamentalist. But he did not speak them at length, nor in their hard-core, most militant versions, which, had he done so, might have alienated fellow travelers who considered themselves conservative evangelicals rather than fundamentalists. That is, Falwell moderated his language doctrinally and, in some ways, politically, so as not to exclude evangelicals. At the same time, Falwell's jeremiad in other ways positively included conservative evangelicals who wanted less cultural and political accommodation and more militancy, just not too much, from their leaders. Both fundamentalists and evangelicals, Falwell argued, each in different ways were silent about, and therefore culpable for, the escalating moral confusion and decay all around them in America. Together they formed the "sleeping church" that Falwell and others were awakening.

Falwell's jeremiad rhetorics enlisted both fundamentalists and evangelicals and united them in an alliance on behalf of moral reform. In addition, there was one more rhetoric audible in Falwell's Temple Baptist sermon that actually erased the boundary between fundamentalist and evangelical Christians—and, for that matter, between them and pentecostal and charismatic Christians, namely, the rhetoric, the narrative, of secular humanism. Cobbled together by various preachers and writers during the 1970s and early 1980s, the critique of secular humanism created a transcendent conservative Christian point of view that was by definition morally engaged in the world. The transition from the earlier critique of modernism fashioned by fundamentalists in the 1910s and 1920s to the critique of secular humanism not only united diverse kinds of conservative Protestants, it helped insure that their return from exile would be an enduring one.[5]

Secular humanism was the new Christian folk history of twentieth-century America. It was most powerfully articulated by Francis Schaeffer IV in his 1979 book and videotape series, *How Should We Then Live?* According to Schaeffer, America was founded on Judeo-Christian principles which guided the nation for much of its first two hundred years. Secular humanism, according to Schaeffer, a godless philosophy with long historical roots and many manifestations, including Communism, took root in America during the nineteenth century. It grew stronger, especially after World War II, when it became the prevailing influence in many American cultural, social, and political institutions, most notably in American public education and the media.

That America was occupied, in Falwell's terms, by "satanic emissaries" was nothing new, but the critique of secular humanism changed a fundamental assumption of the separatist fundamentalist critique of modernism. The earlier critique abandoned the world to Satan; the later critique argued forcefully, as Franky Schaeffer put it, that the whole world belongs to God. In Falwell's words, *You cannot separate the sacred from the secular. Everything is sacred to God. You and your work, that is sacred to God. Your family is sacred to God, your work is sacred to God, your health is sacred to God. You can't separate the two.* With the echoes of earlier charges of Communist conspiracy and takeover at full volume, Falwell argued that Satan has temporarily occupied America, creating the illusion that it is a secular nation, through his global war against the little children and secularistic and amoral instruction that teaches them *there's nothing absolutely right or absolutely wrong, there are no absolutes in society, that there is no infallible Bible, there's no biblical standard of righteousness.* According to the secular humanist critique, it is the duty of all true Christians to take back America, the world, for God. The point is not to reform the world—history is still, after all, regressive—but to return it to its owner, and thus stay God's wrath for "a little season."

These were some of the ways Falwell's jeremiad worked as a rite of passage for its insiders, not only assuring and fortifying true Bible-believing Christians, but also refashioning them. His sermon also worked effectively as a rite of impasse for its outsiders, alerting, alarming, and agitating them in a variety of ways. My professional anthropological training and four years of listening to fundamental Baptist language enabled me to bracket the ways in which I disagreed with Falwell on political and moral issues. But they did not protect me from the exclusionary forces at work in his rhetoric. I was irritated by his full-volume, double-barreled baritone voice. I found his wording often awkward and inelegant. His list of woes seemed to me arbitrary, clichéd, and at moments quite loopy. His reasoning struck me as, well, unreasonable, irrational. I could not avoid thinking that he sounded self-righteous, intolerant, and judgmental. In short, I was undergoing a modern, or liberal, reaction to fundamentalism. I was reacting to the militancy of Falwell's language, to the very quality that distinguishes more moderate Christians and non-Christians from fundamentalists. Their militancy rendered fundamentalists unfit for modern public life from a moderate point of view, at the same time as it drew a line in the sand for fundamentalists. Falwell's implicit as well as explicit message to me that night was that I was on the wrong side of the line; I was beyond the pale. No matter how much I consciously resisted his explicit message, I could not resist the implicit ways the forms of his speech excluded me.

Preachers carve out their audiences, in part, by the voices—the preaching traditions—they ply and merge. They speak in little dialects and codes that bob and weave, unite and divide, contest and harmonize. At a time of political mobilization, preachers fashion new constituencies by merging previously disparate voices, dialects, and codes. Martin Luther King, Jr., joined blacks and liberal whites in a coalition during the late 1950s and 1960s by "merging voices" from black folk and white liberal Protestant preaching traditions.[6] As effectively as King's rhetoric created insiders, it created outsiders—not only those antipathetic to the cause of racial equality, but also those left out or excluded by his forms of speech.

Likewise, Falwell's speech forms defined and excluded its cultural others. Most willfully and fully in sync with the content of his speech, they excluded all kinds of "liberals"—Protestant, Catholic, Jewish, and agnostic. But they also, unwillfully, excluded many others—conservative Protestants, Catholics, Jews, white, black, and Hispanic—who may have agreed with some of his political and moral positions, but who were unaffected or positively put off by Falwell's fundamentalist and evangelical rhetorical forms. His forms of speech simultaneously hailed and repelled listeners according to their religious, intellectual, moral, and political affiliations.[7] They also marked the movement, in spite of its leaders' protestations, as a white—not a racially integrated—movement. Finally—and here Falwell's content and his rhetorical forms agreed again—they marked the movement as male centered.

Although the Moral Majority in all its manifestations—as a movement organization, public lobby, media link, and public rhetoric—was most renowned for its pro-family agenda, the family was for the most part addressed only obliquely in Falwell's jeremiad. Indeed, even when the family was his topic in his Sunday and weekday church sermons back home at Thomas Road Baptist Church, after uttering a few well-worn words about wifely submission, God's chain of command, one-man-for-one-woman-for-one-lifetime, and the sanctity of marriage, Falwell invariably veered off in other directions. His forte was discussing the enemies of the traditional Christian family—not the family as such—Satan's global war against the children: pornography, drugs, teen suicide, sex maniacs, single parenthood, divorce, homosexuality. In Falwell's speech, that which was sacred, whole, and moral emerged out of—or rather, was left implicit in—that which was not.

How are we to understand this obliqueness, this indirectness, on Falwell's part in addressing the ostensible focal point of his movement, the family? Perhaps he gave us a clue that night in Detroit when he spoke of the one woe, the one sin, namely, divorce, in which he directly implicated Christians. This clue also opens up a surprising complexity in Falwell's polemical speech. Though his language seems simply harsh, fixed, and hard, it is at the same time streaked with signs of fluidity, pliancy, and give. Even in the midst of a full-bore jeremiad, we find an extraordinary instance of fundamentalism's flexible absolutism.

Falwell's lament regarding single-parent families in America quickly turned into a plaint about divorce that was aimed at those present: *You know it's such a tragedy, that a man and a woman, for selfish reasons, for self-satisfaction, for causes of hedonism, or immorality—you name the reason—forget what they said in the marriage altar, that when they said to one another "till death do us part." And ignore the fallout and the impact and the repercussions on the little children. They are tossed back and forth like footballs. So go ahead and leave one another and head off and start new homes and new families.* Without pause, he then offered a remarkable personal affirmation of marriage that was nevertheless full of ribald cross-currents of meaning, hierarchy, humor, and (feigned?) hostility:

My wife and I have been married twenty-eight years. The night we were married we made a deal: divorce is no option. We may have our problems, we may have our difficulties, and down the road of life there may be lots of differences of opinion between us, but divorce will never be an option. And in twenty-eight years, we have never one time talked, even mentioned, even discussed, the option of divorce. And I want to

tell you in twenty-eight years we've had some knock-downs and drag-
outs. [Laughter] I've lost every one of them. [Laughter] I tell you, men,
the best thing you can do is quickly raise your hands and unconditionally
surrender because you're gonna lose. [Laughter] Amen? [Amens] And,
in all these twenty-eight years, though, not one time have we, have
I ever thought of divorce. Murder a few times [Laughter], but never
divorce.

Heard literally, that is, for its plain meaning, Falwell, in this passage of
his sermon, seemed to tell us that his marriage survived its conflicts because he ignored God's chain of command in marriage, which requires
male headship and wifely submission. More generally, he seemed to tell
us that it was better to ignore male headship and wifely submission—it
was better for husbands to raise their hands and *unconditionally surrender*
to their wives—than to divorce. Of course, these are not plausible interpretations, as those who heard him that night in Detroit knew, otherwise
they would not have laughed. There was a touch of nervous tension in
the air as Falwell played topsy-turvy with his marriage, but his audience
accepted his joking, his slippage into ironic humor. Still, his marriage,
marriage in general, God's chain of command in marriage—these were
very odd things to joke about in the middle of a Moral Majority jeremiad.
Once again, Falwell's speech had produced a gap, an excess, an instability
that required interpretive work. If he did not mean what he plainly said,
what did he mean?

Upon closer inspection, Falwell's joke was a glimpse, an intimation,
of kaleidoscopic changes in the realm of contemporary fundamentalist
family and gender relations. The joke had some of the qualities of an
open secret, of speaking in code, at once displaying and concealing things
everyone was dimly aware of but never discussed or barely acknowledged. That Christians lived in, or ought to live in, Christian families
was an idea with roots centuries long, but what that had come to mean
during the 1970s and 1980s bore little resemblance to what it meant
among, say, fundamentalists earlier in the twentieth century, or even in
the 1950s and 1960s. Always in the name of staying the same, both family
practices and rhetorics had changed a great deal, so much so that what
they called "the traditional Christian family" was a relatively recent invention. Still, more indirectly, Falwell's joke signaled tension and flux in
the realm of public male authority. The conditions of masculine privilege

and its production outside the family, in the Christian public arena, had also changed a good deal.[8]

Paul admonished the early Christians in Ephesus: "Wives, submit yourselves unto your own husbands, as unto the Lord. For the husband is the head of the wife, even as Christ is the head of the church: and he is the savior of the body. Therefore as the church is subject unto Christ, so let the wives be to their own husbands in every thing" (Ephesians 5:22–24). Protestant preachers in America have cited these verses in defense of the Christian family and Bible-based marriages in the face of feminist reforms for over a century.[9] By the 1920s wifely submission had come to summarize the growing theological bias against women among conservative Protestants—against women in leadership in the home and the church and against femininity in general.[10] During the 1940s and 1950s, John R. Rice proof-texted much of his advice to wives and husbands on Ephesians 5:22–24 in his widely read and highly influential writing and preaching on home, marriage, and the family. During the 1960s and 1970s, Bill Gothard's family seminars popularized the verses as the basis of God's chain of command (the husband is head of the wife as Jesus is head of the husband and the church), which achieved the status of unquestioned folk doctrine across a wide spectrum of conservative Protestant communities.[11] On into the 1980s and 1990s, proliferating born-again Christian family advice rhetoric cited Ephesians 5:22–24.

But over the years, the nature of the marriage authorized by the verses metamorphosed. Early on, preachers, especially self-described fundamentalists, talked about wives as "helpmeets," "the weaker vessel," and they equated submission with silence and railed against newfangled, devil-wrought notions of companionate marriage. Writing in 1945, John R. Rice argued that *God expects women to feel their duty to obey their husbands, good or bad, saved or unsaved.*[12] If anything, the folk doctrine of wifely submission as an overall description of woman's domestic role intensified in the late 1940s and 1950s.[13] At the same time, though, other, more moderate gender rhetorics began to emerge and gathered a hearing in the 1960s and 1970s.[14]

Although an explicit critique of wifely submission and male headship never surfaced among fundamentalists, they moderated what they meant by the terms. By the late 1980s, most younger fundamentalists took for granted that husbands and wives were companions, friends, partners. The

marital relationship was complementary. Wives and husbands were different but equal. A man's responsibility for making final decisions
sounded more like a job than a privilege. In this context, it became something of a struggle to figure out what submission and headship meant.
The widespread finesse went something like this: Yes, the husband has
final authority in all major decisions, but he must consult with his wife
in all of them. Ideally, they will come to a mutual agreement. If not, the
final decision is in the husband's hands. He should realize, however, that
his wife often has more insight and better judgment in family-related
matters. If they disagree, he often might do well to decide to do what
she, rather than what he, thinks best.[15]

An acknowledgment of this widespread finesse of wifely submission
was the serious message to husbands embedded in Falwell's Temple Baptist rendering of Ephesians 5:22–24. His joke implied: "Don't be legalistic
about male headship. Let your wife have her way—I do. Just remember,
even when she gets what she wants, you're still making the decision." At
the same time, his jokiness, his caricature of his marital decision-making
process, acknowledged how prickly husbands might feel about the contemporary contortions required to maintain male authority in the family.
And, as he sketched the decision-making scene with his wife, he took
advantage of the moment to poke fun at the prevailing companionate
notions of marriage. His was hardly a sketch of good marital communication, which he and his ministry otherwise advocated.[16]

The aversion to companionate marriage which prevailed among fundamentalists earlier in the century was the flip side of their particular commitment to the ideology of "separate spheres." "One dimension of fundamentalist separatism was its careful monitoring of the interaction
between the sexes: the ideal was to keep their worlds as distinct and
separate as possible."[17] Fundamentalist leaders argued vigorously that
both social and family order depended on, indeed consisted of, men and
women occupying their distinct, and ranked, social and psychic realms
of work and family.[18] Over the decades of the twentieth century, fundamentalist wives and mothers probably worked outside the home at rates
and in jobs comparable to other wives and mothers, but such work was
not recognized and not valued. And, "Though often physically absent

from the home, the fundamentalist father expressed his love through discipline and sacrifice. Like God the Father, he exercised daily care for his children only indirectly, by the threat of punishment and the presence of material provision."[19]

In the 1940s and 1950s, when the family became a fast-growing topic of fundamentalist sermons and advice literature, sex-segregating rhetorics and practices actually intensified. According to evangelist Robert G. Lee in 1942, the home was a man's *fortress in the warring world where a woman buckles on his armor in the morning as he goes forth to the battles of the day and soothes his wounds when he comes home at night.*[20] "As it was formulated in the 1950s . . . the doctrine of submission, with its heavy emphasis on marriage, assumed that the proper sphere of the Christian woman was the home; outside activities were clearly secondary. Women's new career was marriage."[21]

Bill Gothard's seminars were the most popular source of family advice among fundamentalists during the 1960s and 1970s. Gothard articulated a strong version of God-ordained sex differences but modulated the hierarchical implications by arguing that men and women were equal in essence but not in function. Gothard and his successors—including, among Falwell's community, Ed Hindson, and, on a national scale in the 1980s and 1990s, James Dobson—still argued on behalf of biblically and biologically prescribed sex roles. But they, and the Christians who took their counsel, played them out very differently by the 1980s. In 1945, John R. Rice had advised a husband against making his wife work for wages so that she could devote all her time to making a good Christian home.[22] In 1982, Ed Hindson advised a husband to accept his wife's commitment to her career and to carry his weight in making theirs a Christian home and family.[23]

Evangelicals, as they separated themselves from fundamentalists and fashioned a self-conscious fellowship in the 1940s and 1950s, continued to share with fundamentalists their rhetorics and practices regarding male authority in the home and church. In fact, the strong subcultural links created and sustained between the two larger fellowships by family-focused evangelists and teachers such as John R. Rice and Bill Gothard were among the enabling conditions of the Christian Right movement of the 1980s.

The evangelical experience, however, did differ from that of the fundamentalists in one major respect. Less insulated from intellectual and political currents in the larger society, evangelicals encountered feminists
and feminism earlier and more directly than did fundamentalists. Indeed,
a strong, internal evangelical feminist critique of the traditions of masculine leadership within the church and the family emerged in the late
1960s and 1970s.[24] Paralleling the brief history of evangelical discussion
around abortion (see chapter 7), modestly liberal positions were initially
given a hearing in major national evangelical periodicals such as *Christianity Today* and *Eternity*. Debate ensued and grew acrimonious in the 1970s
as it came to include the ostensible implications for the truth and authority of the Bible. The truth of Ephesians 5:22–24 was specifically at stake.
If that text, which reads "wives submit to your husbands, as unto the
Lord" and "the husband is head of the wife," were not true then the
truth of the whole Bible was in jeopardy. Conservatives, who argued in
defense of the Bible's plain meaning with respect to wifely submission
and male headship, won the day in terms of public position, and evangelical feminists were marginalized or left their churches and teaching posts.
The experience prepared conservative evangelicals to respond sympa-
thetically when Falwell and other fundamentalist preachers pitted the
Moral Majority against feminism in the 1980s.

Fundamentalist and evangelical rhetoric in many ways continued to
highlight and privilege full-time wives and mothers, but public disdain
for women working declined markedly, and their work outside the home
won some recognition and even admiration.[25] Women in Falwell's
Lynchburg community who worked outside the home were sometimes
quite vocal on behalf of their public image. In 1982, they organized a
panel and workshop to showcase how much support there was for wives'
working if they wanted to, and to show how common it was in their
community. At the same time, men had become substantially more involved in family life, especially in terms of how they represented themselves and were represented in preacherly rhetoric. Family life no longer
threatened masculinity, it now enhanced it. For married men, being a
good Christian depended on being a good husband, and for those with
children it depended on being a good father as well.

In short, the fundamentalist regime of separate gender spheres ended
sometime around 1980. Statistically, the transformation registered as a

matter of degree—wives and mothers had always worked—but experientially it was more like a rupture. More married fundamentalist and
evangelical women probably worked outside the home, but their experience of that work changed most dramatically because it had become
more visible and valued. For married women with children, being a good
Christian depended on being a good wife and mother, but it could now
also depend on being a good doctor, or teacher, or computer program-
mer. At the same time as the work sphere became accessible to women,
the family sphere opened up to men. But unlike work outside the home
for married women, family work was not optional for married men—
they must participate actively in it. So both work and family among
fundamentalists were, in terms of gender, dramatically desegregated during the 1970s and 1980s.

Another realm of dramatic change, as we have seen in earlier chapters,
was the matter of parietal rules, the rules of personal separation. While
Falwell continued to endorse the principle of holy living, in the 1970s
he began to preach against legalism, against overly strict or restrictive
rules of personal conduct. More specifically, he preached against preachers preaching legalism. Partly, he wanted them to stop policing each
other in ways that prevented their alliance for other purposes. Though
he never said as much, he was also calling on preachers to get out of the
business of micromanaging family life, just as he was explicitly calling on
fathers and husbands to be more involved. I found in my interviews with
couples in Lynchburg that they still worried a good deal about where to
draw lines of personal separation. But what lines they worried about—
regarding movies, rock 'n' roll music, wine—and where to draw them
varied. More to the point, they felt it was up to them, not their pastor,
to decide.

So, I heard little pulpiteering about parietal rules from Falwell or his
co-pastors. Nor did I hear much from them in the way of policing
women in particular. At least in Lynchburg, the day was gone when the
most popular collection of sermons among fundamentalists—especially
women—was John R. Rice's *Bobbed Hair, Bossy Wives, and Women
Preachers*.[26] Falwell chose to preach on other topics and to leave the new
Christian family-making rhetoric to others—men and women, preachers, psychologists, and popular writers—who produced a still-growing
cascade of Christian family advice texts, audiotapes, and seminars. Even

as more and more conservative Protestants came to agree with the language of Ephesians 5:22–24, it had become less and less obvious to them what the language of submission and headship meant and how to live it in their daily lives. So the business of Christian psychology and family counseling emerged to let them know.

Although Falwell never openly described these social changes, he acknowledged them everytime he narrated his family history, which he did often. An especially well-developed family portrait which he published in 1992 in *The New American Family* etched the shifts in sharp relief.[27] Falwell's father *never went to church* and had a *blustery, ambitious, often belligerent approach to daily life*. His father, Falwell said, was a good parent but not a family man, while his mother was *a faithful churchgoer, an example of godly love, not interested in social events, happy to stay home and tend house and family*. Falwell's wife, Macel, likewise devoted herself full time to her family and home, but she was a more active member of Falwell's church, serving as its lead pianist and on the board of directors of his combined ministries, among other duties. Falwell, on the other hand, portrayed himself as a fully converted version of his father. Aside from being a godly man and a man of God, Jerry Falwell was the furthest thing from an absentee father. Indeed, Falwell sounded very much like a premature Promise Keeper, a harbinger of the men's movement that swept through evangelical communities in the mid-1990s. He described himself tucking each of his three children into bed and listening to their prayers every night when he was in town. He said that he never let his other obligations interfere with anniversaries or birthdays, and that he faithfully attended sports events, graduations, and "every one of Jennie's recitals."[28] In the late 1980s, he proudly watched his children and his wife graduate from Liberty University. His oldest son became a lawyer, his daughter a surgeon, and his youngest son worked with him on the business side of his ministry. All were married and juggling careers and children.

Falwell's portrait may be read as a narrative of upward mobility or as the blessing by God of a Christian family. But it is also a narrative of changing family and gender practices. The pivot appears to be in Jerry's own family, when male headship, defined here as a father's active role in family rites, was restored. But the pivot was also the end of separate

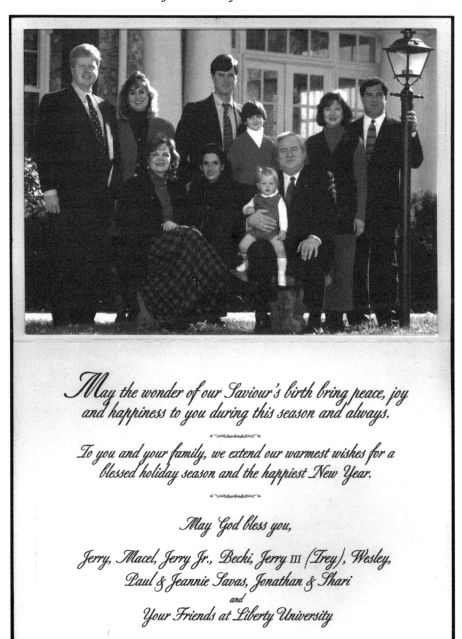

May the wonder of our Saviour's birth bring peace, joy and happiness to you during this season and always.

To you and your family, we extend our warmest wishes for a blessed holiday season and the happiest New Year.

May God bless you,

Jerry, Macel, Jerry Jr., Becki, Jerry III (Trey), Wesley, Paul & Jeannie Savas, Jonathan & Shari
and
Your Friends at Liberty University

Figure 6.1 Christmas greetings from all the Falwells in the late 1980s.

spheres—work for men, family for women. Jerry and Macel took the first steps, and their children, most powerfully represented by the daughter, Jennie—wife, mother, and practicing surgeon—completed the process.

In the context of this narrowing of the consequences of gender among fundamentalists, we may hear Falwell, as he joked in 1986 at Temple Baptist Church about surrendering unconditionally to Macel, articulating some of the mixed feelings among men about these shifts, which included increased family responsibilities at the same time as their authority was circumscribed. We heard the mixed feelings, and the circumscription, when he assured us that Macel got what she wanted because he let her have it. And again when he said that, while he had not thought of divorce, he had thought of murder a few times, yes.

The anger and the threat of force here were ironic but still served as little reminders of men's ostensible physical authority, their "power-in-reserve." More unambiguously, this flash of rhetorical violence revealed to whom the entire joke about his marriage was addressed. It was addressed to men. In this way it not only upheld public male authority, it enacted it. Indeed, the whole sermon, the entire Moral Majority jeremiad, and fundamentalism in general were addressed to men. The joke, the sermon, the jeremiad, and fundamentalism were essentially men's movements, public speech rites that enacted male authority.[29] Not that they were "for men only" but that they, their rhetorics, were addressed primarily, or rather directly, to men. Women were meant to overhear them.

Falwell's joke about his marriage thus revealed the structure of fundamentalist public address. It is an address system that implicitly privileges men through its rhetorical forms and in its content, which in many and varied minute ways create a two-tiered audience with men "up front" and women "in the back." Gender-stratified address among orthodox Protestants, like gender-stratified space in an orthodox Jewish synagogue, which physically situates men inside and women looking in, produces and instills male authority in both men and women. Even as Falwell's joke seemed to surrender men to female authority, it articulated a regime of male authority and inscribed both men and women in it. Men were central, and women were on the margins.

Listening to the rest of Falwell's Temple Baptist sermon and the corpus of his Moral Majority jeremiad in these terms further clarifies its gender dynamics. Falwell's unrelenting baritone voice, his sharp, confrontational language, his aggressive, angry tone, his military and sports metaphors all scan as masculine. His lamentations were primarily occupied by and addressed to men. His woes, the sins that are destroying America, were peopled with male figures. Even when women were full participants, they shadowed the men and became the victims of men's sins. Pornography, drugs, teen suicide, single-parent families, divorce, homosexuality, even abortion and hunger, all happen because men have lost control, most often sexual control, of themselves. Yes, women were running amok too, but moral order and discipline were the responsibility of men. Over and over again in his jeremiads, Falwell called upon Christian men to assert their leadership in the family, in the church, and in the nation. Their doing so would not stop the sinful behavior of non-Christian men and women, but it would rebuild the wall, it would stanch the moral decay and restore moral order and discipline.

A man-centered structure of public address may be as old as Christian preaching, but it was much intensified by late nineteenth and early twentieth century conservative Protestant preachers, who also relied heavily on the language of gender as they elaborated their critiques of the world, modernity, and liberal churches and theology. They associated liberal and secularizing trends with feminist reforms, with the feminization of the church, with women, and with femininity itself.[30] *Lord save us from off-handed, flabby-cheeked, brittle-boned, weak-kneed, thin-skinned, pliable, plastic, spineless, effeminate, sissified, three-carat Christianity*, Billy Sunday declared in 1916.[31] *Many of the subtle and dangerous and seductive heresies and perversions and distortions of the gospel of Jesus Christ have sprung from the brain of woman*, Clarence Macartney wrote in a 1929 polemic against the ordination of women.[32] If during the nineteenth century American women acquired the status of the morally superior sex among Protestants, conservative Protestant leaders and their fundamentalist descendants took it away from them as the century turned. "During the 1920s fundamentalist men began to take on the role as guardians of orthodoxy and women lost their standing as the morally superior sex, becoming not just morally but psychologically inferior to men."[33]

The growing bias against women and femininity among fundamentalists paralleled, or rather was thoroughly entwined with, the emergence
of the aggressive, militant, macho persona of preachers. Nineteenth-century revivalists cultivated a masculine ethos, but fundamentalist evangelists and preachers pushed that ethos into an "offensive weapon."[34] As
representatives of muscular Christianity, they were fearless, fierce, aggressive, heroic, harsh, uncompromising, manly, full-blooded, and vig-
orous. In contrast to *little infidel preachettes*, the fundamentalist preacher
packs a punch for the Lord, and *hits the devil with both fists, then jumps
on him with both feet.*[35]

"Fundamentalists always valued the spoken word," and they "reserved
their greatest rewards for eloquent men, equating masculinity and power
with a spell-binding platform presence and confrontational preaching
style."[36] Preaching was necessarily confrontational, hence masculine,
whereas women, as a "type of church," were expected to be submissive
if not entirely silent; taught, not teaching. Having thus established the
pulpit as a male preserve and men as the privileged audience of preaching,
fundamentalist leaders eventually barred or removed women from virtually all leadership positions within the church. Especially after World War
II, the two areas of church work in which women had prospered, foreign
missions and Bible teaching, were closed off to women—and wifely submission was the rationale.[37]

Most of those who attended Jerry Falwell's Moral Majority jeremiad
in Detroit in 1986 had grown up when this strong regime of public male
authority within the church was in full force. They had also seen it relax
in certain ways in the 1970s and 1980s. The hypermasculine rhetoric
gradually disappeared. As harsh as Falwell's Temple Baptist language was,
it was soft core, militant-lite compared to the rhetoric of his predecessors.
It specifically relied much less on gendered terms to value (virile) friends
and vilify (effeminate) foes. Moreover, in terms of their role within the
Christian public arena, women regained full access to some realms of
church work and activity, including foreign missions and Bible teaching.
They also created new arenas—women's organizations and literature
proliferated after 1980.

Falwell did not invent his masculine persona and preoccupations. He
inherited them. They were a part of his fundamentalist legacy. Nor did
he intensify them—if anything, he muted them, and muted them more

and more over the years. Or rather, he developed new voices that were more moderate and less gender stratified, which he spoke alongside and entwined with his somewhat muted masculinist-fundamentalist registers. His audiences, at least his fundamental Baptist audiences, were aware of this complexity, these complex twists and turns, and they went along with him. All this—the complexity and the complicity—was tucked between the lines of his joke about the knock-downs and drag-outs of his marriage.

Given their intense and rhetorically pervasive commitment to male authority at home and in the church, it is not surprising that the 1970s feminist movement came as a "deep shock" to both evangelicals and fundamentalists.[38] But it is also clear that their response to feminism was more complex and heterogeneous than their public polemics suggest, and that they were responding not just to feminism but also to an array of shifts in family and gender relations in their own communities. Theirs was not a simple crusade in defense of unchanging family values but a multifaceted, multilayered rearrangement of family and gender practices and rhetorics. The principle of male headship of home and church was upheld at the same time as the interpretive and social practices that translated that principle into two gender-segregated spheres were gradually replaced by practices that integrated in some ways both home and church in terms of gender. While the genders remained stratified in certain ways in both spheres, the hypermasculinist and the antifeminine extremes of speech and practice declined markedly.

The earlier generation of fundamentalist leaders had separated themselves from their less biblically correct brethren by feminizing them and masculinizing themselves. At the same time they dramatically separated men and women, rhetorically and practically, within their subculture. In other words, fundamentalist cultural, political, and personal separation from the world paralleled a process of internal gender segregation. The two parallel sets of practices and rhetorics also declined simultaneously. Were they linked? Did one entail the other? It could be argued that early fundamentalist leaders inverted the power relations of the world they vilified as they fashioned their own subculture. Exiled from the national public sphere, they created local Christian spheres—both family and church—in which they were the authorized speakers, the exilers rather than the exiled. Perhaps the end of their exile in larger public spheres reduced their stake in exiling women from their local Christian spheres, enabling them to soften made headship at home and in church.

Still, during the 1980s public fundamentalism was unambiguously male-centered. The pulpit was as exclusively male as ever, as was the deaconry. Preaching rhetorics were not hypermasculine, but they were certainly masculine-friendly, rife with angry, confrontational language and sports and military metaphors. And the structure of public address, which centered men and marginalized women, was intact. Like the masculine-friendly rhetoric, the structure of public address was no doubt moderated during the 1980s, but it still functioned alongside other rhetorical forms and content to maintain male headship in the Christian public arena.

Fundamentalists and conservative evangelicals explain their commitment to male headship and wifely submission as a simple matter of following God's Word. Does a true Bible, a Bible that comes true, that comes alive, in the present, in some way depend on maintaining a regime of male authority? Fundamentalists and conservative evangelicals would say the Bible—that is, God, most clearly speaking through Paul in Ephesians 5:22–24—mandates such a regime, and to dilute or discard the plain meaning of the text would, they argue, set them on the slippery slope toward a world in which there were no absolutes and no moral order. However, we have just seen how much that plain meaning, those absolutes, that moral order, can change during the course of a decade or two. Ephesians 5:22–24 may underwrite quite distinct gender arrangements, including ones that would have counted as unbiblical in the prior regime. It is also the case that many, more moderate, born-again Christians have disavowed the principles of male headship and wifely submission, yet still consider themselves devoted to Bible truth.

The slippery slope argument and, more generally, the strict Bible inerrancy polemic cover up the variety of interpretations of a text that coexists even within one church. And they cover up the speed with which interpretations, including official ones, can be revised—or even forgotten altogether. In the 1950s and 1960s, Genesis 9:22 and 24–25 were often cited as biblically mandating segregation, as they had been during the nineteenth-century abolition movement in defense of slavery. Noah cursed his son Ham and his descendants after Ham saw "the nakedness of his father and told his two brothers without." Noah said, "Cursed be Canaan"—Ham's descendants, which, according to popular theology in the South at the time, included Africans and African Americans—"a servant of servants shall he be unto his brethren." As support for segregation gradually eroded during the late 1960s and 1970s, there was no debate about the truth of these Bible verses. They simply stopped being cited. They, or rather their prevailing interpretation which had been considered to be the biblically inerrant truth, ceased to be part of the spoken Bible.

The question is not really whether Bible-believing born-again Christians can harmonize, historicize, or collectively forget a text such as Ephesians 5:22–24 without sacrificing Bible truth or Biblical inerrancy. They can.[39] Nor is the question really what would happen to the true Bible if they sacrificed male headship. Nothing about the interpretive practices that produce Bible truth or a true, living Bible requires specifically *male* authority.

Perhaps there is, however, a link between a naturally or supernaturally authorized social hierarchy and the kind of speech mimesis between preacher and congregation that fashions and sustains fundamentalist and conservative evangelical communities. Perhaps that kind of speech mimesis depends on a category of interpreters, in this case men and men of God, with unambiguously greater access to the truth. Gendered categories of people, men and women, fortified by the age categories of adult and child, serve as templates for a still more essential distinction between teacher and taught. Practically speaking, it is certainly true that the Christian family, insofar as it operates as a training ground for gender and age hierarchies, undergirds the interpretive authority of preachers and thus the practice of speech mimesis. Male headship then serves an ecclesiastical function. It is a socially embodied conduit for apostolic authority.[40]

Figure 7.1. Dust jacket from Falwell's 1986 pro-life book.

CHAPTER SEVEN

The Pro-Life Gospel

Someone else's words introduced into our own speech inevitably
assume a new (our own) interpretation and become subject to our
evaluation of them; that is, they become double-voiced. All that can
vary is the interrelationship between these two voices. Our practical
everyday speech is full of other people's words; with some of them
we completely merge our own voice, forgetting whose they are;
others, which we take as authoritative, we use to reinforce our own
words; still others, finally, we populate with our own aspirations,
alien or hostile to them.

—M. M. BAKHTIN, 1984

THE BEDROOM scene on the dust cover of *If I
Should Die before I Wake* . . . evokes a sense of innocent remembrance, a
wistfulness, a moment you will never forget, a moment laced with
haunting, foreboding feelings.[1] The room is bare. The bassinet is empty.
Something's missing. The ellipsis in the book's title bespeaks incompleteness as well. More literally, the title alludes to the nearness of death,
appropriating an old, familiar Protestant prayer (Now I lay me down to
sleep/ I pray the Lord my soul to keep/ If I should die before I wake/ I
pray the Lord my soul to take), and converting it into an eerie allusion
to abortion. Not any abortion—it could have been me, it could have
been you. The empty cradle flashes back and forth between womb and
coffin, a spooky place that mingles sleep and terror, birth and death,
safety and danger, innocence and error.

Jesus Christ, the Lord of the prayer, silently brackets the title. He is imaged in the light, accompanied by the Holy Spirit in the gentle wind, coming through the window, bringing hope and the possibility of overcoming evil. He merges with the visible sense that "something is missing," a phrase that appears frequently in conversion stories. Christ is the "something" that is missing. Christ and the missing baby coalesce. The bassinet intimates the manger and the empty tomb. Abortion echoes crucifixion, the slaughter of innocents. Saving babies partakes of Bethlehem, the resurrection, salvation, and the Blesséd Hope.

In the words of the dust jacket blurb: If I Should Die before I Wake . . . *is the story of Falwell's dedication to creating an alternative to abortion—but with an unusual twist. Jennifer Simpson, one of the first young women to join the Liberty Godparent Homes program (providing homes for pregnant teenagers) tells the story of the decision she made. With chapters alternating between Falwell and Jennifer, If I Should Die before I Wake . . . breaks down the barriers of misunderstanding by offering a hopeful alternative to this overwhelming issue.*

The two voices, Jerry's and Jennifer's, and their stories unfold and intertwine across twelve chapters. Their narrative moves are interdependent. She must choose, twice, whether to sacrifice her unborn child. He is called, twice, and must choose how to sacrifice himself on behalf of the unborn. The fetal person is passed back and forth between them, first aborted, then newborn. Her stories prepare the ground for his action; she participates, speaks upon, jointly produces, becomes the landscape for his heroic response, his sacrificial action, which then opens the way for her narrative to move on, indeed, changes the world around her so that her story may have, through her reciprocal sacrificial action, a new ending, a new beginning. She bears her baby; he bears the world in which her baby may be born.

If I Should Die before I Wake . . . is a masterfully seductive and intimate missive of almost love-letter intensity from its preacher-author to his people-readers. Jerry Falwell's born-again readers know they are handling a gospel text—a life-changing text of love, death, and redemption—if not from his name alone, then from the dust cover intimations of something missing. If they read *If I Should Die* as they read the Bible, its juxtaposed and laminated stories will pile up, talk to each other, and narrate a multidimensional world that speaks to readers, pulls them into its inner spaces, and becomes truth. The text will prepare a place for its readers, a kind of gospel passage, through a series of sacrifice stories that are perpetually incomplete, marking a loss, an absence, something given and not returned—an empty cradle—and engendering a desire, a longing, for wholeness, completion, return—rebirth. Readers may fill in what is missing by contributing substantially to the gospel at hand and, more meaningfully, they may be themselves infilled by the Holy Spirit, that is, they may undergo subtle and much sought-after changes of habit and of heart.

These born-again cries and whispers would likely be lost on unborn-again readers, especially unborn-again feminist readers, who might be more inclined to read through the name Jerry Falwell, the book's title, the dust jacket, and all the stories to a polemical subtext about abortion, sexuality, gender, family, feminism, and patriarchy. The sentimental language of *If I Should Die* would become translucent—like a veil thinly disguising what the book is "really" about—reaffirming gender differences, vilifying abortion and feminism, revitalizing patriarchy, and raising money. Jerry and Jennifer's enticing labyrinth of stories of sacrifice, redemption, and unearthly love would give way to something more sinister, monolithic, authoritarian, conspiratorial, and profitable. This and other hypothetical unborn-again readings are not necessarily wrong, but they tell us more about feminist than fundamentalist subjectivity.[2]

Falwell's book is an instance of born-again Christian language whose principal interlocutor is feminism. The text—and Falwell's pro-life gospel more generally—appropriates a central feminist narrative ("women are sexual victims of men and patriarchy, and abortion liberates them"), renarrates it from a born-again point of view, and thus produces and reproduces that point of view in willing readers. The language of *If I Should Die* does not express or reflect, say, male domination as if it were a code underlying the text. Rather, the text is more like a workshop producing born-again Christian subjectivity out of raw materials provided by the feminist, and particularly the pro-choice, movement. That is, the book, and the pro-life campaign generally, performs an act of cultural domination, one in which born-again language appropriates and converts feminist language to its terms.

The fact that *If I Should Die* is written as a collection of vignettes, rather than, say, a polemic, is what makes it productive, subjectively

speaking, for born-again readers. Bible-based story-telling transfers access
to born-again Christian discourse, as a whole and in its parts. Being born-
again means figuring oneself and one's world in biblically framed stories,
on a narrative landscape which simultaneously speaks biblical and con-
temporaneous dialects, submitting the latter to the terms of the former.
If I Should Die's biblically framed stories of transformation fashion a narrative rite of passage, which, as readers undergo it, as they infill its strategic
gaps, transfers narrative authority to them: the right, the ability, and the
desire to speak the pro-life gospel and to bring about the world it speaks.

The transfer of born-again narrative authority from speaker to listener
depends on gender, on a difference between "male" and "female," in
two ways: it is a movement across the gender boundary from a "male"
(saved, speaker, author) to a "female" (lost, listener, reader) position; and
it is a moment of rebirth, a second (spiritual, Fathered) birth that over-
takes the first (fleshly, mothered) birth, converting the lost into the saved,
"female" into "male."

Modern feminism challenges fundamental gender asymmetries, hence
the very mechanism by which born-again Christian subjectivity is reproduced. The narrative rituals of *If I Should Die* contest the feminist challenge in a number of ways: first, through its reiterated enactments of
gendered asymmetries, both in and across male and female bodies; second, by inventing a born-again, that is, biblically framed, tradition of
opposition to abortion; and third, by reconfiguring and occupying the
cultural turf claimed by feminism, the space of women's reproduction,
before and after birth.

If the dust cover scene intimated that the languages of gender and born-
again Christianity would intersect in *If I Should Die*, its prologue ("Who
Will Answer the Challenge?") carries the whole project in embryonic
form. The opening scene, an encounter between Falwell and a presumably secular female reporter, transforms, or converts, Falwell and launches
him on his journey across the landscape of women's bodies, authorizing
both his book and his mission. Cornered by reporters in a nameless airport, flashbulbs popping, microphones thrust into his face, Jerry Falwell
endures another impromptu press conference. Just as he breaks away, a
young newswoman, also nameless, tags him with one last question, as
Falwell reports: *"You say you are against abortion . . . but what practical*

alternative do pregnant girls have when they are facing an unwanted pregnancy?" "They can have the baby," Falwell replies. The reporter persists: *"Do you really think it's that simple?"* Falwell is taken aback. *I looked at her for a moment in silence. This was not just a reporter's question, asked to fill space in a paper or on the evening news. The look in the eyes of that reporter made me feel that her question came from deep and private places down inside her. . . .*

"Most of the girls in this country facing an unwanted pregnancy are young and poor and helpless," she said, *taking advantage of my silence. . . . "Is it enough to take a stand against abortion,"* the woman concluded, *"when you aren't doing anything to help the pregnant girls who have no other way?". . . . Out of that confrontation a dream was born. I decided that the reporter was right. It wasn't enough to be against abortion. Millions of babies were being killed, and I would go on fighting to save their lives, but what about the other victims of abortion, the mothers of those babies who desperately need help to save their babies?*[3]

The encounter appears mundane but it is charged with born-again Christian allusions and biblical pre-texts. Echoing of Paul's encounter on the road to Damascus, Falwell's appropriation of women's reproductive issues is an oblique replay of Christian conversion in which a spiritual birth mediated by the Father subverts, overcomes, natural female birth. As a story of Falwell's election to answer the challenge, the encounter recalls biblical tales of God's calling prophets and apostles in which unwitting moral inferiors figure as messengers, momentarily occupying the "male" position of superior speech as they deliver God's word to a man of God. *Out of that confrontation a dream was born* implies an annunciation of sorts and reinforces the figuring of Falwell in the "female," or listening, position.

Born-again readers come to a gospel text prepared to place themselves in its stories in the "female" position and to undergo its transformations. Falwell makes this understanding between himself and his readers explicit at the end of the prologue, where he begins to fashion the sacrificial passage and to prepare a reciprocal place for his readers, both men and women. He makes plain that his sacrifice will soon enough call forth theirs: *This book is my answer to that reporter's question. I've asked Jennifer Simpson . . . to tell her dramatic true story in chapters that alternate with mine. You may know a young lady like her. Or you may be*

*facing this problem now, just as she did. Or you may be simply watching
the abortion battle from the sidelines, as I once did, trying to decide what
you believe and whether or not to become involved. "Is there no other
way but abortion?" I believe we have found an answer to that reporter's
question. Read on and see if you agree.*[4]

What's missing in the airport encounter? The lack, the incompleteness, in the scene is opened up by the reporter's question: the space
of reproduction, women's bodies, will become the ground for redemp-
tive speech and action. As Falwell ("man") publicly acknowledges the
right of the reporter ("woman") to speak for herself and other women,
he acquires the right to appropriate her concern, in effect, her power,
and with it strikes out to fashion a new pro-family rhetoric. The reporter
is a working woman, assertive and articulate, representing women's point
of view. She stands for feminism, though a feminism domesticated before
it is even spoken—she hails him as "Dr. Falwell." Her words do not
close off but rather open up the subject—women, their reproductive
power and problems—to him, his gaze, his speech. It is she who portrays
women who need abortions as young, helpless, poor victims. It is she,
not he, who places them under him and, like the babies they carry, in
need of his help.

She, in effect, delivers him the feminist story line, which he then re-
imagines. The feminist image of a woman gaining control over her body
and her life through abortion rights becomes *the other victim of abortion*, a helpless girl who is driven to abortion because she has no other
way. With a few more strokes of a pen, *If I Should Die* converts another
feminist image, that of men opposing abortion rights to deprive women
of elemental, bodily equality and liberty, into an image of a born-again
male hero rising up in the country of reproducing women, a man-father-
Father figure who will save girl-mothers, as well as babies, from the maw
of abortion.

We are forewarned that this occupation of the rhetorical territory
claimed by feminism with born-again narrative figures and frames will
be a complex one by the unusual gender arrangements in the encounter:
a female reporter asks Jerry Falwell a question he cannot answer, and
Falwell, silenced, opens up, listens to this brassy young woman who
throws him off guard in public. Their exchange is intimate—she holds
him with her speech at some length, and he looks into her eyes, into

deep and private places down inside her. As her words enter him, his gaze enters her, and he is infilled with a dream. Together they become, in a way, the first Liberty Godparents. What is unusual, of course, is the role reversal in the reproductive metaphor: she takes on a "male" privilege, public speech, and he is feminized in the encounter by submitting, by listening, to a woman and giving birth to a dream—the Liberty Godparent gospel and ministry.

Men may occupy the "female" position and women the "male" position in Christian dialogues; but the point is not that men and women are equal, any more than the fact that the "male" speaking position is marked "superior" means that men necessarily dominate women. The gender reversals in the encounter between Falwell and the female reporter are not "really" about bodily men and women; instead, the reversals engender, and reengender, the essential subject positions in born-again discourse. The point is that gender differences produce born-again Christian subjectivity, not the reverse. Gender differences are, of course, created in the process of being deployed, but as a side effect or, rather, an a priori supplement of born-again discourse. Gender is both the rib and the "without which not" of born-again Christian identity formation.

To the extent that feminism made gender a public issue and declared war on its asymmetries, the movement was liable to provoke a reaction from born-again Christians, who speak themselves through a submerged display of asymmetrical gender meanings. How abortion rights came to be such an incandescent issue for born-again Christians is somewhat less straightforward.

Catholics drew on a long tradition of speech and action to protest promptly the 1973 Supreme Court decision *Roe v. Wade* repealing state bans on abortion. Evangelical Protestants did not respond immediately, but by the early 1980s they had become formidable abortion foes, contributing much materially, organizationally, and rhetorically to what had become known as the pro-life movement. Social movements often seem to arise abruptly, but a little historical inquiry usually reveals precedents and roots, a network of premovement organizations and ideas that anticipated and gave form and content to the movement. No such prior history exists in the case of the born-again movement against abortion.

The mid-nineteenth-century campaigns which banned abortion in many states were led by physicians, not Protestant preachers. There is little record of organized public opposition to abortion by conservative Protestants in the twentieth century until the late 1970s.[5] Debate over abortion in the late 1960s and early 1970s was largely limited to evangelical scholars and physicians who disagreed about the conditions under which therapeutic abortion was advised—and they generally agreed that therapeutic abortions were permissible under some circumstances. In 1968, an institute run by *Christianity Today*, the leading evangelical magazine, organized a symposium on the subject of birth control and abortion. A variety of positions were aired but the official publication of the symposium affirmed the principle that "the Christian physician will advise induced abortion only to safeguard greater values sanctioned by Scripture. These values should include individual health, family welfare, and social responsibility."[6] A special issue of *Eternity* magazine on abortion in 1971 still presented a range of opinions on the circumstances under which abortion might be advised.[7]

A more extreme position that opposed abortion under any circumstances first emerged around the same time in the course of internal debates among conservative Protestants. The forums organized by *Christianity Today* and *Eternity* marginalized that position, but the tables turned in the middle and late 1970s. After the 1973 *Roe v. Wade* decision, which rendered legally moot the whole category of "therapeutic abortion" by defining abortion as a woman's right, a half dozen conservative evangelical scholars intensified the critique of the moderate evangelical position, "laying the deeper scriptural and social reasons for opposing abortion."[8] A consensus against any notion of "abortion-on-demand," which is how conservative evangelicals generally defined a woman's right to abortion, crystallized very quickly, and gradually prominent supporters of therapeutic abortion either publicly changed their minds or stopped speaking out.[9] By the mid-1980s, most conservative Protestants were convinced that a strict pro-life position was both God's word and the traditional Christian position.

Occasionally, there appeared public evidence that a number of theologically conservative Protestants continued to support a less strict position on abortion rights. In 1984, when pro-life campaigns were reaching their peak, an attempt by the student government of Wheaton College, the nation's premier evangelical liberal arts college, to adopt a strong anti-abortion resolution produced such a heated public debate among the faculty and the college-at-large that no public resolution was possible. And according to 1992 figures, 50 percent of the white evangelical Protestant voters surveyed said they were pro-life, but the rest did not, including 25 percent of regular church attendees who said they were pro-choice.[10] The point, therefore, is not that conservative Protestants all agree about abortion rights—they do not—but that during the course of the 1980s a "pro-life gospel" was invented, traditionalized, and became so dominant among them that dissenters seemed to disappear. Moreover, the formation of this consensus was a major, perhaps the major, linchpin of both born-again Christianity as a cultural hybrid and the New Christian Right as a political movement.

The born-again pro-life tradition came together in three overlapping stages and venues. The first was the above-mentioned internal debate among evangelical scholars and intellectual leaders that heated up after the 1973 *Roe v. Wade* decision. Much of the debate was published in *Christianity Today*, which became markedly more conservative after Harold Lindsell took over the editorship from Carl Henry in September 1968, a month after the *Christianity Today* symposium on birth control and abortion. The second stage, the effort to convert conservative Protestant leaders more generally to a stricter anti-abortion position, was launched in 1975 when Billy Graham convened a two-day leadership meeting to "determine a proper Biblical response to abortion-on-demand."[11] That meeting produced the Christian Action Council dedicated to challenging existing abortion policies as well as to internal education.

Perhaps the most important event in this second stage was the production and distribution in 1978 of the five-part film series *Whatever Happened to the Human Race?*. The film and an accompanying book with the same title were written by Francis Schaeffer IV and C. Everett Koop, then surgeon-in-chief at the Children's Hospital in Philadelphia and later to become Ronald Reagan's surgeon general.

Schaeffer and Koop starred in *Whatever Happened to the Human Race?*, which was scripted and directed by Francis Schaeffer's son Franky, and it is widely credited with turning the tide of popular evangelical opinion against abortion. Schaeffer and Koop were disappointed by the turnout for the seminars they conducted after the film was released, but the film itself, which was distributed to churches all over the country, took on a life of its own.[12] It probably did directly, or indirectly through hearsay, convert many conservative Protestants to an anti-abortion position. More importantly, it created and popularized a good many of the subsequently staple pro-life rhetorical stances, including highly compelling ethical, historical, and biblical rationales for born-again Christian activism more generally.

The film series, first of all, never tried to proof-text opposition to abortion or to certify its position in narrow biblical literal terms. Instead, the film grounded its opposition in a version of biblical inerrancy that had become Schaeffer's signature. He argued for the truth of the whole Bible, for the presuppositional truths regarding the existence and character of God upon which the Bible's truth rests.[13] The personhood of the fetus, according to Schaeffer, logically follows from the facts of God's existence and his nature, and because all persons are made in God's image, abortion, like the killing of any other innocent person, violates God directly. The film also exploited scientific disagreements and the changing legal definitions of fetal viability, arguing that such uncertainty could only lead to a constant erosion of constraints. Koop may or may not have invented the practice of reciting in graphic detail how every available abortion technique actually terminates the life of a fetus, but his recitation, as the camera panned slowly over a thousand naked baby dolls scattered on the dimly lit salt flats of the Dead Sea, was perhaps the film's most disquieting episode.

The film also featured the faces, voices, and lives of ordinary men, women, and children who had been saved by heroic medical measures as infants under Koop's care, but whom other doctors, Koop said, would have let languish and die. Koop argued passionately that passive infanticide and euthanasia were already occurring in many hospitals and nursing homes. He and Schaeffer asserted over and over that, if tolerated, these practices would inevitably result, first, in active, and then in state-managed, mandatory infanticide and euthanasia of unwanted individuals and groups.

All this was coming about because of the *Roe v. Wade* decision and the deeper social change it signaled, the eclipse of the Judeo-Christian consensus as the moral and legal basis of Western society. *Roe v. Wade* was possible because the Judeo-Christian consensus and its "high view of human life" had been displaced by humanism (materialism, naturalism) and its "low view of human life." This is another one of Schaeffer's signature arguments, as was the slippery slope-ism that saturated *Whatever Happened to the Human Race?*. Because abortion is permitted, passive infanticide and euthanasia are increasingly tolerated, and later all three will be mandated, and then we will be living in a state exactly like Nazi Germany. Eerie, dark images of shackled blacks, old-world Jews, elderly men and women, handicapped children, and babies in cages combine with the film's voice-over to fashion a rhetoric of equivalence between slavery, the holocaust, abortion, infanticide, euthanasia, and state control.[14]

In the immediate context of the debates among conservative Protestants during the 1970s over the validity of therapeutic or partial abortion rights, the film's coup de grâce was its failure even to acknowledge any internal conflict. There was one not-Christian, humanistic, position, which would permit abortion under some or all circumstances, and there was one Christian position, which would not.

Whatever Happened to the Human Race? did not create overnight legions of pro-life born-again cadres as Schaeffer and Koop had hoped it would, but it produced and disseminated the grounds for that mobilization. Through the starkness of its terms, its powerful, memorable visual and verbal rhetorics, and its national grassroots distribution to conservative Protestant churches of all stripes, the film established the framework within which opposition to abortion rights came to be understood as the modal, "traditional" Christian position. During the early 1980s, in the third stage in the formation of the tradition of born-again opposition to abortion, this framework was customized and filled in by hundreds of local and national ministries. And it was this process that created pro-life cadres, men and women who would sacrifice themselves financially and otherwise in New Christian Right campaigns against abortion.

This final stage of born-again cultural mobilization against abortion was similar to what happened among American evangelical Protestants in the North in the 1830s, when rhetoric against slavery rather suddenly intensified, shifting from a commitment to gradual abolition to a call for immediate abolition. Preachers, each in their own idiom, reinscribed slavery as the ultimate expression of sinful self-gratification, and the commitment to immediate abolition became a kind of rebirth, hence a sign of whether or not someone was truly saved. Abolition accordingly became, like faith in Christ itself, a form of evangelism and preaching the gospel of abolition, a sacred vocation.[15]

In the early 1980s, preachers and lay leaders around the country "biblicalized" total opposition to abortion each in their own idioms, piling up varied ways of figuring and framing the abortion issue in both theological and vernacular terms that resonated with their communities. Overall, they pulled opposition to abortion into the very heart of what it meant to be a born-again Christian, made it a sign of faith and a gospel that must be preached far and wide. For Jerry Falwell, the Liberty Godparent Home campaign also presented the opportunity for him to combine two major dialects, his natal fundamental Baptist tongue and the more mainstream conservative evangelical tongue he was in the course of acquiring.

Early in the evolution of his pro-life rhetoric, Jerry Falwell, in his sermons and in the literature produced by his ministry, demonstrated God's opposition to abortion in the conventional fundamentalist manner. He and his collaborators cited dozens of biblical verses that "prove" God opposes abortion; he also embedded the "sin of abortion" in the premillennial vision of the end-times, a period of rampant immorality and social decay that precedes the rapture, the Great Tribulation, the Battle of Armageddon and the Second Coming of Christ.[16] Although resistance to more liberal sexual practices and gender relations is audible here, Falwell and his co-pastors did not directly elaborate the sin of abortion as an attack on the family or family values. Rather, from the beginning, they figured it as an ultimate violation of the relationship between person and God. Probably borrowing from Schaeffer and Koop, they put abortion, on a par—a slippery slope—with murder, the holocaust, the slaughter of innocents, and, they added, the crucifixion of Christ.

Falwell's Liberty Godparent campaign intensified and expanded this process of biblicalizing opposition to abortion. In terms of imagery, the campaign's major innovation was to place the womb and the fetus in the background and instead to foreground pregnant girls—the female bodies, lives, and experiences that surround endangered fetuses. In *If I Should Die*, this ground, the embodied landscape upon which Falwell acts, is most fully fashioned by Jennifer, in other words, by a woman-in-need-of-abortion elaborated as helpless victim.

Falwell's own early chapters, on the other hand, narrate the birth of the hero who would save her as they describe Falwell's gradual conversion to pro-life activism. Thus we are given to understand that even before he met the reporter in the airport or formed the Moral Majority, he was at least on the road to Damascus. Given the agreement of born-again readers to undergo the transformations of anointed authors, Falwell's story becomes his readers', and his prehistory becomes their experience. Falwell's story, though only lightly marked by biblical cues, also manages to nest abortion and anti-abortion activism fully in the central narrative frames that transfer—reproduce—authority in born-again culture, that is, within the frames of the gospel of Christ's death, burial, and resurrection. Later on in her chapters, Jennifer takes on and embodies this rhetorical innovation.

One of the "credentials" of hard-core pro-life activists is that they can remember where they were and what they were doing the day the *Roe v. Wade* decision came down.[17] In his first chapter in *If I Should Die*, Falwell describes reading about the decision in the newspaper as his eggs, bacon, raisin toast, and coffee grew cold—and, behold, anti-abortion rhetoric came fully formed into his head. Indeed, it had been there a long time:

I will never forget the morning of January 23, 1973. . . . The Supreme Court had just made a seven to two decision that would legalize the killing of a generation of unborn children. I couldn't believe that seven justices on that Court could be so callous about the dignity of human life. Were they misinformed? Had they been misled? Were they plunging the nation into a time of darkness and shame without even knowing what they were doing? . . . I had preached on abortion and its meaning to my people and had used abortion as an example in several sermons over the past ten years.[18] But, as I read the paper that day, I knew something more had to be done, and I felt a growing conviction that I would have to take my stand among the people who were doing it.[19]

There were other signs, small moments of *growing conviction*—for example, when Jerry *saw a full-color picture of an unborn child . . . a tiny, trusting child whom God had created*—but he *still hesitated to take a public stand.*[20] It was his children who officially mediated his actual conversion to political action. During family devotions, when Falwell laments *the legal murder of millions of America's unborn children*, his children call him to task: *"Why don't you do something about it, Dad?" my spunky red-headed son finally interrupted, rising up on one elbow and looking me in the eye. "Yeah," chimed in my daughter. "Do something for the babies."* [21] His children hounded him for weeks. He prayed and argued, his *convictions began to grow*, and he finally overcame his fundamentalist scruples about activism and *jumped into the political arena feet first*. If God later would use a woman, the reporter, to deliver Falwell access to women's reproductive issues, he first used children to give him access to the plight of the unborn.

Still, according to the official record, years passed between this moment and Falwell's public debut as a political leader, when he formed the Moral Majority. Falwell occupied the time, it turns out, educating himself, reading everything he could get his hands on concerning the issues, voraciously consuming all manner of texts, academic and popular, legal, medical, scientific, and political. When, in his second chapter, Falwell takes us through what he learned, we find ourselves caught up in a welter of stories of fetal life and death.

Jerry tells us about the dumpster in Los Angeles stuffed with the remains of 1,700 human babies, mutilated, tiny fetal bodies all torn to pieces, hands chopped off, and the incinerator of burning bags of dead babies from a hospital in Wichita. He lifts the terror briefly to envision how Jennifer's first baby would have developed had she (yes, "she") lived, only to recount, in graphic detail, how she was torn from her *liquid nursery*, her *secret sanctuary*, and disposed of by medical personnel. *There would be no monument for the courageous struggle for life the baby mounted until she died.* [22] Lengthy, detailed, vivid descriptions of abortion methods follow. *Picture it.* Cutting the body into pieces, crushing the head, extracting, sucking the pieces into a container.

Falwell's recounting here is, for him, notably free of biblical citations which would prove that the fetus is "life" and abortion "murder." He refrains from overtly sacralizing the first birth, and, instead, renders it in secular terms and deploys "scientific facts" to construct abortion as murder. The account's relentless, detailed facticity squares with the tradition of "common sense empiricism" in fundamentalism, and also with Falwell's personal narrative, by generating the worldly ground upon which he will take his public stand—and enjoin his readers to take theirs.[23]

Still, there is a way in which Falwell's figuring of fetal life and death in *If I Should Die* worms its way into the core of born-again discourse. Any narrative reiteration of life versus death would, but the fetal struggle also has the potential of meta-commentary, of commenting on Christian discourse itself, which Falwell's account fully realizes. In effect, he figures abortion as the death of the first ("female") birth, a death which precludes the second ("male") birth and thus disrupts the narrative transfer of spiritual authority.

All that chopping and cutting, the excessively vivid, repeated dismembering of little unborn babies resonates, not automatically, but as an outcome of preacherly rhetoric, as sinful sacrifice, as ritual action that defiles and destroys the relationship between person and God, as abolishing the very context in which the relationship might be restored. Among fundamental Baptists, as we have seen, the first birth prefigures the second birth in the same way that Abraham's willingness to sacrifice Isaac prefigured Christ's death and resurrection. The first story frames, enables, anticipates the second story. It marks an incompleteness which the second story fills, fulfills. The second story depends on, cannot happen without, the first story. What if Abraham had disobeyed God in the end and actually killed his son? No Isaac, no Christ. That, Falwell's rhetoric implies, is what abortion does. It destroys the first story/birth ("female," flesh) which prefigures the second story/birth ("male," spirit), thus cutting, chopping the narrative channel which transfers born-again authority. Constituted in these terms, the right to abortion puts the very heart of born-again Christianity—the central narrative frames and figures by which it produces, and reproduces, subjectivity—at stake.

Jennifer's chapters weave in and out of Falwell's, unfolding the intimate, vulnerable, embodied landscape upon which Falwell, and other born-again preachers and believers, must act. He invites his readers to look at abortion from "the woman's point of view," first implicitly in his long review of the physical and psychological damage (ranging from uterine perforations to drug addiction, from bad marriages to suicide) inflicted on women who have abortions, and then explicitly just before Jennifer begins her abortion story. *Try to feel how she felt that awful day her baby died.*[24] But it is she who takes up where the reporter left off and constitutes the born-again version of the woman's point of view, filling the feminist space of "adult women exercising control over their bodies" with the image of "a teenage girl who needs help."

Whereas Falwell was inventing born-again tradition in fashioning a prehistory and new biblically-based narrative grounds for anti-abortion activism, Jennifer works against the grain of a born-again interpretive legacy regarding teenage unwed mothers. That legacy would cast girls like Jennifer in a war against sin, vilifying them as sexual transgressors, framing the maternity homes, the homes for unwed mothers, as places to hide in shame, and posing childbirth and child rearing as the price that must be paid for sin. With Falwell's help, Jennifer reinscribes the girls as innocent, in the sense of naive or abused, victims. The home for unwed mothers becomes a place where teenage lives are restored, and out-of-wedlock childbirth, God's will. It turns out that the better way which Falwell conceives in his prophet-making scene with the reporter includes giving up for adoption the babies saved from abortion, and, accordingly, the Liberty Godparent Home is at once a pleasant maternity home for teenage girls and an adoption agency for married, born-again Christian couples.

It seems that Falwell and his collaborators were not simply responding to feminism but also adjusting their language and practice to certain facts of born-again life in the 1980s. Even in their communities, more teenagers were having sex, girls were getting pregnant and having abortions, and (white) couples who wished to adopt were finding (white) babies scarce.[25] The adjustment was not an easy one, however. By what narrative logic may girls be led to give their babies up for adoption after so much ink has been spilled convincing them to save them from abortion? Several chapters of *If I Should Die* are devoted directly to making this "difficult decision," and Jennifer's and the other Liberty Godparent Home girls' stories seem to work overtime on behalf of "adopting out." Their stories lean toward adoption most notably in their portrayal of the girls as innocent and dependent victims whose lives need to be restored, in the ongoing sacralization of the fetus-child, and in the radical marginalization of the biological father. Ultimately, and rather miraculously in the sense of being utterly unprecedented, adopting out is constituted as the second birth anticipated by the first birth, at least in the lives of unwed teenage girls.

While Falwell's story is one of steady if slow progress toward the pro-life light, Jennifer, as we shall shortly see, goes way down before she goes up. As she moves through her moment of maximum descent, the abortion, through the turning point when she decides to save her second baby, to her triumphant arrival at the Liberty Godparent Home in Lynchburg, Jennifer's story accumulates biblical tropes which exculpate her, demonize abortion, and sanctify giving birth—all without naturalizing the relationship between biological mother and child.

Details of time and space frame Jennifer's abortion as an anti-worship service, as sacrilegious sacrifice: Jennifer and her parents drive past their church on their way to the abortion appointment at 11:00 one Sunday morning. *Nobody noticed us drive by.* The sky is overcast, storm clouds are piling up, the wind is blowing dirty paper plates and empty beer cans across the highway, and by the time they arrive at the Planned Parenthood clinic (anti-church), they are irritable and grumpy—and scared. The waiting room is full of naive girls, frightened and listless, many of whom had been there before. The nurse (anti-Sunday School teacher) lectures them on abortion procedures. *I suppose we didn't really listen to the nurse for the same reason passengers on an airplane don't really listen to the warnings of the stewardess. Who wants to hear the bad news* [anti-good news]?[26]

I'll always remember how embarrassed I felt that day when the young male doctor [anti-pastor] *entered the room to find my two bare legs sticking almost straight up into the air and my hands gripping the table* [anti-altar] *for dear life.*[27] Jennifer glimpses the suction tube in the doctor's hand just before he injects the anesthesia: *I don't know what he did to me after that. I woke up on a bed. A nurse was removing a bloody pad from between my legs. It was gross. . . . I lay there thinking I was going to die when the receptionist entered the room and placed a glass of milk and a plate of Oreo cookies beside me. . . . I felt terribly foolish. It didn't look anything like a last supper* [anti-bread and wine]. *The abortion was over. The little intruder was gone forever. I felt weak and dizzy and high.*[28]

The "last supper" spins an explicit thread between the abortion and Christ's sacrifice that clinches the web of allusions implicit in the situating details. It also evokes the last meal of a convicted murderer and intimates "the wages of sin is death," at the same time as Jennifer's naive narrative voice and the image of milk and cookies deflect those connotations from her and suggest that she is innocent.

Abortion is evil—it carries the full weight of sin—and Jennifer emerges scathed but untainted. She is the girl next door, a sixteen-year-old middle-class Baptist Georgia city girl whose father is a deacon, her mother the church secretary. Neither she nor those who counseled her to get an abortion—her parents, the Health teacher, a Baptist pastor—denies the personhood of the fetus. They are oblivious to it. *Nobody thought about the baby. Not even me,* Jennifer laments in retrospect.[29] Ignorance, not sin, was the culprit as far as these otherwise good Christians are concerned.

If Jennifer's abortion is an anti-worship service, the moment she decides to save her second baby is a cross between an annunciation and a salvation experience. Her parents had *just seen a special on TV about a place in Virginia* and thus knew about a better way when Jennifer told them she was pregnant again. She balks at the idea of going there to have her baby, but then, while driving alone about midnight on a highway, she runs out of gas, pulls into a filling station that was closed for the night (a liminal time, place, and circumstance with connotations of sexual danger and a sign of spiritual hope—the filling station) and has a revelation. Having called a friend to come get her, she curls up in the back seat of her car to wait and watches a moth fly into a hot light and sizzle to death.

I pictured myself fluttering and dancing about the light. I determined that this time I would be smart enough to fly away to safety. That awful night was one of the best things that ever happened to me. There beside the filling station in the middle of nowhere, something changed within me. I grew up. "Dear Lord, please help me." I hadn't prayed for a long time, not a real prayer, not like this one. "I'm in real trouble again, Lord, and I don't know what to do about it." I stared out into the darkness trying to find God out there.[30]

Jennifer's moment of decision echoes of Mary's annunciation—an unmarried girl visited by a messenger, a male birth foreshadowed. Those echoes are mixed with allusions to Christ's death—a meaningful death: he died so that we might live. And something changed within Jennifer.

That night she submits to God (*Dear Lord, please help me*), and the next day she tells her parents she wants to go to that place in Virginia. Jennifer chooses life over death, joins God's plan, and the hidden meaning of things and events will begin now to infill her.

The biblical connotations and allusions break the textual surface when Jennifer arrives at the Liberty Godparent Home. As the director, Jim Savley, ushers Jennifer and her parents into his office, she notices the pictures of his wife and family, a framed telegram from President Reagan, certificates and diplomas, and *an impressive painting of Mary riding on a donkey carrying the baby Jesus in her arms. Joseph walked close by.* Jennifer tries to remember the story, *but all I could see was the look in Mary's eyes as she stared lovingly into her baby's face.* Mr. Savley, answering her unasked question, tells her that Mary and Joseph were fleeing to Egypt *to save the life of their baby.*[31] *I understood why the painting was chosen for his office. My family and I had traveled to Lynchburg for a similar reason—to save my baby. There was an unborn child growing inside me and this time the baby would not die.*[32] Jennifer becomes Mary; Liberty Godparent Home, Egypt; and, by narrative implication, the abortionists are King Herod bent on slaughtering the innocents. Falwell, the absent author of it all, casts a decidedly supermundane shadow. This time, the baby—Christ—will be spared.[33]

Jennifer's arrival scene at Liberty Godparent Home foreshadows, as did the filling station scene, a male birth and clinches the equation, first intimated on the dust cover, between Christ and the baby-saved-from-abortion. It also cleanses Jennifer, wrapping her in Mary's mantle, symbolically restoring virginity to the unwed, pregnant teenage girl threatened by the specter of abortion-Herod, at the same time as it locates her reproductive issue squarely in God's plan, not in her hands, much less in the hands of the biological father. These threads are spun out in the rest of Jennifer's story and in Jerry's, which begins to merge with Jennifer's once she enters Liberty Godparent Home.

When her parents first told Jennifer about the Liberty Godparent Home, she imagined *a haunted house with army nurses and big needles behind locked doors and barred windows,* in effect, a place where she would be punished, drilled, and terrorized.[34] Before Jennifer got there, Falwell, in an intervening chapter, assures his readers that nothing could be further from the truth, rewriting the maternity home from darkness to light, from shame to self-confidence: *We now know that an unwanted pregnancy makes a teenage girl feel ugly, embarrassed, and unwanted. . . . The young woman feels like hiding her shame from the world. . . . That's why it becomes so easy to kill the baby, to end the nightmare, and to try to begin again. That's why Liberty Godparent maternity homes provide a sense of permanence, safety and beauty to restore the self-confidence and self-worth in the pregnant girls it exists to serve.*[35] And, of course, Jennifer is greeted by the warm, intuitive Mr. Savley, not an army nurse, and the place is surrounded by oak trees and blue jays, green lawns and bright yellow flowers, and inside there were bay windows overlooking the garden, Early American maple tables and chairs, and a chef, her arms brimming with grocery bags.

Jennifer and Jerry collaborate in reconfiguring the maternity home, converting a nineteenth- and early-twentieth-century figment of anti-sex rhetoric into a 1980s anti-abortion sanctuary. Accordingly, the stories of how Jennifer and the other girls at Liberty Godparent Home became pregnant portray them as passively, not actively, sexually transgressive, not as sinners but as victims. When she was sixteen, surrounded by the tempting music, visual images, and banter of teen culture, Jennifer feels her body changing and stirring (*just brushing past a boy going through a classroom doorway made me feel excited and curious and a little afraid*) and vulnerable to any boy's attention (*I felt ugly and rejected and alone most of the time*).[36] She spends a weekend unchaperoned at a summer cottage with some other girls; boys arrive one night; she finds herself alone on the dunes with a strange boy and . . . *the romantic dream became a nightmare.*[37] After her abortion, she is *miserable and angry most of the time* and *desperately needed someone or something* [to make her] *feel good again.*[38] That someone is Jeff, that something is sex, and she gets in trouble again.

The other Liberty Godparent Home girls fall into two camps, sexually speaking. There are girls like Jennifer, victims of physical urges, low self-esteem, teen culture, and lack of supervision, who "made mistakes," implying that "these things happen even in (middle-class) Christian families." And there are other girls to whom unthinkable things happen, (lower-class, not Christian) victims of incest, rape, pornography, poverty, negligence. Missy, age thirteen, was abused by her father and impregnated by a stranger. JoAnn's alcoholic father beat his four daughters, sexually abused three of them, and got JoAnn pregnant at fourteen. An unnamed fourteen-year-old girl called the Liberty Godparent Home hotline operator from Baltimore and said her father sexually abused her, made pornographic movies with her and her two-year-old brother, and had just killed their mother. Either way, whether they are victims of bad boys or evil men, the girls are let off sin's hook lightly as the causes of their pregnancies are narratively dispersed in circumstances rather than lodged in the girls, in their sinfulness or their "sin nature."

The victimizers lurk on the margins of the girls' stories, misguided boyfriends who mislead girls who make mistakes and cruel fathers/strangers who rape defenseless girls. Just once, in a few lines, Falwell casts a light on the boys, pointing out that some of them try to change, some try to help the girls they have hurt, not all of them are irresponsible and uncaring, though, by implication, the rest, and all the adult men who impregnate teenage girls, are.[39] Their narrative banishment—the erasure of the natural father—combines with the mariological insinuations surrounding the girls to intensify the sense of fetal divinity and denaturalize the relationship of fetus-child to both its parents. Biological fathers are given no say in the fate of the babies, before or after birth, and, while the girls must make the difficult decisions, it is absolutely clear, given that fetuses belong to, are essentially of, God, that the first birth ought not be aborted.[40] It is not so clear—or rather it must be clarified with much storied attention—what the girls ought to do with God's issue after birth.

Alongside tales of personal and spiritual growth, that is, restoration, at Liberty Godparent Home, Jennifer narrates her painful search for the right thing to do for the baby as she listens to other girls make up their minds and talks over her qualms with the women who work at Liberty Godparent Home. Falwell, in his parallel chapters, is likewise much preoccupied by the choice the girls must make between keeping their babies and giving them up for adoption. Its importance, delicacy, and complexity is forcefully indicated by the narrative space it occupies—Jennifer and Jerry slow down the pace of their storytelling, expand the details, and fill the margins of their thoughts with inset tales that explore other options and outcomes. Although other choices are permitted fairly good endings, the girls are under unequivocal narrative pressure to "adopt out," right-fully to sacrifice their children for their own good to Christian couples.

Andrea kept her son and started a new life in Lynchburg, but working full time meant long hours in daycare for little Brian and the abrupt end of her own adolescence; the failure to make a timely sacrifice called for other sacrifices with uncertain, open-ended consequences. Tammy kept her baby even though she, at age fourteen, had been counseled that adoption was the preferred option, but later we find her happily married to a tall, blond seminary student from Chicago who told Falwell, "I don't agree with all your politics . . . but you saved my son and I'll always love you for that."[41]

JoAnn did not, as did Tammy, have a middle-class home to return to, and her story, drawn out over several pages, accentuates the costs of keeping the baby. A fourteen-year-old victim of incest, poverty, and neglect, JoAnn took her baby back home to the perils of her father's house. Falwell said, *I selected JoAnn's story because struggling with her kind of complex and confounding reality is the responsibility of any person who takes a serious stand against abortion. . . . JoAnn's story isn't over yet. We don't know what God has in mind for her little girl. Whatever it is, we are glad and grateful that God will have His chance in her life. It is risky business reaching out to people in despair. It is risky business helping babies be born into our world.*[42]

The echoes of a second birth deferred are strong in this passage. *JoAnn's story isn't over yet. . . . We don't know what God has in mind. . . . It is risky business reaching out to people in despair*—these are phrases out of in-house meta-gospel talk, forms of speech used among soul winners consoling themselves over lost souls who said "no" when they heard the message of Christ's saving grace. Though the timing is always ultimately given back to God, no born-again Christian has any doubt that the better way, if not necessarily the only route to narrative completion, is to choose Christ (adopt out to a born-again couple) now.

Jennifer decides to give her child up for adoption shortly after witnessing a conversation between thirteen-year-old Missy and Rosemary, a Liberty Godparent Home volunteer who herself had given her baby up for adoption a few years before. Rosemary tells Missy, *You love your baby too much to keep her. You don't have a home or a family or a husband to offer your baby. You can't provide anything you want her to have. . . . There is a young couple right this minute who cannot have a baby of their own. They have a good income. They have a beautiful home with a nursery and toys and baby clothes and an empty cradle. They are praying for a baby, Missy. They can take care of the baby. They can give the baby what you want to give her.*[43]

There is that empty cradle again, that sense of something missing, no longer the consequence of abortion, now the space of awaiting adoption. Jennifer, like Missy and several other girls, decides to fill, to fulfill, that other empty cradle, but their decisions are labored, even belabored.

Jennifer agonizes over adopting out for months, worrying if she will have the courage to stick to it, dwelling on the moment when she will have to give up the baby. The sense that she is engaged in making a rightful sacrifice is clinched when she receives word of her baby's sex and name by way of Falwell: *I had chosen Stephen for my baby's name. I was convinced I was going to have a boy after Dr. Falwell had preached on Stephen, the first Christian martyr.*[44] Just before he is born, Jennifer wrote Stephen a letter he will never receive: "*You were not un-wanted. . . . I want the very best for you, and if I could give it to you, don't think for a moment that I wouldn't. God has a very special plan for you and right now it's for you to have both a mother and a father. . . . I love you.*"[45] Some thoughts are being precluded through all this self-denial, most especially any suggestion that giving Stephen up for adoption was the "convenient" thing for Jennifer to do.

Jennifer, the other girls, and Falwell—their pro-life gospel—must sanction adoption for teenage girls without resorting to language which born-again Christians impute to feminism. They must suppress any implications that babies are "unwanted" or "inconvenient," that they get in the way with girls resuming their adolescence, going to college, having a career, or getting properly married. Hence, the sacrificial excess: "*Do you know that I love you, son?" I whispered into his tiny ear. "Will you remember? We have to trust God now. He'll take care of you. Will you forgive me? Will you love me anyway?" Words poured out of me. Stephen looked as if he was trying to understand. . . . When they took him back to the nursery, I pulled the thin yellow blanket up so that the nylon edge was touching my face. The heavy drapes covered the huge windows. It was twilight outside. The room was almost dark. I was alone again.*[46]

This bedroom scene completes, fulfills, the one on the dust cover. Jennifer has sacrificed herself so that Stephen might live. Although we are given to understand it is a blessing of God, a free gift, not a motive, Jennifer's death-unto-self also marks her own rebirth as she walks boldly back into a middle-class adolescence restored and brimming with possibilities. By the time she reappears in Falwell's final chapter, which jumps ahead a few years and narrates a Memorial Day celebration on the grounds of Liberty Godparent Home in memory of "the unborn children who have died from abortion," Jennifer has become a communications major at his Liberty University and is emerging as a national spokesperson for Liberty Godparent Homes. Clearly, God blesses those who seek and follow his will.

When Falwell finally makes his appeal, in the penultimate chapter, for readers to assume their place in the sacrificial landscape unfolded for them, it is relatively soft and pro forma, concluding with a vague entreaty, *Will you seriously consider joining us in helping save the unborn babies of our nation?* [47] Although the book rehearses all the moves of gospel speech, marking out a multitude of "lacknesses" for readers to complete, *If I Should Die* is a gospel text not so much for the unconverted as for the converted. It is a training manual, comparable to a collection of sermons, for the elaboration and refinement of gospel speech. Instead of building toward a moment of salvation in which pro-life rhetoric is acquired, the stories assume saved readers and effect a continuous transfer of advanced Christian narrative authority. [48]

The stories of Jerry Falwell's pro-life campaign appropriated and displaced feminist rhetorics in ways that were crude and simple. Much was blotted out: feminism and the feminist movement were never named in *If I Should Die*, and adult women and married teenage girls who choose abortion made no appearances. Feminist positions, images, and story lines were caricatured. All of the women who need abortions were unmarried teenage girls, all of them were sexual victims, and all of them needed help. Jennifer, by dint of dependency, age, name (Falwell's children's names begin with "J") resonated as a daughter to Falwell's father/Father. Such choices and devices plainly tilted the narrative campaign in favor of Falwell's authority.

"They cared about me and helped me save my baby."

"At sixteen I got pregnant. Abortion seemed like the only solution—even to my parents.

"But nobody told us that such a quick, easy answer would have such a lasting, devastating effect. No one mentioned the guilt and the grief.

"At eighteen I got pregnant again. But this time I was determined to find another solution. That's when I met some people who cared enough about me to help save my baby."

Jerry Falwell's *If I Should Die Before I Wake . . .* is the rest of Jennifer's story. A true account of compassion and hope that tells how you can become part of the solution.

Available now in all B. Dalton, Waldenbooks, and other fine bookstores.

Figure 7.2 Direct-mail appeals such as these two from the mid-1980s explained how to help Jerry and Jennifer *save the unborn babies of our nation.*

Yet in other ways the campaign was nuanced and complex. It deployed the most powerful and sophisticated narrative resources of born-again Christian culture, resources which have countless times proven themselves capable of reconfiguring the subjective springs of action. The campaign, in figuring abortion as the death of the first birth, saving babies as the first birth, and adopting out as the second birth, lodged the pro-life movement in the discursive heart of born-again culture, in the irresistible play of reciprocal sacrificial action across stories, written, spoken, and lived.

The stories of *If I Should Die* did not represent preexisting asymmetries as fixed eternal truths that must be swallowed whole. They generated the asymmetries anew and transferred them from author to reader with tremendous force and tenderness through the narrative logic of prefiguration and fulfillment. Repeatedly, "superior" persons, terms, stories, and rhetorics appropriated and transcended their "inferior" counterparts. The logic binding "inferior" and "superior" is neither literary nor causal, but divine, foreordained, indelibly written by God. If Isaac, then Christ. If first birth, then second birth. If "female," then "male." If Jennifer, then Falwell-as-maternity-homemaker.

Born-again preachers and pro-life leaders were able to engage their communities in an escalating movement against abortion by embedding it in the greatest story ever told. What they, in collaboration with their followers, achieved as they traced out alterations of character, motif, motive, action, and circumstance across sequences of stories and events was nothing less than the further working out of God's will in history.

If I Should Die ends with Jennifer Simpson making her debut as a public speaker at the Memorial Day celebration. As Jerry Falwell sits on the platform and listens to her, he ponders what would have happened *if people hadn't cared enough to save* the babies of the girls at Liberty Godparent Home. *I imagined their children sliced into pieces and suctioned from their mother's womb or burned and blackened by salt poisoning and born dead. . . . "You are alive, little Brian," I said quietly to myself. "Thank God, Stephen, you are alive."* [49]

In the book's opening scene, the female reporter handed Jerry Falwell the feminist story line and the woman's point of view, and Jennifer and Jerry renarrated them in born-again terms across their intertwining chapters. Together they converted the cradle emptied through abortion

into the cradle filled, and fulfilled, through adoption. In the book's closing scene, once again, a woman speaks in public while Falwell listens,
but this time it is he who created the grounds upon which she speaks,
even as she embodied the landscape upon which he acted. Although
Jennifer has a public voice, she acquired it through Falwell's sacrificial
action. The hint of feminism carried by the female reporter has finally
been erased.

CHAPTER EIGHT

The Creation Museum

Since 1960, creationism has done more than any other issue except abortion to inflame the cultural warfare in American public life.
—MARK NOLL, 1986

DURING the 1950s, fundamentalist preachers such as Carl McIntire, Billy James Hargis, and Edgar Bundy rallied conservative Protestants nationwide in anti-Communist crusades and thus lent support to McCarthy's public interrogations of suspected Communists. Liberal public intellectuals—academics, journalists, novelists, playwrights, and filmmakers—interpreted these activities in their writings as expressions of the same disregard for individual rights that had led to the anti-evolution campaigns of the 1920s. In both periods, it was said, Fundamentalism promoted a right-wing, extremist, conspiratorial politics in which a majority threatened essential civil liberties. In this renascent folklore of liberalism, "the Scopes trial came to symbolize a moment when civil libertarians successfully stood up to majoritarian tyranny."[1] In effect, liberal intellectuals, as they updated modern representations of Fundamentalism in the 1950s and 1960s, conducted a revival of the cultural verdict of the 1925 Scopes trial.[2]

Inherit the Wind was surely the masterpiece of the Scopes revival. In the form of a play, it was performed and published in 1955, and in 1960 it was made into a major motion picture starring Spencer Tracy, Frederick March, and Gene Kelly.[3] *Inherit the Wind* did not pretend to be historically accurate—names and details were changed and the play was set in the present day. Still, the play's essential drama was that of the Scopes trial, or rather the Scopes trial legend: two old white men arguing about

Darwin, the Bible, and a schoolteacher's right to teach evolution. The play's authors "did not intend to present antievolution as an ongoing danger—to the contrary, they perceived that threat as safely past; rather, their concern was the McCarthy-era blacklisting of writers and actors."[4]

Inherit the Wind took for granted that old-time religion, Fundamentalism, as embodied in the figure of Matthew Harrison Brady (Bryan), was the source of the threat, current and past. It confirmed as well the Scopes trial legend that religion, specifically Fundamentalism, is anti-science. And, via its portrayal of Brady, the play presents Fundamentalism, and religion generally, as mindless and reactionary at worst, and hopelessly anachronistic at best.[5] Midplay, at the close of a scene in which Brady seemed to glimpse the danger of religious extremism, he turned to Drummond (Darrow) and said: "We were good friends once. I was always glad of your support. What happened between us? There used to be a mutuality of understanding and admiration. Why is it, my old friend, that you have moved so far away from me?" Drummond responded: "All motion is relative. Perhaps it is *you* who have moved away—by standing still."[6]

If the revival of the Scopes trial legend provoked a response among conservative Protestants, we do not have a record of it.[7] Certainly, they did not perceive it, to the extent they perceived it at all, as a threat to the de facto truce which held sway after the 1930s regarding the teaching of evolution in public schools. Most of the thirty-seven anti-evolution laws introduced in state legislatures during the 1920s had failed to pass, and those that did pass were not actively enforced. But the issue was moot because evolution was scarcely taught, or not taught at all, in many school systems. After the Scopes trial, textbook publishers, acutely sensitive to controversy due to their thin profit margins, enacted a self-imposed ban on the teaching of evolution. For the next thirty years, public school science textbooks avoided mention of evolution, referred vaguely to Darwin if at all, and neglected biology generally, reducing it to morphology and taxonomy.[8] In effect, according to the terms of this textbook truce, Fundamentalists, though they had lost the war of national public opinion, had won the battle regarding the teaching of evolution in public schools.

All this changed in the late 1950s. It did not change as a result of liberalism's critique of domestic anti-Communism but, ironically, as a result of liberalism's own anti-Communism in the form of Cold War politics. In 1958, largely in response to the launching of Sputnik and the Soviet space program, the National Science Foundation (NSF) launched a $100 million program to reform science curricula in the public schools. The Darwin centennial celebration of 1959 further mobilized biologists in particular on behalf of educational reform. During the 1960s, new biology curricula, developed with NSF funding and emphasizing evolutionary principles, were introduced in nearly 50 percent of the nation's schools. Moreover, in 1970, a new social science curriculum, "Man: A Course of Study" (MACOS), developed with NSF funding, was introduced in the public schools. "MACOS was clearly treading on sensitive ground. . . . The course is not only built on evolutionary assumptions, but it denies the existence of absolute values, thus explicitly teaching just those controversial ideas that fundamentalists have long suspected were implicit in the teaching of evolution."[9]

The federally sponsored biology and social science curricula reforms of the 1960s and 1970s created the occasions for renewed conflict around the teaching of evolution and evolutionary principles in the public schools. So also did annual textbook reviews by state school boards. The resulting controversies between Bible-believing Christians and public school officials were widely publicized by the nation's press. State school board battles over textbook adoption in California and Texas during the 1960s and 1970s received much in-depth attention; so did the textbook protests, at times violent, in Kanawha County, West Virginia, in 1974, and the local and national protests about the MACOS curricula in the mid-1970s.[10]

Contests such as these transformed at the same time they resurrected the political landscape of the 1920s with regard to evolution and the Bible. Outright censorship of evolution in biology texts and curricula was no longer politically feasible, even at the local level, but faith in Genesis and contempt for evolution among conservative Protestants could still be tapped and elaborated politically. Instead of attacking biology curricula, the new focus of Bible-based protest was social science and humanities curricula and texbooks that assumed, or seemed to assume, evolution, and that promoted, or seemed to promote, cultural relativism.

While the campaigns were only partially successful in their attempts to suppress most targeted social science and humanities textbooks, they virtually eliminated all of the MACOS texts and curricula. The latter campaigns against MACOS, furthermore, provoked a broader attack on the National Science Foundation that spelled the beginning of the end of its role in reforming public school curricula.[11]

These political campaigns did not simply tap into a stable, homogeneous reservoir of creationist belief. Belief in special creation may have actually increased during the 1960s and 1970s. Moreover, what conservative Protestants believed about creation changed rather dramatically during that period.[12]

During the 1920s, the "day-age" position, which held that a day of creation may have lasted thousands of years, was common sense among Bible-believers. The other belief common among conservative Protestants until the 1960s was known as the "old earth" position or the "gap theory," which supposed that millions of years may have passed between "In the beginning" and the six days of Edenic creation.[13] Both positions allowed that many thousands, if not millions, of years may have passed since the events recorded in Genesis and thus permitted conservative Protestants to accommodate much mainstream geology and even some evolutionary views in the form of theistic evolution. But Bible-believing common sense changed after the 1960s, when a veritable creationist revival displaced these positions with a new, "strict creationist" position. According to strict creationism, "God created man pretty much in his present form at one time within the last 10,000 years."[14] The strict position, also called "young earth" and "day-day" (a Genesis day is a twenty-four-hour day), "virtually co-opted the creationist label" from the old orthodoxy.[15] By 1991, 47 percent of all Americans surveyed by Gallup pollsters reported that they believed in "a recent special creation."[16]

The main force behind the promulgation of a recent special creation was Henry M. Morris and his associates. A Ph.D. in hydraulic engineering from the University of Minnesota and professor of civil engineering at the Virginia Polytechnic Institute, Morris published, with co-author John C. Whitcomb, Jr., *The Genesis Flood* in 1961. They argued against the prevailing "progressive creationist" (old earth) orthodoxy, asserting that Bishop Ussher's chronology was essentially correct—the earth was six thousand, at most ten thousand, years old, and the six days of creation were just that, six literal days. To account for the fossil record, Whitcomb and Morris relied heavily on the work of George McCready Price, a Seventh-Day Adventist and self-taught geologist who argued that the geologic column was laid down, layer by layer, as a result of a single biblically recorded catastrophe, the worldwide flood at the time of Noah.

Confronting as it did the conservative Protestant establishment in the name of a more biblically literal truth and simultaneously steeped in scientific and scholarly trappings, *The Genesis Flood* was an instant sensation. "Strict creationists praised it for making Biblical catastrophism intellectually respectable again, while progressive creationists and theistic evolutionists denounced it as a travesty on geology that threatened to return Christian science to the Dark Ages."[17] The threat, as it turned out, was very real. Over the next twenty-five years, *The Genesis Flood* went through twenty-nine printings and sold over 200,000 copies, and its position became the new conservative Protestant orthodoxy.[18]

Whitcomb and Morris's insistence on young-earth and strict, day-day positions enabled them to reclaim the authority of scriptural literalism with regard to the Genesis account, authority which had been lost in the Scopes trial finale when Darrow decried the inconsistency of Bryan's day-age position. Morris, like Price before him, was convinced that Bryan's voicing of a day-age theory had not only lost the trial but had also made it "a turning point in the intellectual and religious history of mankind."[19] But Whitcomb and Morris hoped to do more than recoup lost ground by promulgating a strictly literal creationist position. What made their rhetoric of strict creationism culturally productive and innovative rather than merely reactive was its assumption of the very apparatus that had defeated them, the apparatus of science. In effect, the popularizers Whitcomb and Morris and, even more effectively, their collaborators over the decades following the publication of *The Genesis Flood*, created creation science, also known as scientific creationism. According to historian Ronald Numbers, by the mid-1970s: "Instead of denying evolution its scientific credentials, as Biblical creationists had done for a century, the scientific creationists granted creation and evolution equal scientific standing. Instead of trying to bar evolution from the classroom,

as their predecessors had done in the 1920s, they fought to bring creation
into the schoolhouse and repudiated the epithet "anti-evolutionist." Instead of appealing to the authority of the Bible, as [even] John C. Whitcomb, Jr. and Morris had done in launching the creationist revival, they
downplayed the Genesis story in favor of emphasizing the scientific aspects of creationism."[20]

In 1972, Henry Morris and his allies established the Institute for Creation Research near San Diego, California, to promote their amalgamation of science and religion. Although the Institute's research program
and graduate school faltered, its staff of ten research scientists, all with
Ph.D.'s, published fifty-five books in its first decade alone, and a widely
circulated newsletter, *Acts & Facts*, and countless pamphlets.[21] During
the 1970s and early 1980s, Morris, Duane Gish, and several other Institute staff scientists staged dozens of debates with evolutionary scientists
at secular colleges and universities all over the country. In the public
presentations as in their writings, they articulated the case for special
creation and the case against evolution within the intellectual apparatus
of science—using its language, its evidentiary rhetoric, and paraphernalia
of overhead projectors displaying charts, diagrams, photos, and citations.
The debates were largely coups for the creationists—such forums were
not really suited to science or scientists. In effect, they restaged repeatedly
the great final debate between Darrow and Bryan and, if only for their
Christian audience, reversed, over and over again, the cultural verdict of
the Scopes trial.

In 1977, the Institute set up the first museum of creation and earth
history. Composed of a one-room collection of exhibits supporting creationism and the biblical record, the museum was substantially expanded
and upgraded to a "state of the art" nine-room museum in the late 1980s.
The first few rooms of the expanded museum, as of 1997 when I took
a tour, presented the topic of creation as such (of the universe, the earth,
plants and animals, and man); the middle rooms exhibited catastrophes
and catastrophism (the Flood, volcanoes, the Ice Age, the geological column); the final rooms addressed history (ancient, recent European, and
modern American). If the early and middle rooms were exercises in mixing biblical and scientific rhetorics, in melding Genesis with astrophysics,
biology, and geology, the final rooms were an exercise in redividing

them. Religion and science were not opposed but were rather two hostile "worldviews" that had struggled for the soul of mankind since the beginning of time. One worldview was grounded in creationism, the other in evolutionism. Orthodox Judaism, orthodox Islam, and biblical Christianity were creationist, and all other religions were evolutionist: "Atheism, Pantheism, Humanism, Polytheism, New Age-ism, Confucianism, Evolutionism, Buddhism, Hinduism, Sikhism, Taoism, Janism, Animism, Shintoism, Occultism, Liberalism, Marxism, Fascism, Maoism, and others."

The connection between evolutionary thought and evil was explicit and intense in the two rooms where visitors learned that human sacrifice, Nietzsche, the holocaust, Communism, imperialism, racism, promiscuity, homosexuality, child abuse, slavery, and abortion are all "fruits of evolution." The museum's ostensible goal, to take people back for God, was thus complemented by several other projects: to take science back for God and to discredit evolution as science, to reveal its sinister implications, indeed, to align evolution with the devil himself. By the end of the tour, not only had creationism been melded with science, but evolution had been separated out from science and turned into an originary, pernicious philosophy.

A number of other creationist organizations, strict and progressive, were active during the 1970s and 1980s, but it was the Institute of Creation Research and its affiliates that made creationism, or rather creation science, a political issue during the period. Specifically, the Institute was the source of legislation that was passed, and subsequently overturned, in Louisiana and Arkansas requiring that the theory of scientific creation be given "equal time," that it be taught alongside the theory of evolution in public schools.[22] In 1973, an earlier version of equal-time legislation had been passed in Tennessee (the law under which Scopes was tried having been repealed only in 1967), but it was overturned in 1975 on the grounds that it established religion. Attempts to pass similar legislation in several other states likewise faltered. In 1978, Institute staff attorney Wendell Bird developed new equal-time legislation in a *Yale Law Review* article, arguing it would not violate the First Amendment.[23] In 1981 bills were introduced in about twenty states requiring, in effect, that the Genesis account of creation, *as science*, with all biblical references deleted, be taught alongside evolution.

The bill was passed and signed into law in Arkansas and Louisiana. A hugely publicized federal court case followed in Arkansas. Though it was heralded as Scopes II, the tables, in some ways, were turned: most of the experts testifying on behalf of the law were scientists, and most of those testifying against it were clergy. The latter argued that scientific creation was indistinguishable from the biblical account of creation and that the law thus violated the First Amendment. The judge agreed, so did the judge in the case against the Louisiana law three years later, and so did the Supreme Court in 1987.

As with so many of the born-again Christian campaigns of the 1980s, the campaign for creation science failed politically in the long run but was hugely successful culturally. The triumph of the strict creationist position of creation science was one of several processes that marginalized liberal and moderate evangelicals within the wider body of conservative Protestants. Their marginalization was, in turn, one of the processes that constituted born-again Christianity in the 1970s and 1980s. Through the lens of creation science, the moderate positions—theistic evolution and progressive creationism—were deemed accommodating and scripturally unsound and lost their internal claim of greater scientific credibility. Rather than reconciling science and religion, creation science appeared to appropriate science, to submit it to the Bible. Its premise was that, if the Bible is true, then geology, archaeology, and history will provide evidence for its truth against any nonbiblical position. Creation science thus rhetorically performed an act of cultural domination. It subordinated science to the Bible.

The careers of many creation scientists also enacted and embodied the same act of cultural domination. They acquired advanced graduate degrees from secular universities; some of them held teaching positions at those universities; they joined secular professional science organizations; and they created their own Christian professional science associations. Expert publicists, they knew how to use academic forums and the media to disseminate their images and ideas in ways that won followers and enraged foes. And they had access to vast internal, born-again Christian media and academic—not to mention church and parachurch—networks. In short, creation scientists seized the forces of representation, and with their fusion of religion, science, and politics, turned left-liberal clichés about equal time, pluralism, advocacy politics, participatory democracy, and the tyranny of experts inside out. For those who followed their lead, they occupied the terrain of science, reason, and education with the Bible and thus recaptured cultural ground lost during the earlier Fundamentalist movement. They were Davids slaying the Goliath of secular science, expertise, and the nation's cultural elite with their slingshot, the counterdiscourse of creation science.

When *The Genesis Flood* came out in 1961, Henry Morris was a member of a moderate Southern Baptist Convention church in Blacksburg, Virginia. His pastor decided that Whitcomb and Morris's book was likely to cause controversy in his congregation, so he relieved Morris of his Sunday School teaching post and "in effect ushered him to the church door."[24] Morris responded by starting an independent Baptist church in his own home. It prospered and shortly enabled him to build a church proper. Morris invited evangelists from around the region to help him build attendance, and among them was the Reverend Jerry Falwell, pastor of a fast-growing church in Lynchburg. Virginia Polytechnic Institute eventually also put pressure on Morris to leave his teaching position there. He did so in 1970 and joined forces with the Reverend Tim La-Haye, one of Falwell's associates in the Baptist Bible Fellowship. LaHaye, like Falwell, was starting a Christian college that year, in California near San Diego, and offered Morris both an academic affiliation and the funds to build the Institute for Creation Research.

Back in Lynchburg, Jerry Falwell and his colleagues at Lynchburg Baptist College relied heavily on the Institute materials and models as they developed the college's biology curriculum during the 1970s. In the early 1980s, it came to the attention of the American Civil Liberties Union that students trained in creationism at LBC were teaching biology in public high schools. The ACLU filed a complaint with the Virginia Board of Education challenging the qualifications of Liberty graduates to teach biology. The college responded by moving the teaching of creationism out of the biology department and into a new unit called the Center for Creation Studies. The letter of the law was abided in that creationism was no longer taught to students in biology classes. However, now all students were required to take a course in creation studies taught by biology professors at the new center.

It was a delicate moment for Falwell when he announced the resolution of the crisis in the fall of 1984 at the quarterly preaching conference of the Baptist Bible Fellowship. He spoke to an audience composed of both old-fashioned separatist preachers and more moderate fundamentalist preachers like himself who were in the process of loosening separatist principles. Falwell passed around a "fact sheet" that described the terms of the resolution in detail (see fig. 8.1). There was a little murmuring among the audience at the time, and Falwell's administrative assistant told meafter the conference that some preachers continued to disagree with Falwell on one or both counts—arguing that evolution should not be taught at all and Falwell should not have accommodated the Virginia State Board of Education in any way. But Falwell convinced most of the assembled preachers, and, as they agreed with him, together they stepped farther away from old-fashioned fundamentalism and into born-again Christianity.

To be sure, the Baptist Bible Fellowship pastors accepted Falwell's resolution of the conflict because they felt he had not compromised. Indeed, Falwell convinced them that, if anything, he had used the crisis to intensify the teaching of and commitment to creationism at Liberty. Creation would be taught to all students as fact, and evolution as an unproven theory (the law could not require it be taught as truth) to all biology students. In effect, Falwell had arranged for creationist biology professors to perform pedagogically the subordination of evolution to creationism. And then, of course, the rationale for the new arrangements was exquisite: Liberty Baptist College graduates, including some of the sons and daughters of the preachers present, would have the credentials they needed to teach biology, or to pursue graduate degrees and professional careers, as Bible-believing Christians.[25]

Jerry Falwell also urged his co-pastors at the preaching conference in 1984 to visit another instance of Liberty's intensified commitment to creationism, the new Museum of Earth and Life History. The museum, which claimed to be, and probably was at the time, the world's largest creation museum, was designed by Lane Lester, the newly appointed director of Liberty's Center for Creation Studies. Lester had earned a Ph.D. in genetics from Purdue University and worked for many years as a research scientist at Morris's Insititute for Creation Science. His museum was located in a large room on the back side of the college library,

============A FACT SHEET ON LIBERTY BAPTIST COLLEGE AND SCHOOLS============
September 24, 1984

1. Liberty Baptist College is a fundamentalist and separatist liberal arts college founded in 1971 by the Thomas Road Baptist Church and its pastor, Dr. Jerry Falwell, with a student body that first year of 144. For the school year 1984-85, 4,566 students are enrolled. This is an increase of 235 over last year.

2. Liberty Baptist College and Schools include liberal arts undergraduate programs, the Institute for Biblical Studies, Liberty Baptist Theological Seminary, and other graduate programs, various adult education programs, and the Lynchburg Christian Academy.

    A total of over 6,000 students are enrolled in these school systems.

3. Liberty Home Bible Institute, a multi-year correspondence Bible school, has over 15,000 students presently enrolled. Dr. Harold Willmington serves as Dean of the Institute.

4. Liberty Baptist College received full approval by the State Council of Higher Education in April 1974.

5. Liberty Baptist College was fully accredited by the Southern Association of Colleges and Schools in 1980.

6. Liberty Baptist College was accepted into the NCAA (National Collegiate Athletic Association) in 1981. We are presently competing in the Division I and the Division II levels.

7. Our masters programs (Master of Divinity, Master of Religious Education, Master of Arts in Education, and Master of Arts in Religion) received candidacy status with the Southern Association of Colleges and Schools in December 1983. It is anticipated that full accreditation will be forthcoming in December 1984. Doctoral programs will then be developed.

8. Liberty Baptist College and Schools will become Liberty University in the late 1980's.

9. Liberty Baptist College offers 66 majors at this time, including pre-law and pre-med.

10. Liberty Baptist College has 9 teacher education programs in
    a. Business
    b. Elementary Education
    c. English
    d. Physical Education
    e. History
    f. Social Sciences
    g. Mathematics
    h. Music
    i. Biology

11. Each of the nine teacher education programs was certified by the Virginia Board of Education in 1982.

    This approval by the Virginia Board of Education provided immediate certification of our schoolteachers in 34 states which have reciprocal agreements with Virginia.

12. The American Civil Liberties Union challenged the certification of our biology education program because of our position on origin, and a three-year battle ensued; however, in July 1984 the Virginia Board of Education certified our biology education program by a 6-2 vote over the protests of the ACLU.

Figure 8.1 A two-sided circular distributed to preachers and church workers attending the 1984 Superconference at TRBC during the accreditation controversy.

and it survived until the mid-1990s when it was closed, apparently as a cost-cutting measure.

For all appearances, the Museum of Earth and Life History was a natural-history museum. It was an ensemble of display cases, dioramas, charts, mobiles, reconstructed animals—one that roared when you pushed a

<table>
<tr><td colspan="2" align="center">FACTS ABOUT THE BIOLOGY EDUCATION PROGRAM AT LBC
AND ITS STATE CERTIFICATION</td></tr>
</table>

A. Since Liberty Baptist College is training future medical doctors, scientists, and other professionals, and since we want our graduates in biology and pre-med to be academically ready for admission to accredited graduate schools, it is imperative that we prepare them to pass every test and meet every demand of the profession into which they plan to enter.

B. Since our graduates must be prepared to academically and professionally compete in order to enter these fields as fundamentalist Christians, we must therefore teach them all the scientific data in the science classes—which includes the theory of evolution (which in no way means our professors espouse that theory).

C. However, Liberty Baptist College and Schools believes in Biblical creation. It is a part of our doctrinal conviction and statement.

D. All eight biology professors, like all other instructors at Liberty Baptist College and Schools, are born again fundamentalists who annually sign our statement of faith—which includes a belief in the inerrancy of Scripture and, of course, a commitment to the accuracy of the Genesis account of creation.

E. These biology professors enjoy total liberty and academic freedom in their classrooms to present all the scientific data as it relates to their disciplines. There is no "gag rule" which limits them in any way as to which scientific data they may present and discuss. All instructors at LBC have this academic freedom to present various ideas in their respective fields.

F. No professor is ever asked to teach anything as proven fact that violates his or her religious convictions. To our knowledge, no professor has ever done this, nor has the Virginia Board of Education requested that they do so.

G. However, we not only have the mandate to prepare students for professional performance and competence, but, even more important, we are committed to grouping these same students in Biblical philosophy. And it is our conviction that the cornerstone of the Christian message is a correct understanding of Biblical creation—just as evolution is the cornerstone of secular humanism. Therefore, we are now developing the Liberty Center for Creation Studies.

H. The Liberty Center for Creation Studies will be in place for the 1985-86 school year, which we trust will be on the East Coast what Dr. Henry Morris' Institute for Creation Research is on the West Coast. LBC will then be, to our knowledge, one of only two accredited schools in the world which examine creation in such depth. Every LBC student must study at this Center to graduate.

Dr. Lane Lester, one of our biology professors and a former staff member of the Institute for Creation Research, will head up the Center.

In summary, the same biology professors who teach our students in the science classes also teach all our students the scientific data related to the concept of creation in the interdisciplinary philosophy course on origins.

I. Every LBC student is also required to take a course presently entitled "The Problem of Origins" which is team taught by Associate Professor of Biology, Mr. James Hall, along with the philosophy and Bible departments. Scientific data related to origins are presented and discussed in this interdisciplinary philosophy course.

J. Science professors have total academic freedom to present and discuss all scientific data in the science classrooms, and may answer any students' questions at any time without hedging—just as professors do at state universities and other private colleges.

K. Our constitutional attorney through all these struggles, Mr. William B. Ball, from Harrisburg, Pennsylvania; our Liberty Baptist College Board of Trustees; our faculty and administration; and our students—all agree that we are enjoying our full constitutional rights while in no way violating our theological integrity—and further, that we are operating in full compliance within all Constitutional parameters.

The American Civil Liberties Union and at least one fundamentalist newspaper disagree.

The October 1984 issue of the *Fundamentalist Journal* magazine contains three articles dealing in detail with this matter, They are:

LBC: The Dream and the Dilemma, page 8
Creationism and Biology at LBC, page 12
Liberty Center for Creation Studies Announced, page 61

button—and canned voices that episodically came forth from the ceiling. The Museum of Earth and Life History occupied the cultural space of a museum of natural history, but of course it did not reproduce natural history's animating meta-narrative of evolution. Visitors knew what to expect from the fundamental Baptist credentials of the university and its chancellor, Jerry Falwell, and even a casual reading of the legends confirmed that this was an "anti-museum of natural history." Rather than replicating, it repeatedly inverted the evolutionary premise and assumptions that encode natural-history museums and recoded the displays of man and beast with the presumptions of creation science.

A tour of the museum revealed that the creation science on display accomplished more than mixing religion and science. Certainly it was not just a matter of dressing up religious views in scientific terms and paraphernelia. Nor was it enough to say that the terrain of evolution had been occupied and colonized by the Bible-based forces. Such formulations might have seemed adequate had it not been for one display that defied them. The display devoted to the work of Dr. Anthony Cianco indicated that the museum's creation science was a more complex cultural hybrid with a broader aim. The museum aimed not simply at evolution but toward releasing fundamentalists, and conservative Protestants generally, from the terms of modernity, from the images and clichés and parodies, clinched in the Scopes trial.

Only one case in the Liberty museum was devoted specifically to overturning the evolutionary story of the emergence of man from his primate ancestors, but it was the most densely argued of all the displays. A large *National Geographic* magazine chart hung on the back wall of the display case. While it visually and textually evolved modern *Homo sapiens* out of eight fossil precursors, the creation science legend to its left disrupted and replaced the chart's evolutionary story line. The chart, the legend argued, *illustrates an important point about the "hominid fossil record," that is, the poor quality of the fossils of our so-called ancestors. In fact, all of the known human fossils could be piled on one dinner table.* Lacking any complete skeletons, the legend continued, evolutionists "fill in" the missing bones and the "soft parts" with their imagination, having decided in advance whether the fossil is more or less human. The legend concluded that the names *Australopithecus* and *Homo* could just as well be replaced by the words Ape and Human.

Here, as elsewhere in the museum, was a transmogrification of secular science origin theories—or rather common sense, popular versions of them—into creation science. Gradually, there emerged from the exhibits an oxymoronic beast with the body of the fossil record and the head of the Book of Genesis.

The fossil record was not thrown out by the Liberty Museum; it was converted to Bible-believing Christianity. Perhaps the most dramatic conversion was the rewriting of the Yale Peabody Museum's poster depicting the evolution of plant and animal life in successive geological ages. The adjacent creation text, entitled "The World before the Flood," reported that *fossil deposits from the different geological systems do indeed have the remains of different living things in them. The evidence is strong, however, that all these creatures perished in the Flood, and their remains were preserved in the earth. Therefore, these pictures can give us an idea of what different parts of the earth looked like at the time of the Flood.*

The museum imitated and inverted secular science theories with a kind of clumsy precision. Its exhibits seemed willfully amateurish, hardly intent on evoking an aura of authenticity, always tottering on the edge of credibility. Yet the displays managed to effect the illusion of a natural-history museum, however topsy-turvy, as well as the impression that creation scientists literally believe what they say they believe, however burlesque it may have sounded to me. At least it seemed so until I came upon "the Work of Anthony Cianco, Ph.D., creation scientist, Vienna Museum of Earth and Life History."

Dr. Cianco's work included three exhibits of evidence of the Flood: a bird's nest containing a fragment of Noah's diary (Birdis Nestialis Noahinsis); a piece of Indian Corn extracted from the mouth of a woolly mammoth (Acornius Copi); and a black frame case with a dozen small animal bones sticking out of a bed of unadorned plaster of paris. The bones are entitled "Trampled before the Flood," and the legend read: *In the wild race to get to the ark, many of the animals were trampled to the ground under the feet and hooves of the swift. Of course, only two of every kind would ever make it. This section of petrified material clearly points out that all of these creatures lived at the same time, contrary to popular evolutionary belief that millions of years separated the existence of these different creatures.* The bones "identified as coming from the stampede" included those of a miniature dinosaur, a bone-headed dinosaur, a human tibia, a lemur femur, a mongrel jaw fragment, a moray eel spiny skeleton, a cat tail bone, and a chicken sternum. "This specimen," the legend concluded, "was found at the base of Mt. Ararat . . . by Dr. Anthony Cianco."

Midway through the legend about animals "trampled on the way to the ark," the museum winked at me. Or did it blink? Or, God forbid, was it a parody of a wink? Or an imitation of a parody of a wink? What started out as a moment of interpretive discomfort rapidly disintegrated into a state of epistemic shock. I for one was not prepared for this sudden encounter in the Cianco case with what appeared to be self-conscious parodic pastiche. It was one thing to make fun of evolution, but quite another to spoof creation science, if it was a spoof. Was it? In an instant, the twinkling of an eye, I was no longer absolutely certain that these fundamentalists simply believed what they said they believed.

A hoax is a joke that does not openly declare itself a joke, a deception of sorts that pitches the viewer into an agitated state of having "to get to the bottom of this." Close readings of the Cianco exhibits, which were all overtly preposterous, did not settle the matter because nothing in the end clearly stated "this exhibit is a joke." Why not call Lane Lester, the museum's curator, and ask him? In fact, several years after my first visit I did ask him, and he admitted it was a joke, one concocted by some of his students. But many faithful fundamentalist visitors did not bother to find out whether it was a joke, or if they did, they did not think it was funny. They complained, and the exhibit was eventually taken down.

Dr. Cianco's exhibit produced an element of interpretative instability that led to his downfall, but it also revealed layers of cultural tension and complexity otherwise obscured. The exhibit revealed the tension between the contrary readings enabled by the museum. On the one hand, the museum performed the serious reading of the Genesis account of creation that Falwell's more fundamentalist constituency expected. On the other hand, it performed a parody of science—even creation science—which especially delighted a circle of savvy, higher-educated, one might even say more cosmopolitan, postfundamentalists. In this way, by juxtaposing and intertwining the two readings, by putting up and taking down the Cianco exhibit, the museum performed the ongoing contest between points of view within Falwell's community.

The Cianco exhibit also indicated that creation science was a more complex object than met the eye. The museum, creation science, and even the Cianco exhibit, it could be argued, reproduced an inerrant Bible. Dr. Cianco, even if he was joking, submitted to an orthodox reading by setting the record straight. He revealed, in effect, that even creation science does not prove creation, does not produce truth. He confirmed without stating what is taken for granted by believers—that the

Bible, not science, makes creation true. But this reading, either as a direct reading by a believer or a meta-reading by an ethnographer, does not come to grips with Cianco or the Liberty museum. Its displays were not single-minded, monolog'ɔ voices speaking either the Bible's inerrancy or preexisting fundamental Baptist cultural structures. They were each intersections of multilayered allusions, of criss-crossing, upending, one-sided dialogues, of incongruous, contentious voices. The exhibits opened up gaps in meaning that could be closed only by willful interpretive acts, and then only partially, only momentarily.

The creation museum as a whole, and creation science in general, was built on permanent breaks between discourses, signifying fault lines that generate meaning precisely by resisting closure, by disorienting, destabilizing, coming out of the blue, slipping and sliding, always on the brink of escalating into reckless gobbledygook. This is precisely how parody works—through mimicry. Creation science is spoken from within the discourse of science, and it claims to be a voice of science, but it produces objects, propositions, assumptions, and so on which other speakers recognize as not-science, or anti-science.

Dr. Cianco's exhibit thus called attention to the extent to which the creation museum as a whole relied on parody. Its primary mission—to discredit scientific origin theories—was deadly serious, but its means were hardly serious. The sober tasks of edification and rectification were effected throughout by mimicry, caricature, misreading, mockery, and unmasking. Tacky, plastic, and plaster-cast imitations of scientific thought were displayed as if they were "real science," then verbally ridiculed by calling attention to their human authorship and all its foibles, to the stories embedded in theories of evolution and how the stories transform minutiae into "evidence," to the iffyness of the evidence and how easily it can be suborned to "prove" another story or theory, including creationism.

Inside the museum's parody of science lay another parody—of higher criticism. The interpretive moves made against science in the museum imitated the interpretive moves made against orthodox biblical thought in the eighteenth and nineteenth centuries by modern theologians. Those moves, called "higher criticism," actually literalized the Bible. They put it on trial as a representational text. They severed biblical stories, which were once one with the world, from events, from history.

They spotlighted and interrogated biblical narrators and imputed them with ulterior motives. And they mercilessly undermined the plausibility of biblical stories as literal depictions of "reality." By such means, higher critics, according to those who resisted them, attempted to discredit the Bible and render it a heap of myths and legends. Evolutionary theory came ultimately to occupy the space opened up by the descent of Genesis. Thus, by subjecting scientific "stories" to the same higher critical moves and supplanting evolution with creation science, the Liberty museum mocked, and reversed, the course of secular intellectual history.

The museum wrote creation science into the space opened up by its aggressive misreading of secular scientific discourse and of higher criticism. It did not transform scientific and critical theories into fundamentalist discourse, but rather, in a manner unsettling from all points of view, the fundamentalist creation story emerged like an alien from the belly of its discursive foes. The museum spoke, was spoken by, all three discourses. Creation science is a monster composed of three mutually exclusive voices occupying an uninhabitable intellectual space. And yet, miraculously, it walks and talks, it publishes and pickets and boycotts and lobbies and litigates.

And then, just to top it off, to tip it over the edge, "Dr. Cianco" winked. If only by not stating whether he was joking, Cianco destabilized the whole museum, coming dangerously close to declaring it and creation science a self-conscious farce. In doing so, he revealed that the museum was, finally, a parody of the modern point of view, and its image of the literal believer as a monolithic, single-minded creature, incapable of polyphony, double-coding, reflexivity, irony, parody, or self-parody. The museum permitted, indeed, incited, a reading of Fundamentalists as premodern, antimodern, one-dimensional biblical literalists—that was the museum's official outcome, its ostensible point. But the practices by which this image of biblical literal identity was constituted revealed its artifice, its polyglot, mercurial, and deeply political character, and performing this complexity was a piece of the transformation of Fundamentalists into born-again Christians.

In creation science and its museums, we witness, we encounter, the politics of a people deformed by the emergence and eventual dominance of modern liberal and secular discourses. But banishing God and Fundamentalists from the modern garden, that is, in this case, from natural science, also enabled a sequel in which they returned.

The Genesis debate, given its central role in the Scopes trial as the origin myth of secular modernity, was a necessary site of reconfiguration if conservative Protestants were going to reenfranchise themselves politically and culturally. After the trial, some Protestant scientists and theologians developed their theories of progressive creation and theistic evolution; others denied Genesis any role as a historical account. Their voices, their modus operandi, were, according to modern logics, recognizable or reasonable.[26] They sought relief from the grip of modern caricatures by articulating views that did not pretend directly to challenge or upend science, or higher criticism, but rather could be reconciled with modern scientific discourses.

The public power of fundamentalists-cum-born-again Christians came precisely from their capacity to destabilize and undermine the cultural opposition between Fundamentalist and Modern by fashioning a third, studiously ambiguous, figure which joins the incongruous terms. In the language of creation science, the dreaded biblical literalist and the modern scientist and higher critic are stitched together into a savvy, multistoried, code-switching, self-conscious, playful, confident, absolutely certain, old-fashioned, born-again Bible believer.

Creation science's reliance on parody is itself a riposte to its modern discursive foes, for Fundamentalism—that is, Bible-believing Protestantism from the modern point of view—is nothing if not a parody, a willful, strategic, deauthorizing misreading of fundamentalism and Protestant orthodoxy in general. Fundamental Baptists, above all their preachers, responded to the modern parody of supernaturalist white Protestants during the middle half of the twentieth century by embodying aggressively its caricature of them. But under the regime of born-again Christianity in the late 1970s and 1980s, fundamentalist preachers, in this instance allied with creation scientists, licensed themselves to enter and occupy a whole range of worldly practices hitherto off-limits by turning modernity's parody of them into their parody of modernity.

CHAPTER NINE

The Last Days

I trust you will gain a greater understanding of Bible Prophecy, but will also catch part of the vision that has motivated this ministry through the years—and now especially in these last days as we begin the 1980s, the Decade of Destiny.

—JERRY FALWELL, 1980

A TOUR of Israel conducted by Jerry Falwell's Old-Time Gospel Hour Tours has a good deal in common with a tour of Greece sponsored by a secular tourist agency. Familiar historical landscapes and events and figures come alive, and what was a two-dimensional story about the past, about the origins of our civilization, pops vividly into three dimensions. One feels and sees oneself walking within history. History thus embodied becomes more real, truer. But the Israeli and Greek tours are also absolutely unlike each other. For Jerry Falwell's Holy Land tourists also find themselves inside the future, walking upon its landscape, knowing its actors, foreseeing its events. They walk within the scenes of Jesus Christ's First Coming two thousand years ago, and of his Second Coming, which they know will be soon. They know that they are living in the last days, the end-times, and that shortly Christ will rapture them, bodily lift them up, off the earth. They will enjoy seven years in heaven while all those left on earth will endure a terrible tribulation culminating in Israel in the battle of Armageddon. Then they will return to earth with Christ to rule with him on earth during the Kingdom Age of one thousand years.

So real, immediate, specific, and unarguable is the future foreseen that the Old-Time Gospel Hour tour guide and Bible prophecy teacher, Harold Willmington, buried a Protestant Bible in one of the caves in the Valley of Petra. He wrapped it in plastic and buried it for the Jews who will hide in those caves after the destruction of the Jews begins during the "great tribulation."[1] Willmington recalled in his account of that trip that W. E. Blackstone, a nineteenth-century scholar of Bible prophecy, *felt that someday the terrified survivors of the antichrist's blood bath will welcome the opportunity to read God's Word*, so he hid thousands of copies of the New Testament in the caves of Petra.[2] Willmington, like Blackstone, *knew*, on the basis of Scripture, that those Edomite caves would be the *special hiding place* where *one-third of Israel will remain true to God* and come to know Christ as their savior during the tribulation.[3] Willmington was more modest than Blackstone, leaving the remnant just one large Bible, but he was no less certain of the future. In the Bible he inscribed this note: *Attention to all of Hebrew background: This Bible has been placed here on October 14, 1974, by the students and Dean of the Thomas Road Bible Institute in Lynchburg, Va., U.S.A. We respectfully urge its finder to prayerfully and publicly read the following Bible chapters. They are: Daniel 7 and 11; Matthew 24; II Thesalonians 2; Revelation 12 and 13.*[4]

No doctrine, no preacher, instructed Harold Willmington to bury a Bible in the caves of the Valley of Petra. Nor did Willmington bury it there in hopes of changing the future. Whatever Harold Willmington did in 1974, whatever he or anyone else does at any time before the rapture, Jews in the tribulation will hear the gospel and be converted in the Valley of Petra before the battle of Armageddon. This unequivocal knowledge of the future makes born-again Christian apocalypticism, or Bible prophecy, a moving, thrilling sort of faith. So does the particular relationship posited between what happens now and what happens later. It is through this relationship that Bible prophecy effects action, if obliquely, on the plane of human history. Prophecy converts born-again Christians into historical agents who operate according to a typological theory of historical causality and agency.

Typology remains the reigning mode of reading the relationship between past and future events in many born-again Christian communities.

As we have seen in earlier chapters, what comes before prefigures or typifies what comes after; what comes after fulfills or completes what came before. New Testament events fulfill Old Testament events, and the New Testament establishes a point of view from which to read the Old Testament. Likewise, tribulation events, as foretold in both Testaments, establish a point of view from which to read current history, and that record, the testament of current history, is being written, is being enacted, now.

To the born-again ear, biblical stories are not allegorical, nor do they merely represent history. They *are* history, past and future. Nor are the storied events that prefigure and fulfill each other connected by mere cause and effect, for much might intervene between the two to change the outcome. The historical tissues connecting biblically storied events are the sinews of divine design, and nothing interrupts God's plan, by definition. Former events do not bring about later ones but rather reveal in advance God's plan. Christians through their actions today cannot alter God's plan, but they may be enacting it. Their actions may prefigure or typify the events of the Second Coming of the Lord. Thus, born-again Christians, through the lens of Bible prophecy, read history backwards. Future events, which are fixed and known, determine—if only in the sense of enabling Christians to imagine—the shape, the content, and the significance of present events and actions.

Revivalists understood these typological springs of action perfectly, for it was they, beginning with Dwight L. Moody in the late nineteenth century, who fashioned Bible prophecy's vision of the future into one of the most powerful evangelistic tools in their kit.[5] Not wanting to be here for the tribulation and knowing that it could begin at any minute, including this very minute, has convinced many malingering souls to receive Christ. And knowing that the Bible foretells the spread of the gospel to all nations before Christ comes again has motivated them to become world-class missionaries.

Harold Willmington, along with all "true Christians," is locked out of the tribulation events by the rapture, which will situate them on high, seated beside Jesus in Heaven, to watch the tribulation unfold below. Apart from getting saved, living piously, and evangelizing, nothing they do now matters. Yet they may, each in their own small way, hope them-

selves in, if not will themselves into, God's plan for the last days. So
Harold Willmington, in the thrall of his foreknowledge of the minute
details of tribulational geopolitics, buried a Bible in the Valley of Petra
on his tour of Israel.

For much of this century, fundamentalist and pentecostal preachers and
evangelists cited Bible prophecy on behalf of separatism as well as evangelism. They argued that modern theology and liberal Protestantism were
signs of the times, that is, Bible-based evidence that the world was approaching the end of history. The appropriate response of true Christians
to growing apostasy within the Church was ecclesiastical separation, so
preachers urged their people to foresake their denominations and form
new associations dedicated to Bible truth. Moreover, according to the
conventions of Bible prophecy preaching, all social reform activities, including politics, were folly. Before Christ returns for his millennial reign,
the course of history is hopelessly regressive. It cannot be reversed by
human actions. During the last days, the pace of social and moral deterio-
ration accelerates rapidly, so preachers counseled true Christians to maintain personal as well as ecclesiastical separation from the world and its
ways. It seemed that Bible prophecy "was and is primarily a *religious*
movement." Its "paramount appeal is to personal and religious sentiments," not social and political causes.[6]

Given this legacy, one might have expected preachers to abandon,
moderate, or minimize their apocalyptic rhetorics as they became more
politically active and outspoken during the 1970s and the 1980s. Eschatology, or the doctrine of last things, moreover, has long been a source of
division among American Protestants, and that too might have motivated
preachers to hold their prophetic tongues as they attempted to ally across
doctrinal lines. Indeed, officially, within the fundamentalist and pentecostal networks subscribing to Bible prophecy, there were no great doctrinal battles and no major eschatological shifts.[7] But unofficially, in the
realm of popular apocalypticism, preachers did not hold their tongues.
The late 1970s and 1980s were an apocalyptic boomtime, and politically
interested preachers were among the most ardent and productive voices.

Apocalyptic narrative frames and figures became the ground for a nationwide conversation among born-again Christians about current

events and what must be done. The conversation was not a small one. Christians for whom Bible prophecy is a matter of doctrine—largely fundamentalists and pentecostals—numbered ten to fifteen million in the 1980s. Another ten to fifteen million Christians—largely charismatics and conservative evangelicals—came to share the vision not as doctrinal but as narrative believers. In a word, Bible prophecy was the lens through which twenty to thirty million Bible-believing Christians in America read current history and the daily news.[8] Nor were these Christians a desperate lot, driven to their apocalyptic visions by the poverty or violence of their lives. Born-again Christians in America today have roughly the same class, educational, and occupational profile as the population as a whole. For these Christians, apocalypticism was not just a set of beliefs, conscious or unconscious. It was a specific narrative mode of reading history; Christians for whom Bible prophecy is true do not inhabit the same historical landscape as nonbelievers.

Popular apocalyptic voices multiplied and mingled during the 1970s and 1980s, and their story lines shifted in many small ways. Gradually, the many small changes effected a big change in the narrative pattern of Bible prophecy. It came to counsel American Christians to engage rather than disengage in the world, to take rather than disdain moral and political action during the last days of human history. Again, prophecy preachers and writers did not effect this transformation on the level of official doctrine. Instead, they altered the historical narratives, the folk histories, authorized by those doctrines. Nor would it be correct to say that millennial visions literally caused born-again Christians to mobilize politically in the 1980s. The relationship between vision and action was more oblique. Bible prophecy of the 1980s enabled them to read history in a particular way, and it enabled them to understand the significance of born-again activism in terms of God's unfolding plan for mankind. Reading this history backwards from the future, they knew it was time to act differently.

It was a dramatic rearrangement, if not reversal, of the terms in which Christians might imagine and shape themselves in the end-time. But it did not mean that suddenly Bible prophecy became a political tool or movement rather than a religious one. For one thing, its "appeal to personal and religious sentiments" persisted, undiluted. For another, there were ways in which Bible prophecy was already, and always had been, political. That is, it was always a kind of cultural politics. More precisely, it was always a kind of narrative politics.

Bible prophecy as it is practiced in everyday life is not so much a system or set of religious beliefs as it is a narrative mode of knowing current history. Current events and the daily news are not neutral, secular phenomena that exist independently and are subjected to religious interpretation by Christians. They are signs of the times. They are inside Bible-based history. They are evidence that God and his enemy are coming to final blows over the fate of the Jews and of all mankind.

Go to any one of the thousands of Baptist, Brethren, charismatic, pentecostal, and nondenominational churches in America for whom Bible prophecy is doctrine and listen to sermons and Bible studies on the end-times, the tribulation, and the millennium. Listen to the cornucopia of apocalyptic audiotapes; read prophetic articles and journals; browse through the brimming racks of books on prophecy in your local Christian bookstore. Take a look at the videos documenting the rapture and the tribulation. Explore the topic of Bible prophecy on the Internet and CD SOFTWARE.

Then talk to any of a wide variety of Bible-believing Christians about how God is dealing with America now. Ask them what the Bible says about the AIDS crisis, the New Age movement, satanic cults and demonic principalities, about the epidemic of abortion, pornography, homosexuality, divorce, crime, and drugs. Ask them about Israel, about what God has in store for Israel. Ask them about the Persian Gulf war, or the Mid-East peace treaty. Ask them what the election and reelection of Bill Clinton meant for America. Ask them about the North American Trade Agreement, General Agreement on Tariffs and Trade, the European Economic Community, about borderless travel between nations, the Internet, transnational business and finance, and UFOs and alien abductions.

If you listen to their sermons and read their publications on unfulfilled biblical prophecies, you will hear them talk about current events. If you ask them about current events, you will hear them talk about those events in terms framed by Bible prophecy. Popular apocalypticism is not always political in the sense of advocating specific actions that count as political in American culture, but it is always political. It is a kind of narrative politics that contests the dominant secular or modern voices of journalists and academics for control over the definition and meaning of current events and of history more broadly.

Whether the tense is biblical, present, or postrapture, popular prophecy produces a point of view from which history is narrated. It constitutes those on behalf of whom history is directed ("we") and those to whom history happens ("they"). Bible prophecy presents itself as a set of fixed doctrines or specific beliefs, but it is spoken as a complex, shifting, flexible, pervasive interpretive field, a wide range of narrative figures and frames. It is a living cultural narrative that maps out history, geopolitics, current events, the forces and trajectories of history, its agents, its benefactors, and its victims—all from a biblical point of view.

Theologically conservative Christians articulated a variety of Bible prophecy schemes during the 1980s. Some schemes foresaw no rapture of Christians and asserted that the tribulation in which Bible prophecies were being fulfilled was well under way. One scheme, called Christian Reconstructionism, asserted that, for true Christians alone, the Kingdom Age had already begun and they set about creating the elements of a Christian theocracy that would soon rule the world. By far the most important scheme for interpreting Bible prophecies, in terms of both doctrinal and narrative belief, was dispensationalism, or dispensational premillennialism. The scheme is premillennial because it argues that Christ will return before the millennium, not after, as postmillennial schemes assert. Dispensations are successive periods of human history, each one defined by a distinct mode, or covenant, by which men and women know God. In the current dispensation, called the Church Age, lasting from Christ's death to his Second Coming, we may know God through Christ alone.

These labels, however, do not identify the doctrine that most distinguishes dispensational prophecy from other prophetic schemes, namely, the doctrine of the rapture. The instantaneous rapture of all true Christians, dead and alive, will be an unambiguous event that ends history as we know it and starts the clock of biblical prophecy ticking again. The Bible contains dozens of unfulfilled prophecies and all of them will be fulfilled after the rapture. None of them will be fulfilled before, while

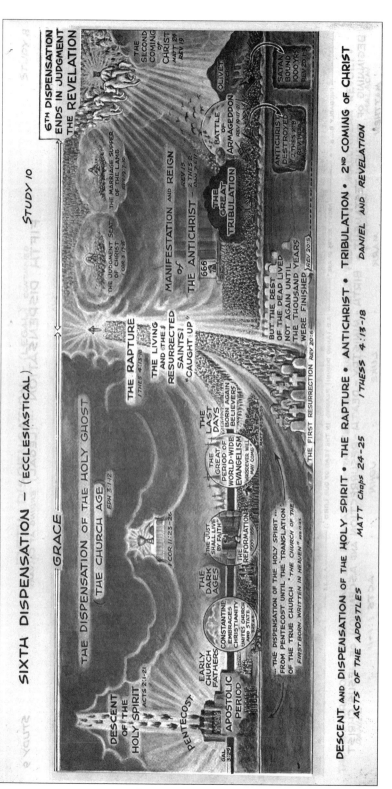

The dispensation of grace, or the Church Age, is the period between Pentecost and the Second Coming of Christ. We are currently living in the last days before the rapture of the saints, living and dead. (From Alfred Thompson Eade, *The New Panorama Bible Study Course.* © Baker Book House Co., 1975.)

Christians are still on earth. Hence orthodox dispensational believers are called "futurists"—because the fulfillment of their prophecies is always deferred, always in the future, never in the present. Belief in the rapture is often credited with removing Christians from history, of separating them, in the last days as surely as it removes them from earth during the tribulation. As we shall see shortly, however, not all rapture beliefs are the same, and there is more play in the rapture than meets the eye. Moreover, there were ways in which even the old-fashioned rapture belief that willfully separates Christians from history also engages them in history.

John Nelson Darby, an Irish Brethren preacher, invented what came to be called dispensationalism in the mid-nineteenth century. He brought it to America in the 1860s, and it spread through various networks of conservative preachers in Brethren, Baptist, Methodist, and Holiness denominations during the late nineteenth century. It was codified and reproduced in study Bibles, Bible institutes, and seminaries during the early twentieth century. And throughout this century it has been preached as doctrine in thousands of fundamentalist and pentecostal pulpits around the country. Dispensational prophecy was invented in the nineteenth century but not out of whole cloth. It reworked well-worn premillennial dreams that were circulating widely in Britain and America in the wake of the French Revolution. And it took on the task of asserting and protecting the veracity of Bible prophecies in the face of higher criticism with exceptional vigor.[9]

In particular, by positing a pretribulational rapture and by arguing that its date is not known and cannot be known, dispensationalists placed the fulfillment of unfulfilled Bible prophecies in the future and drew an incontrovertible line between now and then. As long as true Christians are on earth, unfulfilled Bible prophecies, strictly speaking, are not coming true. God will fulfill unfulfilled prophecies, which apply only to the fate of Jews and Israel, during the tribulation. Meanwhile, in the Church Age, speculations about how current events might be preparing the way for tribulation prophecies are just that, speculations. The Bible is literally silent about current history, about Christians in current history, and about America. In this way, the dispensationalist scheme exempted believers from having to prove one of the things that higher critics argued they had to prove if the Bible was "really true." Namely, they had to demonstrate that unfulfilled Bible prophecies have come true or are coming true. The scheme removed this onus but, through the pretribulational rapture which is so soon yet so absolutely not now, did so in a way that assured believers that Bible prophecies are perpetually about to come true.

Higher critical readings of the Bible not only undermined its transcendent authority, they also opened up ground for the development of modern scientific and historical discourses. "Modern" here means secular, that is, accounts of nature and history in which God played no part. During the late nineteenth and early twentieth centuries, modern historical discourses were fashioned in many settings—educational, literary, journalistic, popular, governmental, religious. Gradually they quarantined and displaced religion as a public arbiter of reality. Bible believers continuously contested and continue to contest this displacement. They specifically contest higher critical interpretations and their degradation of Bible truth in the form of official doctrines, popular polemics, cultural critiques, and counterdiscourses—among them dispensationalism. It is in this respect that dispensationalism, even when its speakers argue for radical separation from the world, works as a kind of cultural politics.

Modern nineteenth-century narratives of history—world history, social evolution, Marxist theories—were grand totalizing schemes of human history arranged into a sequence of epochs or stages or modes of production. Dispensational prophecy occupied the same terrain, the same grand narrative landscape, and also divided history into stages (dispensations), but the similarity ends there and the contrasts begin.

Modern biblical critics submitted the Bible to history and found the Bible wanting. Dispensationalists submit history to the Bible and find history wanting. Modern historians expelled deities from history. Dispensationalists entrench God and Satan and the conflict between them as the very pattern of history. The interpretive strategies deployed by dispensationalists as they biblicalize history and current events are the very ones most repugnant to the modern, critical eye and ear—biblical proof-texting, typologizing, and erratic literalizing, that is, sometimes reading for "plain meaning," other times not at all. And dispensationalists specifically read literally, plainly, the biblical texts modern readers find most disturbing, most incredible, and the most violent—the apocalyptic texts, which invariably foretell a dreadful death to any and all who reject their absolute truth.[10]

Dispensationalists, moreover, refuse the progressive story line of modern history and its implicit assumption that human nature is good and educable. Instead, they pronounce history, overall and in each of its stages, irreversibly regressive precisely because human beings are by nature sinful. The logic of dispensational history is not an unfolding of rational forces but rather a timeless struggle between good and evil that dwarfs human comprehension. The rise of the West, the development of capitalism, and the expansion of American hegemony are not central stories in world history. History instead is centered in the Middle East and narrated as a relentless road toward the fulfillment of biblical prophecies in which reemergent biblical empires plunge into war, all ultimately in pursuit of the apple of God's eye, Israel and the Jews—with whom God has some unfinished business.

All historical discourses constitute subjects—persons from whose point of view history is narrated and directed—as well as objects—historical events, periods, forces, and figures. Dispensationalism casts the subjects of modern theories of history, namely, enlightened men and women, as, at best, hapless agents of Satan, at worst, villains with demonic designs. It casts Bible-believing Christians, on the other hand, as temporary victims and the ultimate heroes of history. Christians, whether engaged or disengaged politically, emerge as the subjects of current history, and modern men and women become historical objects whose behavior requires study and explanation.

Features such as these render dispensational prophecy a kind of madness from the modern point of view, and that, I would argue, makes it compelling from a Bible-believing point of view. Dispensational premillennialism is a willfully mad rhetoric, and speaking it is a political act, a constant dissent, disruption, and critique of modern thought, specifically, of the modern theories of history that shape prevailing knowledge about world events, past and present, in America.

But dispensational prophecy would eventually yield to more literal politicking as well. How did this happen?

For one thing, even as doctrine, dispensational prophecy is not a uniform universe. There are long-standing disputes about many things, including the timing of the rapture. Few would claim to know when the rapture will occur, but many wonder whether it is in fact scheduled to happen before the tribulation. Perhaps it will happen during the tribulation. Or even at the end.[11] And then pentecostals and fundamentalists disagree about how supernatural gifts of the spirit square with Bible prophecy. Pentecostals interpreted the outbreaks of supernatural gifts after 1906 as signs that Christ was not only coming soon but arriving early in the Latter Rain of miracles. Indeed, they seemed more than signs—they were a fulfillment of prophecy that confirmed what many believed already, that the tribulation had begun and Christians would be raptured later. Fundamentalists, who honed to the orthodox, pretribulational rapture, not only disagreed, they interpreted such spiritual and doctrinal deviations as signs that Satan was loose in the church.

In addition to doctrinal disputes and disagreements such as these, there is enormous free play in the interpretative zone between current events and biblical imagery. That is, as a folk practice, Bible prophecy is a complex, flexible, shifting, polymorphous field of fluid stories. Everyone prognosticates, even those who believe strictly that no Bible prophecies are coming true in the present. Invariably, they find signs that prophecies are about to be fulfilled or have been partially fulfilled by current events. And sometimes events happen—in particular, the founding of the state of Israel in 1948, the Six-Day War in 1967—which so resemble pivotal Bible prophecies that the line between now and then begins to wobble badly.[12] The heterogeneity, instability, and partiality of dispensational narrative framings of current events undermine the absolute futurism of Bible prophecies. Again, even those who know for certain that no Bible prophecy can be fulfilled before the rapture find themselves wondering whether events are signs or fulfilled prophecies.

Queries such as these had always opened up gaps in dispensational premillennialism. The gaps, and new gaps and instabilities stimulated by other nondispensational schemes, became settings during the 1980s in which God showed Christians that he had more in store for them, and for American Christians in particular, than had hitherto been gathered. Christians were more directly implicated in Bible prophecies than had been previously supposed. It became clear that Christians would, after all, figure—ever so slightly perhaps—in the events that bring Christ back finally to stanch the dreadful downhill slide of history.

Such subtexts, side stories, and trajectories always characterized dispensationalism—it, as a living narrative tradition, never was as purely futurist as it presented itself to be. But, until the 1980s, these speculations did not congeal into a serious reinscription of Christians in history, and dispensational narratives seemed remorselessly to cast Christians in the wings of public life in America. During the 1980s, major popular Bible prophecy teachers, most of them dispensational preachers and writers, fashioned some bold new narrative frames that not only cast Christians onto history's center stage but, at least momentarily, reversed the course of immediate human history. The overall course of human history was still hopelessly regressive, but it seemed the present moment in America was a window in the end-times, a window in which Christians might actually affect the course of human history.

Although future events—the trials of the tribulation period—are absolutely fixed according to dispensational Bible prophecy, what Christians know about the history of the tribulation changes constantly as they update Bible prophecy in relation to current events. What is consistent is the instruction to read history backwards, to interpret the significance of present events as signs that tribulational prophecies are incipiently coming true, that future events are unfolding now. Bible prophecy thus landscapes the terrain of current history with events, figures, organizations, and trends that foreshadow the cataclysmic future known and fixed by God.

Before the 1980s, the sermons, writings, journals, films, tapes, and conferences on Bible prophecy, insofar as they addressed current history at all, were devoted to analyzing global events for any sign of gathering storms that would culminate in the war to end all wars in Israel: earthquakes, typhoons, famines, wars; arch-villainous leaders, and men who preached world unity and peace; global communications, the space age, and the computer revolution; rapid population growth, the rise and collapse of great economic systems; the Common Market, the Cold War, and the end of the Cold War; shifting political alliances and borders in Africa, Asia, Europe, and, above all, the Middle East. All these world-scale events and many more were seen as fashioning the future leaders and armies which will converge in the Valley of Megiddo.

What about America? What about domestic events? Christians, American and otherwise, following Matthew 28:19, had one duty, one task, to complete in current history: "Go ye therefore, and teach all nations, baptizing them in the name of the Father, and of the Son, and of the Holy

Ghost." In short, save souls. Aside from this, their Great Commission, Christians at home, in America, could only wait, live holy lives, support Israel, and read domestic events as signs of the times. Local signs of impending doom included any evidence of growth or development in education, technology, communications, transportation, population, material well-being, liberal theology, secularization, ecumenism, atheism, witchcraft, Satanism, astrology, Communism, crime, drug use, and divorce. The outcome of these domestic trends was straightforwardly the demise of America as an economic and political power in the last days. America might not even survive the rapture as a nation and, by dint of the Bible's silence to this effect, most certainly had no role in the events of the tribulation.

Some Bible prophecy preachers and writers plying political agendas in the 1980s forsook this conventional, pretribulational rapture scheme in whole or in part.[13] But many did not. Instead, they opened up Bible prophecy substantially as a mode of millennial dreaming. Major national preachers and writers, including Hal Lindsey, Tim LaHaye, Billy Graham, and Jerry Falwell, created a new kind of time within the end-times, a potentially progressive period in what was otherwise a hopelessly regressive era. The tribulation, as ever, was a time when God would judge the Jews according to immutable, irreversible, Bible prophecy. But the outlines of another, pretribulational, judgment, a "little tribulation" that preceded the great tribulation, also precipitated out, one that had not been clearly foretold in the Bible. The period before the rapture, the end-time, was now understood to be a time in which God would judge Christians, as opposed to Jews. And his judgment was not fixed by biblical prophecies. It was, in other words, reversible. If Christians responded to God's call through holy living *and* moral action, God would spare them and the American nation. Thus, with this little tribulation, Bible prophecy teachers opened a small window of progressive history in the last days, a brief moment in time when Christians could, and must be, agents of political and social change.

Hal Lindsey was by far the most popular Bible prophecy writer in the 1970s. *The Late Great Planet Earth*, published in 1970, reportedly sold eighteen million copies and was described by the *New York Times* as the "number-one non-fiction best-seller of the decade."[14] *The Late Great Planet Earth*, in line with other mainstream dispensational writing and preaching in the 1970s, aggressively constituted born-again Christians as a marginal people and America as a marginal nation in the end-times. In *The 1980s: Countdown to Armageddon*, published in 1980, Lindsey delivered one of the first small narrative shifts that would shortly open history to Christian action. He argued that, if Christians got involved in preserving this country, it was possible that America would remain a world power through the last days. Christians should live as if Jesus could come today, and *that means that we must actively take on the responsibility of being a citizen and a member of God's family. We need to get active electing officials who will not only reflect the Bible's morality in government, but will shape domestic and foreign policies to protect our country and our way of life.*[15] Lindsey did not build a reputation as a political writer, but his altered vision was a piece of the political placement of born-again Christians in historical time during the 1980s.

During the 1970s, preacher and best-selling author Tim LaHaye, like Lindsey, argued that American Christians had nothing else to do with their lives on this earth but pray, live right, and save souls. In 1980, he too began to construct a more elaborate end-time history, in his widely read book, *The Battle for the Mind*. LaHaye read domestic signs of the times as the effects of the liberal humanist effort to take over the country, an effort which amounted to what he called a pretribulation tribulation that could destroy America. However, it was not too late to save America. The great tribulation, he said, *is predestined and will surely come to pass. But the pre-Tribulation tribulation—that is, the tribulation that will engulf this country if liberal humanists are permitted to take total control of our government—is neither predestined nor necessary. But it will deluge the entire land in the next few years, unless Christians are willing to become much more assertive in defense of morality and decency than they have been during the past three decades.*[16] LaHaye urged Christians to pray and witness, as usual, and also to help the victims of humanism (unwed mothers, divorced partners, children being raised by single parents). Christians should join the national drive to register Christian voters, campaign for pro-moral candidates, and expose amoral candidates and incumbents. They should educate themselves and their friends, run for public offices, join pro-moral organizations, and speak out and write vigorously on moral issues. And they should contribute money to and work for pro-moral causes.

Billy Graham, in *Approaching Hoofbeats: The Four Horsemen of the Apocalypse*, published in 1984, also identified the present time as a kind of pretribulational tribulation. But Graham did not fashion himself a Christian Right preacher and did not articulate the right-wing agenda of the moment. The four horsemen Graham discerned were not signs of the true or great tribulation, which he still figured as irreversible. They were signs of a forthcoming judgment of God, an armageddon which was conditional, as opposed to the Armageddon which was unconditional. Graham's signs, the four horsemen, were familiar in their broad strokes— deception, war, famine, and plagues. But Graham's precise rendering of each sign did not square with the moralism of the day, and the Jesus who he promised would soon liberate us rang of the modernists' social gospel as well as the gospel of personal salvation. Indeed, in his rendering of war, Billy Graham was even more liberal. He targeted the nuclear arms race, declaring it sin and not God's will. He foresaw "total cosmocide," yet argued that war is not necessary and called on Christians to work for peace, an end to the nuclear arms race, and nuclear disarmament.[17] While Graham thus contributed to the bending of Bible prophecy toward social and political activism, his distinct articulation of that activism proved that the Christian Right's agenda did not follow logically or necessarily from the dispensational scheme of things to come.[18]

Jerry Falwell was of course the perceived leader of the Christian Right during much of the 1980s. As head of the Moral Majority, an organization that rode piggyback on networks of fundamental Baptist churches, Falwell was also the main mobilizer of doctrinally committed dispensational pastors and church people.[19] In his speech, his writings, and his actions during the 1980s, Falwell constructed grounds for political action where before he had argued there were no grounds. He enabled himself to say that Christian political activism mattered, that it was necessary, even that it would be efficacious, that Christians could and should change history. More than any of the other preachers, Falwell converted, or rather diverted, dispensational Bible prophecy from a rationale for separation from the world into a rhetoric of urgent engagement with the world.

Falwell argued that the moral crises which led him to organize the Moral Majority were simultaneously irreversible and reversible. They were signs of the times, indications that Christ is coming very soon, and matters that American Christians must take into their hands and try to do something about. *Is there hope for our country? I think so. I believe as we trust in God and pray, as we Christians lead the battle to outlaw abortion, which is murder on demand, as we take our stand against pornography, against the drug traffic, as we take our stand against the breakdown of the traditional family in America, the promotion of homosexual marriages, as we stand up for strong national defense so that this country can survive and our children and our children's children will know the America we've known.*

As we pray and preach and lead, Christian friends, I think there is hope that God may one more time bless America. . . . I believe that between now and the rapture of the Church, America can have a reprieve. God can bless the country and before the rapture I believe we can stay a free nation. . . . I believe that we can pray and that God is able to deliver us out of tribulations.[20]

World history is hopelessly regressive, careening pell-mell into Satan's maw, and it may seem as if America is plummeting down the same dark tunnel, but, not necessarily, not if Christians act now.

Here was Falwell's signature innovation in the Bible prophecy revisions of the 1980s: in order to do the only thing Bible prophecy prescribed them to do in the end-times, namely, spread the gospel to the four corners of the world, Christians must do more than that. Falwell reversed the political valence of the Great Commission prescription so that, instead of counseling against politics, it enjoined political action. He argued that unless born-again Christians acted politically they would lose their "freedom," religious and political, which was what enabled them to spread the good news at home and abroad, that is, to fulfill Bible prophecy.

This is the message Falwell gave his audience of students at Moody Bible Institute in 1984: *On the Christian campuses all over America kids are not only winning souls and loving the Bible and loving Christ, they're becoming good citizens. They are getting registered to vote; they are getting informed. They are determining that we are no longer going to lose by default. . . . We're going to do something, we're going to have revival, and we're going to have restoration, and the rebuilding of this great nation, so that out of a society and an environment of freedom we*

might evangelize the world in our generation, and before the rapture,
take a multitude on to heaven with us.[21]

The exact terms in which Falwell framed the conflict varied quite a
bit during the 1980s, but throughout his most politically visible and vocal
years he deployed the lens and logics of Bible prophecy to render, to
fashion and refashion, the historical moment, himself, his opponents, his
allies and audience, and their mission.

The core of the Christian Right in the 1980s was composed of men
and women who believed, consciously or unconsciously, in dispensational Bible prophecy. Their leaders, their spokesmen, the men (and, in
pentecostal and charismatic communities, women) who spoke church
people into political existence, spoke to them in historical terms framed
by Bible prophecy. They fashioned Christians—their identity and agency
as political actors—their opponents, and what counted as problematic,
symptomatic, emblematic, and ameliorative in terms of end-time and
tribulational scenarios. Although politically conservative born-again
Protestants fell far short of casting secular humanists out of power in
American society and politics, they succeeded in reenfranchising themselves politically and culturally. Their theorization of the little tribulation
did not simply reflect or effect the redistribution of political voice. It *was*
the shift, culturally speaking, insofar as it renarrated the pattern of history
and the place of born-again believers in that history.

Although we cannot foresee how Bible prophecy will mutate anew as the
third millennium begins, we know that shifts in prevailing apocalyptic
scenarios matter. If we listen carefully to them, to their details and nuances, we may learn how born-again Christians are resituating themselves
as agents in and of history. We may read their politics, and perhaps also
perceive the present and the future from their point of view.[22]

Contemporary Christians caught up in the little tribulation unfolding
before the rapture have a wider range of actions open to them than they
had before the 1980s. Their definition of holy living has been broadened
to include all sorts of political, cultural, economic, and moral actions,
actions which may stave off God's conditional judgment on America.
But the temporal window they opened up was in fact just a window. It
could be shut at any time. It did not alter the basic structure of history,
of either the end-times or the great tribulation, and Christians continue

to operate according to a specifically antimodern causal logic, one more divine than human. Their prayers and activities on behalf of saving America may stay God's hand, but they may not. And either way, the world is going to hell. Moreover, their moral campaigns also foreshadow and partake of the ultimate struggles between the forces of God and Satan during the great tribulation. Christians were thus perched precariously by the 1980s innovations in Bible prophecy within a bifocal vision of present history. Both Satan and God are winning, and Christians are double agents, at once inside and outside, the history of the future.

CHAPTER TEN

The Born-Again Telescandals

*Wrestling is not a sport, it is a spectacle. The spectator is not inter-
ested in the rise and fall of fortunes; he expects the transient image
of certain passions. Thus the function of the wrestler is not to win;
it is to go exactly through the motions which are expected of him.
What is expected is the intelligible representation of moral situations which are usually private.*

—ROLAND BARTHES, 1972

IN MARCH of 1987 the evangelist Oral Roberts
announced that God had told him to raise $8 million within two weeks.
If he failed, God said he would take Roberts "home." Roberts retreated
to his prayer tower, a space-needle-like structure located at the center of
Oral Roberts University in Tulsa, Oklahoma, to pray for the massive gift
that would spare his earthly life. A few days before his time was up, a
dog-track owner stepped forward with a check for $8 million, and Rob-
erts was released from his challenge. When queried whether he had
qualms accepting money that was earned by gambling, Roberts replied
that *all money is green.*

In retrospect, Oral Roberts's bold appeal was the opening episode in
a year-long sequence of scandals that rocked the world of televangelical-
ism in the late 1980s. Before the dust had settled around that episode,
its sequel took off with the exfoliating revelations of the misdeeds of
Jim and Tammy Faye Bakker. There were multiple charges of financial
misconduct against their Praise the Lord ministry (PTL)—of deceitful
fund-raising practices, missing millions, and hare-brained building plans.

Jim was accused of sexual misconduct—of having a tryst with Jessica Hahn and possibly engaging in homosexual activities. Both Jim and Tammy Faye were accused of extravagant bad taste—of owning several huge, opulently appointed houses, of having a carpeted, air-conditioned dog house, of tacky melodrama in their public appearance and performance. The revelations, which continued to erupt for months, were compounded by the entry onto the scene of Jerry Falwell and his entourage in the role of white/black knight. Was he there to save Jim and Tammy Faye's ministry or to take it over—that was the question. Finally, Jim Bakker stood trial on charges of financially defrauding his partners, the thousands of men and women who had bought shares in his theme park ministry, Heritage USA. After much histrionics and moralizing, Jim was convicted by a jury of peers and sentenced by the judge to ten years in jail.

Some time after the PTL revelations died down but before Jim Bakker was tried, early in 1988, the third and final major scandal broke out when Jimmy Swaggart was caught red-handed visiting a prostitute in New Orleans by a fellow Assemblies of God preacher, who, reportedly motivated by revenge to pursue long-circulating rumors about Swaggart, was tailing him. The prostitute Swaggart visited joined the chorus with her exclusive story in *Playboy*, then others stepped forward to say they "knew" Jimmy Swaggart. On national television, Swaggart confessed his sins and asked Jesus Christ, his wife, his son, his family, and his church people to forgive him. A few months later he was caught again in New Orleans with another prostitute.

Pat Robertson's campaign for the presidency in 1988 was a risky venture under any circumstances. In the context of the televangelical scandals, it acquired the air of yet another scandal. Journalists scoured his background, organizations, and oratory for infelicities which, however minor or however well Robertson finessed them, inevitably loomed larger as they resonated with the more sensational infelicities of his fellow televangelists. More generally, the very idea of a televangelist running for the nation's highest public office, of his orchestrating his bid for delegates in the nation's primaries through local churches, of his pronouncing on public policy from an aggressively partisan religious point of view, was unseemly. It was especially so for non-born-again Christians, but many Bible believers also voiced qualms. They had been able to accept the politicking of New Christian Right preachers as a kind of moral activism, but they were unable to abide a preacher's entry into partisan electoral politics. Thus, alongside the scandals surrounding the sexual and financial misconduct of his co-televangelists, many Americans read Robertson's move on the presidency as itself an instance of political misconduct, that is, as another piece of that scandalous whole.

As a representative of the prior generation of high-profile national televangelists, Oral Roberts was a peripheral figure in the 1987–1988 scandals. The Bakkers, Swaggart, Falwell, and Robertson, on the other hand, were the central figures in the reign of the televangelists. At the time, it seemed like the controversy that embroiled them for two years spelled the end of televangelism and the political movement associated with it, the New Christian Right. In some ways, the crisis did bring to an end the televangelical reign. But it did not constitute the kind of comprehensive finale that was effected by the Scopes trial in 1925. In fact, I would argue, the moment had the opposite symbolic effect. Instead of marking the exile, or reexile, of conservative Protestants from public life, it marked their installation, or reinstallation, as routine participants in the cultural and political life of the nation.

Episodes of revival and religious enthusiasm in the history of American Protestant evangelicalism frequently have been occasioned, and sometimes have been cut short, by scandal and controversy. Scandals are an extreme instance of the cultural instability that is an integral and productive force in American Protestant evangelistic preaching. One route to greatness, at least as measured in terms of the magnitude of one's reputation, available to evangelistic preachers is controversy. As we have seen, evangelistic preachers narrate and act out strategic indeterminacies—gaps, excesses, anomalies, breaches—that their followers harmonize and critics intensify. An evangelist's survival depends on his or her skill at maneuvering the gaps in a way that enables their followers to read miracles where their critics read scandals. From time to time, an evangelist produces gaps that his people cannot or will not close up or harmonize, and then they too read scandal, not miracle, and fall away.

The last time scandals broke out among American Protestants on a scale comparable to 1987–1988 was in the late 1950s and early 1960s. Charges of gimmickry, personal ambition, drunkenness, womanizing, extravagant living, fraudulent fund-raising tactics, financial mismanagement, and fake miracles broke up the postwar tent healing revival.[1] There were trials then too, the most famous in 1956, of Jack Coe, for practicing medicine without a license. The charges were dismissed, but for his followers and co-evangelists a much more troubling verdict came in when Coe was diagnosed shortly after with polio and died. What was God trying to tell them?[2]

Around the edges of every preacher of renown who taps the narrative force of controversy, there is gathered another force that routinizes scandals in American evangelical Protestantism, namely, "the market for religious controversy."[3] A preacher's critics both inside and outside the faith have a stake in widening gaps, deploring excesses, intensifying anomalies and missteps, and in using every means possible to disseminate—to spread, to advertise—the bad news. The audience for such conflicts has been enormous throughout American history. During the nineteenth century, religious controversies of all kinds—about doctrinal disputes, failed prophecies, unusual practices, and preacherly misconduct—became a commercial source of entertainment for the American public. The main stage for the controversies, the nation's newspapers, expanded to include radio and television during the twentieth century. Thus the major narrators of religious controversies were, and still are, the nation's journalists. Insofar as religious controversies attract mass audiences, they are not simply news. They are also big business.

So the televangelical scandals of 1987–1988 were in several senses business as usual within American evangelicalism. Their outcomes were also predictably dire. As the reputations of the principal scandalizing evangelists, the Bakkers and Swaggart, collapsed, so did the sacrificial giving that funded their empires and, hence, so did the empires. The Bakkers' operation folded completely when Jim Bakker went to jail, and Jimmy Swaggart's domestic empire shriveled. The other great national televangelical empires also shrank as their financial supporters shifted their contributions to their church outreaches and smaller parachurch organizations which seemed easier to monitor and less driven by personalities that might run amok.

The decline of the major national televangelists and their empires marked a collective end as well, for they were not simply replaced by the next generation. Other national television preachers did emerge, but they occupied much less television time, and they were smaller scale and more modest in other respects. The era of flamboyant, high-profile, national-celebrity televangelists was over. Their crises and decline triggered a wider cleansing movement within the community of born-again Christian institutions. Sermons and articles and books poured out for years examining the spiritual and practical sources of the crisis, speculating on the role of Satan, and attempting to set the houses of God in order once more.[4] The decline of the national televangelists in the late 1980s, finally, also marked the end of the period of their public leadership of the New Christian Right.

So again, at first blush, the scandals would seem to be the modern dream come true: pompous misplaced preachers brought down by their own greed, lust, and hypocrisy, a moment of predictably grotesque narrative closure on a pesky little chapter in the unfolding subtext of modernity marching on. But the moment did not, after all, reiterate the symbolic work of the Scopes trial in 1925. Had it done so, the downfall of the televangelists and their empires would have reinstated the cultural opposition between religious orthodoxy and secular modernity. Religious orthodoxy would have been restigmatized as unfit for the modern world, and conservative Protestants would have withdrawn, retreated, to a lower profile role in national life. Clearly, that did not happen. Instead of reiterating the symbolic effect of the Scopes trial, the scandals and controversies of 1987–1988 reversed its effect. Or rather, they publicized the fact that the cultural verdict of the Scopes trial had been reversed. The era of relatively unrivaled modern religious and secular dominance in public life was over.

In order to examine this effect of the televangelical scandals, we must focus not on the preachers' misdeeds but on how those misdeeds were represented on television and in the newspapers. Focusing on the scandals as representational struggles—that is, focusing on the *telescandals*—brings into view the scandalized as well as the scandalizers. The parallel with the Scopes trial becomes apparent. Once again two sides contested for control over public representations of what had been called Fundamentalism and was now called born-again Christianity. In addition to the reputations of the televangelists, images, value judgments, story lines, points of view, social identities and rank, and history itself were at stake. Throughout the 1980s, born-again Christians had contested the commonsense, cultural narrative of modern America as intrinsically secular.

The telescandals, instead of marking the defeat of born-again Christians, were the moment in which their revolt reached its most fevered pitch.

The telescandals fragmented the illusion that Fundamentalism, or born-again Christianity, was a homogeneous whole. They accentuated the similarities between Fundamentalist and Modern, between born-again Christian and the modern religious and secular world. And they stripped away the storied ploys that rendered modern America secular, the ones that would hide it as a story and present it instead as history, as objective reportage, as reality. The outcome of these representational movements was more like a spectacle than a story—a narrative-free zone in which history, fiction, and the Bible were equivalent sources of narrative figures and frames, and the boundaries between religious and secular, fictional and factual, authors and characters, participants and observers were called into question, interrogated, transgressed, suspended, relocated, and multiplied. The effect was to disrupt—indeed, to deconstruct—dramatically the terms of secular modernity, to effect "the end" of its hegemonic regime and to complete the process of reinscribing Fundamentalism begun in the late 1970s with the emergence of born-again Christianity and the New Christian Right.

Ted Koppel represented the voice of modernity for millions of Americans throughout the born-again telescandals, which yielded sixteen blockbuster *Nightline* programs. In May 1988, he aired an hour-long prime-time special report intended to settle once and for all, as he put it, "what this has got to do with." None of the scandalizers (Roberts, the Bakkers, or Swaggart) were present, nor were the scandalous events reviewed in any descriptive way. This particular episode in the telescandals was for exegeses, commentary, and midrash by and for the scandalized.

The title of the show, "The Billion Dollar Pie," its opening collage of talking heads, and Koppel's initial sally of remarks all had the same vector: to unmask televangelism, to reveal its real and vulgar business nature, rendering not just the scandalizers but all its preachers false prophets, worthy of chastisement and a touch of satire.[5] In fact, what Koppel produced was a bald caricature of social-scientific explanation, one that undermined his own ostensible detachment, that inspired a cascade of mixed metaphors, wild intertextualities, and backtalk from his guests, and began to erase the very distinction between him and "them" which he had to establish in order to have any authority at all.

In the opening visual and verbal collage of "The Billion-Dollar Pie," Ted Koppel laid out the show's thesis. Images flashed across the screen—proliferating icons of television ministries, a pie with money-colored filling, a graph depicting the declining birthrate across the century—while Koppel talked about televangelism's "shrinking donor base." Then Jack Sims, a "religious-market analyst," vividly narrated another version of the thesis, punctuated midway by a checkerboard of talking heads from the PTL telescandal:

> TED KOPPEL [voice-over]: In all, there are sixteen hundred television ministers. Sixteen hundred. And of the $1.5 billion grossed annually by television ministries, just three of them—Pat Robertson's, Jimmy Swaggart's, and Jim Bakker's—took in close to $500 million. It's a big pie, but the slices are anything but evenly divided. And because the birthrate in this country dipped sharply in the 1930s, there are fewer people in their fifties replacing those among the big givers who are dying off. The donor base is shrinking. And for televangelism, rocked by scandals, it couldn't have come at a worse time.
>
> JACK SIMS (religious-market analyst): Last March, it was as if the aging evangelicals were like dinosaurs that walked onto an iceberg. The end of March, when Roberts announced that he was being kidnapped by God and held for ransom, the iceberg broke off and began to float south. Atop the iceberg, the aging evangelical dinosaurs began to fight.
>
> MAN [news clip of John Ankerberg]: The Reverend Bakker has been involved in episodes with prostitutes, and he has also been involved in homosexual incidents.
>
> REV. JIM BAKKER (televangelist) [news clip]: If anyone has raised these charges against me, I want them to come forward publicly with this proof.
>
> REV. JIMMY SWAGGART (televangelist) [news clip]: I don't appreciate preachers that get mixed up in adultery and every other type of sin that one can imagine, and then blaming Jimmy Swaggart for it.
>
> MAN (Bakker's lawyer) [news clip of Norman Gruttman]: There is smellier laundry in his hamper than the laundry that he thought was in Reverend Bakker's.

> REV. BAKKER [news clip]: There was a plot to hostilely take over the PTL by Jimmy Swaggart.
>
> REV. JERRY FALWELL (televangelist) [news clip]: If he decides he wants to come back, he'll preside over a funeral. The funeral of his ministry.
>
> MRS. BAKKER [news clip]: I wake up every morning wishing that they had killed me.
>
> REV. FALWELL [news clip]: Their own clandestine behavior brought this terrible thing upon them.
>
> MR. SIMS: But the real story of American religion is not the dinosaurs, it's the iceberg. It's floating south and melting, and all the aging evangelical electronic dinosaurs are going to die.

Jack Sims, himself an odd crossbreed—religious market analyst—mixed up Darwin, Disney, and the Book of Revelation in his tale of electronic evangelical dinosaurs in a way that foreshadowed the hybrid scene setting and boundary blurring that ensued. Koppel greeted his television audience from a huge, plush, packed Memphis church and introduced his guest preachers: Jack Wimber, Jerry Falwell, E. V. Hill, James Kennedy, Jack Hayford, James Robison, and, via satellite on a television screen, Robert Schuller. Everyone—Koppel, the celebrity preachers, the satin-robed choir, and the brimming congregation—seemed at home in this pastiche of the religious and the secular, news and entertainment, postmodern electronics and a premodern God. But it was hardly a propitious setting for a serious discussion of the complex conditions that brought about the televangelical scandals. Koppel, leaving Jack Sims out in the cold, abruptly shifted metaphoric gear and called his guests "hogs at the trough" in his opening punch. Within minutes he was caught in a quagmire of pious backtalk—Falwell essentially retorted to Koppel, "So are you," then Hill and Hayford mystified all by wrestling over the sinfulness of sex.

> MR. KOPPEL [on camera]: I must tell you that over the past couple of years, as many of you know, we have done a great many programs on *Nightline* on some of these problems that televangelists have been having, particularly the Bakkers and Jimmy Swaggart. You know what the sources of our information are? Not private detectives, not our own great reportorial skills. Other preachers. You guys. Other preachers. I conclude from this that what's going on here is a battle royal in the business world.

This has got nothing to do with saving souls. This has got nothing to do with evangelical Christianity. What this has got to do with is a huge billion-dollar pie. [Applause] Or to put it in a somewhat different sense, we've got a bunch of hogs at the trough here. And they see that one way of elbowing the other hogs away from the trough is this business of sexual infidelity.

REV. FALWELL: That's true. And of course that's going on today, as you well know in the journalism world, the business world, and every vocation under the heaven, which in no way vindicates or justifies this happening in the religious world.

REV. E. V. HILL (Mount Zion Baptist Church): This is reducing sin to sex. And so when you say, "I've sinned," everybody wants to know, "Who'd you have?" But I submit that there are—and you're dealing with it—I submit that there are some sins here in Proverbs 6:16. The last one closes out with, "He that soweth discord among the brotherhood." And here are the sins that God hates the most, so he wrote, and sex ain't in it. [Applause, laughter] Sex ain't in it.

MR. KOPPEL: See, you're, you're missing—

REV. HILL: Wait a minute, let me just say it.

MR. KOPPEL: Reverend Hill—

REV. HILL: ". . . a lying tongue—

MR. KOPPEL (motions "time-out" with hands): —hold it, hold it.

REV. HILL: —. . . innocent blood [Applause, laughter], wicked imagination, running into mischief, and sowing discord." He hates these the most, and sex ain't on the list. And we have towns and churches torn apart because of lying lips and sowing discord, as you said, among the ministry.

MR. KOPPEL: Yeah. Now, what I—

REV. JACK HAYFORD (Church on the Way): I don't doubt the validity of that list, that's scriptural. But I would recall to you, dear brother, there's another list I read somewhere of ten, and sex is on it.

MR. KOPPEL: What I'm trying to get at here is money. We're not just talking about sins. We're talking about people who are competing for millions and tens of millions of dollars. [Applause]

And so the show went on, the metaphors slipping and sliding; the preachers resisting and disrupting Koppel's withering story line as they drew from a spellbinding panoply of theological voices crafted through the ages to thwart each other and to astound and stupefy unbelievers. The show dissolved first into a mishmash of arguments among the preachers over fine points of Scripture, doctrine, and ecclesiology, and then into a kind of staged populist inquisition as members of the audience stood and leveled Bible-based charges against the electronic preachers, who in turn spoke back in a splendid jumble of artfully humble voices.

Koppel never lost his composure, but he certainly lost control of the discussion as well as his privileged position as the man who would un- mask these bandits once and for all. Surely, television production values interrupted Koppel's effort to expose the material causes, the ostensible reality, behind the scandals. That is, he himself, Mr. Modern Secularity, was torn between story and spectacle. But the spectacularizing forces that disrupted the cultural story line that excluded Fundamentalists from modern America—on Koppel's show, in the telescandals, and through- out the decade of born-again rhetorical eruptions—were much bigger than television. Far from coming across as premodern anachronisms, the televangelical empires emerged as often quarrelsome, always proliferating religious vanguards, first, of a hitherto hidden born-again world which had become a kind of frontier zone in which premodern, modern, and even postmodern cultural forms were intermingling and reproducing wildly; and, second, of a born-again cultural diaspora, a movement into the unborn-again world that would blur so many of the boundaries be- tween the two worlds that it might seem only a miracle could resurrect the myth of modernity.

The story lines of secular modernity depended on a totalizing rhetorical opposition between the social worlds and worldviews grounded in super- natural faith on the one hand and in science and reason on the other. While the telescandals seemed to ratify that opposition in a general way, they also flooded the country with images and information that steadily undermined and subverted it. With each new scandalous revelation in 1987 and 1988, the nation's press gathered up and repackaged the shock- ing—from a modern point of view—facts about white conservative Prot- estants in America and delivered them anew to their television, radio, and print audiences. Thirty, forty, or fifty—depending on how you count them—million Americans were "born-again." They are everywhere, flourishing where least expected, in big cities, in areas of rapid economic growth and social transformation. They occupy all manner of occupations, all echelons of society. They have built a vast infrastructure of schools, colleges, and universities, and they are fully present and increasingly vocal inside the nation's public school systems, liberal arts colleges, and research universities. Their churches, denominations, networks, and parachurch organizations are growing and seem especially robust and booming alongside the majority of mainline white Protestant churches and denominations that are steadily declining.

Such facts, which have gradually lost their shock value, were public glimpses of the social and historical landscape of white conservative Protestantism in America that had been veiled by the myths of secular modernity. The telescandal narrators did not, could not, reconstruct Fundamentalism as a uniformly strident, backward, rural, southern, uneducated, mindless mass stuck in the past. It was multifarious. It had many names and a history, or, rather, many histories. And those histories were as complex and as enmeshed as the histories of other American peoples in the modern, late modern, or postmodern macrohistories of capitalism, nation and state making, technology, and cultural production.

Televangelism was born in the 1940s and 1950s. Its first two giants, Billy Graham and Oral Roberts, represented neither the fundamentalist nor the pentecostal movement but rather their postwar offspring: evangelicalism and the charismatic movement. Both Graham and Roberts were pioneers in the use of television for evangelism and faith healing. Most of the electronic churches that dominated the airwaves in the 1980s also had their origins in the 1940s and 1950s, in relatively modest local churches and ministries. By the 1970s, hundreds of entrepreneurial pastors and evangelists had parlayed their local operations into corporations, extending their reach far beyond the limits of church walls and local crusades via radio, television, music, and publishing operations. By the time of the PTL crisis, the dozen biggest electronic empires took in hundreds of millions a year, mostly in the form of small contributions. They each employed over a thousand men and women and paid out many millions of dollars in payroll every month. They hired ad agencies, market consultants, and corporate lawyers, and their preacher bosses justified their six-figure salaries by saying they were paid no more than the CEOs of other major corporations.

The electronic empires, then, were, as Koppel had suggested, as much businesses as they were churches. Indeed, the 1980s electronic churches were anomalous, mercurial, protean creatures, at once religious, economic, and political. Far from being premodern relics, atavisms of an earlier age, the televangelists were a late capitalist crossbreed of symbolic production, consumption, and social reproduction. They were harbingers of an emerging political economic order in which the stakes were collective identities, cultural ideas, and symbols as well as profits, markets, political power, and lost souls.

Most of the second-generation of television preachers were charismatics or pentecostals, and many of them, most notably Pat Robertson and Jimmy Swaggart, also mixed in selected fundamentalist forms of faith, revival, and activism in the world. Jerry Falwell and Jim Bakker, on the other hand, kept the fundamentalist and pentecostal forms separate and, more than any of the other television preachers, exaggerated their distinguishing features—Falwell was Mr. Modern Fundamentalism and Bakker was Mr. Postmodern Pentecostalism.[6]

Jerry Falwell's world in Lynchburg, Virginia, was a very serious, solid, industrious kind of place. The language, architecture, ceremonies, and rites of daily life of Thomas Road Baptist Church communicated its singular commitment to reach out to a world of lost and dying men and to win their souls to Christ. What distinguished Falwell from his fellow fundamentalists from the beginning was his entrepreneurial zeal. The same year in which he founded his church, 1956, he started his television ministry, and by 1967 he was broadcasting his Sunday service as the Old-Time Gospel Hour. In other words, he used television "literally," to broadcast his church services exactly as they were performed. Later, he upscaled the services somewhat with light pop gospel tunes and select Christian celebrity singers, but he never really formatted his shows for television; he never used television to generate its own realities. Likewise, although his message opened up to more current events and moral issues, it never strayed too far from its fundamentalist gospel core. Above all, Falwell used television to spread the Word, the linear story of Christ's death, burial, and resurrection, which offered irreversible transformation to all who would accept it. Ignoring television's built-in preference for visually dramatic performance, Falwell seemed to be all story and no spectacle.

Through it all, as we have seen, Jerry Falwell and his fundamentalist allies were fashioning a distinct Christian conservative middle-class counterculture and using higher education, the national news, and national politics to chip away at the cultural hegemony of its opposite number, the alleged secular, liberal middle class. This was very serious business. Jerry Falwell, his empire, and his allies stood for production, hard work, restraint, sacrifice, delayed gratification, steady growth, contained crises, hierarchy, male dominance, sexual repression, obedience to Godly others, the Word, narrative structure and authority, fixed identity, place, authenticity, depth, and centeredness.

Meanwhile, another entrepreneurial movement was emerging in pentecostal Christendom during the 1950s, 1960s, and 1970s, one that turned all those serious fundamentalist terms upside down. This movement, drawing from somewhat lower class factions than Falwell's movement, reached its apogee in Jim and Tammy Faye Bakker's Heritage USA, a kind of late modern or postmodern pentecostal mecca. Their "inspirational theme park" conspicuously celebrated consumption, play, excess, indulgence, immediate gratification, wild swings of growth and crisis, antihierarchy, feminization, polymorphous sexuality, the godly powers of ordinary men and women, visual images, spectacle and narrative fragmentation, disposable identities, movement, artifice, surfaces, and decenteredness.[7]

The cultural and theological reversals at Heritage USA were not accidental. The significant "cultural other" against which prosperity pentecostals fashioned their discourse and practice was not the world defined by the liberal, secular middle class, but the world defined by fundamentalism. The early healing evangelists of the 1940s and 1950s had themselves worked against the grain of the more fundamental voices of pentecostal church pastors, but in the late 1970s, Jim and Tammy Faye Bakker set out to build a little world in the image of their version of "the positive gospel." Jim Bakker liked to compare his kingdom to the camp meetings of his youth: *During boyhood summers in Michigan, Jim Bakker attended camp meetings where he had his most moving spiritual experiences in an old tabernacle with a sawdust floor. Even then, looking beyond the stuffy cabins with lumpy mattresses, looking beyond the muddy swimming holes and "outdoor plumbing" he dreamed of a day when God's people could come together in beautiful, pleasant surroundings.*

Aware that lifestyle was changing in twentieth century America, Jim knew that drab, outmoded campgrounds would no longer appeal to Christians. . . . God impressed on Jim . . . the need to carry the spirit of the camp meeting movement into the twenty-first century, and the concept of Heritage USA came into being.[8]

So, in Fort Mills, South Carolina, Heritage USA became a place, a language, and a practice that performed a ceaseless if implicit critique of fundamentalism's restraint, its sacrificial logic, its obsession with authority, hierarchy, and rules. Heritage USA was an ensemble of replicas, relics, facades, imitations, simulations, props, and sets drawn from biblical Jerusalem, the Old West, small-town America, Hollywood, modern suburbs, and tourist resorts. Nothing simply was itself; everything was palpably a production, a reproduction, or a performance.

Just inside the entrance to Heritage USA, you could visit Billy Graham's "actual" boyhood home. In the study, on the wall, a series of photographs depicted Billy's home being dismantled, brick by brick, and rebuilt on the edge of Heritage USA property, the displacement and appropriation of Graham's home having become part of its significance.[9]

Heritage's centerpiece was a "man-made water park" with a three-story waterslide. Nearby was the Grand Hotel and Main Street shopping mall, a hodgepodge of pastel-colored Victorian and colonial surfaces, and down the road past the water park, the tennis courts, condos, and campgrounds, healing and prayer were available twenty-four hours a day in the Upper Room, an "exact replica" of the building where Jesus and his disciples had their Last Supper, except that this one looked like a replica. Across the road was another self-proclaiming replica, an ancient amphitheater where several nights a week the Passion Play was performed, complete with special effects, new characters (mainly, Satan incarnate), and new episodes, all intended to "heighten the dramatic tension" of Christ's final days.

Church services and camp meetings at Heritage were held in the television studio and an adjacent auditorium, which in no respect resembled a church. The Bakkers never used television to represent the traditional rituals; instead, their television realities, including their TV personalities, broke through the screen and expanded into the empirical world. The accent was always on performance, visuals, excess, spectacle, not on words or the Word, at least not as fundamentalists understood the

Word. The linear, irreversibly life-changing story of Christ's death, burial, and resurrection, of suffering and of sacrifice, gave way to a cornucopia of miracle stories of God's healing, restoration, infinite love, and bountiful gifts.

From the beginning, Heritage troubled many Christians who noticed the internal countercultural message—its suppression of sacrifice theology—but few guessed how far the Bakkers had gone in the direction of antinomian heresy, of rejecting all earthly restraints. At the time of their fall, the Bakkers not only promised their partners material abundance and well-being but were refining a gospel of infinite forgiveness, a folk theology that seemed almost to sanction sinning by guaranteeing God's perpetual forgiveness in advance.

It is not so surprising then that the two folk theologies represented by Falwell and the Bakkers' televangelical empires cast the born-again scandals in dramatically different terms. The fact that this conflict assumed center stage in the PTL crisis, however, virtually undermined the possibility that the voice of the third folk tradition entering into the fray, that of secular modernity, would ever get a solid grip on the telescandals.

The PTL scandals of 1987 and 1988 spread two grand dramas across America's television screens. One was composed of the sensational misdeeds of Jim and Tammy Faye Bakker—his night with Jessica Hahn, her blackmailing him, more sexual improprieties, gross financial misconduct, tax fraud, bankruptcy, million-dollar spending sprees, and so on. The other drama was born when Jerry Falwell's friendly takeover of PTL turned into a hostile one and launched a gaudy series of media skirmishes, known at the time as a "holy war," between the two Christian camps during which Falwell's forces and the press successively revealed and endlessly reiterated, interrogated, and dissected the Bakkers' misdeeds before a national audience.

The cultural theorist Roland Barthes might have said the PTL scandal was a boxing match that kept dissolving into a television wrestling match. An orderly bout, based on the demonstration of excellence and directed, like a story, toward an outcome—the definitive downfall of the Bakkers—kept evolving into a more chaotic bout in which each moment was immediately intelligible as spectacle and the most natural outcome was baroque confusion. As Barthes put it, "Some fights, among the most successful kind, are crowned by a final charivari, a sort of unrestrained fantasia where the rules, the laws of the genre, the referee's censuring and the limits of the ring are abolished, swept away by a triumphant disorder which overflows into the hall and carries off pell-mell wrestlers, seconds, referee and spectators."[10]

Perhaps the essence of spectacle is the loss of a unitary authorial point of view, a proliferation of points of view such that stories pile up fantastically, realities clash and mingle indiscriminately, and the total effect of everyone vying for narrative control is an irrepressible sense of events-out-of-control, of confusion, disorder, and a constant instability of genres, borders, roles, rules. The disordering forces at work in the PTL telescandal that kept it from settling into a singular storied tradition were, first, the unholy and profoundly unstable authorial alliance between the fundamentalist and journalistic points of view; second, the spectacularizing desires of the narrators themselves—their allusory excesses, feuds, and histrionics; third, the ever-anarchic words and deeds of the scandalizers; and fourth, a fistful of competing sideshows, of secular scandals grabbing for public attention. Such forces spectacularize—in this instance, specifically disrupting efforts to narrate the scandals from a modern point of view—by destabilizing the boundary between Fundamentalist and Modern, by highlighting the processes of fabrication, of fabulation, and by constantly juxtaposing contradictory points of view.

Take, for example, the profusion of allusions. In measured doses, literary and historical allusions help "make sense" of events by suggesting narrative frames that, in effect, interpret characters, plots, subplots, motives, climaxes, tragic flaws, and moral meanings. In excess, they produce "a sort of unrestrained fantasia." During the PTL crisis, the Bakkers, for their part, were figured, among others, as Elmer Gantry, Imelda and Ferdinand Marcos, Adam and Eve, David and Bathsheba, Ivan Boesky, Catholics buying and selling indulgences, and Gary Hart. Falwell, meanwhile, was figured—usually, he figured himself—as, among others, a Protestant reformer, Lee Iacocca, Nathan, the Securities and Exchange Commission, God in the Garden after the Fall, and Christ cleaning out the money changers. The scandal as a whole was compared to *The Scarlet Letter*, the sinking of the *Titanic*, the Book of Revelation, the television series *Dynasty*, and the war between Iran and Iraq. Such hyperfiguration spectacularized events by calling attention to the narrative process, to the narrators as "telling stories" and therefore "having a point of view," which helped break whatever spell of truth they might have cast.

The major narrators also kept bringing each other into focus as narrators by calling attention to their "motives," "interests," and "biases." Journalists made several attempts to "unmask" Jerry Falwell, to find evidence of his plotting to take over PTL, and constantly speculated about his "real motives" (for example, he wanted to appropriate the PTL television network, or the PTL audience, or simply have the free prime-time exposure). Falwell, of course, argued back that, at least when reporters turned on him, they were displaying their secular liberal bias. In the process, the press lost some of its pretense of standing outside the fray, detached, disinterested, objective, reporting events. At the same time, Falwell's pose as a selfless man of God was compromised.

Nor were the press and Falwell above all histrionics. Early on Ted Koppel and his *Nightline* crew orchestrated the most frenetically embroiling episode of the telescandals per se, a three-night series of shows in late May 1987. The series opened with a full, heated, but indecisive, airing of the charges against Falwell. The second show was the first live interview with Jim and Tammy Faye Bakker since the scandal broke, and it was pure spectacle. Twenty-three million people watched the Bakkers be themselves, with a touch of remorse and lots of "love." The series concluded, inconclusively, with a "prognosis" on televangelism, featuring, of all people, Jerry Falwell.

Falwell produced his own fireworks on the morning of the third day of the *Nightline* series by calling a press conference to display evidence that the Bakkers were not truly repentant. He waved a letter from the Bakkers asking for money, homes, cars, benefits, guards, and a full-time maid, and he told a new version of that night in the Clearwater motel with Jessica Hahn, exactly what Jim and his confederates, John Wesley Fletcher and an unnamed third man, did to her. As performances go, it was still rather rhetorical, but nonetheless stunning—spectacular, in a way—to hear the sordid details spill from Falwell's lips. His role as chief of Heritage USA also inspired some performances from the usually stiff Falwell, reaching a peak when he finally, on September 10, 1987, slid down Heritage Island's three-story Typhoon waterslide. After posing with a person dressed up as "Allie the Alligator" atop the slide, Falwell took the plunge, arms crossed at his chest and dressed in a business suit, looking like he was about to be baptized—or buried.

The scandalizers—those about whom the narrators narrated—were another spectacularizing force, as they kept resisting and disrupting narrative frames, characterizations, plottings, and climactic moments. After every barrage of charges leveled at the Bakkers, they were still standing when the smoke cleared, smiling and chatting about God's love and forgiveness. They refused to be shamed into oblivion, escaped narrative grips, and talked back, irrepressibly, from their own point of view. They would not simply die and go away. Indeed, lingering in the wings was a potential narrative frame, which, if only they could slip it into place, would produce the greatest of all spectacles. If only Jim and Tammy Faye could fashion themselves as innocent victims, slain by the forces of evil, they might rise again.

Finally, compounding the sense of spectacle was a backdrop of secular telescandals (Irangate, the Hart affair, the Marine spy case, Ivan Boesky, Wall Street drug raids), a whole host of lesser televangelists, hungry, waiting for the titans to fall, and the unshakable sense that we, the audiences, were inside the telescandal too—that it had caught us up, variously, and put us down somewhere else, changed imperceptibly perhaps—that just possibly, for instance, the line between the Modern and the archetype of premodernity, the Fundamentalist, had moved in some way that made us all different.

Of course, the story did not end there. The spectacularizing forces of the telescandals did not abolish the cultural narrative of modern America. Confused and confounded it, yes, but modern subjectivity actually needs an occasional feast of Fundamentalists, for it emerges out of the contradictory processes of internalizing and expelling Fundamentalist otherness. Just as surely as Ted Koppel orchestrated "The Billion Dollar Pie" as a spectacle in which his "hogs at the trough" thesis was lost in a cascading melee of excited criticism, proof-texting, and posturing, he also in the end did his best to pull his modern point of view out of the fire.

Ted Koppel's evening in the spring of 1988 in the Memphis church concluded with thousands of people standing up and cheering Jerry Falwell's assertion, *I do believe the Bible is the infallible Word of God*. This moment, bore no apparent relationship to the scandals or to televangel-

Figure 10.1 Jerry Falwell takes the plunge down Heritage Island's Typhoon waterslide. (Photo courtesy of Lynn Hey.)

ism; as a biting retort to a hostile question from a fellow Baptist in the audience, it further fractured the Fundamentalist whole; the sight of thousands cheering the literal Bible was spectacular from any point of view; and insofar as it was "great TV," it confirmed Falwell's innuendo that Koppel was also a hog at the trough. But it was also the moment which, from the modern point of view, most categorically distinguished Koppel from Falwell, who was Koppel's otherwise disconcertingly cool, reasonable, and remarkably well regarded co-author during the telescandals, by stigmatizing Falwell as an unrepentant biblical literalist.

> AUDIENCE MEMBER: I have heard at least five of you on the tube, and when I hear you, you've got all the answers. I'm surprised and amazed at your humility. You know exactly how we're supposed to understand the Bible; you won't consider any other view; you know exactly who's going to be saved and who's not going to be saved. I believe that at least you, Mr. Falwell, and Mr. Robison [also a Baptist preacher] believe that the Bible is the totally inspired word of God, without any admixture of any kind of error. Genesis 17:7 and 8 says that God made an eternal covenant with Israel. Eternal covenant. And yet it is my understanding that both you gentlemen somehow must think he has abrogated this covenant, because you think it is your Christian duty to convert Jews. I believe there's a contradiction in this, and I'd like you to explain it.
>
> REV. FALWELL: All right. First of all, let me ask you this. Which Baptist church are you a member of?
>
> AUDIENCE MEMBER: Prescott Memorial. [Laughter and some boos]
>
> MR. KOPPEL: Wait, does that have some meaning?
>
> AUDIENCE MEMBER: What difference does that make?
>
> MR. KOPPEL: Does that have some meaning? Well, I'm not sure I'd like to know. Does it make any difference?
>
> REV. FALWELL: Well, most Baptists believe in the inerrancy of the Bible. Do you?
>
> AUDIENCE MEMBER: No, I don't.
>
> REV. FALWELL: All right. Fine. I just wanted to know where you were. Now, the fact is I do believe the Bible is the infallible Word of God. I do—[Over half the audience, the choir, the arrayed preachers stand up, applaud, cheer, and shout "Amen"]

AUDIENCE MEMBER: May I respond? May I respond to that?

REV. FALWELL: You've had your time; be quiet for a moment.

AUDIENCE MEMBER: The ovation means they agree with you; that doesn't necessarily mean you're right.

REV. FALWELL: Hush! Let me tell you something. Now, the Bible—because we do believe the Bible is the inerrant Word of God, and because that Bible says Jesus is the way, the truth, the life, and no man cometh under the Father but by me. Jesus doing the talking. I don't have a plan of salvation, God does, and I believe that Jews, gentiles, Moslems, blacks, white, rich, poor, all come the same way, through the death, burial, resurrection of Christ, whom we learn about in an inerrant Bible.

Shortly after Falwell's declaration of faith, Koppel said good night to his church guests and then tacked on a clip for his television audience that would be his last grasp at the modernity narrative. It was a nostalgic scene featuring the pastor of a little Virginia church, John Sherfey, whom Koppel had introduced in his opening collage.[11] With a country gospel tune in the background, we pan in on Sherfey's church from above and find ourselves sitting in the pews with Ted and John, dressed in flannel shirts, and looking a little like distant cousins.

SINGER: Oh, I love to walk with Jesus like the publicans of old/ when he gathered them about him and the blessed tidings told.

MR. KOPPEL: John, I want to end where we began right here in the pews of your church. Is there a lesson in all this that you can draw for us?

REV. SHERFEY: Yes, I think so. I think a lot of times, Ted, what I tell my people here is, don't get their eyes fastened on man. Look to God. Because man'll let you down. Of course, I do want to be a pattern, as I go in and out of this church. As I go up and down these rows, as I walk the streets of Stanley, wherever I'm at. I want to live so that I'd be a pattern for them to follow. But I still don't want them to get their eyes fastened on me and take them off Jesus. See. Set your mind and your fixings on things above and not on this earth. [Short clip of Rev. Sherfey shaking the hands of his people as they leave church and saying, "Bless you, Brother, and praise the Lord."]

SINGER: I will follow/ all the way, Lord/ I will follow Jesus all the way/ Oh I love to walk with Jesus like the man of long ago—

A touching scene and a bit of a spectacle—Koppel and his television crew in a little church in the hills of Virginia, concocting the image of a good preacher (read preentrepreneurial, prepolitical, premodern, pre-postmodern) who told us the lesson of all this is that we must keep our eyes on God, not man. But visually, musically, and idiomatically, Koppel had nonetheless reconstituted the quaint premodern Fundamental other and ceremoniously cast him into the Southern countryside where we may presume Koppel is telling us such folk belong.

Of course, Ted Koppel and his co-reporters were not working alone to save the modern point of view. During the 1980s and on into the 1990s, dozens if not hundreds of scholarly panels, meetings, and publications visited and revisited questions of secularization, religion and modernity, and the revival of fundamentalism and religious orthodoxy. The single most ambitious effort was funded by the MacArthur Foundation. Beginning in 1991, with a $5 million, five-year MacArthur Foundation grant, the Fundamentalism Project convened hundreds of scholars from around the world to discuss and write about the origins, folk and official theologies, social organizations, and political practices of "fundamentalisms" all over the globe. The term "Fundamentalism" had already been expanded by scholars and journalists beyond its original American Protestant reference to refer to certain sects of Islam and Judaism. In the 1990s, with a big boost from the Fundamentalism Project, the term billowed once again to include as well certain Hindu, Buddhist, and even animist and new religious sects.[12] The emphasis on textual literalism as a defining feature of Fundamentalism all but disappeared and left absolutism and zealotry in its place. Indeed, if the movements now loosely dubbed "fundamentalist" by outsiders have anything in common, it is their capacity to alarm the managers and agents of secular nation-states. In short, it could be argued that, rather than disappearing, the rhetorical opposition between "Fundamentalism" and "Modernity" has been revamped and globalized, and that a ruffled, humbled moral superiority has been tentatively restored to the Modern, or at least the not-Fundamentalist, point of view. It may be difficult to find anyone willing to declare themselves "Modern" in the sense the term was used in the Protestant controversies early in the twentieth century. But the modern religious and secular points of view are still hard at work implicitly, shaping stories, the possibilities of action, thought, and faith—indeed, shaping persons, events, and history itself.

Much money and many raconteurs can do wonders, and there are many ways to fabulate a Fundamentalist, but it seems doubtful that the specifically secularizing version of the story of modernity—and the regime of secular modernity it sustained—can be put back together again. That version proposes that, when we look upon the television preachers and their electronic empires and escapades, their "moral majorities" and "traditional value coalitions," and the vast panoply of white born-again Christian churches, organizations, publications, and paraphernalia that still envelops the country, we see figures and scenes from the past. In fact, it makes more sense by now to say we are gazing into the future.

In retrospect, Jack Sims provided the perfect prefatory fable to the Koppel show. With respect to the fate of the big television preachers, he may have accurately fabulated what came to pass, but his language, the manner of his fabulation, was indubitably precise. His wild imagery vividly conveyed the exquisite unexpectedness and improbability of the characters and events that composed the telescandals—aging evangelical electronic dinosaurs crawling onto an iceberg, fighting tooth and nail, as the iceberg floats south, melting, to the inevitable doom of all. The tale speaks ending, but the language, its cyborg creatures and mixed metaphors and mythic time and space, speaks beginning—the opening up of a new world composed of preposterous cultural hybrids and antic transgressions of social boundaries. Religious mingles with secular, churches become businesses, Christ dispenses grace and miracles on TV, preachers call themselves CEOs and run for president, faith healers build ultramodern hospitals, AT&T hires New Age consultants and churches hire religious-market analysts, creationists call themselves scientists, and scientists discover the ineffable. If something is ending, perhaps it is the world in which the things forming these zany amalgamations were kept apart, separated, in their place, properly ordered and moving progressively toward some end.

Postscript

$\mathbb{A}$MERICAN fundamentalists once described themselves, and were widely described, as being opposed to modernity. They appeared to be, and wished to be seen as, outside and apart from modernity, holding fast to their traditions. However, fundamentalists were in fact always fully inside modernity.

The modern point of view emerged from a web of cultural practices that traditionalized—that rendered traditional, anachronistic, or backward—peoples deemed outside industrial societies and national cultures.[1] Under the sway of the modern perspective, nonindustrial agriculturalists became "peasants." Non-national polities became "tribes" and "ethnic groups." Noninstitutionalized religions became "magic" and "cults." Publicly supernaturalist religious believers became "orthodox" and "old-fashioned." And supernaturalist religious believers who actively contested modern perspectives and realities became "Fundamentalists." These traditional peoples and their cultural practices gave shape and substance to modernity by representing and enacting what modernity was not, what modernity had "lost" or "left behind." They were thus not only inside modernity, they helped produce it. They helped make modernity seem distinct and real and better.

From the modern point of view, it appeared that the faith of Fundamentalists, in America and elsewhere, was hardened as a result of their opposition to modernity. Modernity, so the story goes, naturally disenchanted the world.[2] In the context of powerful secular, naturalistic, and scientific modes of thought, religious beliefs in things transcendent, supernatural, and mysterious no longer made sense experientially, no longer could be taken for granted as common sense. In response, some faiths accommodated their beliefs to modern modes of thought. Some faiths withered away. And some bunkered themselves from an increasingly hostile world. Among the latter, it was said, religious convictions endured but were altered. On the defensive, they became more doctrinal, legalistic, dogmatic.

Bible scholar Hans Frei most convincingly rendered this transformation as it related to the biblical interpretive practices of European and American Protestants. In his terms, a premodern "realist" mode of understanding the Bible privileged literal and historical, rather than allegorical or spiritual, interpretations. And it incorporated "extra-biblical thought, experience, and reality into the one real world detailed and made accessible by the biblical story."[3] It was a "pre-critical" mode of interpretation that survived as long as it was not effectively challenged. Biblical stories and the story of the Bible as a whole "underwent ceaseless revision," yet they "remained the adequate depiction of the common and inclusive world until the coming of modernity."[4]

The biblical realist approach, according to Frei, was undermined as modern interpretive practices spread through seminaries and pulpits in the eighteenth and nineteenth centuries. As soon as biblical realism had to defend itself, it became something else. Gradually, theologians, preachers, and their faithful no longer simply *knew* that the Bible was true; they had to *believe* it. Once the threat of modern biblical criticism "is even vaguely in the air, the biblical narratives' literary unity is in unadjustable tension with the depiction of temporally sequential reality. The [biblical] story itself no longer rendered the reality of the history it depicted."[5]

Thus Frei joined many other modern observers in arguing that modernity produced a universal disenchantment in which faith, if it survived, was deformed and ever after felt mediated rather than simply given. In America, Protestant fundamentalist preachers and theologians collaborated with this view of their faith as they promulgated (and still promulgate) polemics regarding the unchanging "fundamentals of the faith" and the "absolute truth," "infallibility," and "inerrancy" of the Bible. Taken at their word, fundamentalist spokesmen represent their doctrines and beliefs as fixed and inflexible in the face of worldly forces that would "undermine the authority of the Bible" by accommodating faith to modern logics and moral codes that do not presuppose God.

Modern and fundamentalist polemics about how fundamentalists interpret the Bible thus converge in many ways, however much their evaluations of those reading practices differ. The modern observer considers

fundamentalist beliefs rigid; for the fundamentalist preacher, they are un-
yielding. "Absolute truths" scandalize one and gladden the other, but
both agree that true Bible believers cleave to them. Such representations
are not entirely wrong, but nor are they accurate depictions of fundamentalist faith. As we have seen throughout this study, Bible-believing
interpretive practices are quite complex, and Bible truths are varied and
in certain ways dynamic, even protean. Let us say that the reports of the
death of biblical realism have been greatly exaggerated.[6] Bible stories still
render the reality of the events they depict among the people and preachers I came to know. Fundamentalists, and born-again Christians generally, do not simply *believe*, they *know*, that the Bible is true and is still
coming true, that God speaks to them, and that Jesus died so that they
might live. There is no gap between story and event, between Bible-
based language and reality. Or, more accurately, like biblical realists before the coming of modernity, modern Bible believers effectively and
perpetually close the gap and so generate a world in which their faith is
obviously true.

By way of concluding, let us review some of the other ways in which
Jerry Falwell, his fundamentalist/evangelical community, and the larger
fellowship of born-again Christianity defied rather than fulfilled modern
expectations of a traditional, premodern, fundamentalist people.

Jerry Falwell, as a public speaker during the late 1970s and 1980s, dexter-
ously mixed and merged voices to remake, expand, and diversify his
reputation and audience. As he crafted his public postures on political
and moral issues, he borrowed language from the right side of debates
within evangelicalism and blended it with certain fundamentalist distinguishing features while discarding others. He selectively absorbed and
Christianized secular rhetorics, thus occupying the terrain of his opponents and particularizing their positions. Overall, he juggled several distinct and partial identities to command the attention of discrete audiences. The fact that he was an emblematic, card-carrying fundamentalist
making claim to a national political voice won the nervous attention of
non-born-again Christians. That he was a fundamentalist ventriloquizing
evangelicalism won the hostile attention of his most separatist and militant brethren. That he was the first nationally visible spokesman to articulate their hitherto inchoate point of view won the grateful attention of

conservative evangelicals and moderate fundamentalists. The combination catapulted Jerry Falwell and his marbled voice onto the national public stage for nearly a decade.

The fact that Falwell did not himself borrow and blend most of the language attributed to him—his ghostwriters did—further amplified the sense of him as a man without a center. Many of his in-house ghostwriters, such as Elmer Towns and Ed Hindson, were themselves bicultural, having many times crossed over the line between evangelicalism and fundamentalism in their careers. And Falwell's most published ghostwriter, Mel White, who ghostwrote *Strength for the Journey* and *If I Should Die before I Wake*, had little contact with historic fundamentalism and considered himself an evangelical. It was his ghostwriters who enabled Falwell to flex his identities as much as he did, to remix his styles, to reach across generational as well as folk-theological boundaries. The tension here between an officially singular authorial voice in the foreground and multiple authors in the background was hardly novel—it was as old as the Bible. The point is that on some level it was understood by all. To flexibility, fluidity, and hybridity we may add instability as a characteristic of Falwell's public persona. As we have seen, Falwell's reputation relied on his taking risks, on his continually troubling his people's perceptions of him so that they in turn might repeatedly make the little leaps of faith that bound them to him. Even his ghostwriters collaborated with him in this, one of them committing an offense so grave (adultery) that he was banished for a decade, and another an offense so grave (unrepentant homosexuality) that he was banished forever.

More broadly, 1980s Bible-believing Christianity itself also appeared to be very much a creature of, if not ahead of, its times. Aside from the aggressively entrepreneurial quality of especially the superchurches, the surrounding institutional and oratorical contexts of the churches were decentralized and diversely responsive to new conditions. Bible-believing Christianity functioned without a pope, without a Rome, without centralized, hierarchical, and costly denominational bureaucracies, and without a unifying written doctrinal statement. Instead, it was managed by loose, fragmentary pastoral networks or weak denominational structures and a huge host of parachurch organizations. Hardly anachronistic, it operated as a multifaceted, enormously agile apparatus capable of generating rapid local, regional, and national responses to changing political, social, and cultural conditions. A decentralized organizational structure enabled the whole movement, as well as components of it, to morph relatively quickly in response to new conditions. Thus, for example, the Moral Majority of the 1980s gave way readily to the Christian Coalition of the 1990s as the prevailing political manifestation of Bible-believing Christianity.

Oratorically as well, heterogeneity not homogeneity, hybridity not purity, fluidity not fixity, characterized the movement at every level. One's identity as a Bible-believing Christian was not narrowly defined or stationary; there were dozens of culturally distinct ways of being "born-again," and more emerged every day. Even the rhetorics unifying born-again Christianity were multiversioned and versatile. One such source of unity was a shared, yet variously inflected, elementary folk theology of Jesus that crusaders like Billy Graham and Bill Bright had cultivated and George Gallup, Jr., rendered visible. Another source, which produced partial but overlapping affiliations, was the multifarious and shifting field of millennial theories, crosscut and further interconnected by an updated polyvocal Christian folk history of America, secular humanism. And, of course, the conservative Christian moral rhetorics of the decade generated a compelling illusion of unity across myriad lines of theological and subcultural difference.

Tuning in to Bible-believing interpretive practices, we see not simple, static rote but a complex medley of literary devices, moods, and genres. Nostalgia, mimesis, parody, pastiche, double-voicing, intertextuality, and deconstruction were all at work in the cultural texts of Bible believers. Even absolutism, the attribute that most famously distinguishes the true Bible believer from others, was not quite what it appeared to be. The traditional Christian family designed by God for all time, as both rhetoric and practice, changed quite a bit during the twentieth century, including in its most sacred aspects. Creationism was not only a new tradition but it was a Bible-based absolute that came in at least five major named versions (ultra, strict/young earth, old earth, theistic, and design). The strict pro-life rhetorics that dominated public debate disguised an internal diversity of opinion among born-again Christians about abortion rights. In most surveys, nearly a majority of born-again Christians were found to support some degree of abortion rights. And stricter pro-life Protestant positions (there were several of them) and their

attendant rhetorics were cobbled together—that is, the evangelical Protestant pro-life tradition was invented—between 1978 and 1984. In short,
what we are looking at is a kind of "flexible absolutism," or, more precisely, a rhetorical capacity and will to frame new and internally diverse
cultural positions as "eternal absolutes."

When Charlotte and her son, David, visited me in New York City on
Easter weekend in 1985, I saw it as another small episode in the movement of contemporary American fundamentalists to abandon their
historic separatism from the secular world. Charlotte and her family had
taken me into their home when I stayed in Lynchburg, and she tutored
and guided me in my work there in many ways. They had traveled a
good deal but had never been to New York City and were eager to visit.
They wanted to see everything—Central Park, FAO Schwartz, Tiffany's,
Rockefeller Center, St. Patrick's Cathedral, Grand Central Station, the
New York Public Library, Times Square, the Empire State Building,
the Village, the World Trade Center, and even Liberace at Radio City
Music Hall.

They responded to the city's sites much as many first-time visitors do,
alternately overwhelmed and charmed, repelled and allured, excited and
exhausted. They took almost everything in stride. Even the city's aggressive secularity did not phase them—they made no comment, for example, about the World Trade Center brochure entitled "The Closest Some
of Us Will Ever Get to Heaven." But Charlotte did on several occasions
"adequately depict" the city in biblical realist terms, incorporating its
reality into "the one real world detailed by the biblical story." In my
account of the language of fundamentalism in the 1980s, I have emphasized the similarities, the space of overlap, between fundamentalist
and modern, religious and secular, Bible belief and unbelief. Charlotte
always wanted me to remember the difference, specifically, between
Bible belief and unbelief. As we stood one morning on the top floor of
the Empire State Building, she had an evangelistic vision of New York
City that reminded me once again of the difference, but also, once again,
of the similarity.

We had spent half an hour naming everything we could see from the
observation deck. David and I had gone inside and were browsing
through the souvenir stand when Charlotte came up to us looking very

distressed. David responded immediately. "What's wrong, Mom? What happened?" Charlotte hesitated, then spoke directly to David, making me her audience.

David, you are going to laugh when you get back to Lynchburg about how your mother cried on top of the Empire State Building. I was look-ing down on the city, and I thought about all those people down there who've never heard the gospel. I wondered, what does God see when he looks down on New York? And it just broke my heart. All the lost, lonely, destitute people, crowing for identity, their lives empty and cold without Jesus. There are millions of people down there who have never heard the Word, who don't know how much God loves them and that Jesus died for them. I saw a cross coming down from the sky reaching right into the city. It's the channel of communication God has given us if only we will open our hearts. So many people here, convinced they are all alone, that no one can help them. But they are so wrong. If only they would ask, the Lord will help them, he's their true friend, and he's there for everyone.

Charlotte caught us up in her evangelistic vision for about ten minutes, then dried her eyes and suggested we go to lunch. Before we left, she put a tract, a little pamphlet explaining God's plan for salvation, on the window ledge.

Thomas Road Baptist Church
Statement of Doctrine

WE AFFIRM our belief in one God, infinite Spirit, creator, and sustainer of all things, who exists eternally in three persons, God the Father, God the Son, and God the Holy Spirit. These three are one in essence but distinct in person and function.

We affirm that the Father is the first person of the Trinity and the source of all that God is and does. From Him the Son is eternally generated and from Them the Spirit eternally proceeds. He is the designer of creation, the speaker of revelation, the author of redemption, and the sovereign of history.

We affirm that the Lord Jesus Christ is the second person of the Trinity. Eternally begotten from the Father, He is God. He was conceived by the virgin Mary through a miracle of the Holy Spirit. He lives forever as perfect God and perfect man: two distinct natures inseparably united in one person.

We affirm that the Holy Spirit is the third person of the Trinity, proceeding from the Father and Son and equal in deity. He is the giver of all life, active in the creating and ordering of the universe: He is the agent of inspiration and the new birth; He restrains sin and Satan; and He indwells and sanctifies all believers.

We affirm that all things were created by God. Angels were created as ministering agents, though some, under the leadership of Satan, fell from their sinless state to become agents of evil. The universe was created in six historical days and is continuously sustained by God; thus it both reflects His glory and reveals His truth. Human beings were directly created, not evolved, in the very image of God. As reasoning moral agents, they are responsible under God for understanding and governing themselves and the world.

We affirm that the Bible, both Old and New Testaments, though written by men, was supernaturally inspired by God so that all its words are the written true revelation of God, it is therefore inherent in the originals and authoritative in all matters. It is to be understood by all through the illumination of the Holy Spirit, its meaning determined by the historical, grammatical, and literary use of the author's language, comparing Scripture with Scripture.

We affirm that Adam, the first man, willfully disobeyed God, bringing sin and death into the world. As a result, all persons are sinners from conception, which is evidenced in their willful acts of sin; and they are therefore subject to eternal punishment, under the just condemnation of a holy God.

We affirm that Jesus Christ offered Himself as a sacrifice by the appointment of the Father. He fulfilled the demands of God by His obedient life, died on the cross in full substitution and payment for the sins of all, was buried, and on the third day He arose physically and bodily from the dead. He ascended into heaven where He now intercedes for all believers.

We affirm that each person can be saved only through the work of Jesus Christ, through repentance of sin and by faith alone in Him as Savior. The believer is declared righteous, born again by the Holy Spirit, turned from sin, and assured of heaven.

We affirm that the Holy Spirit indwells all who are born again, conforming them to the likeness of Jesus Christ. This is a process completed only in heaven. Every believer is responsible to live in obedience to the Word of God in separation from sin.

We affirm that a church is a local assembly of baptized believers, under the discipline of the Word of God and the lordship of Christ, organized to carry out the commission to evangelize, to teach, and to administer the ordinances of believers' baptism and the Lord's table. Its offices are pastors and deacons, and it is self-governing. It functions through the ministry of gifts given by the Holy Spirit to each believer.

We affirm that the return of Christ for all believers is imminent. It will be followed by seven years of great tribulation, and then the coming of

Christ to establish His earthly kingdom for a thousand years. The unsaved will then be raised and judged according to their works and separated forever from God in hell. The saved, having been raised, will live forever in heaven in fellowship with God.

APPENDIX B

Sources of Jerry Falwell's Sermons

SOME of the sermons discussed in this account have been published in books, and I have cited those sources. Other sermons were recorded on audiocassettes or printed in church literature; they are not publicly available. I list here in descreasing order of accessiblity major sources of Jerry Falwell's sermons, noting the titles of sermons discussed at any length in my account.

- http://www.trbc.org, Thomas Road Baptist Church's website, contains recent sermons preached by Falwell.
- *Capturing a Town for Christ* (Falwell 1973) contains six sermons preached by Falwell in 1972.
- *Jerry Falwell: Aflame for God* (Strober and Tomczak 1979) contains long excerpts from various 1970s sermons by Falwell (1977 "Miracle Day" sermon on Liberty Mountain).
- *America Can Be Saved* (Falwell 1979) contains eleven Sword of the Lord revival sermons by Falwell ("Let Us Reach the World Together," "Seven Things Corrupting America," "A Day of Many Solomons," and "The Establishment").
- Jones Memorial Library in Lynchburg, Virginia, has three issues of the church publication *Word of Life* from 1958 which contain sermons by Falwell ("Segregation or Integration, Which?").
- Liberty Archives at Liberty University has copies of some of Falwell's later sermons ("America Back to God"), and one early sermon ("Ministers and Marchers"). The archive also has a copy of *How You Can Help Clean Up America* (Falwell 1978) which has reprints of three 1978 sermons ("Abortion: Is It Murder?").

• In the early 1980s the Old-Time Gospel Hour Cassette Ministry kept masters of church and chapel sermons. Copies were available for $4 each from the OTGH Cassette Catalog ("Inside the Cup II," Franky Schaeffer's "Christianity Is Truth Rather than Religion," and Francis Schaeffer's "What Really Is Christianity?")

• OTGH also made available many sermon videos ("America Declares War against God") and audiotape series (Ed Hindson's "Liberty Family Seminar" and "Dr. Jerry Falwell Teaches Bible Prophecy").

• Church people loaned me audiotapes of sermons preached at TRBC before 1982, and I recorded sermons on my trips to Lynchburg and elsewhere ("The Spiritual Renaissance in America").

Notes to the Chapters

PREFACE

1. When conservative Protestants say that "the Bible is the inerrant Word of God," they mean that it is, like God, flawless and without error. Simply stated, the "plain truth" of the Bible has long been a commonsense assumption among many American Protestants. It was named "biblical inerrancy" and fashioned into a formal doctrine by theologians at the Princeton Theological Seminary early in the twentieth century in defense of Bible truth against modern higher criticism.

2. The approaches used in this account draw on many hours of conversation with Kathleen Stewart and Harry Berger Jr. as well as a wide variety of texts, among them Alter 1981, 1985; Alter and Kermode 1987; Auerbach 1953, 1959; Bakhtin 1981, 1984; Barthes 1972; Basso 1996; Bauman 1977; Bercovich 1978; Berger 1988, 1989, 1997; Borker n.d.; Boyarin 1990; Brooks 1984; Burke 1941, 1966, 1989; Chambers 1991; Culler 1981, 1997; Favret-Saada 1980; Fish 1980; Foucault 1972, 1979; Frei, 1974, 1986; Freund 1987; Friedman 1987; Frye 1976, 1982; Girard 1977, 1986; Handelman 1982; Haraway 1991; Harris 1977; Habershon 1974; Jules-Rosette 1976; Kermode 1979, 1986; Landow 1980; Latour 1993; Laymon 1971; Macaulay 1994; McConnell 1986; Miller 1992; Morson 1989; Radway 1984; Rimmon-Kenan 1983; Said 1978; Silverman 1983; Stallybrass and White 1986; Sternberg 1987; Stewart 1996; Tompkins 1980; Volosinov 1973; White 1987; Williams 1991.

INTRODUCTION

1. There were, of course, exceptions, as noted below. Also, note I am using the term "fundamentalist" here narrowly to describe conservative Protestants whose preachers called themselves "fundamentalists" and who identified themselves in some way with historic fundamentalism (see the Guide to Terms). In fact, many of the students and church people I talked with in Lynchburg did

not think of themselves as "fundamentalists," but simply as "Christians," and were only vaguely aware of the history of fundamentalism in America. On the other hand, as Christian Smith has demonstrated in his recent study, *American Evangelicalism*, a wide variety of conservative Protestants will describe themselves as "fundamentalist" when their other options are to call themselves "evangelicals," "mainline," "liberal," or "other" (Smith 1998, 240, 243).

2. I use the term "dialect" here because it is more familiar, but linguists reserve that term to describe regional and social, or class-based, variation in language. A more precise term for the variation I am describing here would be "register." Ronald Macaulay (1994, 217) defines a "register" as "a variety of language used in connection with a particular activity or body of knowledge. Football, preaching, chemistry, music, and linguistics all have specialized vocabularies and manners of speaking that constitute their registers."

3. Stott 1982 describes preaching as "bridge-building" between the biblical world and the modern world. The image of a man standing in the gap for God comes from Ezekiel 22:30. God said: "And I sought for a man among them, that should make up the hedge, and stand in the gap before me for the land, that I should not destroy it: but I found none."

4. This formulation of the Bible as "old language" and of religion as a process of reshaping old language in new contexts was suggested to me by Becker's discussion of proverbs (1996). Keith Basso's discussion of "ancient speech" was also very useful (1996).

Scholars of the Bible as literature whose work is especially helpful in thinking about the Bible as ancient speech which may be brought back to life include Alter 1981, 1985; Auerbach 1953, 1959; Frei 1974; and Sternberg 1987.

5. During the 1980s, Falwell's sermons were aired on over three hundred local television stations and over five hundred radio stations (Lloyd 1988, 20). Falwell's audience during the 1980s is a matter of dispute. For example, Falwell claimed fifty million people watched his weekly televised sermons in 1980, whileHadden and Swann estimated his weekly audience at fewer than 1.5 million (1981, 47).

6. According to interviews with ministry staff.

7. See Moore 1994.

8. On the two types of Christian masculinity, see Bendroth 1993, 80.

9. Falwell and Towns 1971, 40–41.

10. Falwell 1987, 360.

11. According to the BBF website in March 1998 (http://www.bbfi.org/). Also, the doctrinal statement published on TRBC's website (http://www.trbc.org) was the same one distributed by the church in the early 1980s (see Appendix A).

12. "Evangelical" has another, broader meaning, too, one which dates from the colonial period when "established" churches were distinguished from "evangelical" churches (such as Methodist and Baptist churches), which recruited members by evangelizing. This broader usage, which has been revived recently in popular discourse, includes fundamentalist, pentecostal, and charismatic, as well as more narrowly defined evangelical churches. See the Guide to Terms.

13. See Marsden 1987.

14. Rozell and Wilcox 1996, describe the Christian Right in the 1980s as "a disorganized, decentralized social movement." "It was a decentralized collection of social movement organizations and leaders, with little cooperation or coordination" (4).

15. "Born-again Christianity" usually refers to these four sorts of "confessional" Protestants and specifically excludes Mormons, Jehovah's Witnesses, and Seventh-Day Adventists. (Many born-again Christians do not consider these nineteenth-century denominations truly Christian, arguing that they "amended" the core Christian doctrine (or "confessions of faith") summarized in the Nicene and Apostle's Creeds and "added" to Scripture. In his 1983 study (141), James Hunter distinguished "confessional" and "conversional" Protestants, but I am lumping them together here.

16. Such elementary salvational language had been spread by revivalists and shared widely at other moments in American history.

17. Gallup 1982, 31–32.

18. The origin of the term "moral majority" is often attributed to the New Right leader Paul Weyrich. He and other New Right leaders met with Falwell in Lynchburg, Virginia, in May 1979 and convinced him to create an organization by that name. In his 1987 autobiography (361), Falwell himself implied that Weyrich came up with the phrase "moral majority," and Weyrich said as much in an interview with William Martin in 1995 (Martin 1996, 200). However, according to a story in the March 23, 1979, issue of Falwell's *Journal Champion* (which later became *The Moral Majority Report*), Falwell had been preaching at "I Love America" rallies around the country that *a moral majority must stand up and support goodness, rightness and virtue along with Christian principles* to combat *the moral decay which is rearing its ugly head across America.* In other words, Weyrich may have realized "moral majority" would be a good name for the new organization, but the term originated within Falwell's organization.

The after-the-fact attribution of the origin of the term "moral majority" to Weyrich may be another instance of Falwell casting himself, and being cast, as having received a call, a message, from an outsider. Falwell also narrated the moment he disavowed racial segregation (see discussion later in this chapter) and the moment in which he committed himself to pro-life politics (see chapter 7) as outcomes of messages from outsiders. As we shall see, these moments were thus framed as biblical, or God-given, events.

19. 1980 was in fact a very busy year in this respect; see FitzGerald 1986 and Martin 1996.

20. Robertson 1986, 281–82.

21. See the Guide to Terms.

22. See Carter 1993.

23. The "Ministers and Marchers" sermon pamphlet which I found at the LBC's Liberty Archives had the following note penned across the front: *My Aunt in Atlanta says Jerry would like to buy this back. But here's one free. ha! ha! A friend of Bob Jones from Greenville sent me this!*

24. In an interview in 1984, O. C. Cardwell, a black Civil Rights leader in Lynchburg during the 1950s and 1960s, told me that Falwell was known at the time as a spokesman for "race separation." It is, however, difficult to document this from written sources inside Falwell's community. Liberty Archives, which has dozens of printed sermons by Falwell from the 1970s and 1980s on file, had none, apart from "Ministers and Marchers," from the 1950s and 1960s. I was told by two members of Falwell's staff that he had recalled written texts of his 1950s and 1960s sermons to prevent their being used against him. The only three sermons I was able to locate from that earlier period, all of them from 1958, were at the Jones Memorial Library in Lynchburg. One of them, "Segregation or Integration, Which?," was entirely devoted to defending racial segregation, citing Genesis 9:18–27, Noah's curse on Ham, as its biblical basis. The other two sermons addressed "Marriage, According to God's Word," and Falwell's "Elim Home for Alcoholics."

25. From one of Falwell's early national crusade sermons, "America Back to God" (Falwell 1976). Also see "I Love America!," "Seven Things Corrupting America," "A Day of Many Solomons," and "The Establishment," sermons which Falwell preached to other fundamentalist preachers in the middle 1970s, in Falwell 1979.

26. FitzGerald 1986, 129. FitzGerald notes that Falwell's "repudiation of the sermon makes it clear that his change of position was little more than a political change from support of the status quo to attack upon it. The civil rights movement was the turning point. It showed Falwell that preachers could be politically effective and removed one important reason for his support of the status quo. Ironically, it may have benefitted Falwell and other white fundamentalists as much or more than it benefitted blacks in the south" (171). Falwell's distancing

himself from segregationist views also had an important payoff as it enabled him to fashion a national, rather than a southern, profile after 1970.

27. Boyd 1977, 119.

28. Until about 1970, self-described historically fundamentalist churches were virtually all white. Those, such as Falwell's, which have since then "broken the color barrier," are still mostly all white. Self-described fundamentalist churches that were founded more recently or had come out of a different, more pentecostal lineage, such as Chuck Smith's Calvary Chapels, include more Asian-Americans and Hispanics, but not significantly more African Americans.

29. This discussion is based on Miller 1992.

30. Falwell 1986, 294–96.

31. FitzGerald 1986, 188; Martin 1996, 211.

32. Martin 1996, 70.

33. In a 1982 interview, Falwell claimed his views on segregation began to change in the early 1960s.

34. See Martin 1996, 68–73.

35. See chapter 7; and note 18, above.

36. Alter 1981, 49, 51, 60.

37. One former TRBC member dated a crisis of faith in his life to 1965–67, when he could not square his sense that segregation was wrong with the teachings of his parents and his pastor. And two of Falwell's leading co-pastors told me that, when they had joined Falwell's staff, one in 1970 and the other in 1974, they told Falwell that they opposed racial segregation and could not work for his church unless it, and he, did too.

38. Of course, neither Falwell nor his church people consciously or explicitly fashioned themselves as biblical characters or authors of ongoing books of the Bible. This is my interpretation of their cultural practices.

James B. Hurley (1986) made a similar argument when he remarked that evangelist Francis Schaeffer's "functioning and self-concept" was in the mold of Elijah, "who spoke God's message to the nation of Israel at the turning point in its history" (1986; 280–81). Hurley hastened to add, "Please note: I am not suggesting that Schaeffer considered himself a prophet like Elijah. That would be a travesty. I am suggesting that he felt that he was preaching God's truth (revealed in the Bible) to a nation at the turning point in its history and that his preaching might be a crucial factor in preventing a departure from God's law which will ultimately bring judgment on the nation. His message to the churches might be compared to what was undoubtedly Elijah's message to the schools of the prophets: preach the Word faithfully, unsparingly, regardless of the opposition" (281). Michael Walzer also argued in this vein regarding "revolutionaries" and the biblical figure of Moses in his book *Exodus and Revolution* (1985), as have those who have written about jeremiad preaching (see, for example, Bercovitch 1978).

CHAPTER ONE

1. James 1906, 158.

2. Here I am summarizing Heirich 1977, 653–80.

3. Whitehead (1987) provides an excellent, critical review of this literature in her study of conversion among Scientologists.

4. Christian social scientists and theologians have studied the secular literature on conversion and generated their own. Elmer Towns, dean of Jerry Falwell's Liberty Baptist Seminary and a nationally known researcher in the "science of church growth," told me that the highest rate of conversion occurred among prisoners, the second highest among the bankrupt; he also emphasized the importance of personal networks and of reaching people while they are "in transition" of some kind. The difference between Towns and secular social scientists is that Towns would never suggest any of these factors really causes conversion; the Holy Spirit convicts sinners and Christ saves them.

5. Borker n.d., 1, 3.

6. This is how Bakhtin (1981, 282) described ordinary dialogue from the speaker's point of view: "The speaker strives to get a reading on his own word, and on his own conceptual system that determines this word, within the alien conceptual system of the understanding receiver; he enters into dialogical relationships with cetain aspects of this system. The speaker breaks through the alien conceptual horizon of the listener, constructs his own utterance on alien territory, against his, the listener's, apperceptive background."

7. Hill 1985, 26.

8. Jules-Rosette 1976, 135.

9. Favret-Saada 1980, 22.

10. Favret-Saada 1980, 16.

11. Bauman 1977, 15–24.

12. Graham 1983, 203.

13. Alter 1981, 69.

14. Compare the Reverend Campbell's language here with these words, which God spoke to Ezekiel regarding the nation of Israel (16:4–6): "And as for thy nativity, in the day thou wast born thy navel was not cut, neither wast thou washed in water to supple thee; thou wast not salted at all, nor swaddled at all.

None eye pitied thee, to do any of these unto thee, to have compassion upon thee, but thou wast cast out in the open field, to the loathing of thy person, in the day that thou wast born. And when I passed by thee, and saw thee polluted in thine own blood, I said unto thee when thou wast in thy own blood, Live; yea, I said unto thee, when thou wast in thy blood, Live."

15. See Alter 1981, passim.

16. Auerbach 1953, 73.

17. Frei 1974, 1.

18. In fact, the listener can never really make the speaker's speech his own. Here is how Bakhtin (1981, 293–94) described the dialogue from the listener's point of view: "As a living, socio-ideological concrete thing, as heteroglot opinion, language, for the individual consciousness, lies on the borderline between oneself and the other. The word in language is half someone else's. It becomes 'one's own' only when the speaker [that is, the listener becoming a speaker] populates it with his own intention, his own accent, when he appropriates the word, adapting it to his own semantic and expressive intention. Prior to this moment of appropriation, the word does not exist in a neutral language . . . , but rather it exists in other people's mouths, in other people's contexts, serving other people's intentions: it is from there that one must take the word, and make it one's own. . . . Expropriating it, forcing it to submit to one's own intentions and accents, is a difficult and complicated process."

19. "It seems to me that to explain what is involved in [witchcraft] situations simply by talking of the effect of suggestion is not sufficient, for this is to do no more than to give a name to the very thing which is doubtful. . . . So the touchstone of witchcraft is not so much the simple realization of a prediction or malediction, as the fact that it is taken up by the bewitched, who becomes the unwilling agent of fate" (Favret-Saada 1980, 113–14).

20. Perhaps, as William James concluded about the divine, the only certain evidence of the reality that preoccupies ethnographers, of shared unconscious knowledge, is experiential. Faye Ginsburg (personal communication) put it this way: "Anthropologists approach self-alteration as a mode of knowing. Our epistemology requires that we alter ourselves in order to know." And Barbara Myerhoff, in her last film, *In Her Own Time*, said, "This is what anthropologists are taught to do. You study what is happening to others by understanding what is going on in you, and you yourself become the data-gathering instrument. You come from a culture, and you step into a new culture, and how you respond to the new one tells you about them, and it tells you about the one you came from."

CHAPTER TWO

1. My major sources for this retelling of the Scopes trial include the trial transcript edited and compiled by Allen 1967; accounts of the trial, its historical context and principle figures by Marsden 1980, Daniel 1986, Furniss 1954, Gatewood 1969, Tompkins 1965, Vanderlaan 1925, Larson 1997, and Levine 1965; articles in the *New York Times, Baltimore Evening Sun, Richmond Times-Dispatch, Knoxville Journal, Chattanooga Times, Moody Bible Institute Monthly, Bible Champion, Presbyterian and Herald Presbyter, Christian Century*; and a variety of modernist and antimodernist theological tracts by figures such as Shailer Mathews, Harry Emerson Fosdick, John Horsch, and John Roach Straton.

2. Larson (1997) argues that it was subsequent treatments of the trial, written in the period between 1931 and 1960, that produced what he calls "the modern Scopes legend" (225 ff.). I argue that the initial coverage also produced "the modern legend," which later treatments reproduced, elaborated, and intensified.

3. See the Guide to Terms regarding "Fundamentalist" and "Modern" (in contrast to "fundamentalist" and "modern").

4. See note 1 for sources. John Scopes was fined $50 for violating the law against teaching evolution in a public school. The conviction was overturned on a technicality a year later by the Tennessee Supreme Court, which saw "nothing to be gained by prolonging the life of this bizarre case" (Larson 1997, 220–21).

5. From the conservative camp, for example, John Horsch wrote in his *Modern Religious Liberalism*, published in 1920, that "Modernist theology discredits and destroys the foundations of Christianity as it has been known in all ages from the time of its origins" (5). From the liberal camp, Shailer Mathews wrote in *The Faith of Modernism*, published in 1924, that "every age has its Modernist movement when Christian life, needing new spiritual support, has outgrown some element of ecclesiastical coercion and incarnated some new freedom of the spirit" (3).

6. From an editorial in *Watchman-Examiner*, July 1, 1920, by Curtis Lee Laws, quoted in a sermon he delivered at the Moody Bible Institute and reprinted in the *Moody Bible Institute Monthly*, September 1922. Although Laws invented the term "fundamentalist," "fundamentalism" as a movement is usually derived from *The Fundamentals*, a series of small volumes written by Bible scholars and popular writers and published from 1910 to 1915. Two Southern California oil millionaires, Milton and Lyman Stewart, conceived of and financed the project. "They financed free distribution to every pastor, missionary, theological profes-sor, theological student, YMCA and YWCA secretary, college professor, Sunday School superintendent, and religious editor in the English-speaking world, and sent out some three million individual volumes in all" (Marsden 1980, 119).

7. According to Norman Furniss, who published in 1954 the first major academic rendering of the Protestant disputes of the 1920s, "the Scopes trial was a part, actually the climax, of the fundamentalist controversy" (3). At the other end of the spectrum, a history of fundamentalism co-edited by Jerry Falwell in 1981 represented the event in virtually the same terms: "The Fundamentalist Movement was brought to an abrupt halt in 1925 at the Scopes trial" (90).

8. Evangelical historian George Marsden (1980, 184 ff.) comes close to destabilizing modernist frames by concentrating on the ways in which the trial and fundamentalists were (mis)interpreted in the press, implicitly calling into question the status of the "events" as such. Marsden also argues that some fundamentalists shortly came to fulfill modernist stereotypes with a vengeance, thus fueling more ridicule and leading "moderate" orthodox Protestants to fall away. In this way, he concedes some "truth" to modern stereotypes, but only after the fact of their invention. See Marsden 1980, 189 ff.

9. Tompkins 1965, 57–58.

10. Trial coverage in the *Richmond Times Dispatch* (Virginia) was provided by the Associated Press and the Universal Service. Local reporters provided occasional, relatively low-key side stories about reactions in Richmond to the trial ("Ministers Here Discuss Evolution but Few Will Talk of Scopes Hearing," July 10, 1925), and there were sober-minded editorials ("Did [Scopes] violate the laws of the State of Tennessee? That is the sole question before the court of Judge Raulston and before his jury. All the rest of the talk as to 'eternal truths' is sheer bunk"; July 11, 1925). Even major papers in Tennessee such as the *Knoxville Journal* and *Chattanooga Times* relied on the news services for detailed coverage of the trial and its principals, though they also had reporters in Dayton reporting directly, as well as reporters and editors at home gathering and formulating commentary. While the latter wrote relatively low-key, sober copy, the on-site correspondents conveyed more of the "carnival atmosphere" ("Dayton Disappointed/Huge Crowds, Expected for Weeks, Fail to Put in Appearance/Concessionists Storm Lawn/Medicine Men, Auction Sales, Itinerant Musicians and Old Man of the Mountains among the Carnival Attractions—Much Religious Literature Offered for Sale"; *Chattanooga Times*, July 11, 1925.)

11. *New York Times*, July 10, 1925.

12. *New York Times*, July 17, 1925.

13. *Baltimore Sun*, July 13, 1925.

14. Tompkins 1965, 40.

15. Tompkins 1965, 50–51.

16. *New York Times*, July 10–11, 1925.

17. Scopes and Presley 1967, 98–99.

18. Allen 1967, 156–57.

19. When I first sketched this reframing of Bryan's performance—as it might have been rendered from a fundamentalist point of view that resisted modernist insinuations—it was purely speculative. Since then, the encounter between Bryan and Darrow has been reinterpreted along these lines by various writers, including Wills (1990, 97–114). Wills casts Darrow and Mencken as consciously collaborating in a Social Darwinist plot to discredit fundamentalism by "diabolizing" Bryan, whom Wills figures as the benign, unassuming, well-intentioned victim. Wills concludes that the Scopes trial did not represent the triumph of evolution. On the contrary, "Just as the lawyers and journalists left Dayton, laughing and congratulating themselves that they had slain fundamentalism, the teaching of evolution was starting its decline in America, one from which it would not recover until the 1960s" (113).

20. *New York Times*, July 21, 1925.

21. *Presbyterian & Herald Presbyter*, August 6, 1925, 14.

22. See Larson 1997.

23. See, for example, Schaeffer 1976, LaHaye 1980, Hitchcock 1982, Whitehead 1983, and Peretti 1986, 1989. Also see Neuhaus (1984, 1986) and Carter (1993) for less conspiratorial critiques of secular America.

24. According to recent studies (see Hunter 1983, 49 ff., and Kellstedt et al. in Guth and Green 1991, 139 ff.), the born-again Christian, or (broadly defined) evangelical Christian, population is only moderately more southern, more rural, and less educated than either the American population as a whole or other major religious categories (mainline or liberal Protestant, Catholic, non-Christian, secularist.) See also Smith 1998. Nancy Ammerman's account of a northern Protestant congregation that is at once fundamentalist and mainstream is particularly striking (1987, chapter 3). Shibley (1996) and Miller (1997) also amend stereotypic images of evangelical faith in America in a variety of ways.

25. Wardin 1980, 35.

26. Wardin 1980, passim. See Dollar (1973, 1983) and Beale (1986) for much longer and more complete lists of independent Baptist fellowships, and for full discussions of fundamentalist Methodist, Presbyterian, and other organizations.

27. Wardin 1980, 36. At the time the list was drawn up, Falwell's church was out-of-fellowship with the Baptist Bible Fellowship; see chapter 3.

28. *Fundamentalist Journal*, December 1984, 54.

29. In a 1992 survey, 10 percent of mainline Protestants and 13 percent of Catholics considered themselves "spirit-filled" (Smidt et al. 1996, 226).

30. George Marsden uses the term "conscious fellowship" to describe postwar evangelicalism in his introduction to *Evangelicalism and Modern America* (1984, xvi).

31. Other institutions central to evangelicalism's rapidly increasing growth and influence as a cultural formation during the 1940s, 1950s, and 1960s were

Fuller Seminary, *Christianity Today*, Billy Graham Evangelistic Crusade, Wheaton College, Charles Fuller's Old-Fashioned Gospel Hour, Youth for Christ, Campus Crusade for Christ, Zondervan Publishing, and William B. Eerdmans Publishing.

32. See Martin 1996, 40, and Peirard 1984, 164.

33. As late as 1976, a relatively discrete national campaign by Bill Bright, a well-known conservative evangelical leader, and Arizona Congressman John Conlan to promote religious conservative candidates to public office was derailed when an evangelical magazine, *Sojourners*, exposed its operation. Mere exposure from inside the evangelical community—and by a left-leaning journal at that—was all it took, so strong still was the sentiment among evangelicals against "mixing" religion and politics. See Peirard 1984, 169. See also Diamond 1995, 173.

34. See Martin 1996, 102–16, on Anaheim, and 119–43 on Kanawha County; see Nelkin 1982, 47–51, on "Man: A Course of Study" (MACOS).

35. Of course, black Protestant churches had already manifest a vibrant supernatural religiosity in American public culture during the 1950s and 1960s. Modern religiosity, however, was premised on the exclusion of white, not black, supernatural Protestantism, and the Civil Rights movement, insofar as it mobilized the white liberal Protestant community—and liberal Catholic and Jewish communities—may actually have strengthened the hegemony of modern—or liberal—religiosity. Still, two qualifications are in order: born-again Christian churches and organizations, especially those affiliated with pentecostalism, did include some blacks; and, as we saw in the Introduction and shall see again in chapters 4 and 6, white born-again activism was, and still is, engaged in a complex dialogue with the activism of historically black Protestantism.

36. As of course it had been until the late 1920s. See Marsden (1980) for his account of "the great reversal" which began in the post–Civil War years and culminated with the Scopes trial.

CHAPTER THREE

1. My notion of "miracles," and, specifically, of the narrative production of miracles, is indebted to David Edwards (1989) and Michael Gilsenan (1982, especially chapter 4).

2. During the Second Great Awakening revivals of the early nineteenth century, Arminian (after Jacobus Arminius) and Calvinist (after John Calvin) doctrines and practices were mingled in many varying degrees and manners in many northern denominations. The doctrines were also mixed in the Southern Baptist

groups that forebore Falwell's Baptist Bible Fellowship fundamentalist Baptists. I do not mean to unscramble those omelettes here, just to note the "more Arminian" shape to pentecostal/charismatic conversion and election stories, in contrast to the "more Calvinist" shape of the fundamentalist/evangelical stories. The basic difference is rooted in the way respective ideas about "reversible" and "irreversible" salvation give shape to vernacular traditions of narrating the conversation experience.

3. Swaggart 1984.

4. Bakker 1976, 10.

5. Robertson 1972.

6. As may be apparent by now, this account of Falwell is neither an exposé that attempts to "get to the bottom" of Falwell and show what he is "really up to," nor a defense of Falwell that weighs some of the "negative evidence" but ultimately finds him a worthy man. Instead of rendering a judgment on Jerry Falwell's reliability or character, I am, as I found his church people do, reading across his (auto)biographical corpus to produce a specifically fundamental Baptist charismatic authority figure.

In this manner of reading Falwell's corpus, I am negotiating a dilemma. Church people were continuously troubled, some more, some less, by what I call "gaps and excesses" in Falwell's stories. Some finally decided to leave his church because of their doubts about him, but many did not. Those who stayed did not ignore or deny his lapses and their qualms about them but rather worked with him, with his narrative voice, to interpret them benignly, if not divinely, and to build his ever-amplifying reputation. My question is: How did they do it?

7. In the hands of fundamentalist theologians and in the polemics of fundamentalist preachers, the Bible is an object of hermeneutic, not poetic, analysis. The point is to determine what its author, God, meant. But I think fundamentalist folk interpretive practices are best described as poetics, not hermeneutics.

Jonathan Culler contrasts these two sorts of interpretive practices in literary studies as follows: "Poetics starts with attested meanings or effects [of a text] and asks how are they achieved. (What makes this passage in a novel seem ironic? What makes us sympathize with this particular character? Why is the ending of this poem ambiguous?) Hermeneutics, on the other hand, starts with texts and asks what they mean, seeking to discover new and better interpretations" (1997, 61). Fundamentalists, unlike literary scholars, do not consciously ask such questions, of course, but, I would argue, their interpretative strategies begin with "attested meanings or effects" rather than "texts," hence are more poetic than hermeneutic.

By calling folk fundamentalist interpretation a poetics of faith rather than a poetics of suspicion, I mean to say that it is a practice which presumes meaning is knowable, determinate, and ultimately designed, rather than the reverse.

8. I rely heavily, if somewhat indirectly, in this analysis on the work of Robert Alter (1981, 1985) and Meir Sternberg (1987), especially in the latter's discussion of "the system of gaps" in Hebrew Bible stories.

9. Falwell, like the rich, powerful, and famous eccentrics described by Marcus (1995) is a multiply authored man who exercises no direct control over many of his authors. My attention here is on those parts of his "self-making" corpus that he has publicly spoken about or that was written under his name. Although he probably composed little of that corpus (he has had many ghostwriters over the years), he authored it in the sense of controlling it editorially and claiming it as his own.

10. Pingry 1980, 15. Note that Pingry fashions Jerry as the younger Jacob even though he, Jerry, was the older twin, a detail which is suppressed.

11. Falwell 1987, 47.

12. Falwell 1987, 47.

13. Falwell 1987, 58.

14. Falwell 1987, 48.

15. Falwell 1987, 92–93.

16. Mel White ghostwrote *Strength for the Journey*. White, whose career by then included teaching and filmmaking as well, also ghostwrote for many of the major national preachers and evangelists during the 1980s, including Billy Graham, Frances Schaeffer, W. A. Criswell, Pat Robertson, Jim and Tammy Faye Bakker, E. V. Hill, and James Kennedy. In 1991, White wrote a letter to Jerry Falwell in which he revealed that he was a homosexual and requested a meeting with Falwell. Falwell refused, and White, during the course of the following year, came out more publicly as an advocate of gay evangelicals. He established a large evangelical gay church in Dallas, and later became the Minister for Justice of the national Metropolitan Church. See his book *Stranger at the Gate: To Be Gay and Christian in America* (1994).

17. Falwell 1987, 98–100.

18. Falwell and Towns 1971, 22. The details of this story—why Jerry went to church that night and how he and Jim picked their girls—vary quite a bit among different versions.

19. Falwell and Towns 1971, 27.

20. Falwell and Towns 1971, 29.

21. Falwell and Towns 1971, 29.

22. Strober and Tomczak 1979, 30.

23. D'Souza 1984, 65–66.

24. Falwell 1987, 153–54.

25. Falwell 1987, 169.

26. One former TRBC member told me that "the new pastor was quite a bit more liberal" than the dissidents. But liberal in what sense—theological or political? Dinesh D'Souza (1984, 69), on the other hand, implies that the split was a squabble, the kind that occurs "frequently in fundamentalist churches because of doctrinal hair splitting and fetish about proper conduct." The complete silence surrounding the nature of the dispute in all other accounts suggests Falwell and his founding church members were defending a position they no longer avow.

27. Falwell 1987, 170.

28. Strober and Tomczak (1979, 30) suggest there was a BBF rule against a new pastor's starting a church in his hometown.

29. Falwell 1987, 173–74.

30. Falwell 1987, 175–78.

31. Falwell also narrates his change of heart as an outcome of two "special messages from God" sent to him by strangers (1987, 384–86).

32. Falwell preached an earlier version of this sermon in October 1980, as discussed in FitzGerald 1986, 188–89.

CHAPTER FOUR

1. Koppel 1988.

2. Falwell 1987, 332. Figures vary.

3. FitzGerald 1986, 153.

4. Falwell 1987, 273.

5. Strober and Tomczak 1979, 73.

6. Strober and Tomczak 1979, 76.

7. Strober and Tomczak 1979, 76. Falwell's biographers claim that $2.5 million was raised, and the same figure appeared in a story about LBC in *Faith Aflame* (July–August 1977), a church publication. I consider this figure and many of the other figures on church finances "soft." In this case, two publications happened to report the same figure, but figures often vary wildly between accounts. Fundraisers, of course, are generally under pressure to overestimate, and, it seems, some fundamentalists feel special pressure in the name of witnessing for Christ. In a chapel service for college students in the mid-1980s, for example, Jerry Falwell recounted that his old friend and mentor, B. R. Lakin, once advised him to say he was well fed even if he were starving, lest he suggest to an unbeliever that God did not in fact provide.

On the other hand, Falwell, in his autobiography, said that "lying, half-truths, and exaggerations should be off limits for everybody in public life, especially for those who follow the One who said, 'I am the truth . . .'," and that church finance statistics were "close to accurate" (1987, 328). Fortunately, for my purposes accuracy is not paramount. Figures and statistics quoted and culled from fundamentalist accounts may be read as figments of a story, of a construction of reality, not literally, not as facts.

8. Strober and Tomczak 1979, 79–81.

9. These figures are soft because sources vary so much. I have used here Falwell's report of his ministry's 1973 income (1987, 332), and a church publication report of ministry income for 1976–77 (*Faith Aflame*, July–August 1977).

10. Falwell 1982, 404.

11. Falwell 1982, 406.

12. Willmington 1981c, 921.

13. Habershon 1974, 11.

14. Habershon 1974, 22.

15. Harris 1977, 6.

16. Falwell 1978, 659.

17. Habershon 1974, 11.

18. Ironically, it was the polemics of fundamentalist preachers themselves that suppressed typological terminology. They could not defend it as a transparently literalist mode of interpretation.

19. Three sermons from the late 1950s kept in a local library archive, Jefferson Memorial Library, also survived. See Introduction, note 24.

20. D'Souza 1984, 87.

21. Strober and Tomczak 1979, 54.

22. D'Souza 1984, 87.

23. Falwell 1987, 310.

24. Falwell 1987, 310.

25. D'Souza 1984, 87.

26. D'Souza 1984, 88.

27. Strober and Tomczak 1979, 58.

28. Falwell 1987, 322.

29. Strober and Tomczak 1979, 55.

30. Strober and Tomczak 1979, 65.

31. Strober and Tomczak 1979, 66.

32. Strober and Tomczak 1979, 66.

33. Strober and Tomczak 1979, 70–71.

34. Strober and Tomczak 1979, 63.

35. Falwell 1987, 333.

36. Falwell 1987, 333, 315.

37. Strober and Tomczak 1979, 152.

38. The pentecostal "gospel of giving" embedded in pentecostal "health and wealth" theology is efficacious—gifts to God do induce him to give back blessings to those who give.

39. Strober and Tomczak 1979, 151.

40. FitzGerald 1986, 152 ff.; *The Old-Time Gospel Hour News*, 1971–1973.

41. I am grateful to Peter Brown for this formulation.

42. Falwell and Towns 1984.

CHAPTER FIVE

1. In his autobiography, Falwell indicated that he was out of fellowship with the Baptist Bible Fellowship for fifteen years, that is, from 1956 to 1971 (Falwell 1987, 178). However, according to Elmer Towns (cited in Vaughan 1984, 119), the BBF Missions Board only began accepting graduates from Liberty Baptist College for overseas assignment in 1976. And Falwell's administrative assistant, Nelson Keener (interview), told me Falwell's church was not re-enrolled in the BBF until 1978. He explained that Falwell's fellow BBF pastors were concerned about his position on "gifts of the spirit" (and pentecostalism) because he had hired Doug Oldham, a well-known charismatic vocalist, to tour with his crusades. Falwell had to convince his brethren he still maintained an orthodox fundamentalist position against gifts before they would readmit him to the BBF.

2. See Appendix B for a list of sermons and sources.

3. On Rice's career, see Carpenter 1997, Sumner 1982, and Dollar 1973.

4. Falwell 1979, 41.

5. Falwell 1979, 11, 12.

6. Falwell 1979, 116.

7. Falwell 1979, 116, 120.

8. Ribuffo 1989, 145–46.

9. Hariston 1987, 12.

10. Staff interview.

11. Nelson 1978, 154–55.

12. By the time William Martin wrote his book (1996) about the Religious Right of the 1980s, Schaeffer's analysis of "pietism" as a barrier to fundamentalist activism had been taken up by others. "Falwell recognized that riding into the political arena in such a visible vehicle [the Moral Majority] constituted a direct

challenge to fundamentalist pietism, which traditionally manifested itself not only in disciplined devotional practice and strict standards of personal morality, but also in a general stance of separation from 'the world.' As Dobson [one of Falwell's leading co–pastors during the 1980s] explained, pietists felt that 'the political world—the public square—should not be part of a Christian's priority. Our priority is to love God and to love our neighbor. Forget about politics. That pietistic idea was predominant in the mind of the average person in the average pew in a fundamentalist church in America. The miracle of the Moral Majority was that, in just a matter of months, that whole concept was shattered, and [fundamentalists] began registering to vote and getting involved' " (1996, 201–2).

13. This is a dubious claim. To count as "member" of the Moral Majority, one only had to subscribe to the *Moral Majority Report*, so at best it is a weaker claim than it appears to be. In addition, there was, as far as I know, never any serious internal or external analysis of who was on the subscriber list. I was a "member" of the Moral Majority for most of the 1980s, and I was never asked about my religious affiliation. Finally, a 1982–83 survey of Moral Majority Political Action Committee contributors revealed that "the organization draws no backing whatever from socially conservative activists among Roman Catholics, Orthodox Jews, or Eastern Orthodox." The survey showed strong support for the Moral Majority from fundamentalist Protestant communities and from Mormons, but weak support or opposition from the majority of theologically conservative Protestant church bodies (Guth and Green 1996, 35).

14. The *Fundamentalist Journal*'s statement of purpose neatly etched the path it was blazing: *This magazine is committed to the historic fundamentals of the Christian faith, biblical separation, moral absolutes, the priority of the local church, and world evangelization. Although no magazine or individual can speak for the overall Fundamentalist movement, it is our desire to create a forum to encourage Christian leaders and statesmen to defend biblical Christianity. We will examine matters of contemporary interest to all Christians, providing an open discussion of divergent opinions on relevant issues. The Fundamentalist Journal will also reaffirm our history and heritage, as well as point the way to the future.*

15. Falwell et al. 1981, 163.

16. Falwell et al. 1981, 219–21.

17. Falwell et al. 1981, 221–23.

18. Kantzer, notes from 1982 meeting.

19. Others present were John Aker, Hudson Armerding, Bob Dugan, David McKenna, John Walvoord (President, Dallas Theological Seminary), Richard

Chase. Invited but not present were Ed Clowney (President, Westminster Theological Seminary), Adrian Rogers, George Sweeting (President, Moody Bible Institute).

20. Wells 1986, 241.

CHAPTER SIX

1. Temple Baptist Church in fact had a ban that barred black members. It was in force for ninety-four years and was overturned a few months after Falwell spoke in 1986. "Redford Church Ends Ban on Blacks," *Detroit Free Press*, September 29, 1986.

2. "Aide: Sex Call Cost Pastor Job," *Detroit Free Press*, June 22, 1988.

3. Accounts of this incident and of Norris's pastorate abound. See, for example, Hankins 1996, Russell 1976, Carpenter 1997.

4. Bercovitch 1978. Much of Francis Schaeffer IV's writtings also follow the classic form of the jeremiad according to Ronald Wells (1982) in his incisive critique *A Christian Manifesto*. Also see Wells 1986.

5. See 23, chapter 2.

6. Miller 1992.

7. Guth and Green 1996, 35.

8. The major sources for this section are Bendroth 1993, DeBerg 1990, McDannell 1986, Douglas 1977, Gillis 1996, Fishburn 1981, Bederman 1996, Juster 1992, Watt 1991, and Carpenter 1997.

9. Bendroth 1993 and DeBerg 1990.

10. Bendroth (1993, 49) describes growing bias in terms of dispensationalist theology (see also 55–56). DeBerg (1990) also extensively documents this trend.

11. Rice 1945, chapters 6–8. Patricia Gundry, writing in 1980, said that chain-of-command thinking "is so widely accepted among believers that it is seldom questioned at all" (cited in Bendroth 1993, 126). Margaret Bendroth noted in 1993 that Gundry's observation "still describes many conservative evangelicals today" (126).

12. Rice 1945, 105; see Watt 1991, 98.

13. Bendroth 1993, 98.

14. Watt 1991, 99 ff.

15. For a more manipulative version of this advice, see the widely read *Total Woman* by Marabel Morgan (1973); also see *The Power of the Positive Woman* by Phyllis Schlafly (1977). See Judith Stacey's *Brave New Families* (1990) for an extended discussion of finessing among evangelical couples.

16. Thanks to the thoughts of Pat Pudip here.

17. Bendroth 1993, 113.

18. "Despite periodic pleas for more involvement from fathers, fundamental-ist mothers embraced the family as their common prerogative" (Bendroth 1993, 100).

19. Bendroth 1993, 75, 104.

20. Bendroth 1993, 100.

21. Bendroth 1993, 96

22. See Rice 1945, chapter 3; Watt 1991, 97–99. The only women's work outside the home that Rice endorsed was Christian service, such as Sunday School teaching (Bendroth 1993, 111, 113). According to Watt (1991, 98–99), Billy Graham and many other evangelical leaders, as well as Rice, voiced opposition to women working for wages during the 1940s, 1950s, and 1960s. They warned, for instance, "that a wife's working outside the home had to be considered an emergency measure and that such jobs might lead to sexual frigidity" (99).

23. Hindson 1976 (3:2); Hindson interview.

24. Bendroth 1993, 118 ff.

25. While most of the older married women I interviewed had quit their jobs after their children were born, the younger women, many of whom described themselves as having careers, not jobs, planned to continue working outside the home after having children or at least did not assume they would quit.

26. In Rice's heyday, women "often noted the salutary effects of its teaching on non-Christian husbands." Bendroth 1993, 113.

27. Falwell 1992, 21–23.

28. When read closely, the account by Falwell (1992, 27–28) of his family feats sounds exaggerated—it was perhaps not meant to be read literally—but Falwell was indeed an early advocate of active fathering. He hired Larry Coe, who had trained with Bill Gothard, to set up family-oriented services in the early 1970s, and his 1970s Sword of the Lord sermons contained admonitions to men, such as, "*Love is the spiritual lubricant that puts the home together and keeps it together. And the man who is so busy in his work that he does not have time to love his family is just too busy. It could not be God's work he is doing, for duties never conflict* (1979, 143).

29. Bendroth 1993, 30: "Fundamentalism was meant to appeal first, though not exlcusively, to men." Her book as a whole substantiates this in many ways—with respect to biblical inerrancy and dispensational doctrines, to revivalism, to the preacher's persona, to the operation of fundamentalist schools, missionary organizations, and churches, to preaching rhetorics, and so on. Bendroth argues that this masculine bias did not automatically make fundamentalists hostile to-ward women and femininity, but did so under certain circumstances (see her chapter 2).

30. Quoted Bendroth 1993, 6

31. Quoted in DeBerg 1990, 89.

32. Quoted in Bendroth 1993, 58–59.

33. Bendroth 1993, 9.

34. Bendroth 1993, 64 ff. See also Bendroth 1993, 14, 76, and Carpenter 1997, 64–69.

35. Bendroth 1993, 66, 77.

36. Bendroth 1993, 80.

37. Bendroth 1993, 10.

38. Bendroth 1993, 11.

39. Watt 1991, 93–117.

40. At a coffee break during a Word of God conference I attended in 1986, I overheard a gay man ask Richard John Neuhaus, one of the most influential and thoughtful of the politically active conservative theologians in the 1980s, if Christian orthodoxy would ever accept "loving loyal homosexual relationships as equal" to those formed by vows of marriage or celibacy. The two men had gathered a small crowd around them as the gay man, Michael, introduced himself to Neuhaus and told him about his coming-out to his church and how painful it had been to endure its censure of his life. The encounter was so unlikely—I would have thought impossible—that it had mesmerized those of us who had gathered around. When Michael asked his question, time stood still. What would Neuhaus say? He paused briefly and said, "We don't know, but it seems improbable." To those of us accustomed to hearing questions answered in ways that met the standard of biblical inerrancy, Neuhaus's response was astonishing. It was an answer that openly recognized the complexity and contingency of what at the time was generally understood to be an unambiguous moral, doctrinal, biblical absolute. The answer was so off-key relative to the prevailing public conservative Christian polemics about homosexuality, Neuhaus might as well have said, "Probably."

I wonder what an earnest, historically savvy conservative theologian might say if he or she were asked whether Christian orthodoxy would ever forsake its commitment to male headship and wifely submission.

CHAPTER SEVEN

1. Falwell 1986.

2. *If I Should Die* also presents certain conundrums of authorship which might elude unborn-again readers but not believers. Although Falwell appears on the book's dust cover and in the credits as sole author, the chapters are clearly co-

authored with Jennifer Simpson, a subsuming which neatly implies that he is her author. Nor did Falwell make a secret of the fact that Mel White ghostwrote the book for both of them.

Such authorial ambiguities, rather than casting doubt on the text's veracity, enhance it by recalling debates over the authorship of biblical books and thus nesting *If I Should Die* in a corpus whose authority (authorship) is accepted as a testament of faith. As we have seen, it is the responsibility of faithful readers to "unify" the authorial and narrative voices in their interpretation and to "harmonize" the text with other texts, spoken and written, so that it comes "true." Falwell's words, like the words of all men of God, are always already double-voiced in any case, in the sense that it is never entirely clear whether he or God is the author.

3. Falwell 1986, 10–11.

4. Falwell 1986, 11.

5. Many conservative Protestant ministers spoke out against feminism in the late nineteenth and early twentieth centuries, and they sometimes included abortion when listing sins associated with feminism and modern society. John R. Rice, for example, condemned abortion (as well as birth control) in his 1945 manual on the Christian family. But Protestant preachers were not active participants in the campaign to criminalize abortion. See Bendroth 1993, DeBerg 1990, and Luker 1984.

Regarding Falwell's position on abortion, see, for example, Falwell 1973: *Some come* [to Falwell's church] *seeking forgiveness, as a young father who was guilty of pressuring his wife to get an abortion; he wondered if God would forgive him for murdering an unborn child* (53). (Elmer Towns ghostwrote this early text.)

In 1976, abortion appeared on Falwell's list of "America's sins" in his bicentennial "I Love America" crusade sermons and tracts, but it was just one among many other sins, not the cause célèbre it was to become. Elmer Towns told me in an interview that it was he who finally convinced Falwell, in spring 1978, to speak out at length against abortion—and that he, Towns, wrote Falwell's first pro-life sermon. Still, it was a while before the issue took off; *How You Can Help Clean Up America* (Falwell 1978) reprints the sermon "Abortion: Is It Murder?" (probably the one Towns was talking about), but *America Can Be Saved* (Falwell 1979) does not mention abortion.

The chapter on abortion in *Listen America!* (1981) is Falwell's first extended treatment in print; it relies heavily on right-to-life rhetoric, on the work of Bernard Nathanson, an "abortionist" who converted to the pro-life movement, and on Francis Schaeffer and Dr. C. Everett Koop's *Whatever Happened to the Human Race?* (1979), the first highly successful born-again polemic against abortion.

6. Spitzer and Saylor 1969, xxvi.

7. *Eternity*, Februrary 1968.

8. Paul Fowler 1987, 72. Fowler mentions Harold O. J. Brown, John Warwick Montgomery, Clifford Bosgra, and Richard Ganz.

9. See Fowler 1987, 72–77.

10. Regarding Wheaton, see Fowler 1987, 83; for 1992 figures, see Green et al. 1996, 251, 283. This evidence of internal conflict argues against the notion that pro-life mobilization emerged, as if inevitably, out of a preexisting "worldview," a position most fully developed by Luker (1984).

11. Fowler 1987, 73.

12. Fowler 1987, 73.

13. See Schaeffer and Koop 1979, 117.

14. See Burke (1989). Burke describes Hitler's use of a similar rhetorical technique, which Burke calls "associative merger," in *Mein Kampf*. It is common in much political rhetoric and enables the formation of larger, conglomerate, political identity groups.

15. See Scott 1959.

16. A list of proof-texts called "Scriptures for Life" invariably accompanied pro-life literature put out by the LGH campaign. It listed twenty-three Bible passages (there are others) as "proof-texts" against abortion; that is, they prove that God opposes it. For example, and oft-cited, is Jeremiah 1:5: "Before I formed thee in the belly I knew thee; and before thou camest forth out of the womb I sanctified thee." Inscribed on the Monument to the Unborn, a huge gravestone placed on Falwell's Liberty University campus, is Matthew 18:6: "But whoso shall offend one of these little ones which believe in me, it were better for him that a millstone were hung around his neck and to be drowned in the sea."

17. Ginsburg 1989. *If I Should Die* presents itself as "true stories" and, we may ask, "true" in what sense? As we have seen, "truth" in born-again culture is authenticated by its author; everything in the Bible is "true" because God wrote it, and everything Jerry Falwell (a man anointed by God) says is "true" because he said it. Discrepancies in parallel stories are not unsettling (because stories do not represent a fixed natural reality) but, rather, revealing (because the alterations constitute the working out of God's will).

18. As noted above in 5, I found no evidence that Falwell had preached on abortion before 1973; what evidence there is suggests that he realized the potential and importance of the abortion issue gradually during the late 1970s and early 1980s.

19. Falwell 1986, 31–32.

20. Falwell 1986, 36.

21. Falwell 1986, 37.

22. Falwell 1986, 67.

23. See Marsden 1980, 16–19. Note here Falwell's discursive interlocutors on the matter of abortion as such; those whose authority he would appropriate seem to be scientists, doctors, lawyers, justices, politicians, as well as feminists.

24. Falwell 1986, 47.

25. Teenage sexuality (once an unthinkable juxtaposition of terms for born-again Christians, especially fundamentalists) became in the mid-1980s a frequent topic of sermons, books, and seminars. Josh McDowell, a widely read writer on the subject, reported that "between 55 percent and 60 percent of evangelical Christian youth are involved in sexual activity" (1987, 15).

I was told in Lynchburg that the waiting list of Christian couples who wish to adopt LGH babies was a long one and that they pay substantial "fees" for the privilege, conditions which suggest that the success of Falwell's Liberty God-parent campaign may be as much due to its adoption as its anti-abortion aspect.

26. Falwell 1986, 55.

27. Falwell 1986, 56.

28. Falwell 1986, 57.

29. Falwell 1986, 29.

30. Falwell 1986, 95.

31. Falwell 1986, 125.

32. Falwell 1986, 126.

33. Note here that Jennifer's discursive interlocutors, whose authority she is displacing, include Catholics and Jews as well as feminists.

34. Falwell 1986, 91.

35. Falwell 1986, 110.

36. Falwell 1986, 14, 15.

37. Falwell 1986, 23.

38. Falwell 1986, 85.

39. Falwell 1986, 191–92.

40. *If I Should Die* establishes the primacy of the fetal-God relationship (and the independence of the fetus from the mother) through largely narrative means, but its readers bring other arguments to that effect to the text. Perhaps the strongest among them is the argument that the fetus is a "person," which lodges opposition to abortion in the founding premise of Protestantism, "the priesthood of the believer"—that the relationship between person and God is mediated by no man, or woman. ("The personhood of the fetus" is, of course, originally a

Catholic doctrine, yet in the mouths of these Protestants it acquires a slight anti-Catholic spin.)

41. Falwell 1986, 211.

42. Falwell 1986, 158–59.

43. Falwell 1986, 139.

44. Falwell 1986, 194–95.

45. Falwell 1986, 202.

46. Falwell 1986, 202–3.

47. Falwell 1986, 191.

48. Pointed demands for money, "a sacrificial gift of $400 to save the life of a baby," come in televised and direct-mail fund-raising pitches. *If I Should Die* figured in these pitches as a persuasive force after the fact, that is, as a "free gift" given in return to those who sacrificed themselves by sending in $400 to became "Liberty Godparents."

49. Falwell 1986, 216.

CHAPTER EIGHT

1. Larson 1997, 238. Joseph Wood Krutch used the term "folklore of liberalism" in a May 1967 article, "The Monkey Trial," in *Commentary*; Krutch had attended the Scopes trial as a reporter and attempted to correct widely circulating inaccuracies about it. See Larson 1997, 241, 244.

2. Relevant sources on the period include Larson 1997, Ribuffo 1983, Brinkley 1982, Hofstader 1965, Bell 1963, Hixon 1992.

3. The play was written by Jerome Lawrence and Robert E. Lee. While most reviews criticized the play and the movie as a caricature of the Scopes trial, both versions were immediately successful and remain so. Spencer Tracy was nominated for an Academy Award as best actor for his performance of Drummond/Darrow but lost, to Burt Lancaster, who won the prize for his portrayal of the title-role preacher in *Elmer Gantry* (see Larson 1997, 301–2, footnote 49).

4. Larson 1997, 240. See Larson 1997, 241 ff., for a discussion of the specific ways in which the play worked as a critique of McCarthyism.

5. Larson 1997, 241.

6. Lawrence and Lee 1955, 60.

7. Howard J. Van Till, a longtime opponent of anti-evolution within the evangelical community, reported to Edward Larson (1997, 245) that "many members of the conservative Christian community" think of the Scopes trial "as an episode in which William Jennings Bryan was skillfully manipulated by

a skilled but unprincipled lawyer representing an antitheistic scientific estab-lishment."

8. Nelkin 1982, chapter 1; Larson 1997, 230–31.

9. Nelkin 1982, 51. My main sources for this discussion are Nelkin 1982 and Larson 1997.

10. See Nelkin 1982.

11. Nelkin 1982, 51, and her chapter 8.

12. The following discussion is based on Numbers 1992, xi, and 299–301. See also Larson 1997.

13. Numbers 1992, x.

14. Numbers 1992, ix.

15. Numbers 1992, 299.

16. Numbers 1992, 300.

17. Numbers 1992, 204.

18. Numbers 1992, 209, and his preface.

19. Larson 1997, 237.

20. Numbers 1992, 242.

21. Numbers 1992, 287.

22. Nelkin 1982, 97 ff., and 139.

23. Bird 1978.

24. Numbers 1992, 212.

25. A similar conflict over accreditation and the teaching of creation occurred at LaHaye's Christian Heritage College a few years earlier; see Morris 1984, 228 ff.

26. See Numbers 1992, 212; Noll 1986, 191.

CHAPTER NINE

1. Willmington wrote about his gift to the future in his commentary on the Book of Revelation in his *Guide to the Bible* (1981c, 562–63), and Elmer Towns, the dean of Liberty Seminary, mentioned it in his sermon on "Iraq in Bible Prophecy" during the Persian Gulf War.

2. Willmington 1981c, 563.

3. Willmington 1981c, 562.

4. Willmington 1981c, 563. The tradition was taken up again by Tim La-Haye and Jerry Jenkins in their best-selling end-time novel, *Left Behind*. After the rapture, which occurs at the beginning of the novel, church members who were not truly saved and thus "left behind" find a videotape that explained and proof-texted the rapture and what would follow it. Their raptured pastor had left it for them so that they might be finally truly saved.

5. Weber 1983, 9, 32 ff.

6. Weber 1983, 229.

7. At least not in official doctrine. Debates among theologians are complicating dispensational theory and may eventually produce more formal shifts and adjustments. See Blaising and Bock (1993) for a sample of some of the current discussion in theological circles.

8. See Wilson 1977, 12; Weber 1983, 274; and Boyer 1992, 2–4. Weber (1983, 274) provides a list of the denominations doctrinally committed to dispensationalism or composed of large numbers of doctrinal believers. The Baptist Bible Fellowship, the General Association of Regular Baptist Churches, the Conservative Baptist Association of America, the Baptist General Conference, the Evangelical Free Church of America, the Independent Fundamental Churches of America, Plymouth Brethren, Grace Brethren, the Bible Presbyterian Church, and the Baptist Missionary Association are "predominantly premillennialist denominations." In addition, Weber notes, many independent and Bible churches are dispensationalist, as are most Pentecostal denominations, including the Assemblies of God, and there are large and vocal factions of premillennialists in nonpremillennialist denominations, including the Southern Baptist Convention.

Boyer distinguishes between doctrinal believers and "believers who may be hazy about the details of Biblical eschatology [the doctrine of "last things"], but who nevertheless believe that the Bible provides clues to future events. . . . This group, comprising many millions of Americans, is susceptible to popularizers who confidently weave Bible passages into highly imaginative end-time scenarios or promulgate particular schemes of prophetic interpretation" (1992, 2–3).

9. See Marsden 1980 and Weber 1983; also see Weber 1982.

10. See Noll et al. for a similar reading of dispensationalism as "strikingly anti-modernist. In many respects it looked like the mirror image of modernism. Modernism was optimistic about modern culture; dispensationalism was pessimistic. Most importantly, each centered around an interpretation of the relation of the Bible to history. Modernism interpreted the Bible through the lens of human history. Dispensationalists interpreted history exclusively through the lens of Scripture. Where modernism stressed the naturalistic, seeing social forces as being crucial to understanding religion, dispensationalists accentuated the supernatural, making divine intervention the direct solution to the modern problem of explaining historical change" (1983, 331).

11. Weber 1983, 240–41.

12. For extensive discussions of the shifting "signs of the times" in this century, see Wilson 1977, Weber 1983, and Boyer 1992. Marsden (1987, 71, 73) describes the wobbling of Arno Gaeblien (in *Our Hope*) and Wilbur Smith in

this regard. Wilbur Smith, for example, asserted the impossibility of equating current events/persons with prophecies, yet "found a remarkable number of prophetic statements that seemed to refer to the present era" (cited in Marsden 1987, 73).

13. According to Timothy Weber, turn-of the century advocates of a post-tribulational rapture were routed by the pretribulational party, which so succeeded in establishing its position as the orthodox and original one that "many dispensationalists today believe posttribulationalism is new" (1983, 241).

Posttribulationalism was revived after World War II by a host of evangelical scholars critical of orthodox dispensational biblical hermeneutics. The popular revival came later, was less explicit, and overlapped in many of its moves with the innovation of the "little tribulation," described shortly. The posttribulational view was popularized by Jim McKeever (1978) and more obliquely by Pat Robertson (1986; Robertson and Slosser 1984). See Weber 1983, 222–24, 241. On Robertson's position, see Harrell 1987, 143–49.

The major postmillennial elaboration within the New Christian Right was Kingdom Now theology (a.k.a. Dominion Theology and Christian Reconstructionism) associated with Rousas John Rushdoony and Gary North.

14. Hal Lindsey has written many Bible prophecy books. His titles include *The Rapture, There's a New World Coming, Satan Is Alive and Well on Planet Earth, Terminal Generation, The 1980s: Countdown to Armageddon, The Promise*, and *Combat Faith*. Books by other mainstream dispensational authors (Tim LaHaye, John Walvoord) also gained large readerships, but none on the scale of Lindsey's. Although some observers think a prophecy boom began in the 1970s, it probably makes more sense to think of the dispensational audience growing more gradually after World War II, fueled as much by the increasing level of education among born-again Christians as by the steadily growing circulation of books, pamphlets, movies, and crusaders (foremost among them, Billy Graham) articulating dispensational themes.

15. Lindsey 1980, 157.

16. LaHaye 1980, 218–19.

17. Graham 1983, 137, 129, 128. Graham, in fact, was not stepping out on a limb here but rather taking up an appeal made as early as the late 1940s by evangelical theologians such as Carl Henry and Harold Ockenga. According to Marsden (1987, 76), Henry and Ockenga, "while remaining premillennialist in a general sense, abandoned the central dispensationalist preoccupation with reading the prophetic signs so as to indicate that the present was incontrovertibly the end time." Graham did not go so far. He did not abandon those dispensationalist preoccupations, but he did, like Henry and Okenga, his friends and mentors, draw "on a view of history more characteristic of the mainstream of

the Reformed theological tradition. Modern culture, in this view, is not beyond hope, and Christians have the task of transforming culture to bring it more in conformity with God's law and will."

18. Weber 1983, 226.

19. The network was composed of churches in the Baptist Bible Fellowship (some three thousand of them, with membership rolls of 1.5 million by 1980) plus hundreds of fellow-traveller churches and preachers (such as Charles Stanley and W. A. Criswell's Southern Baptist churches).

20. Falwell, "1980 Bible Prophecy Update," *Old-Time Gospel Hour* audiotape.

21. Jerry Falwell's "Founder's Week Sermon," February 1, 1984, Moody Bible Institute audiotape FW84–5.

22. Not surprisingly, the Reverend Jerry Falwell was greatly alarmed by the 1992 Democratic National Convention and the election of Bill Clinton as president of the United States. For months after the election, my mailbox overflowed with "Letters from Jerry," mostly about Clinton's campaign to destroy both the military and America by letting "the gays" take over. In February 1993, he preached a sermon called "America Declares War on God," which concluded with his usual appeal to spiritual, moral, and political action in order to save America. But in his depiction of current events under Bill Clinton, "the country's first New Age president," Falwell deployed overtly tribulational imagery, that is, the language of irreversible cataclysm. At the very least, it seemed the Reverend Falwell was splicing his 1980s little tribulation with sounds and images from the great tribulation.

Other preachers and writers in the late 1980s and 1990s even more aggressively imagined America and Bible-believing Christians inside the great tribulation in their blockbuster best-selling Christian thrillers (Peretti 1986, 1989; Robertson 1995; LaHaye and Jenkins 1995, 1996, 1997, 1998, 1999a, 1999b).

CHAPTER TEN

1. Harrell 1975, 132–44.

2. Harrell 1975, 62.

3. Moore 1994, chapter 5.

4. Wiersbe 1988; Horton 1990; Schultze 1991. See also *Christianity Today* and *Charisma* articles in the late 1980s.

5. Koppel 1988.

6. Falwell was not a "typical" fundamentalist; nor were the Bakkers "typical" pentecostals. Instead, their communities exaggerated certain features of the cul-

tural trappings of their religious traditions in ways that seem to mimic the distinction between modern and postmodern cultural forms in secular architecture, literature, and popular culture. While both communities, relative to others like them, mixed and melded an unusually wide range of religious and cultural styles and idioms, both also worked hard to distinguish themselves from, and even repudiate, certain styles and idioms, in this instance, each other's.

7. See Hassan 1987 regarding the modern versus postmodern cultural contrasts.

8. Bakker and Bakker 1986, 91.

9. Coincidentally, "the house Jerry [Falwell] was born in was a gentleman's house that [his father] Carey had moved piece by piece from Rivermont, the wealthy section of town" (FitzGerald 1986, 144).

10. Barthes 1972, 23.

11. Ted Koppel did not actually discover John Sherfey. Jeff Todd Titon, an ethnomusicologist and folklorist, had been working with Sherfey and his Appalachian community for ten years, and they were the subject of a major monograph Titon published that year (1988).

12. See Said 1997, xvii. Said suggests that the Fundamentalism Project "was started precisely with Islam in mind," and he goes on to make a case that Islamic fundamentalism, or simply Islam, has replaced both Protestant Fundamentalism and Communism as the premier Western pariah.

POSTSCRIPT

1. See Chakrabarty 1992, Rofel 1999, Gupta 1998, Ivy 1995, Ferguson 1990, and Latour 1993.

2. "Disenchantment" is Max Weber's term, and he was the theoretical source of most work in the social sciences on modernization and secularization. Sociologists produced the strongest versions of the story of modern disenchantment under a variety of rubrics—modernization theory, development theory, theories of capitalism, nationalism, and state-making. Most of the theorizing focused on objects other than religion or religiosity, but religious modernity was invariably implicated as an aside, a side-effect, or a presupposition.

Briefly, social scientists told us "the modern era" was the outcome of the development of industrial capitalism and modern nation-states and their attendant processes, the great modernizing "-ations"—urbanization, immigration, class formation, institutional differentiation, bureaucratization, rationalization, and secularization. Each of these processes was understood to be intensifying, spreading, becoming more global over time—that is, each provided modern history with a trajectory, a telos.

Of them all, secularization was the most derivative: it was the inexorable outcome of urbanization and immigration, which increasingly juxtaposed and therefore relativized discrepant worldviews. It was an intrinsic aspect of bureaucratization and rationalization, which produced generic zones and codes of action and speech that homogenized cultural differences. And it was the result of social differentiation, which increasingly privatized religions as other institutions, mostly governmental, appropriated many of its social functions.

Secularization was derivative but central in that the disenchantment of the world, the world's desupernaturalization, was an essential, defining feature of the modern era. The story of modernity naturalized secularization and the cultural domination of those who accommodated to secularizing processes by making them appear to be the inevitable—natural—outcomes of transhistorical processes during the late nineteenth and twentieth centuries.

3. Frei 1974, 3.

4. Frei 1974, 3.

5. Frei 1974, 48. According to Frei, Christian writers increasingly came to see events, history, and the "real" world as autonomous from and prior to biblical description. Events had to be fitted into a biblical framework, not vice versa. "There is now a logical distinction and a reflective distance between the stories and the 'reality' they depict" (5). Efforts to bridge the steadily growing gap between biblical narrative and reality took a variety of forms, but they invariably failed. Attempts to verify Bible stories only confirmed the autonomy of events. Figural readings that once presumed and produced a unity of biblical and historical events looked "like a forced, arbitrary imposition of unity on a group of very diverse texts. No longer an extension of literal reading, figural [or typological] interpretation becomes a bad historical argument or an arbitrary allegorizing of texts in the service of preconceived dogma" (37).

6. It is also quite likely that, at least with respect to Christianity, the forces of disenchantment are nothing new either. According to Cameron (1991), the first Christians in the Roman empire were surrounded by and actively in dialogue with skeptics and rationalists.

Bibliography

Allen, Leslie H., ed. 1967. *Bryan and Darrow at Dayton: The Record of the "Bible Evolution Trial."* New York: Russell and Russell.

Alsdurf, James, and Phyllis Alsdurf. 1989. *Battered into Submission: The Tragedy of Wife Abuse in the Christian Home.* Downers Grove, IL: InterVarsity Press.

Alter, Robert. 1981. *The Art of Biblical Narrative.* New York: Basic Books.

Alter, Robert. 1985. *The Art of Biblical Poetry.* New York: Basic Books.

Alter, Robert, and Frank Kermode. 1987. *The Literary Guide to the Bible.* Cambridge, MA: Harvard University Press.

Ammerman, Nancy Tatom. 1987. *Bible Believers.* New Brunswick, NJ: Rutgers University Press.

Ammerman, Nancy Tatom. 1990. *Baptist Battles: Social Change and Religious Conflict in the Southern Baptist Convention.* New Brunswick, NJ: Rutgers University Press.

Ammerman, Nancy Tatom. 1991. North American Protestant Fundamentalism. In *Fundamentalisms Observed*, edited by M. E. Marty and R. Scott Appleby. Chicago: University of Chicago Press.

Ammerman, Nancy Tatom. 1993. *Southern Baptists Observed: Multiple Perspectives on a Changing Denomination.* Knoxville: University of Tennessee Press.

Ammerman, Nancy Tatom. 1994. The Dynamics of Christian Fundamentalism: An Introduction. In *Accounting for Fundamentalisms: The Dynamic Character of Movements*, edited by M. E. Marty and R. Scott Appleby. Chicago: University of Chicago Press.

Auerbach, Erich. 1953. *Mimesis: The Representation of Reality in Modern Literature.* Princeton, NJ: Princeton University Press.

Auerbach, Erich. 1959. *Scenes from the Drama of European Literature.* New York: Meridian Books.

Bakhtin, M. M. 1981. Discourse in the Novel. In *The Dialogic Imagination: Four Essays by M. M. Bakhtin*, edited by M. Holquist. Austin: University of Texas Press.

Bakhtin, M. M. 1984. *Problems in Dostoevsky's Poetics.* Minneapolis: University of Minnesota Press.

Bakker, James, and Tammy Faye Bakker. 1986. *Heritage Village Church*. Toronto: Boulton Publishing Services.

Bakker, Jim. 1976. *Move That Mountain!* Charlotte, NC: PTL Television Network.

Balmer, Randall. 1989. *Mine Eyes Have Seen the Glory: A Journey into the Evangelical Subculture in America*. New York: Oxford University Press.

Barthes, Roland. 1972. *Mythologies*. New York: Noonday Press.

Basso, Keith. 1996. *Wisdom Sits in Places: Landscape and Language among the Western Apache*. Albuquerque: University of New Mexico Press.

Bauman, Richard. 1977. *Verbal Art as Performance*. Prospect Heights, IL: Waveland Press.

Beale, David O. 1986. *In Pursuit of Purity: American Fundamentalism since 1850*. Greenville, SC: Bob Jones University Press.

Becker, A. L. 1996. The Biography of a Sentence: A Burmese Proverb. In *The Matrix of Language: Contemporary Linguistic Anthropology*, edited by D. Brenneis and Ronald H. S. Macaulay. Boulder, CO: Westview Press.

Bederman, Gail. 1996. The Men and Religion Forward Movement. In *A Mighty Baptism: Race, Gender, and the Creation of American Protestantism*, edited by S. Juster and Lisa MacFarlane. Ithaca, NY: Cornell University Press.

Bell, Daniel. 1963. *The Radical Right*. Garden City, NY: Doubleday.

Bendroth, Margaret. 1993. *Fundamentalism and Gender, 1875 to the Present*. New Haven, CT: Yale University Press.

Bercovich, Sacvan. 1978. *American Jeremiad*. Madison: University of Wisconsin Press.

Berger, Brigitte, and Peter L. Berger. 1983. *The War over the Family: Capturing the Middle Ground*. Garden City, NY: Anchor Press.

Berger, Harry, Jr. 1988. *Second World and Green World: Studies in Renaissance Fiction-Making*. Berkeley: University of California Press.

Berger, Harry, Jr. 1989. *Imaginary Audition:Shakespeare on Stage and Page*. Berkeley: University of California Press.

Berger, Harry, Jr. 1997. *Making Trifles of Terrors: Redistributing Complicities in Shakespeare*. Stanford, CA: Stanford University Press.

Bird, Wendell R. 1978. Freedom of Religion and Science Instruction in Public Schools. *Yale Law Journal* 87:515–570.

Blaising, Craig A., and Darrell L. Bock. 1993. *Progressive Dispensationalism*. Wheaton, IL: Victor Books.

Bockelman, Wilfred. 1976. *Gothard: The Man and His Ministry, An Evaluation*. Santa Barbara, CA: Quill Publications.

Boone, Kathleen C. 1989. *The Bible Tells Them So: The Discourse of Protestant Fundamentalism*. Albany: State University of New York Press.

Borker, Ruth. n.d. The Presentation of the Gospel in Everyday Life. Unpublished manuscript.

Boyarin, Daniel. 1990. *Intertextuality and the Reading of Midrash*. Bloomington: Indiana University Press.

Boyd, Blanche. 1977. *Mourning the Death of Magic*. New York: Macmillan.

Boyer, Paul. 1992. *When Time Shall Be No More: Prophecy Belief in Modern American Culture*. Cambridge, MA: Harvard Unversity Press.

Breasted, Mary. 1970. *Oh! Sex Education!* New York: Praeger.

Bright, Charles, and Susan Harding, eds. 1984. *Statemaking and Social Movements*. Ann Arbor: University of Michigan Press.

Brinkley, Alan. 1982. *Voices of Protest: Huey Long, Father Coughlin, and the Great Depression*. New York: Alfred A. Knopf.

Brooks, Peter. 1984. *Reading for the Plot: Design and Intention in Narrative*. Cambridge, MA: Harvard University Press.

Burke, Kenneth. 1941. *Philosophy of Literary From: Studies in Symbolic Action*. Baton Rouge: Louisiana State University Press.

Burke, Kenneth. 1966. *Language as Symbolic Action: Essays on Life, Literature, and Method*. Berkeley: University of California Press.

Burke, Kenneth. 1989. The Rhetoric of Hitler's "Battle." In *Kenneth Burke: On Symbols and Society*, edited by J. R. Gusfield. Chicago: University of Chicago Press.

Cameron, Averil. 1991. *Christianity and the Rhetoric of Empire: The Development of Christian Discourse*. Berkeley: University of California Press.

Carpenter, Joel A. 1997. *Revive Us Again: The Reawakening of American Fundamentalism*. New York: Oxford University Press.

Carter, Paul A. 1968. The Fundamentalist Defense of the Faith. In *Change and Continuity in Twentieth-Century America*, edited by J. Braeman, Robert H. Bremner, and David Brody. Columbus: Ohio State University Press.

Carter, Stephen L. 1993. *The Culture of Disbelief: How American Law and Politics Trivialize Religious Devotion*. New York: Basic Books.

Chakrabarty, Dipesh. 1992. Postcoloniality and the Artifice of History: Who Speaks for the "Indian" Pasts? *Representations* (37):1–26.

Chambers, Ross. 1991. *Room for Maneuver: Reading (the) Oppositional (in) Narrative*. Chicago: University of Chicago Press.

Cohen, Norman J., ed. 1990. *The Fundamentalist Phenomenon: A View from Within, A Response from Without*. Grand Rapids, MI: William B. Eerdmans.

Cohn, Norman. 1961. *The Pursuit of the Millennium*. New York: Harper and Row.

Colson, Charles W. 1976. *Born Again*. Old Tappan, NJ: Fleming H. Revell.

Colson, Charles W. 1987. *Kingdoms in Conflict*. New York: William Morrow/
Zondervan.

Criswell, W. A. 1979. *Criswell Study Bible*. Nashville: Thomas Nelson.

Cross, Whitney R. 1950. *The Burned-over District: The Social and Intellectual History of Enthusiastic Religion in Western New York, 1800–1850*. New York: Harper and Row.

Culler, Jonathan. 1981. *The Pursuit of Signs*. Ithaca, NY: Cornell University Press.

Culler, Jonathan. 1997. *A Very Short Introduction to Literary Theory*. Oxford: Oxford University Press.

Dalhouse, Mark Taylor. 1996. *An Island in the Lake of Fire: Bob Jones, Fundamentalism, and the Separatist Movement*. Athens: University of Georgia Press.

Daniel, Pete. 1986. *Standing at the Crossroads: Southern Life in the Twentieth Century*. New York: Hill and Wang.

D'Antonio, Michael. 1989. *Fall from Grace: The Failed Crusade of the Christian Right*. New York: Farrar Straus Giroux.

DeBerg, Betty. 1990. *Ungodly Women: Gender and the First Wave of American Fundamentalism*. Minneapolis: University of Minnesota Press.

Diamond, Sara. 1995. *Roads to Dominion: Right-wing Movements and Political Power in the United States*. New York: Guilford Press.

Dollar, George W. 1973. *A History of Fundamentalism in America*. Greenville, SC: Bob Jones University Press.

Dollar, George W. 1983. *The Fight for Fundamentalism: American Fundamentalism, 1973–1983*. Sarasota, FL: Author.

Douglas, Ann. 1977. *The Feminization of American Culture*. New York: Alfred A. Knopf.

D'Souza, Dinesh. 1984. *Falwell before the Millennium: A Critical Biography*. Chicago: Regnery Gateway.

Edwards, David. 1989. Mad Mullahs and Englishmen: Discourse in the Colonial Encounter. *Comparative Studies in Society and History* 31 (4).

Falwell, Jerry. 1978. *How You Can Help Clean Up America: An Action Program for Decency in Your Community*. Lynchburg, VA: Liberty Publishing.

Falwell, Jerry, ed. 1978. *Liberty Bible Commentary: New Testament*. Lynchburg, VA: Old-Time Gospel Hour.

Falwell, Jerry. 1979. *America Can Be Saved*. Murfreesboro, TN: Sword of the Lord Publishers.

Falwell, Jerry. 1980. *The Future, the Bible, and You*. Lynchburg, VA: Old-Time Gospel Hour.

Falwell, Jerry. 1981. *Listen America!* New York: Bantam Books.

Falwell, Jerry, ed. 1982. *Liberty Bible Commentary: Old Testament.* Lynchburg, VA: Old-Time Gospel Hour.

Falwell, Jerry. 1986. *If I Should Die before I Wake.* . . . . Nashville: Thomas Nelson.

Falwell, Jerry. 1987. *Strength for the Journey: An Autobiography.* New York: Simon and Schuster.

Falwell, Jerry. 1992. *The New American Family: The Rebirth of the American Dream.* Dallas: Word Publishing.

Falwell, Jerry, and Elmer Towns. 1971. *Church Aflame.* Nashville: Impact Books.

Falwell, Jerry, and Elmer Towns. 1973. *Capturing a Town for Christ: Saturation Evangelism in Action.* Old Tappan, NJ: Fleming H. Revell.

Falwell, Jerry, and Elmer Towns. 1984. *Stepping Out on Faith.* Wheaton, IL: Tyndale House.

Falwell, Jerry, Ed Dobson, and Ed Hindson, eds. 1981. *The Fundamentalist Phenomenon: The Resurgence of Conservative Christianity.* Garden City, NY: Doubleday.

Favret-Saada, Jeanne. 1980. *Deadly Words: Witchcraft in the Bocage.* Cambridge, UK: University of Cambridge Press.

Ferguson, James. 1990. *The Anti-Politics Machine: "Development," Depolitization, and Bureaucratic Power in Lesotho.* Minneapolis: University of Minnesota Press.

Fish, Stanley. 1980. *Is There a Text in This Class? The Authority of Interpretive Communities.* Cambridge, MA: Harvard University Press.

Fishburn, Janet Forsythe. 1981. *The Fatherhood of God and the Victorian Family: The Social Gospel in America.* Philadelphia: Fortress Press.

FitzGerald, Frances. 1985. The American Millennium. *The New Yorker,* November 11, 1985, 105–96.

FitzGerald, Frances. 1986. *Cities on a Hill: A Journey through Contemporary American Cultures.* New York: Simon and Schuster.

Foucault, Michel. 1972. *The Archaeology of Knowledge and the Discourse of Language.* New York: Pantheon.

Foucault, Michel. 1979. *Discipline and Punish: The Birth of the Prison.* New York: Vintage.

Fowler, Paul B. 1987. *Abortion: Toward an Evangelical Consensus.* Portland, OR: Multnomah Press.

Fowler, Robert Booth. 1982. *The New Engagement: Evangelical Political Thought, 1966–1976.* Grand Rapids, MI: William B. Eerdmans.

Frady, Marshall. 1979. *Billy Graham: A Parable of American Righteousness.* Boston: Little, Brown.

Frank, Douglas W. 1986. *Less Than Conquerors: How Evangelicals Entered the Twentieth Century.* Grand Rapids, MI: William B. Eerdmans.

Frei, Hans W. 1974. *The Eclipse of Biblical Narrative: A Study of Eighteenth and Nineteenth Century Hermeneutics.* New Haven, CT: Yale University Press.

Frei, Hans W. 1986. The "Literal Reading" of Biblical Narrative in the Christian Tradition: Does It Stretch or Will It Break? In *The Bible and the Narrative Tradition,* edited by F. McConnell. New York: Oxford University Press.

Freund, Elizabeth. 1987. *The Return of the Reader: Reader-Response Criticism.* London: Methuen.

Friedman, Richard Elliot. 1987. *Who Wrote the Bible?* New York: Summit Books.

Frye, Northrop. 1976. *The Secular Scripture: A Study of the Structure of Romance.* Cambridge, MA: Harvard University Press.

Frye, Northrop. 1982. *The Great Code: The Bible and Literature.* New York: Harcourt Brace Jovanovich.

Furniss, Norman. 1954. *The Fundamentalist Controversy, 1918–1931.* New Haven, CT: Yale University Press.

Gallup, George, Jr. 1982. *Religion in America.* The Gallup Report. Princeton, NJ: Princeton Religious Research Center.

Gatewood, William B. 1969. *Controversy in the Twenties.* Nashville: Vanderbilt University Press.

Geertz, Clifford. 1968. *Islam Observed: Religious Development in Morocco and Indonesia.* Chicago: University of Chicago Press.

Geertz, Clifford. 1973. *The Interpretation of Cultures.* New York: Basic Books.

Gillis, John. 1996. *A World of Their Own Making: Myth, Ritual, and the Quest for Family Values.* New York: Basic Books.

Gilsenan, Michael. 1982. *Recognizing Islam: An Anthropologist's Introduction.* New York: Pantheon.

Ginsburg, Faye. 1989. *Contested Lives: The Abortion Debate in an American Community.* Berkeley: University of California Press.

Girard, Rene. 1977. *Violence and the Sacred.* Baltimore: Johns Hopkins University Press.

Girard, Rene. 1986. *The Scapegoat.* Baltimore: Johns Hopkins University Press.

Graham, Billy. 1983. *Approaching Hoofbeats: The Four Horsemen of the Apocalypse.* Waco, TX: Word Books.

Green, John C., James L. Guth, Corwin E. Smidt, and Lyman A. Kellstedt, eds. 1996. *Religion and the Culture Wars: Dispatches from the Front.* Lanham, MD: Rowman and Littlefield.

Gupta, Akhil. 1998. *Postcolonial Developments: Agriculture in the Making of Modern India.* Durham, NC: Duke University Press.

Gusfield, Joseph R. 1963. *Symbolic Crusade: Status Politics and the American Temperance Movement*. Urbana: University of Illinois Press.

Gusfield, Joseph R., ed. 1989. *On Symbols and Society: Kenneth Burke*. Chicago: University of Chicago Press.

Guth, James L., and John C. Green, eds. 1991. *The Bible and the Ballot Box: Religion and Politics in the 1988 Election*. Boulder, CO: Westview Press.

Guth, James L., and John C. Green. 1996. The Moralizing Minority: Christian Right Support among Political Contributors. In *Religion and the Culture Wars: Dispatches from the Front*, edited by J. C. Green, James L. Guth, Corwin E. Smidt, and Lyman A. Kellstedt. Lanham, MD: Rowman and Littlefield.

Habershon, Ada. 1974. *The Study of Types*. Grand Rapids, MI: Kregel Publications.

Hadaway, C. Kirk, Penny Long Marler, and Mark Chaves. 1993. What the Polls Don't Show: A Closer Look at U.S. Church Attendance. *American Journal of Sociology* 58:741–752.

Hadden, Jeffrey K. 1989. Religious Broadcasting and the Mobilization of the New Christian Right. In *Secularization and Fundamentalism Reconsidered*, edited by J. K. Hadden and Anson Shupe. New York: Paragon.

Hadden, Jeffrey K., and Anson Shupe, eds. 1986. *Prophetic Religions and Politics*. New York: Paragon.

Hadden, Jeffrey K., and Anson Shupe. 1988. *Televangelism: Power and Politics on God's Frontier*. New York: Henry Holt.

Hadden, Jeffrey, and Charles W. Swann. 1981. *Prime-Time Preachers: The Rising Power of Televangelism*. Reading, MA: Addison-Wesley.

Hammond, Phillip E., ed. 1985. *The Sacred in a Secular Age: Toward Revision in the Scientific Study of Religion*. Berkeley: University of California Press.

Handelman, Susan A. 1982. *The Slayers of Moses: The Emergence of Rabbinic Interpretation in Modern Literary Theory*. Albany: State University of New York Press.

Hankins, Barry. 1996. *God's Rascal: J. Frank Norris and the Beginnings of Southern Fundamentalism*. Lexington: University of Kentucky Press.

Haraway, Donna. 1991. *Simians, Cyborgs, and Monsters: A Regenerative Politics for Inappropriate/d Others*. New York: Routledge.

Harding, Susan. 1981. Family Reform Movements: Recent Feminism and Its Opposition. *Feminist Studies* 7:57–75.

Harding, Susan. 1984. Reconstructing Order through Action: Jim Crow and the Southern Civil Rights Movement. In *Statemaking and Social Movements: Essays in History and Theory*, edited by Charles Bright and Susan Harding. Ann Arbor: University of Michigan Press.

Harding, Susan. 1987. Convicted by the Holy Spirit: The Rhetoric of Fundamental Baptist Conversion. *American Ethnologist* 14 (1):167–181.

Harding, Susan. 1990. If I Should Die Before I Wake: Jerry Falwell's Pro-life Gospel. In *Uncertain Terms: Renegotiating Gender in American Culture*, edited by Faye Ginsburg and Anna Tsing. Boston: Beacon Press.

Harding, Susan. 1991. Representing Fundamentalism: The Problem of the Repugnant Cultural Other. *Social Research* 58 (2):373–393.

Harding, Susan. 1992. The Afterlife of Stories: The Genesis of a Man of God. In *Storied Lives: The Cultural Politics of Self-Undestanding*, edited by Richard Ockberg and George Rosenwald. New Haven CT: Yale University Press.

Harding, Susan. 1992. The Gospel of Giving: The Narrative Construction of a Sacrificial Economy. In *Vocabularies of Public Life*, edited by Robert Wuthnow, New York: Routledge.

Harding, Susan. 1993. The Born-Again Telescandals. In *Culture/Power/History*, edited by Nicholas Dirks, Geoffrey Eley, and Sherry Ortner. Princeton, NJ: Princeeton University Press.

Harding, Susan. 1994. Imagining the Last Days: The Politics of Apocalyptic Language. In *Accounting for Fundamentalisms: The Dynamic Character of Movements*, edited by Martin E. Marty and R. Scott Appleby. Chicago: University of Chicago Press.

Hariston, Julie. 1987. Is PTL's Savior Facing His Own Judgment Day? *The Independent*, May 7–20, 1987.

Harrell, David Edwin, Jr. 1975. *All Things Are Possible: The Healing and Charismatic Revivals in Modern America*. Bloomington: Indiana University Press.

Harrell, David Edwin, Jr. 1985. *Oral Roberts: An American Life*. New York: Harper and Row.

Harrell, David Edwin, Jr. 1987. *Pat Roberston: A Personal, Political, and Religious Portrait*. San Francisco: Harper and Row.

Harris, Ralph W. 1977. *Pictures of Truth*. Springfield, MO: Gospel Publishing House.

Hassan, Ibn. 1987. *The Postmodern Turn*. Columbus: Ohio State University.

Hatch, Nathan O., and Mark A. Noll, ed. 1982. *The Bible in America: Essays in Cultural History*. New York: Oxford University Press.

Heirich, Max. 1977. A Change of Heart: A Test of Some Widely Held Theories of Religious Conversion. *American Journal of Sociology* 83 (3):653–680.

Herberg, Will. 1960. *Protestant, Catholic, Jew*. Garden City, NY: Anchor Books.

Hill, Samuel S. 1985. *The South and the North in American Religion*. Athens: University of Georgia Press.

Hindson, Ed. 1976. *The Total Family*. Lynchburg, VA: Old-Time Gospel Hour. Audio tape series.

Hindson, Ed. 1980. *The Total Family*. Wheaton, IL: Tyndale House.

Hitchcock, James. 1982. *What Is Secular Humanism: Why Humanism Became Secular and How It Is Changing Our World*. Ann Arbor, MI: Servant Books.

Hixon, William B., Jr. 1992. *Search for the American Right Wing: Social Science Record, 1955–1987*. Princeton, NJ: Princeton University Press.

Hofstadter, Richard. 1965. *The Paranoid Style of American Politics, and Other Essays*. New York: Alfred A. Knopf.

Horsch, John. 1920. *Modern Religious Liberalism*. Chicago: Bible Institute Colportage Association.

Horton, Michael. 1990. *The Agony of Deceit: What Some TV Preachers Are Really Teaching*. Chicago: Moody Press.

Hunter, James. 1983. *American Evangelicalism: Conservative Religion and the Quandary of Modernity*. New Brunswick, NJ: Rutgers University Press.

Hunter, James. 1987. *Evangelicalism: The Coming Generation*. Chicago: University of Chicago Press.

Hunter, James Davidson. 1991. *Culture Wars: The Struggle to Define America*. New York: Basic Books.

Hurley, James B. 1986. "Schaeffer on Evangelicalism." In *Reflections on Francis Schaeffer*, edited by Ronald W. Ruegsegger. Grand Rapids, MI: Zondervan.

Ivy, Marilyn. 1995. Discourses of the Vanishing: Modernity, Phantasm, Japan. Chicago: University of Chicago Press.

James, William. 1906. *Varieties of Religious Experience*. New York: Collier Books.

Jencks, Charles. 1977. *The Language of Post-modern Architecture*. New York: Rizzoli.

Jencks, Charles. 1986. *What Is Post-Modernism*. New York: St. Martin's Press.

Jules-Rosette, Benetta. 1976. The Conversion Experience: The Apostles of John Maranke. *Journal of Religion in Africa* 7 (2):132–64.

Juster, Susan. 1992. *Disorderly Women: Sexual Politics and Evangelicalism in Revolutionary New England*. Ithaca, NY: Cornell University Press.

Kermode, Frank. 1979. *The Genesis of Secrecy: On the Interpretation of Narrative*. Cambridge, MA: Harvard University Press.

Kermode, Frank. 1986. The Plain Sense of Things. In *Midrash and Literature*, edited by G. H. Hartman and Sanford Burdick. New Haven, CT: Yale University Press.

Klein, Patricia, Evelyn Bence, Jane Campbell, Laura Pearson, and David Wimbish. 1987. *Growing Up Born Again: A Whimsical Look at the Blessings and Tribulations of Growing Up Born Again*. Old Tappan, NJ: Fleming H. Revell.

Koop, C. Everett, and Francis Schaeffer. 1978. *Whatever Happened to the Human Race?* Westchester, IL: Crossway Books.

Koppel, Ted. 1988. "The Billion-Dollar Pie." Ted Koppel Special Report.

LaHaye, Tim. 1980. *The Battle for the Mind*. Old Tappan, NJ: Fleming H. Revell.

LaHaye, Tim. 1982. *The Battle for the Family*. Old Tappan, NJ: Fleming H. Revell.

LaHaye, Tim, and Jerry B. Jenkins. 1995. *Left Behind: A Novel of the Last Days on Earth*. Wheaton, IL: Tyndale Publishing House.

LaHaye, Tim, and Jerry B. Jenkins. 1996. *Tribulation Force: The Continuing Drama of Those Left Behind*. Wheaton, IL: Tyndale Publishing House.

LaHaye, Tim, and Jerry B. Jenkins. 1997. *Nicolae: The Rise of the Antichrist*. Wheaton, IL: Tyndale Publishing House.

LaHaye, Tim, and Jerry B. Jenkins. 1998. *Soul Harvest: The World Takes Sides*. Wheaton, IL: Tyndale Publishing House.

LaHaye, Tim, and Jerry B. Jenkins. 1999a. *Appollyon: The Destroyer Is Unleashed*. Wheaton, IL: Tyndale Publishing House.

LaHaye, Tim, and Jerry B. Jenkins. 1999b. *Assassins*. Wheaton, IL: Tyndale Publishing House.

Landow, George P. 1980. *Victorian Types, Victorian Shadows: Biblical Typology in Victorian Literature, Art, and Thought*. Boston: Routledge and Kegan Paul.

Larson, Edward J. 1997. *Summer of the Gods: The Scopes Trial and America's Continuing Debate over Science and Religion*. New York: Basic Books.

Lash, Scott, and John Urry. 1987. *The End of Organized Capitalism*. Cambridge, U.K.: Polity Press.

Latour, Bruno. 1993. *We Have Never Been Modern*. Cambridge, MA: Harvard University Press.

Lawrence, Jerome, and Robert E. Lee. 1955. *Inherit the Wind*. New York: Bantam Books.

Laymon, Charles M. 1971. *The Interpreter's One-Volume Commentary on the Bible*. Nashville: Abington Press.

Levine, Lawrence W. 1965. *Defender of the Faith: William Jennings Bryan*. New York: Oxford University Press.

Liebman, Robert C., and Robert Wuthnow. 1983. *The New Christian Right: Mobilization and Legitimation*. Hawthorne, NY: Aldine.

Lienesch, Michael. 1993. *Redeeming America: Piety and Politics in the New Christian Right*. Chapel Hill: University of North Carolina Press.

Lindsell, Harold. 1976. *The Battle for the Bible*. Grand Rapids, MI: Zondervan.

Lindsey, Hal. 1972. *Satan Is Alive and Well on Planet Earth*. Grand Rapids, MI: Zondervan.

Lindsey, Hal. 1970. *The Late Great Planet Earth*. Grand Rapids, MI: Zondervan.

Lindsey, Hal. 1973. *There's a New World Coming*. Eugene, OR: Harvest House.

Lindsey, Hal. 1976. *The Terminal Generation*. Old Tappan, NJ: Fleming H. Revell.

Lindsey, Hal. 1980. *The 1980s: Countdown to Armageddon*. New York: Bantam Books.

Lindsey, Hal. 1982. *The Promise*. Eugene, OR: Harvest House.

Lindsey, Hal. 1983. *The Rapture*. New York: Bantam Books.

Lindsey, Hal. 1986. *Combat Faith*. New York: Bantam Books.

Lloyd, Mark. 1988. *Pioneers of Prime-Time Religion*. Dubuque, IA: Kendall Publishing.

Luker, Kristin. 1984. *Abortion and the Politics of Motherhood*. Berkeley: University of California Press.

Macaulay, Ronald H. S. 1994. *The Social Art of Language and Its Uses*. Oxford: Oxford University Press.

Marcus, George. 1995. On Eccentricity. In *Rhetorics of Self-Making*, edited by D. Battaglia. Berkeley: University of California Press.

Marsden, George M. 1980. *Fundamentalism and American Culture: The Shaping of a Twentieth-Century Evangelicalism, 1870–1925*. Oxford: Oxford University Press.

Marsden, George M. 1984. *Evangelicalism and Modern America*. Grand Rapids, MI: William B. Eerdmans.

Marsden, George M. 1987. *Reforming Fundamentalism: Fuller Seminary and the New Evangelicalism*. Grand Rapids, MI: William B. Eerdmans.

Marsden, George M. 1991. *Understanding Fundamentalism and Evangelicalism*. Grand Rapids MI: William B. Eerdmans.

Martin, William. 1996. *With God on Our Side: The Rise of the Religious Right in America*. New York: Broadway Books.

Mathews, Donald G. 1977. *Religion in the Old South*. Chicago: University of Chicago Press.

Mathews, Donald G., and Jane Sherron De Hart. 1990. *Sex, Gender, and the Politics of ERA: A State and the Nation*. New York: Oxford University Press.

Mathews, Shailer. 1925. *The Faith of Modernism*. New York: Macmillan.

McConnell, Frank, ed. 1986. *The Bible and the Narrative Tradition*. New York: Oxford University Press.

McDannell, Collen. 1986. *The Christian Home in Victorian America, 1840–1900*. Bloomington: Indiana University Press.

McDowell, Josh. 1987. *"What I Wish My Parents Knew about My Sexuality."* San Bernadino, CA: Here's Life Publications.

McKeever, Jim. 1978. *Christians Will Go through the Tribulation*. Medford, OR: Omega Publications.

Mead, Frank S. 1985. *Handbook of Denominations in the United States*. Nashville: Abington Press.

Miller, Keith. 1992. *Voice of Deliverance: The Language of Martin Luther King, Jr.* New York: Free Press.

Moore, R. Laurence. 1986. *Religious Outsiders and the Making of Americans*. New York: Oxford University Press.

Moore, R. Laurence. 1994. *Selling God: American Religion and the Marketplace of Culture*. Oxford: Oxford University Press.

Morgan, Marabel. 1973. *The Total Woman*. Old Tappan, NJ: Fleming H. Revell.

Morris, Henry M. 1984. *A History of Modern Creationism*. San Diego: Master Book.

Morson, Gary Saul. 1989. Parody, History, and Mataparody. In *Rethinking Bakhtin: Extensions and Challenges*, edited by G. S. Morson and Caryl Emerson. Evanston, IL: Northwestern University Press.

Myerhoff, Barbara, and Lynn Littman. 1986. *In Her Own Time*. Film.

Nelkin, Dorothy. 1982. *The Creation Controversy: Science or Scripture in the Schools*. Boston: Beacon Press.

Nelson, Shirley. 1978. *The Last Year of the War*. New York: Harper and Row.

Neuhaus, Richard John. 1984. *The Naked Public Square: Religion and Democracy in America*. Grand Rapids, MI: William B. Eerdmans.

Neuhaus, Richard John, ed. 1986. *Unsecular America*. Grand Rapids, MI: William B. Eerdmans.

Noll, Mark A. 1986. *Between Faith and Criticism: Evangelicals, Scholarship, and the Bible in America*. San Francisco: Harper and Row.

Noll, Mark A., ed. 1990. *Religion and American Politics*. New York: Oxford University Press.

Noll, Mark A. 1994. *The Scandal of the Evangelical Mind*. Grand Rapids, MI: William B. Eerdmans.

Noll, Mark A., Nathan O. Hatch, George M. Marsden, David F. Wells, and John D. Woodbridge, eds. 1983. *Eerdmans' Handbook to Christianity in America*. Grand Rapids, MI: William B. Eerdmans.

Numbers, Ronald L. 1992. *The Creationists: The Evolution of Scientific Creationism*. Berkeley: University of California Press.

Peretti, Frank E. 1986. *This Present Darkness*. Westchester, IL: Crossway Books.

Peretti, Frank E. 1989. *Piercing the Darkness*. Westchester, IL: Crossway Books.

Pierard, Richard V. 1984. The New Religious Right in American Politics. In *Evangelicalism and Modern America*, edited by George Marsden. Grand Rapids, MI: William B. Eerdmans.

Pingry, Patricia. 1980. *Jerry Falwell: A Man of Vision*. Milwaukee: Ideals Publishing.

Pinnock, Clyde H. 1986. Schaeffer on Modern Theology. In *Reflections on Francis Schaeffer*, edited by R. W. Ruegsegger. Grand Rapids, MI: Zondervan.

Radway, Janice. 1984. *Reading the Romance: Women, Patriarchy, and Popular Literature*. Chapel Hill: University of North Carolina Press.

Ribuffo, Leo P. 1983. *The Old Christian Right: The Protestant Far Right from the Great Depression to the Cold War*. Philadelphia: Temple University Press.

Ribuffo, Leo. 1989. God and Jimmy Carter. In *Transforming Faith: The Sacred and the Secular in Modern America*, edited by M. L. Bradbury and James B. Gilbert. Westport, CT: Greenwood Press.

Rice, John R. 1941. *Bobbed Hair, Bossy Wives, and Women Preachers*. Murfreesboro, TN: Sword of the Lord Publishers.

Rice, John R. 1945. *Home, Courtship, Marriage, and Children: A Bible Manual of Twenty-two Chapters on the Christian Home*. Wheaton, IL: Sword of the Lord Publishers.

Rimmon-Kenan, Shlomith. 1983. *Narrative Fiction: Contemporary Poetics*. London: Methuen.

Robertson, Pat. 1972. *Shout It from the Housetops*. South Plainfield, NJ: Bridge Publishing.

Robertson, Pat. 1986. *America's Dates with Destiny*. Nashville: Thomas Nelson.

Robertson, Pat. 1995. *The End of the Age*. Dallas: Word Publishing.

Roberston, Pat, and Bob Slosser. 1984. *The Secret Kingdom*. New York: Bantam Books.

Rofel, Lisa. 1999. *Other Modernities: Gendered Yearnings in China after Socialism*. Berkeley: University of California Press.

Rozell, Mark J., and Clyde Wilcox. 1996. *Second Coming: The New Christian Right in Virigina Politics*. Baltimore: Johns Hopkins University Press.

Ruegsegger, Ronald W., ed. 1986. *Reflections on Francis Schaffer*. Grand Rapids, MI: Zondervan.

Russell, Charles Allyn. 1976. *Voices of American Fundamentalism: Seven Biographical Studies*. Philadelphia: Westminster Press.

Said, Edward W. 1978. *Orientalism*. New York: Vintage Books.

Said, Edward W. 1981. *Covering Islam: How the Media and the Experts Determine How We See the Rest of the World*. New York: Pantheon Books.

Sandeen, Ernest R. 1970. *The Roots of Fundamentalism*. Chicago: University of Chicago Press.

Schaeffer, Edith. 1975. *What Is a Family?* Old Tappan, NJ: Fleming H. Revell.

Schaeffer, Francis A. 1976. *How Should We Then Live? The Rise and Decline of Western Thought and Culture*. Old Tappan, NJ: Fleming H. Revell.

Schaeffer, Francis A. 1981. *A Christian Manifesto*. Westchester, IL: Crossway Books.

Schaeffer, Francis A. 1984. *The Great Evangical Disasters*. Westchester, IL: Crossway Books.

Schaeffer, Francis, and C. Everett Koop. 1979. *Whatever Happened to the Human Race?* Muskegon, MI: Gospel Films. Video series.

Schlafly, Phyllis. 1977. *The Power of the Positive Woman*. New Rochelle, NY: Arlington House.

Schultze, Quentin. 1991. *Televangelism and American Culture: The Business of Popular Religion*. Grand Rapids, MI: Baker Book House.

Scofield, C. I., ed. 1909. *The Scofield Reference Bible*. New York: Oxford University Press.

Scopes, John Thomas, and James Presley. 1967. *The Center of the Storm: Memoirs of John T. Scopes*. New York: Holt, Rinehart and Winston.

Scott, Donald M. 1979. Abolition as a Sacred Vocation. In *Anti-Slavery Reconsidered*, edited by Lewis Perry and Michael Fellman. Baton Rouge: Louisiana State University Press.

Shibley, Mark A. 1996. *Resurgent Evangelicalism in the United States: Mapping Cultural Change since 1970*. Columbia, SC: University of South Carolina Press.

Silverman, Kaja. 1983. *The Subject of Semiotics*. New York: Oxford University Press.

Skaggs, Calvin, Executive Producer. 1996. *With God on Our Side*. PBS television documentary series. New York: Lumiere Productions.

Smidt, Corwin E., John C. Green, Lyman A. Kellstedt, and James L. Guth. 1996. The Spirit-Filled Movements and American Politics. In *Religion and the Culture Wars: Dispatches from the Front*, edited by J. C. Green, James L. Guth, Corwin E. Smidt, and Lyman A. Kellstedt. Lanham, MD: Rowman and Littlefield.

Smith, Christian. 1998. *American Evangelicalism: Embattled and Thriving*. Chicago: University of Chicago Press.

Spitzer, Walter O., and Carlyle L. Saylor. 1969. *Birth Control and the Christian*. Wheaton, IL: Tyndale Publishing House.

Stacey, Judith. 1990. *Brave New Families: Stories of Domestic Upheaval in Late Twentieth Century America*. Berkeley: University of California Press.

Stallybrass, Peter, and Allon White. 1986. *The Politics and Poetics of Transgression*. Ithaca, NY: Cornell University Press.

Sternberg, Meir. 1987. *The Poetics of Biblical Narrative: Ideological Literature and the Drama of Reading*. Bloomington: Indiana University Press.

Stewart, Kathleen. 1996. *A Space by the Side of the Road: Cultural Poetics in an "Other America."* Princeton, NJ: Princeton University Press.

Stott, John R. W. 1982. *Between Two Worlds: The Art of Preaching in the Twentieth Century*. Grand Rapids, MI: William B. Eerdmans.

Strober, Jerry, and Ruth Tomczak. 1979. *Jerry Falwell: Aflame for God*. Nashville: Thomas Nelson.

Sumner, Robert. 1982. John R. Rice: Man Sent from God. *Fundamentalist Journal*, December 1982, 24–25, 34.

Swaggart, Jimmy. 1984. *Crossing the River*. Baton Rouge: Jimmy Swaggart Ministries.

Sweet, Leonard I., ed. 1984. *The Evangelical Tradition in America*. Macon, GA: Mercer University Press.

Taylor, Mark C. 1998. *Critical Terms for Religious Studies*. Chicago: University of Chicago Press.

Titon, Jeff Todd. 1988. *Powerhouse for God: Speech, Chant, and Song in an Appalachian Baptist Church*. Austin: University of Texas Press.

Tompkins, Jane P., ed. 1980. *Reader-Response Criticism: From Formalism to Post-Structuralism*. Baltimore: Johns Hopkins University Press.

Tompkins, Jerry R. 1965. *D-Days at Dayton: Reflections on the Scopes Trial*. Baton Rouge: Lousiana State University Press.

Toulouse, Mark G. 1981. A Case Study in Schism: J. Frank Norris and the Southern Baptist Convention. *Foundations* 24 (1):32–53.

Towns, Elmer L. 1984. *What the Faith is All About: A Study of the Basic Doctrines of Christianity*. Wheaton, IL: Tyndale House.

Trollinger, William Vance. 1990. *God's Empire: William Bell Riley and Midwestern Fundamentalism*. Madison: University of Wisconsin Press.

Tuveson, Ernest Lee. 1968. *Redeemer Nation: The Idea of America's Millennial Role*. Chicago: University of Chicago Press.

Vanderlaan, Eldred C., ed. 1925. *Fundamentalism versus Modernism*. New York: H. W. Wilson.

Vaughan, John N. 1984. *The World's 20 Largest Churches: Church Growth Principles in Action*. Grand Rapids, MI: Baker Book House.

Volosinov, V. N. 1973. *Marxism and the Philosophy of Language*. Cambridge, MA: Harvard University Press.

Walzer, Michael, 1985. *Exodus and Revolution*. New York: Basic Books.

Wardin, Albert W. Jr., 1980. *Baptist Atlas*. Nashville: Boardman Press.

Watt, David Harrington. 1991. *A Transforming Faith: Explorations of Twentieth Century American Evangelicalism*. New Brunswick, NJ: Rutgers University Press.

Weber, Timothy P. 1983. *Living in the Shadow of the Second Coming: American Premillennialism, 1875–1982*. Chicago: University of Chicago Press.

Weber, Timothy. 1992. The Two-Edged Sword: The Fundamentalist Use of the Bible. In *The Bible in America: Essays in Cultural History*, edited by Nathan O. Hatch and Mark A. Noll. New York: Oxford University Press.

Wells, Ronald A. 1982. Francis Schaeffer's Jeremaid. *Reformed Journal* 18 (May):16–20.

Wells, Ronald. 1986. Schaeffer on America. In *Reflections on Francis Schaeffer*, edited by R. W. Rugsegger. Grand Rapids, MI: Zondervan.

Wemp, Sumner C. 1982. *The Guide to Practical Preaching*. Nashville: Thomas Nelson.

Whitcomb, John Clement, and Harry M. Morris. 1961. *The Genesis Flood: The Biblical Record and Its Scientific Implications*. Philadelphia: Presbyterian and Reformed Publishing Company.

White, Hayden. 1987. *The Content of the Form: Narrative Discourse and Historical Representation*. Baltimore: Johns Hopkins University Press.

White, Mel. 1994. *Stranger at the Gate: To Be Gay and Christian in America*. New York: Simon and Schuster.

Whitehead, Harriet. 1987. *Renunciation and Reformulation: A Study of Conversion in an American Sect*. Ithaca, NY: Cornell University Press.

Whitehead, John W. 1983. *The Stealing of America*. Westchester, IL: Crossway Books.

Wiersbe, Warren. 1988. *The Integrity Crisis: A Blemished Church Struggles with Accountability, Morality, and Lifestyles of Its Leaders and Laity*. Nashville: Thomas Nelson.

Wilder, Amos N. 1971. *Early Christian Rhetoric: The Language of the Gospel*. Cambridge, MA: Harvard University Press.

Williams, James G. 1991. *The Bible, Violence, and the Sacred: Liberation from the Myth of Sanctioned Violence*. New York: HarperCollins.

Willmington, Harold. 1981a. *The King Is Coming: An Outline Study of the Last Days*. Wheaton, IL: Tyndale House.

Willmington, Harold. 1981b. *Signs of the Times*. Wheaton, IL: Tyndale House.

Willmington, Harold. 1981c. *Willmington's Guide to the Bible*. Wheaton, IL: Tyndale House.

Wills, Gary. 1990. *Under God: Religion and American Politics*. New York: Simon and Schuster.

Wilson, Dwight. 1977. *Armageddon Now! The Premillennarian Response to Russia and Israel since 1917*. Grand Rapids, MI: Baker Book House.

Wuthnow, Robert. 1988. *The Restructuring of American Religion: Society and Faith since World War II*. Princeton, NJ: Princeton University Press.

Wuthnow, Robert, and Matthew P. Lawson. 1994. Sources of Christian Fundamentalism in the United States. In *Accounting for Fundamentalisms: The Dynamic Character of Movements*, edited by M. E. Marty and R. Scott Appleby. Chicago: University of Chicago Press.

Credits

Portions of chapter 1 first appeared in "Convicted by the Holy Spirit: The Rhetoric of Fundamental Baptist Conversion," *American Ethnologist* (January 1987); and "The Afterlife of Stories: The Genesis of a Man of God," in Richard Ockberg and George Rosenwald, eds., *Storied Lives: The Cultural Politics of Self-Understanding* (New Haven: Yale University Press, 1992). Portions of chapter 2 appeared in "Representing Fundamentalism: The Problem of the Repugnant Cultural Other," *Social Research* (Summer 1991); and "Observing the Observers," in Nancy Tatom Ammerman, ed., *Southern Baptists Observed: Multiple Perspectives on a Changing Denomination* (Knoxville: University of Tennessee Press, 1992). Portions of chapter 4 appeared in the "The Gospel of Giving: The Narrative Construction of a Sacrificial Economy," in Robert Wuthnow, ed., *Vocabularies of Public Life: Empirical Essays in Symbolic Structure* (New York: Routledge, 1992). Portions of chapter 7 appeared in "If I Should Die before I Wake: Jerry Falwell's Pro-life Gospel," in Faye Ginsburg and Anna Lowenhaupt Tsing, eds., *Uncertain Terms: Renegotiating Gender in American Culture* (Boston: Beacon Press, 1990). Portions of chapter 9 appeared in "Imagining the Last Days: The Politics of Apocalyptic Language," in Martin E. Marty and R. Scott Appleby, eds., *Accounting for Fundamentalisms: The Dynamic Character of Movements* (Chicago: University of Chicago Press, 1994). Portions of chapter 10 appeared in "The World of the Born-Again Telescandals," *Michigan Quarterly Review* (Fall 1988); and "The Born-Again Telescandals" in Nicholas B. Dirks, Geoffrey Eley, and Sherry Ortner, eds., *Culture/Power/History: A Reader in Contemporary Social Theory* (Princeton: Princeton University Press, 1993).

Index